The Rise and Fall of British Liberalism
1776–1988

The Rise and Fall of British Liberalism 1776–1988

ALAN SYKES

Longman
London and New York

Addison Wesley Longman Limited
Edinburgh Gate,
Harlow, Essex CM20 2JE, United Kingdom
and Associated Companies throughout the world.

*Published in the United States of America
by Addison Wesley Longman, New York.*

First published 1997

ISBN 0-582-06041-9 CSD
ISBN 0-582-06057-5 PPR

British Library Cataloguing-in-Publication Data

catalogue entry for this title is available from the British Library

Library of Congress Cataloging-in-Publication Data

Sykes, Alan, 1942–
The rise and fall of British liberalism, 1776–1988 / Alan Sykes.
p.   cm.
Includes bibliographical references and index.
ISBN 0-582-06057-5.—ISBN 0-582-06041-9
1. Liberal Party (Great Britain)—History.   2. Liberalism—Great
Britain—History.   3. Great Britain—Politics and government.
I. Title.
JN1129.L32S94   1997   324.24106—dc21
97-25080
CIP

Set by 35 in 10/12pt Baskerville
Produced by Longman Singapore Publishers (Pte) Ltd.
Printed in Singapore

Contents

Acknowledgements

Without the more specialist monographs and articles by other historians, extended surveys such as this would be impossible. My great debt to the authors of the many excellent studies of the British Liberal party is, I hope, fully acknowledged in the footnotes. My colleagues, Hamish Scott and Michael Bentley, both read and commented on a late draft of this book; Bruce Lenman provided valuable guidance to the intricacies of late eighteenth century politics, Paul Vysny to those of the late twentieth. The misjudgements and errors that remain after their advice are, of course, my own. At Addison Wesley Longman, Andrew MacLennan has been the perfect editor on what has been a troublesome project. I would also like to thank Bill Jenkins for seeing it through the press.

Most of this book was written in difficult personal circumstances. My children, 'Tasha, Tom and Claude provided invaluable support, as did numerous friends. I am especially grateful to Peter Burns and Peter Bruce in Australia for chatting through the night hours, to Richard and Monique Paice, Ken and Sandra Duncan and Mike and Sue Broers for talk and hospitality, and to Adrian Berry, Patrick Jess, Jonathan Harfield, Andy Marrison, Simon Phillips and Prem Singh among many others for their kindness. Above all, I am grateful to M just for being there.

Introduction: The Liberal Outlook

Writing of Victorian Liberalism in 1993, Jonathan Parry warned that 'a useful general history of the nineteenth century Liberal movement [is] almost impossible. . . . One might write a casserole of a book . . . but this would be an indigestible dish, of incompatible ingredients.'[1] Whatever unpleasant experience might lie behind this harsh criticism of the humble casserole, the point is well made. Describing the Liberal outlook in Britain alone is, to borrow Lloyd George's description of negotiating with Eamonn deValera, 'like trying to pick up mercury with a fork'. Mercury is funny stuff. Not only does it divide easily; it also tends to evaporate over time. Liberalism shared both these characteristics.

As a specific concept and a self-conscious political movement, liberalism only clearly emerged in the early nineteenth century. Its roots, however, lay far deeper in the British past and in interpretations of that past, particularly those developed during the political conflicts of the seventeenth and eighteenth centuries. Liberalism was pre-eminently a doctrine of opposition, whether to the pretensions of a monarch, a corrupted parliament, a self-serving aristocratic elite, an established church, or, indeed, any authority or regulation that restricted the legitimate liberty of the individual. Its classic formulations dated from the late eighteenth century, took their tone from the need to legitimise revolt, and expressed the Enlightenment's faith in nature, reason and the overwhelming importance of the individual.

Thus, according to the Virginian Declaration of Rights of June 1776, all men were 'by nature equally free and independent, and have certain inherent rights . . . namely, the enjoyment of life and liberty, with the means of acquiring and possessing property, and pursuing and obtaining happiness and safety'. This became almost the standard formula. To the authors of the American Declaration of

---

1. Jonathan Parry, *The Rise and Fall of Liberal Governments in Victorian Britain*, (New Haven: Yale University Press, 1993), p. 2.

1

Independence, it was 'self-evident that all men are created equal, that they are endowed by their Creator with certain unalienable rights, that among these are life, liberty and the pursuit of happiness'. In 1789, the French Declaration of the Rights of Man, 'in the presence and under the auspices of the Supreme Being', more cautiously listed those rights as 'liberty, property, security and resistance to oppression'. Unlike the Americans, the French were apparently prepared to forgo happiness, just as long as they were not oppressed, but they shared the same basic ideas.

In this pattern of ideas, governments existed solely to preserve what the French called 'the natural and imprescriptible rights of man'. 'To secure these rights', ran the American Declaration of Independence, 'governments are instituted among men, deriving their just powers from the consent of the governed . . . whenever any form of government becomes destructive of these ends, it is the right of the people to alter or to abolish it.' The limits of governmental powers were defined in written constitutions in the American states, in the American Federal Constitution of 1787, and in the French Constitution of 1791, each of which thus reconstituted their governments afresh. In their enthusiasm, the revolutionaries in France went further and introduced a new system of dating that made 1792 the Year 1 of Liberty. The experiment was short-lived, but the late eighteenth and early nineteenth centuries saw an efflorescence of constitutions and law codes in Europe, all proclaiming basic individual rights. In the form of declarations of rights safeguarded by constitutions, those essential characteristics of liberalism, individual liberty and personal property secured by the rule of law, were subsequently exported to the world, as a statement of the ideal towards which governments should strive. As the *Economist* observed in 1996, 'In the West, by and large, we are all liberals now.'[2]

Until the 1760s, Americans shared the widely held view, subscribed to not least by the British themselves, that through the settlement which followed the 'Glorious Revolution' of 1688–9, Britain had achieved the best possible system of government. Its mixed constitution of king, Lords and Commons, with checks awnd balances to the power of each section, was, according to the American patriot, John Adams, 'the most perfect combination of human powers in society which finite wisdom has yet contrived and reduced to practice for the preservation of liberty and the production

2. *Economist*, 21 December 1996.

of happiness'.[3] Without the social bases upon which the traditional conception of a mixed constitution was assumed to rest, monarchy, aristocracy and Commons, the American Federal Constitution of 1787 recreated in a functional way the same tripartite separation of powers to achieve what was still thought to be the ideal of power checked and balanced in the interests of liberty.

During the eighteenth century, there were fears that Britain was gradually losing that delicate balance, that the Court was gaining excessive influence in parliament and tilting the constitution too heavily in favour of its executive branch by the insidious extension of government patronage. Perceptions were coloured by the contemporary belief that liberty was a fragile growth, and that it was in the nature of governments to seek to extend their power. English critics of Court influence, the Country faction, whose views circulated widely in the American colonies,[4] warned constantly from early in the century of

> mercenary and dangerous wretches amongst us, who have dared to lead for a dependence of the parliament on the crown; not for that dependence of the several parts of the government on one another, which our constitution hath formed, and on the preservation of which the freedom of our government entirely rests; but for the most indirect the most iniquitous, as well as dangerous dependence imaginable; for a dependence to be created by corruption.[5]

The idea that the British government was conspiring to subvert the historic 'liberties of the freeborn Englishman' gained strength not merely from its treatment of the American colonies after 1763, but from its behaviour at home. Its use of a general warrant to search John Wilkes's house following his criticism of George III in No. 45 of the *North Briton* was unlawful; its order for his arrest whilst he was still an MP was contrary to parliamentary privilege. The continuing pursuit of Wilkes, arranging for his expulsion from the Commons in order to prosecute him, successfully, for seditious libel, gave some substance to his claim in 1763 that his case raised the issue of 'whether ENGLISH LIBERTY be a reality or a shadow'. In 1768, Wilkes's election for Middlesex raised even more fundamental questions. He was again expelled from the House of Commons, re-elected by Middlesex, and re-elected for a third time in

3. Bernard Bailyn, *The Ideological Origins of the American Revolution* (Cambridge, Mass.: Harvard University Press, 1967), p. 87.

4. Ibid. pp. 35–54.

5. H.T. Dickinson, *Liberty and Property: Political Ideology in Eighteenth Century Britain* (London: Methuen, 1977), p. 175.

April 1769 against the government candidate, Colonel Luttrell. Despite this, the Commons declared Luttrell duly elected. Ministers, it appeared, and Wilkes pointed out, had gained such control of parliament as to turn the House of Commons into a self-selecting body, at which point 'the boasted Constitution of England will be entirely torn up by the roots'.[6] The government's disregard for legal rights was sufficiently notorious for general warrants to be specifically denounced by the Virginian Declaration of Rights.

What began as a question of the balance within the constitution thus became a debate on the effectiveness of the constitution to protect individual liberty, and ended as an argument about the proper limits to parliamentary power and the location of sovereignty. In Britain, the debate between popular and parliamentary sovereignty had been resolved early in the century, in favour of the latter. During the crisis of the 1760s and 1770s, there were influential voices raised in favour of some limits on parliament's powers. Both Pitt and his close political ally, the eminent lawyer, Lord Camden, supported the American case to the extent that, as Camden argued, 'taxation and representation are inseparable – this position is founded on the laws of nature; it is more, it is in itself an eternal law of nature; for whatever is a man's own is absolutely his own; no man hath a right to take it from him without his consent . . . whoever attempts to do it . . . throws down and destroys the distinction between liberty and slavery'. There was, according to Pitt, 'no such idea in this constitution, as a supreme power operating upon property'.[7] Such occasional voices affirmed the integral connection between liberalism and property that all accepted, but they did not change the accepted doctrine of parliamentary sovereignty.

Whereas the American colonies ultimately rebelled and proclaimed the doctrines of popular sovereignty and natural rights, the mainstream of British protest concentrated upon the reform of parliament itself. This took two principal forms: the reduction of Crown patronage, and the redistribution of seats away from rotten and pocket boroughs towards the more independent counties and the under-represented, or unrepresented, centres of population such as Greater London, Birmingham or Sheffield, where the size of the electorate would itself reduce the possibilities for corruption. Such ideas were not new. Attempts to reduce the number of royal supporters in the Commons dated back to the early 1690s; proposals for the redistribution of seats to the beginning of the century.[8] Nor

6. Ibid. p. 211.   7. Ibid. p. 216.   8. Ibid. pp. 112–18.

were they mutually exclusive. Both sought, by reducing the power of the Court or increasing the influence of the electorate, to restore the independence of the Commons and the balance of the traditional constitution. Other suggestions that were to become the staple of late-eighteenth- and early-nineteenth-century radicalism such as triennial, or even annual, parliaments and the secret ballot had the same objectives.

The American warcry of 'no taxation without representation', however, moved the debate in a potentially far more radical direction, the extension of the franchise. First mooted by Wilkes in 1776, by 1780 the radical Westminster Association had concluded that 'an equal representation of the people in the great council of the nation, annual elections, and the universal right of suffrage . . . are rights of so transcendent a nature'[9] that no traditional authority could nullify them. It was a radical, yet logical, extension of the accepted view that property was an individual right and could not be taken without the individual's consent. Like liberalism, of which it was an expression, the movement for parliamentary reform that resulted in the Reform Act of 1832 had its roots in the eighteenth-century controversy initiated by the American colonists. The Reform Act demonstrated that, contrary to the belief of the colonists, parliament could reform itself, and thus Britain's historic constitution; that the constitution was, after all, self-correcting.

Britain's position in the late eighteenth century was thus incongruous. Britain was the tyrant against which the Americans asserted their rights, and the principal counter-revolutionary power in the wars against revolutionary and Napoleonic France. Yet the American colonists believed they were defending their rights as freeborn Englishmen, and pillaged English history, legal authorities and theorists to sustain that argument. There was no shortage of sources, simply because the English had had to do the same to justify resistance to the Stuart monarchy throughout much of the seventeenth century. In this history, English liberties were enshrined in English common law. They had been enjoyed in a mythical Saxon past before the coming of the Norman conquest and the imposition of 'the Norman yoke', had been regained in Magna Carta, defended by law and ultimately by force, and most recently reasserted in the 'Glorious Revolution'. The inviolability of private property, participation through representatives in the framing of legislation, consent to taxation, ministerial responsibility, the presumption of

9. Ibid. pp. 214, 219.

innocence until judged guilty, freedom from arbitrary arrest, trial by jury and habeas corpus, all so urgently stated in the Virginian and French declarations of rights, were already established in the British political and legal framework. In many respects, Britain served as a model for other more formal and systematised statements of liberal beliefs whilst her own liberalism remained informally embodied in custom, law and the political practice of a parliamentary regime. The appeal to history, the sense of liberties enshrined in common law and the acceptance of parliamentary sovereignty were both the characteristics and the eccentricities of British liberalism as it emerged from the late eighteenth century.

There were, then, no 'origins of British Liberalism' as such. The victors wrote their own history to legitimise their tenure of power, for, as John Locke observed in his *Second Treatise on Civil Government* of 1690, 'to settle therefore men's consciences under an obligation to obedience, 'tis necessary that they know not only that there is a power somewhere in the world, but the person who by right is vested with this power'.[10] In a country that had developed a deep distrust of standing armies and relied heavily on voluntary agencies for both national and local government, Locke might have added that 'twas also expedient in the extreme that obedience should be freely given. Locke himself justified English resistance to James II not on the grounds of royal infringements of historic liberties, but on the broader basis of man's natural right to life, liberty and property. He took his place amongst the Enlightenment theorists cited by American colonists and English radicals against the Court, but the logic of his arguments went further than most British liberals either wanted or needed to go. There was no difficulty in confounding natural and historic rights. English common law and the British constitution were merely the best way yet devised, at least before 1776, of giving practical expression to rights that were in origin natural, or endowed to man by his Creator. In this nebulous form, God was, for liberals, the first liberal.

Each of the various sections of what became the nineteenth-century Liberal party had their own particular view of the past. The Whigs, in office for much of the first half of the eighteenth century, had no need or desire to look back beyond the Glorious Revolution of 1688–9. The myth of James II's abdication, made credible by his flight, was more comfortable to a connection of wealthy landed Anglican families than the execution of one monarch and

10. Ibid. p. 59.

the expropriation of a second. But for those radicals who felt that their liberties were still not fully established, the Glorious Revolution was an opportunity missed, and missed deliberately, by the landed elite to secure its own power.

> The flaws in the Revolution system left full opportunity for private interest to exclude public good, and for a faction, who by their struggles against former tyrannies had gained the confidence of the people, to create, against the liberties and virtues of their trusting countrymen, the undermining and irresistible hydra, court influence, in the room of the more terrifying, yet less formidable monster, prerogative.[11]

Protestant Dissenters, whose long association with British liberalism gave the movement its characteristic air of moral earnestness, still laboured in the late eighteenth century under the civil disabilities imposed upon them by the Test and Corporation Acts that the Revolution Settlement had left substantially untouched. They enjoyed toleration under the Toleration Act of 1689, but toleration was not an equality of either historic liberties or natural rights. If there was a Dissenting golden age, it lay in the Cromwellian protectorate, before the restoration of the Stuart monarchy, the Anglican establishment and an aristocratic oligarchy. Popular radicalism had to look further back still, to a misinterpretation of Magna Carta, for a declaration of the rights of Englishmen, and to Saxon times for a mythical golden age of English liberty, before those rights were usurped by a despotic monarchy and an avaricious aristocracy. In the late eighteenth century, stimulated by the American and French examples, these elements of the future Liberal party began to coalesce behind the campaign for parliamentary reform.

Reformism demonstrated a sense of reality. Even limited parliamentary reform was for a long time a minority cause, and was achieved only after a protracted struggle. But it also stemmed from the sense of history, and satisfaction at the progressive evolution of that history, which distinguished the Liberal outlook in Britain. British Liberalism retained its oppositional stance in seeking to reform and improve, but it was also part of a historical process. Unlike the American colonists and many European liberals, British Liberals saw no need for a totally new departure. As a result, Liberalism in Britain remained an uncomfortable, even contradictory, compound of historical and natural rights, and contained an even more uncomfortable, or contradictory, accommodation between the

11. Ibid. pp. 204, 233–4.

assertion of those individual rights on the one hand and the acceptance of parliamentary sovereignty on the other.

Parliament, as Burke pointed out in the debate on the Declaratory Act of 1766, had to recognise that in practice there were limits
to its powers, even if this conflicted with its position in accepted
constitutional theory.

> The completeness of the legislative authority of parliament over this
> kingdom is not questioned; and yet many things indubitably included
> in the abstract idea of that power and which carry no injustice in
> themselves, yet being contrary to the opinions and feelings of the
> people, can as little be exercised, as if parliament in that case had
> been possessed of no right at all.[12]

The accommodation survived by parliamentary and royal restraint,
the acceptance by the House of Lords of the reduction of its powers
in 1911, all of which increased the power of the Commons within the
constitution, and the steady extension of the franchise which gave the
impression of greater popular control while in practice conceding
little. It was, and remains, an uneasy and insecure accommodation.

It left Britain with the continuing problem of defining the relationship between the state and the individual without the basis of
a declaration of fundamental rights in a written constitution. In
1859, the foremost exponent of British liberalism in the nineteenth
century, John Stuart Mill, was still grappling with this crucial question. For Mill, the relationship could be reduced to 'one very simple
principle . . . that the only purpose for which power can be right-
fully exercised over any member of a civilised community, against
his will, is to prevent harm to others. His own good, either physical
or moral, is not a sufficient warrant.'[13] But this marked no advance
on the eighteenth century. 'Liberty', according to the French Declaration of the Rights of Man, summarising an already common-
place view,[14] 'consists of the power to do whatever is not injurious
to others.' Its limits were 'only those that assure other members of
society the enjoyment of those same rights; those limits may be
declared only by the law'. But whereas the French Declaration could
then add that the legislature could not make laws that contradicted
the constitution, whereas Americans could appeal to the Supreme
Court in defence of their constitutional rights, Mill had no such
recourse; nor had the British people. The 'harm principle', as it

---

12. Ibid. p. 215.
13. John Stuart Mill, *On Liberty* (London: Everyman edn, 1972), p. 78.
14. See Bailyn, *Ideological Origins*, p. 77 and fn 21.

became known, solved nothing. It, too, remains the subject of enduring controversy.[15]

In other respects, Britain shared the prevailing assumptions about nature and the Creator, the existence of laws of nature that regulated society as they regulated the physical world, and the benevolent effect of those laws. Thomas Malthus, whose explanation of the laws governing the growth of population exercised immense influence on the nineteenth-century imagination, thus observed that 'it seems absolutely necessary that the Supreme Being should act always according to general laws',[16] and that 'the dictates of those laws of nature [are] evidently calculated to promote the general good, and increase the mass of human happiness'.[17] Adam Smith's *Wealth of Nations* (1776) was so successful not just because it argued that markets and trade should be freed, or that a society organised according to the laws of nature was, of necessity, harmonious, but because it appeared to demonstrate how Nature actually did harmonise the interests of self-seeking individuals with the social good. Through the operation of the free market, the individual, though he 'neither intends to promote the public interest, nor knows how much he is promoting it', but pursues 'only his own security and . . . only his own gain . . . is in this, as in so many other cases, led by an invisible hand to promote an end which was no part of his intention'.[18] It was a further proof of the conviction expressed much earlier (1733) in Pope's celebrated couplet:

> Thus God and Nature linked the general frame
> And bade Self-love and Social be the same.

In consequence, the liberty of the individual was not just a moral imperative deriving from the natural rights of man, nor even an imperative deriving from the historic liberties of the freeborn Englishman; it was the most efficient, as well as the right, form of social organisation. Progressively discovered by man through reason and science, the application of the laws of nature to social and political organisation would bring about constant and unremitting, if not unending, improvement. 'In the natural course of human affairs, which is evidently progressive,' wrote the Radical and Dissenter,

---

15. E.g. *Economist*, 21 December 1996.

16. Antony Flew (ed.), *Thomas Robert Malthus: An Essay on the Principles of Population and a Summary View of the Principles of Population* (London: Penguin edn, 1985), p. 205.

17. Ibid. p. 268.

18. Phyllis Deane, *The Evolution of Economic Ideas* (Cambridge: Cambridge University Press, 1978), p. 15.

William Enfield, in his 'Sermon on the Centennial Commemoration of the Revolution' in 1788, 'it must soon come to pass that enlarged views and a liberal spirit will obliterate the maxims of ignorance and bigotry, and that every institution which is manifestly contrary to sound policy and inconsistent with that share of natural or political liberty to which every member of a free state is entitled, will be abolished.'[19] With the spread of education and enlightenment, the future was liberal. Liberals embraced that future with optimism and enthusiasm. In the short term at least they were mistaken. The onset of war with revolutionary France pulled down the shutters on the movement for parliamentary reform and the liberal opinions behind it for more than two decades. The reform movement and liberalism crept cautiously back into Britain after 1815, but only began to gain ground in the 1820s. Not until the 1830s did the term 'Liberal', borrowed from the Continent, enter the everyday vocabulary of politics.

Liberalism and Elitism

British Liberalism, however, stood on cloven feet. It was not simply that, as Liberals of the eighteenth and nineteenth century constantly declared, property was the only sound basis for the right to vote and thus 'when we talk of people with regard to elections, we ought only to think of those of the better sort',[20] but that the possession of property was endowed with superior intellectual and moral qualities. Mill's 'simple principle' was qualified in theory and practice. Liberty, Mill argued, was not applicable to 'backward states of society' or 'to any state of things anterior to a time when mankind have become capable of being improved by free and equal discussion'.[21] Liberals had no scruples about interfering with the poor, even without their consent through the vote, in the interests of improved social morality as they understood it. Alnwick's 'traditional Shrove Tuesday football game' was banished from its traditional streets; cock-fighting and bear-baiting, traditional popular pastimes, were banned. Nor were Liberals any more tender with the poor's only possession, their bodies. The 1832 Anatomy Act made the bodies of paupers who had died in workhouses available for dissection.[22] The advancement of science took precedence over

---

19. Dickinson, *Liberty and Property*, p. 201.   20. Ibid. p. 128.
21. Ibid. pp. 78–9.   22. Parry, *Rise and Fall*, pp. 118, 102, 100.

the sensitivities of the poor, who, in any case, were presumed not to have such fine feelings.

Individual liberty was the constant objective of Liberalism, but rationality and civilisation were the pre-requisites of that liberty. For the Whig elite of the mid-nineteenth century, the coercion of the irrational poor, for their own good as well as that of society, was an essential element of their concept of good government in a well-ordered society. Legislation was intended to have an educative as well as a coercive effect, so that ultimately its subjects would internalise the values law enshrined. The Reform Act of 1832 thus sought to provide 'for the moral as well as for the political improvement of the country', by setting the vote at a level to which thrifty hard-working men could aspire.[23] There were limits to what could be achieved by legislation. As the former Whig secretary at war, Viscount Howick, observed in 1840,

> All the best laws and the best government can accomplish is by assuring to exertion its true reward, by providing for the security of persons and property, by promoting education, and by diffusing religious instruction to encourage the formation of those habits of industry and virtue which alone can be the sources of the welfare and the prosperity either of individuals or communities.[24]

Nevertheless, the assumptions derived from a belief in the laws of nature or Providence remained unimpaired. However much Whigs and Liberals recognised a diversity of interests and opinion, they still expected that conflict could be reduced to harmony through the educative influence of the law, much as the market harmonised those conflicts in the sphere of economics.[25] Free trade became pre-eminent in Liberalism not simply because the repeal of the Corn Laws in 1846 shattered the Conservative party, nor because removing government interference in, and thus responsibility for, economic fluctuations enabled a property-owning elite to present itself as disinterested. The doctrine accorded perfectly with Liberal presuppositions about society and government. Free trade purported

---

23. Ibid. p. 86.   24. Ibid. p. 114.
25. Ibid. pp. 113–14.

Their faith in the ameliorative power of law was based on a theologically inspired rationalism . . . as long as reform was founded upon . . . 'profound views of human nature'. Rational observation of human behaviour would allow the framing of legislation systematic enough to remove obstacles to a more natural state of human society . . . the object of government must be to promote order and liberate that virtue and industry for its Providential purpose.

to be a law of nature, the means by which a benevolent, if remote, Providence intended to secure to man the fruits of his labours. Benevolence, like the morality of legislation, was nevertheless relative. Under Liberal beliefs, whilst animals were saved from working-class cruelty, Irishmen starved in their tens of thousands during the famine of the 1840s.

Famine was one of the positive checks on population, 'the last and most dreadful resource of nature',[26] enumerated by Malthus. The view that population rose in pace with the resources required to maintain it was implicit in Smith's *Wealth of Nations* when he observed that 'the demand for men, like that for any other commodity, necessarily regulates the production of men'.[27] It was developed by Malthus, who found the reason for population growth more straightforwardly in unbridled lust. However, Malthus also concluded that populations expanded geometrically whilst food production could at best only expand arithmetically. The population therefore always threatened to outrun the resources needed to maintain it. The two were kept in balance by either 'preventive' or 'positive' checks. The former consisted of what Malthus called 'moral restraint . . . the restraint from marriage which is not followed by irregular gratifications', although Mill subsequently pointed out that restraint could also be exercised within marriage, and 'vice', such as contraception, abortion and infanticide.[28] Positive checks were those over which man had no control so that, if restraint and vice failed 'in this war of extermination, sickly seasons, epidemics, pestilence and plague advance in terrific array, and sweep off their thousands and tens of thousands. Should success be incomplete, gigantic and inevitable famine stalks in the rear.' However the extermination was achieved, it remained certain 'that premature death must in some shape or other visit the human race'.[29]

The twin assumptions that 'the increase of population is necessarily limited by the means of subsistence' and that 'population does invariably increase when the means of subsistence increase'[30] doomed the mass of mankind to a hard and precarious existence. High wages would only result in an increased population which would in turn bring wages down again to their natural level of mere subsistence.[31] Nor, beyond moral restraint, could much be done to

26. Flew, *Thomas Robert Malthus*, p. 118.
27. Deane, *Evolution of Economic Ideas*, pp. 35–6.
28. Flew, *Thomas Robert Malthus*, pp. 25–6, 250.   29. Ibid. pp. 118–9.
30. Ibid. pp. 119, 79.
31. Deane, *Evolution of Economic Ideas*, pp. 38, 63–4; see also Flew, *Thomas Robert Malthus*, p. 97.

remedy the situation. Pathetic human efforts to distort the operation of the laws of nature were destined to fail, or more frequently to exacerbate the problems they tried to solve. Malthus condemned the redistribution of wealth through parish relief as inflationary, increasing effective demand without increasing the supply of food. Even if the increased demand did stimulate greater production, that in turn would only lead to a rise in population, once again reducing the poor to subsistence. In practice, such redistribution would be counter-productive, encouraging man's natural idleness by removing the pressure of necessity, and giving 'a strong and immediate check to productive industry ... in a short time, not only would the nation be poorer, but the lower classes themselves would be much more distressed'. Thus 'no possible contributions or sacrifices by the rich, particularly in money, could for any time prevent the recurrence of distress among the lower members of society'.[32]

Worse still, the existence of parish relief sapped individual responsibility, discouraged saving and created a destructive culture of dependency. It generated 'that carelessness and want of frugality observable among the poor'. Since population had to be checked, it was clearly 'better that it should be checked from a foresight of the difficulties attending a family and the fear of dependent poverty'[33] than by the four horsemen who waited in the wings. The poor had to be taught to fear 'dependent poverty', and encouraged in moral restraint. The first found legislative expression in the Poor Law Amendment Act of 1834, which, in theory at least, restricted relief to those willing to enter the workhouse, reduced that relief to the lowest level of earnings available on the outside labour market and broke up families by segregating the sexes to enforce 'restraint'. Fear of the workhouse bit deep into the consciousness of the working classes, and remained there well into the twentieth century.

'Moral restraint' was a longer-term problem and an incomplete solution. The poor would never achieve those levels of prudence believed to characterise their social superiors,[34] but would always suffer from 'the natural tendency of the labouring classes of society to increase beyond the demand for their labour, or the means of their adequate support, and the effect of this tendency to throw the greatest difficulties in the way of permanently improving their condition'.[35] Hence, as Malthus observed, 'the improbability that the

32. Flew, *Thomas Robert Malthus*, p. 95.　　33. Ibid. pp. 98–9.
34. Ibid. p. 244.　　35. Ibid. p. 270.

lower classes of people in any country should ever be sufficiently free from want and labour to obtain any high degree of intellectual improvement'.[36] Malthus himself was not completely pessimistic. He believed that 'a spirit of independence still remains among the peasantry',[37] and that there was still room for considerable growth through the reform of 'the institutions of society, and the moral habits of the people'.[38] By reform, Malthus meant liberalisation, since 'the effectual demand of the society, whatever it may be, is best supplied under the most perfect system of liberty'.[39] Nevertheless, ultimately there were limits. Not only Adam Smith and Malthus, but David Ricardo, who published his *Principles of Political Economy and Taxation* in 1817 and whose economic theories achieved, according to Keynes, 'complete domination ... for a period of a hundred years',[40] all agreed that population pressure would eventually bring a halt to economic growth.[41]

The political economists were simplified and bowdlerised by popularisers, misunderstood and misquoted by practical men, whether of politics or business. As the advertisement for Malthus's *Summary View of the Principles of Population*, published in 1830, resignedly observed, 'it has been frequently remarked, that no work has been so much talked of by persons who do not seem to have read it as Mr Malthus's *Essay on Population*'.[42] There were severe limits on what any mid-nineteenth-century government could do about famine, or other positive checks, but the shadow of Malthusian theory loomed over the government's attitude to Ireland, as the shadow of political economy loomed over the poor in general. Moral improvement stood at the centre of any social improvement. The poor could expect only coercion for their habits and neglect of their poverty. Since the laws of nature precluded their intellectual improvement, political economy also sanctioned the continued and virtually permanent rule of an elite which alone had the wealth, independence, leisure and education to render it fully capable of rational judgement. Both propositions were further reinforced by the Creator, at least in his English, Christian manifestation. The poor were not only ever-present, but doomed to be ever-foolish. 'The wisdom of a learned man cometh by opportunity of leisure; and he that hath little business shall become wise. How can he get wisdom that holdeth the plough, and that glorieth in

36. Ibid. pp. 148–9.   37. Ibid. p. 98.   38. Ibid. p. 249.
39. Ibid. p. 246; see also p. 101.   40. Ibid. p. 16.
41. Deane, *Evolution of Economic Ideas*, pp. 36, 38, 63.
42. Flew, *Thomas Robert Malthus*, p. 221.

the goad; that driveth oxen, and is occupied in their labours, and whose talk is of bullocks?'[43]

It accordingly fell to the governing elite to determine which opinions were rational and which were not, and to guide and educate public opinion when it erred. As Lord John Russell declared in 1844, 'if the people were wrong they ought to be put right'.[44] Farmers were wrong in their alarm at the removal of protection; democrats were wrong in their demands for further parliamentary reform in the late 1830s and 1840s; jingos were almost always misled in their support for militarism, and the working classes were mistaken in their support for a sectional Labour party in the early twentieth century. To government also belonged the duty of deciding how best to meet what it deemed justifiable grievances, and indeed to legislate and regulate even if there was no popular demand. 'Those who are called to the business of legislation should follow the deliberate result of their own judgement',[45] for, as Lloyd George later declared, the people 'must be redeemed by others outside'.[46]

Elitism was the bane of Liberal politics. It was expressed in social terms, whether limiting the franchise to property owners in 1832, or by constituency associations rejecting working-class candidates at the end of the century. Property, however, was only a crude rationality test: 'a certain amount of income was the only general and practical criterion of a required degree of intelligence'.[47] Behind social elitism lay intellectual arrogance. Thomas Arnold's view in 1836 that 'vulgar minds never can understand the duty of reform ... and the mass of mankind ... will always be vulgar minded'[48] was echoed nearly ninety years later by Gilbert Murray: 'Liberalism stood for Freedom of Speech and Thought. Thinking men, rich and poor were with them; but the uneducated masses liked neither, any more than the Tories did.'[49] Liberals, whether of the 1830s or the 1920s, would have to do their thinking for them. Liberal pluralism, such as it was, took the form of condescension, of toleration rather than equality.

The exception was Gladstone, or more precisely, the libertarian and populist image of Liberalism that Gladstone presented. That

43. Ecclesiasticus 38: 24–5.   44. Parry, *Rise and Fall*, p. 133.   45. Ibid. p. 89.
46. Speech at Manchester, 1908, in Herbert Du Parcq, *Life of David Lloyd George*, vol. 4 (Caxton Publishing Company, n.d.), p. 637.
47. Norman Gash, *Politics in the Age of Peel* (London: Longmans, 1953), pp. 18–19.
48. Parry, *Rise and Fall*, p. 149.
49. Trevor Wilson, *The Downfall of the Liberal Party* (London: Collins, 1966), p. 283.

image was coincidental, even paradoxical. Gladstone was as convinced of the incontrovertible character of natural laws as the Whigs, and was no less an advocate of good government by an enlightened administrative elite. He had no more faith in the governing capacity of the working classes than Lloyd George, and no hope for the material improvement of the condition of the poor. He did not take opposition lightly, and was doctrinaire in his morality. Yet because of his belief in natural laws, his fiscal reforms to remove indirect taxes and reduce taxation were directed towards emancipating trade and the individual taxpayer; his vision of morality in politics allowed him at least to contemplate a church freed from its association with the state (even if his one action, the disestablishment of the Anglican church in Ireland, was aimed more at abandoning an indefensible bastion in order to safeguard the principle in the rest of Britain); that same vision underpinned his ideal of nationalism and sympathy with small nations 'struggling to be free', allowing him, under extreme pressure, to adopt Home Rule for Ireland.

Above all, the doctrinaire quality of his morality led him to condemn the corruption he saw in the ruling elite in terms that eighteenth-century radicals might have understood. In becoming rich and leisured, Gladstone argued, the elite had become selfish, and lost 'the capacity of right judgement in large and most important questions'. Although this meant no more than that the elite disagreed with Gladstone, the disagreement was vital to the public image of Gladstonian Liberalism. The 'loss of moral equilibrium' that Gladstone perceived in 'large portions of what is termed society', could only be counterbalanced by the morality that Gladstone discovered in the masses who had escaped the 'subtle perils of the wealthy state'. When it came to 'judging the great questions of policy which appeal to the primal truths and laws of our nature',[50] their judgement was superior to that of their social and intellectual betters. In the 1870s and 1880s, Gladstonian Liberalism was in opposition to the establishment in almost all its forms, consciously proclaiming a populist interpretation of reform that credited progress to the morality of the common man. The 'upper ten thousand' as Gladstone called them, had never provided

> the impulse that has prompted, and finally achieved, *any* of the great measures which in the last half-century have contributed so much to the fame and happiness of England. They did not emancipate the

50. H.C.G. Matthew (ed.), *The Gladstone Diaries*, vol. 9 (Oxford: Oxford University Press, 1986), pp. lxiv–lxv.

dissenters, Roman Catholics and Jews. They did not reform the parliament. They did not liberate the negro slave. They did not abolish
the corn law. They did not take the taxes off the press. They did not
abolish the Irish established church. They did not cheer on the work
of Italian freedom and reconstitution. Yet all these things have been
done; and done by agencies other than theirs, and despite their
opposition.[51]

By identifying Liberalism with the masses and against the establishment, Gladstone harnessed popular libertarianism behind formal
Liberal ideology and the Liberal party in a series of liberationist
crusades. It was this that the administrative elitism of the Whigs and
the intellectual elitism of the New Liberals with their more explicitly
coercive and didactic emphasis, signally failed to do.

Much of the New Liberalism of the late nineteenth and early
twentieth centuries was a conscious reaction against mid-Victorian
libertarianism. Its ideas were conditioned by the increasingly influential biological interpretation of man and his world; by the advanc-
ing secularisation that was eroding the cohesive morality which
bound Liberalism together despite its intellectual contradictions,
and by an awareness of the poverty and social injustice to which
traditional Liberalism had no answer. It found in the concept of an
organic society with its own ethical purpose of 'a good human life',
a means to eliminate the tensions evident in Mill's formula. But in
rejecting Mill's 'very simple principle', New Liberalism virtually
eliminated the autonomy of the individual altogether. Within an
ethically purposeful organic society, the individual realised himself
and his liberty in and through society and not, as in Mill's view,
against it. The state, as the embodiment of society's 'common will',
acquired not only the right, but the obligation, to coerce the individual for his own and society's good. These were, in any case,
indistinguishable. Individual liberty was no longer an end in itself,
nor its preservation the purpose of government. It was merely one
condition amongst others for the achievement by society and its
constituent individuals, under the direction of the state, of the
higher end for which it was established, 'the good human life'.

New Liberalism provided the intellectual arguments for the
welfare reforms with which the Liberal governments of 1906–14
laid the foundations of an interventionist welfare state. By continuing to focus primarily on the individual, however, it did not solve

51. John Morley, *The Life of William Ewart Gladstone*, vol. 2 (London: Macmillan,
1903), p. 557.

what was rapidly becoming the main problem for Liberalism at the turn of the century: mass society. Liberalism was never fully at ease with the world of the masses, and never understood the collective and defensive response that the constant insecurity of working-class life evoked. Based on individualism, Liberalism was ill-adapted to encompass individuals in the aggregate within its intellectual framework. Football crowds aroused apprehension of disorder; trade unions, as institutions, appeared to formalise that very sectionalism that Liberals found incompatible with individual freedom on the one hand and social harmony on the other. From the 1870s onwards, Liberals found difficulty integrating trade unions into the legal and political system. By the 1920s, confronted with the growth of union power during the First World War, a resolution was found only by considering trade unions as virtually an expression of irrationality. Inappropriate though it was in view of the extension of the franchise, the spread of education and the development of mass communications, Liberals became more, rather than less, elitist and coercive in the twentieth century. Their demise as a political force occurred in circumstances of a widening gap between the intellectual formulation and the popular understanding of the Liberal creed.

Liberalism contained two intertwined but competing strands, the libertarian and the coercive, which gradually came unravelled. The hegemonic liberal ideology of the mid-nineteenth century was one which believed that society should be organised in conformity with natural laws. To that end rational individuals should be liberated as far as possible from external constraints. Much of the work of mid-nineteenth-century Liberalism was concerned with removing those constraints. Such a stance frequently allowed the Liberals to profit from an identification with the pervasive libertarianism of British culture, rooted in history, which Liberal principles appeared to reinforce. Appearances could be, and were, deceptive, but while they lasted, the Liberal party was paramount.

CHAPTER ONE

The Liberal Party:
A Question of Origins

'Out of the present state of confusion and discordance', wrote Queen Victoria in 1852, 'a sound state of Parties will be obtained and two Parties, as of old, will again exist without which it is impossible to have a strong Government. How these Parties will be formed it is impossible to say at present.'[1] For a monarch seeking a stable government, neither the Liberal party nor a party system existed in the 1850s. Gladstone on the other hand, surveying his party's past in 1874, claimed that it had been 'forty, or more exactly forty-three, years since the Liberal party acquired the main direction of public affairs'.[2] For the leader of the Liberal party, that party existed when the Reform Act of 1832 was passed, and the difficulties that beset the queen were no more than a temporary dislocation.

Historians, having neither regal nor ministerial responsibilities, have been free to continue the debate. Hawkins accepts Southgate's view that the meeting at Willis's Rooms on 6 June 1859 in which Palmerston and Lord John Russell finally agreed to set aside their personal differences, and the Radicals agreed to support Palmerston, marked 'the formal foundation of the Liberal party'. He quotes, in addition, Robert Blake and Derek Beales.[3] John Vincent, meanwhile, in his classic study *The Formation of the British Liberal Party*, dates that formation as 1857–68. For Norman Gash, however, the Lichfield House compact of 1835 in which Whigs, Radicals and Irish agreed to combine to overthrow Peel's minority Conservative

1. Angus Hawkins, *Parliament, Party and the Art of Politics in Britain 1855–59* (London: Macmillan, 1987), p. 8.

2. John Morley, *The Life of William Ewart Gladstone*, vol. 2 (London: Macmillan, 1903), p. 488.

3. Hawkins, *Parliament, Party and the Art of Politics*, pp. 268, 8.

government, was 'the point of origin of the Victorian Liberal party
. . . long before 1841 . . . a recognisable Liberal party was actually
in being'.[4] Jonathan Parry also stresses the events of 1834–5; the
acceptance by the Whigs in 1834 of the principle that the government could appropriate the surplus revenue of the Irish Church
and redistribute it in a way that benefited the entire population was
'probably the most important single step in the formation of the
Liberal party'.[5] That formative process was sufficiently complete for
it to be 'possible to discern an effective Liberal party functioning
by 1841, with a presentable set of values and a stalwart constituency
following'.[6] Central to this was the decision to fight the election
of 1841 on the reform of the Corn Laws, 'a seminal development
in Liberal politics', and the subsequent identification of the party
with the policy of free trade.[7] After the repeal of the Corn Laws in
1846, 'anti-Conservatives . . . definitively adopted the phrase "Liberal party."'[8]

Both starting dates are problematic. The years between 1830
and 1886 were those of almost unchallenged Liberal, or at least
non-Conservative, ascendancy. During that period, the Conservative
party won only two general elections, in 1841 and 1874. After the
Willis's Rooms meeting of 1859, the Liberals themselves gained
an independent majority only four times, three before 1886 (1865,
1868, 1880), and then not until 1906. If the party was not formed
until 1859, it would seem to have been in decline almost from its
inception; 1834–5 at least does justice to the liberal domination of
the middle fifty years of the nineteenth century. Yet for much of
that period, Liberals could win elections, but were unable to keep
a secure grip on office. Disunity was so great that Conservative
support was frequently required to survive at all, and in 1852,
1858–9 and 1867–8 even this was insufficient, resulting in Conservative minority governments. The so-called Liberal party looked and
acted more like a non-Conservative alliance of disparate and discordant groups than a political party; the mid-nineteenth-century
liberal hegemony appears primarily to have been that of a political
mentality.

4. Norman Gash, *Aristocracy and People: Britain 1815–1865* (London: Arnold, 1979),
pp. 161, 163.
5. Jonathan Parry, *The Rise and Fall of Liberal Government in Victorian Britain* (New
Haven: Yale University Press, 1993), p. 108.
6. Ibid. p. 94.   7. Ibid. p. 147.
8. Ibid. p. 167. T.A. Jenkins, *The Liberal Ascendancy 1830–1886* (London: Macmillan,
1994), pp. 45–6.

The Whigs and the politics of reform

A political mentality is not a political party. Parry's theme that 'in the half century after 1830 there was a coherent Liberal approach to politics . . . continuity in fundamental principles . . . which owed most to the Whig tradition, but which was influenced also by Canning and the liberal tories of the 1820s',[9] tends to equate the two. It also assumes that similar principles will result in similar conclusions. Unfortunately for the coherence of liberal action, this was frequently not the case. The Whigs were only one section, an extremely aristocratic section, of that broader political grouping that became the Liberal party, and their liberalism was correspondingly coloured. The changes, and especially the impulse for further change, that the Whig Reform Act introduced into British politics were largely unintentional. It was designed as an aristocratic, restorative and conservative measure at a time when the public had lost confidence in the old political system and 'the universal feeling' made it 'impossible to avoid doing something'.[10]

The something that the Whigs attempted was to attach those 'who possess property and knowledge',[11] essentially the middle classes defined by a £10 householder franchise in the boroughs, to the aristocratic constitution by satisfying 'all reasonable demands and remov[ing] at once and for ever, all rational grounds for complaint from the minds of the intelligent and independent portion of the community'.[12] Far from endangering the interests of the aristocracy, the Whig prime minister, Lord Grey, argued that the act would give them 'a general influence more congenial to their true character, and more effectual for securing to them the weight which they ought to possess'.[13] By removing the taint of corruption and demonstrating the representative nature of the system, reform sought to improve the image of the aristocracy and facilitate the acceptance of legislation; conversely, the aristocracy was to be obliged to fulfil its governing role by being placed under the surveillance of educated opinion to which, in the last resort, it was responsible.[14]

Other sections of liberal opinion disagreed from the first with the Whig view of the nature of the aristocracy, its proper role in

---

9. Parry, *Rise and Fall*, pp. 17–18.
10. Norman Gash, *Politics in the Age of Peel* (London: Longmans, 1953), p. 10.
11. Ibid. p. 15.   12. Ibid. p. 10.
13. J.R.M. Butler, *The Passing of the Great Reform Bill* (London: Cass, 1964), pp. 255–6.
14. Parry, *Rise and Fall*, pp. 87–9.

politics and the sort of harmony that legislation should bring about. The Reform Act of 1832 backfired on its authors. Severe economic and social dislocation which found political expression in widespread agitation for further parliamentary reform gave all governments problems until relative prosperity returned in the 1850s. 'When', Gladstone wailed in 1843, 'will anybody govern anything.'[15] Behind the anxieties of the governing classes, however, lay the political instability that the Reform Act produced within governing circles themselves. Post-reform governments found themselves adrift on a sea of swirling opinion, 'the sport of every wind that blows'.[16] The act intensified politicisation, but evoked not a general will but the fears and expectations of conflicting interests.

The increased influence that the 1832 Reform Act gave to Dissent and to industry alarmed the established interests of church and land. Alexander Baring, MP for Thetford, warned that 'in a reformed parliament, when the day of battle came, the country Squires would not be able to stand against the active pushing, intelligent people who would be sent from the manufacturing districts'.[17] The active pushed. Political Radicals demanded further parliamentary reform, especially the secret ballot; Dissenters the redress of various grievances symbolic of their second-class status and denial of civil rights, above all the requirement to pay church rates; the Irish, under cover of a demand for the repeal of the Union, further emancipation for the Catholic majority. Towards the end of the decade the Corn Laws, as anticipated, came under fire from the manufacturing districts.

All governments were caught in this turbulence. The removal of 'rational grounds for complaint' required further reform; the preservation of the aristocratic constitution set limits that were too tight. The Whigs were under constant pressure from their nominal followers, frequently threatened with their opposition, and equally frequently sought refuge from that pressure in the support of their nominal opponents, the moderate Conservatives. The Whigs were not in an entirely false position. There was liberalism in their outlook, and there was a genuine desire to reform. But they were, in the last resort, aristocratic, landowning and Anglican, part of the very establishment that Radicals wished not simply to reform, but often to destroy. Tension and disruption were unavoidable. The Reform Act of 1832 was intended to be a final settlement of the

15. Ibid. p. 161.   16. Ibid. p. 106.   17. Gash, *Politics in the Age of Peel*, p. 6.

political system, a point which Russell, the most radical of the Whigs, reaffirmed in an unfortunate outburst in November 1837. Nevertheless, the government found itself forced to concede by stages. The secret ballot, which Russell himself feared as the beginning of an attack on aristocracy and property, was made an open question by the government by 1839, and Russell reopened the question of franchise reform in the late 1840s.

The Whigs were broad-church Anglicans who aspired to harmony even in that most contentious of issues in mid-nineteenth-century politics, religion. They were fundamentally Erastian, seeing in the maintenance of the established church a means by which government control could be exercised over any tendency in Anglicanism to either institutional or dogmatic exclusiveness. By removing Dissenting grievances whilst broadening Anglicanism, they hoped that the various sects could be brought to agree on the ethical basis of their common Protestantism. 'I should rejoice', said Earl Fitzwilliam in 1837, 'to see the day come in which the members of the Church of England and the Dissenters . . . should agree together to worship their God within the same walls.'[18] Such unity would strengthen religion in its function as a source of public morality and social stability. To this end, however, the church establishment must remain. 'Our object', as Russell put it, 'is, if possible, to conciliate the Dissenters, and having framed our measures with that end, strenuously to resist the separation of Church and State.'[19]

The assumption that toleration within the framework of an established Anglicanism would satisfy Dissent was itself flawed, but a greater and more immediate difficulty lay in delivering measures of conciliation. Apart from the provision of state registration of births, marriages and deaths, attempts to meet the Dissenters' grievances fell between the two stools of reform and conservation. Russell's marriage bill of 1833 displeased both Dissenters and churchmen, and had to be withdrawn; in the face of Anglican opposition, church rates could not be reformed, still less abolished, and the effort was abandoned in 1838 despite Dissenting campaigns and the formation of the Church Rates Abolition Society in 1836–7; the House of Lords blocked the opening of the entry of non-Anglicans to Oxford and Cambridge. Russell's edu-cation bill of 1839 received qualified support from Dissenters, but did little to relieve their

18. G.I.T. Machin, *Politics and the Churches in Great Britain 1832 to 1868* (Oxford: Oxford University Press, 1977), p. 29.

19. Ibid. p. 47.

general dissatisfaction, and its impact was further reduced by the concessions Russell was obliged to make to Anglican animosity. During the 1830s, Dissenters gained most not from direct attempts to meet their sectarian grievances, but indirectly through the reform of municipal government, which gave them, and thus Liberalism, control of towns across the north and midlands.

The Whig governments of the 1830s fared equally badly with legislative attempts to reconcile Irish Catholicism. The commitment to the preservation of the Union and the church establishment restricted what the government was prepared to offer, whilst, as in the case of Dissent, the latitudinarian approach to religion ensured that much of what it did propose was based on false premises. Russell expected that, in the long run, under good government 'Catholics would become Protestants – at least . . . less Catholics, and therefore more English.'[20] But the payment of Catholic priests, a continuing element of Whig policy towards Ireland, was unacceptable to the Irish Catholic hierarchy. The same reduction of dogmatic religion to Christian ethics lay behind the creation of the national education scheme in 1831 providing undenominational primary education for Catholics and Protestants together, and of the Queen's University in 1850. The critical issue, however, remained that of government appropriation and redistribution of the Irish church's surplus income which would, the Whigs hoped, both make the payment of church tithes more acceptable to the Irish, and provide increased resources for education that emphasised 'the points of the Christian faith common to us all', upon which Whigs placed so much emphasis.[21] The effort, nevertheless, had to be abandoned in 1838 in the face of Anglican opposition. Insofar as Ireland was at all pacified after the tithe war of 1830–2, pacification was achieved by benign administration. Integration through educative legislation was less apparent.

The Irish nevertheless continued to cooperate with the Whigs after the Lichfield House compact and called off the campaign for the repeal of the Union whilst the Whigs were in office. The Radicals, who campaigned for universal suffrage, the secret ballot and annual parliaments in order to destroy that very aristocratic predominance which the Whigs sought to preserve, were far less accommodating. After the election of 1835, the former Whig leader of the House of Commons, Lord Althorp, noted that in the future, as in the past, 'the Whigs . . . will find . . . the Radicals their most

20. Parry, *Rise and Fall*, pp. 107–8, 196.   21. Ibid. pp. 108–9.

bitter opponents'.[22] The Radicals in turn considered their relationship with the Whigs no more than an 'alliance', and in the same year went so far as to attempt to form a separate Radical party. This broke down because of lack of unity even within the Radical section of what was to become the Liberal party, but it exposed the very limited and temporary nature of the Lichfield House compact. It was a means to remove the minority Conservative government that the king had placed in office in 1834, not the beginning of a long-term working relationship, and still less the foundation of a political party.

The Whigs themselves were scarcely more united than the Radicals. To its opponents, government appropriation of Irish church revenues raised a wider issue of principle, the right of parliament to seize church property for state purposes and by extension the survival of the church establishment in Great Britain as well as Ireland. Stanley, Graham, Ripon and Richmond all resigned from the government when it adopted appropriation in 1834, and were subsequently absorbed into the Conservative party. For Ripon and Richmond this was only a reversion to their former allegiance. Richmond, an ultra-Tory, was a surprising recruit to the reform ministry of 1830, and Ripon, as Goderich, had been Tory prime minister in 1827–8. Stanley, the future Earl of Derby, and Graham, who had been a member of the sub-committee of four that had drafted the reform bill, were, however, Whigs of considerable standing. The losses were significant. As a stage in the evolution of liberal principles that brought most Whigs closer to the Radicals and Irish, who felt they shared a common enemy and jointly applauded Russell's announcement of the policy, lay appropriation was significant; as a stage in the formation of a distinct and integrated Liberal party, the episode was counter-productive.

Politics in the 1830s was confused not only by the abrasive independence of Radicalism, but by the centrism of the Whig outlook. After his resignation, Stanley dallied with the idea of a Centre party, but found little support. The idea of party was sufficiently ingrained to prevent such a venture, but amongst the Whigs it went little further. In 1835, Althorp clearly considered that in other circumstances the Whigs might cooperate electorally with the Conservatives against the Radicals, which would have reflected events within parliament itself. Almost from the first, the Whigs relied upon the

---

22. Robert Stewart, *The Foundation of the Conservative Party* (London: Longman, 1978), pp. 109–10.

Conservatives for support against Radicals. In 1833 Conservative votes were required to defeat a Radical motion for triennial parliaments, and in 1834 to defeat a proposal to reduce pensions. Conservative support was also required to reverse the malt tax vote on the 1833 budget. As the government's majority declined, so reliance on Conservative support became more frequent, especially in the difficult years after 1837, when the Whigs decided that association with Radicalism was an electoral liability and a succession of Radical proposals was defeated with Conservative assistance.[23]

The Whig ideal of rule from above by a disinterested but wise and dutiful aristocracy, legislating only after independent deliberation, inhibited both party spirit and the development of party. In contrast to the Conservatives, who whipped strongly against the reform bill in 1831 and developed a high degree of cohesion under Peel's autocratic leadership, Althorp, as leader of the House of Commons, was opposed to whipping on principle.[24] The Whig view of party, summed up by H.D. Goring, Whig MP for Shoreham, as 'those Gentlemen I generally find myself able to support',[25] was informal, the cooperation of like-minded men, but men who, in the words of Lord Brougham, lord chancellor in the Whig ministry of 1830–4, 'want and ought to think for themselves'.[26] The Whigs were also reluctant to foster extra-parliamentary organisation because of their fears of Radical activism, and their awareness that the organisers and the press were markedly more Radical than the leadership.[27] The Reform Association, set up in 1835 to register the Whig-Liberal vote, was not ineffective in that role. The increase in registrations of Conservative voters during the 1830s reflected the shift of opinion towards Conservatism rather than any marked superiority in Conservative organisation. But the Association generally made little impact in its other purpose, to induce the Whigs to adopt more Radical, and thus more sectional, policies that acknowledged the alignment of opinion.

Party clearly existed during the 1830s in the sense that Goring understood it. Both inside and outside parliament, confronted by a straight choice between an MP at an election or a government on a vote that was, or amounted to, a vote of confidence, electors and

23. Jenkins, *The Liberal Ascendancy*, p. 30.
24. Ian Newbould, 'Whiggery and the growth of party 1830–1841: organisation and the challenge of reform', *Parliamentary History* 4 (1985), 142–3.
25. Machin, *Politics and the Churches*, p. 61.
26. Newbould, 'Whiggery and the growth of party', p. 139.
27. Ibid. pp. 145–9.

MPs expressed a party choice: in the emerging language of the time, Liberal or Conservative. When the question is 'yes' or 'no', then 'a plain bi-polar pattern to politics' is virtually inevitable.[28] The registration provisions of the Reform Act encouraged rudimentary party organisation to the extent of ensuring that supporters were included on, and opponents excluded from, the electoral register. The increased politicisation that resulted from the passage of the Reform Act and the prospect of further reform encouraged issue politics: many politicians were expected to define their stand upon certain specific issues. But not all electors had a choice, and not all politicians had to define their position: 'Just over two-thirds of the constituencies were contested in 1832; just over half in 1835; just under two-thirds in 1837; less than half in 1841; and just over two-fifths in 1847.'[29] Uncontested elections did not mean the absence of parties, but they diminished partisanship, and to that extent organisation and strict affiliation, in favour of compromise. This was the centrist consensus-seeking rationale behind the retention of double-member constituencies in the 1832 act.

Within parliament, the Lichfield House compact showed the ability of the discordant elements of the reform coalition to agree at least that Whigs rather than Conservatives should be in office, if only so that Whigs and Conservatives should not form a central coalition.[30] Party inclinations, or at least the preference of individual MPs, were clear enough for both Conservatives and Whigs to calculate relative numbers accurately after the election of 1837.[31] Such an indication of general support, however, does not advance the development of party far beyond Goring's definition. Nor does a demonstration that a solid core of supporters existed for crucial votes, when 'on all but the trials of strength, the [Whig] government was never sure of its support until the questions were debated and amended'.[32] During the 1830s, the Liberal alliance had made little progress towards becoming a coherent party organised around common principles, and what development there was, was soon lost. Even those historians who see stronger party organisations and

28. David Close, 'The formation of a two-party alignment in the House of Commons between 1832 and 1841', *English Historical Review*, 84 (321) (1969), 266–77; P.M. Gurowich, 'The continuation of war by other means: party and politics 1855–1865', *The Historical Journal* 27 (3) (1984), 604–5, 611.
29. Gash, *Politics in the Age of Peel*, p. 239.
30. Newbould, 'Whiggery and the growth of party', pp. 138–9.
31. Close, 'Formation of a two-party alignment', p. 274.
32. Newbould, 'Whiggery and the growth of party', p. 139; Close, 'Formation of a two-party alignment', pp. 272–5.

a vigorous two-party system between 1835 and 1841, admit that this 'was exceptional'.[33]

Nor did Whiggism in the 1830s achieve the hegemony that characterised later more liberal expressions of Liberalism. The ministerial resignations of 1834 were the tip of the iceberg. During the 1830s, some fifty-eight government supporters defected.[34] In this, parliament reflected the views of the electorate. Unprepared by their outlook for the irrationality and contrariness of opinion, the Whigs realised too few of the expectations of their supporters and confirmed too many of the fears of their opponents. Russell encapsulated the dilemma in 1837: 'the difficulty of Whig administrations [is] that their friends expect them to do more than is possible; so that if they attempt little, their friends grow slacker, and if they attempt much, their enemies grow strong'.[35] Radical gains at the general election of 1835 squeezed the Whigs from one side, whilst the Conservatives, who won eighty-one seats, only one of which was from the Radicals, squeezed them from the other.[36] Between then and the defeat of 1841, the Whigs continued to suffer from their association with urban, Radical, Dissenting and Irish interests, however little they did for those interests in practice. Their overwhelming majority of 1832 fell to about eighty after the election of 1835 and to an unreliable twenty after that of 1837. The election of 1841 left them in a minority of eighty-seven, and the Conservatives were back in office. The Whig problem was at least partly self-inflicted. By increasing the number of county seats from 82 to 144 and retaining a considerable number of small boroughs[37] in the provisions of the settlement of 1832, the Whigs created an electorate that was considerably more conservative than the public opinion to which they attempted, however mildly, to respond.

This was especially obvious in the prestigious county seats where the association with urban Dissenting Radicalism led to an agricultural and Anglican backlash. After the 1837 election, Lord Melbourne, still prime minister despite Whig losses, concluded that 'the Church had been too much for us'. The counties, according to the former chief whip, Francis Baring, were lost because 'squires and clergy are dead against us and the county voters are under the

33. Close, 'Formation of a two-party alignment', p. 277.
34. Stewart, *Foundation of the Conservative Party*, p. 117.
35. Jenkins, *Liberal Ascendancy*, p. 29.
36. Stewart, *Foundation of the Conservative Party*, pp. 109, 117.
37. Parry, *Rise and Fall*, pp. 79, 83. Boroughs with an electorate of less than 1000 returned 202 MPs. Jenkins, *Liberal Ascendancy*, p. 17.

sway of the "Church in Danger" cry'. To this, he added the damage done by the association with the Irish which aroused popular anti-Catholicism: 'the great body of the *English* people have been, and are, against anything like liberal government in Ireland'.[38] In 1832 the Conservatives had won only forty-three county seats; by 1835 they had almost achieved parity with the Whigs; by 1837 the Whigs were in a minority winning only forty-seven, and in 1841 they were almost obliterated, winning only twenty-two.[39] Despite their desire for consensus politics and harmonious opinion, the Whigs were becoming, in electoral terms, an urban, sectional interest.

This was the logic of their reforming stance and their acceptance of the importance of public opinion. By the end of the decade, when economic depression greatly increased the pressure for reform, the Whigs capitulated on the crucial question of the Corn Laws as they were to capitulate on the secret ballot. In 1839 almost all ministers voted in favour of corn-law reform, and in 1841 Russell announced a new government policy of a low fixed duty on which to fight the general election. Although arguments were made that the Corn Laws harmed rather than aided agriculture, the government recognised that the counties were a lost cause. In a period of high bread prices and popular distress, corn-law reform accorded with the Whig view that aristocratic government should be, and be seen to be, responsive to popular needs. More pragmatically, corn-law reform was an attempt to regain Radical and Dissenting support, recognising the government's dependence upon the urban vote. In that respect, the Whigs were slowly becoming the Liberal party. Nevertheless, it was a development that they resisted strongly.

Whig centrism

Whig reaction to Conservative success in 1841 belied the old adage that parties define themselves against each other. Triumphant Conservatism did not drive Whigs, Radicals and Irish together in a renewed Lichfield House compact, but reinforced the Whigs in their conviction that association with Radicalism, Dissent and the Irish was ruinous. Following the direction established by the late 1830s, in defeat they moved further towards the centre, and towards the Conservatives. As early as October 1841, Ellice, another former

---

38. Stewart, *Foundation of the Conservative Party*, p. 158.
39. Ibid. pp. 85, 159; Parry, *Rise and Fall*, p. 146.

chief whip who had remained an important background wirepuller, thought that there were virtually no differences between the Whig and Conservative parties.[40] Whig centrism was encouraged by Russell's conviction that in government Peel was likely to lead the Conservative party in a direction 'far more Liberal than the majority of the lords would like', and ultimately destroy his party over the Corn Laws,[41] although the process took longer than the single session that Russell predicted.

Russell was, nevertheless, perceptive. Peel could no more ignore the problems of government than the Whigs. Elected on agricultural apprehension and Protestant fervour, he was caught between the conservatism of the electorate and the requirement to govern at a time of economic depression and widespread agitation both in Great Britain and Ireland. His ministry was engulfed by a tide of mass petitions and mass demonstrations: those of the Chartists for further parliamentary reform could be ignored despite their sometimes incendiary language; Dissenting opposition forced the withdrawal of the education clauses of Graham's factory bill in 1843, but could be met with inactivity; the need to make a positive response to the incendiary repeal campaign in Ireland and the class war agitation of the Anti-Corn Law League brought the government down. Herein lay the paradox of politics between 1832 and 1859; the failure to establish stable Liberal governments when liberal ideology was dominant. Peel had no means of meeting Irish and industrial discontent other than Whig policies founded on liberal principles. Aberdeen, the Conservative foreign secretary, observed to Russell in 1845 that 'a coalition is impossible [but] . . . we perfectly agree with each other on every point'.[42] He overstated the case, but his comment indicated the general affinity of outlook that had developed between Peelites and Whigs in this intellectual climate.

Peel's reasoning, that Irish disaffection was a danger at times of diplomatic tension, and that Ireland would only be efficiently governed if 'the professional middle classes of Ireland identified themselves with the state' which in turn would only come when 'they and their Church were given political and cultural as well as legal equality' mirrored Russell's analysis.[43] Peel's Queen's Colleges, established in 1845 to provide undenominational education where

40. John Prest, *Lord John Russell* (London: Macmillan, 1972), p. 187.
41. Ibid. pp. 186–8; Parry, *Rise and Fall*, pp. 144–7.
42. Prest, *Lord John Russell*, p. 213.
43. Stewart, *Foundation of the Conservative Party*, p. 192; Prest, *Lord John Russell*, pp. 193, 236.

Catholics and Protestants might be educated together, followed the similar objectives of the Whigs' national system of education of 1831. The Whigs incorporated the colleges into Queen's University in 1850. The proposal to increase and make permanent the government grant to the Maynooth seminary in 1845 was even more directly political, seeking to reconcile the Catholic church and detach the priesthood from Irish agitation. Russell had suggested this the previous year,[44] and argued in supporting Peel that it would lead to the endowment of Catholicism, which Peel did not deny. It provoked a wave of Protestant protest from Anglicans as well as Dissenters, and proved too much for the Tory party which split 149 to 148 against it on the third reading, although the measure passed easily with Whig support.

Despite this revolt, Gladstone, at this point in his long career still a troublesome Conservative, continued to believe that 'the numerical and on the whole the moral strength of the party was still entire'.[45] It required the conjunction of Ireland and trade to destroy Peel's government. Shaken by the distress in industrial areas, and intellectually convinced by the arguments of free traders, Peel had already lost confidence in the Corn Laws on economic grounds by 1845, and claimed that he intended in any case to dissolve on the question of repeal in 1846.[46] The Irish famine precipitated the issue, not because repeal would relieve Irish hunger, but to retain English credibility. It was, as Wellington argued, not a question 'of Corn Laws – it is one of *Government*'.[47] Russell pre-empted any move by Peel to outflank the Whigs by committing them to repeal in his 'Edinburgh letter' at the end of November 1845.

Peel resigned on 6 December, but was forced to resume office when Russell, fortuitously but fortunately, failed to form a government, and repeal passed by the combined votes of the Whigs and about a third of the Conservative party. The day after the repeal of the Corn Laws was secure, Peel's proposals for Irish coercion were defeated by the combined votes of Whigs and protectionists. The collapse of Peel's government was another indication of the limits of party. Peel's failure to conciliate backbenchers whom he despised, and his demand for absolute support reinforced by threats of resignation, pushed discipline too far. The resentment which burst out against his liberal policies on Ireland and trade in 1845 was partly the product of earlier mishandling and exacerbated the

44. Prest, *Lord John Russell*, p. 197.
45. Stewart, *Foundation of the Conservative Party*, p. 194.   46. Ibid. p. 201.
47. Parry, *Rise and Fall*, p. 165.

party split. Whilst the majority remained loyal to Protestantism and protection, the bulk of the leadership and just over 100 MPs became 'Peelites', following Peel into political limbo. The less rigorous regime of the Liberal alliance at least avoided the violence of Conservative disruption.

The Conservative collapse had conflicting effects on the Liberal alliance. It handed office back to the Whigs, but it also accentuated political instability, and retarded the development of a coherent Liberal force because of the impulse it gave to Whig centrism. For the Whigs, the secessionist Peelites were infinitely preferable to the Radicals as political allies, provided, of course, that they came into any combination as subordinate partners. Peel's reputation for combining administrative efficiency, purposeful government and liberal policies in contrast to the uncertain handling of affairs by his Whig predecessors made this difficult. The 100 or so Peelites in parliament gave the government general support but were really secure only on free trade. Nevertheless, the Whigs needed allies of some sort. Their nominal majority after the general election of 1847 was lower than the number of unreliable Radicals included within it. The Whigs were able to look both ways, to the Peelites and the centre, or to the Radicals and the left. As in the late 1830s, however, the result was less to make them powerful, than to reopen old divisions and promote indecision.

From the first Russell attempted to incorporate the Peelites in his administration. 'Whigs and Peelites', he told Palmerston at the beginning of 1849, 'ought to govern the country and not to quarrel about trifles',[48] but almost without exception, his offers of office to senior Peelites were rejected.[49] Peel's accidental death in 1850 removed the possibility of his return to office if the Whig government collapsed, and thus the danger that, as Palmerston warned, Russell would be 'obliged to hand your party over to Peel'.[50] Leaderless, the Peelites had no independent future after 1850, which appeared to open the opportunity for the merger of the centre. Ecclesiastical politics prevented this. The leading Peelites were generally high-church Anglicans, out of sympathy with the broad-church, Erastian outlook of the Whigs. A succession of acrimonious disputes over church appointments in the late 1840s kept the differences between the two groups alive. The theoretically unrelated issues of the 'Gorham judgement' and the 'Durham letter' brought them into open conflict.

48. Prest, *Lord John Russell*, p. 292.   49. Ibid. p. 223.   50. Ibid. p. 299.

In 1848, The Revd G.C. Gorham, who had been presented with the living of Brampton Speke by the Whig lord chancellor in the previous year, was excluded by the high-church bishop of Exeter, Henry Phillpotts, because of his allegedly heretical views on baptism. Phillpotts was already a veteran thorn in the side of governments, both Whig and Conservative, but especially the former. Gorham appealed to the Judicial Committee of the Privy Council, which, in March 1850, decided in his favour and ordered his institution. The case, however, raised far-reaching questions: the authority of a civil court to decide on matters of doctrine, and by implication the authority of the state over the church embodied in royal supremacy. It was, as Gladstone declared, 'a stupendous issue'. Gladstone had already expressed his desire for a 'substantial check' on the power of the prime minister over church appointments in 1848 on the appointment of the controversially 'liberal' Professor R.D. Hampden as bishop of Hereford. But whilst Gladstone reacted to the Gorham case with even deeper reservations about state control, Russell reacted equally strongly against high-church assertions of ecclesiastical independence.

With royal supremacy over the church already a matter of public debate, the announcement of the Pope's restoration of the Catholic hierarchy in England and Wales, creating Cardinal Wiseman archbishop of Westminster supported by seven bishops with territorial titles, further inflamed passions on both sides. The politics of the so-called 'papal aggression' merged with those of the Gorham judgement. Russell's 'Durham letter', an open letter to the sympathetic Whig bishop of Durham published on 7 November, denounced not only Wiseman's 'pretension of supremacy over the whole realm of England' as 'inconsistent with the Queen's supremacy', but also the 'mummeries of superstition' manifested in high Anglican ritual, and 'clergymen of our own church' who appeared to be leading Anglicans towards Catholicism. Russell's letter caught, as it was designed to catch, a popular mood of ultra-Protestant nationalism, but as an attack on high-church Anglicanism as much as on papal pretensions, it further alienated the already aggrieved high-church Peelites.

Although only a minority of Peelites opposed the subsequent ecclesiastical titles bill imposing penalties on clergymen other than those of the established churches who took territorial titles, the controversy was enough to confirm the leading Peelites in their refusal to cooperate with the Whigs. Gladstone, in particular, opposed the bill strongly, basing his case on the defence of religious liberty which marked another stage in his transition to liberalism, and was to become increasingly central to his entire understanding of liberalism as a political idea. He repealed the Act in 1871.[51] Thus, when the government resigned in 1851 after defeat on Locke King's motion to equalise the county and borough franchises, the opportunity to forge a central alliance went begging, even though, in the absence of Peel, royal influence was brought to bear in favour of a coalition. After the Conservative Protectionists had failed to form a government, and Lansdowne and Wellington had refused, the Whigs were forced to carry on alone. Further approaches to the Peelites in 1851 and 1852 were also rebuffed.[52] When the Whig government fell in February 1852, the capture of the Peelites, and thus of the political centre, remained unrealised.

Instead, the Whigs themselves fell apart at the top as the growing conflict between Palmerston and Russell also became critical. The 'almost universal' objections to Palmerston's return to the foreign office lay behind Russell's failure to form a government in December 1845. Palmerston's apparently abrasive foreign policy alarmed his Whig colleagues, and was another reason why the Peelites remained aloof, whilst his autocratic behaviour alienated the Court. Reprimanded in 1850 for excessive use of British naval power, he replied by asking, not unreasonably, what British ships were for.[53] His own understanding goes a good way to explaining his popularity in otherwise radically inclined commercial circles: 'it is the business of the Government to open and to secure the road for the merchant'.[54] The occasion of the reprimand, his use of the navy to defend the rights of Don Pacifico as a British citizen against the Greek government, made Palmerston's reputation, and briefly put an end to Russell's plan to replace him.

The doctrine of 'civis Romanus sum' that Palmerston then proclaimed appealed to the popular vision of Britain's liberal empire, and secured a large parliamentary majority, despite the opposition of Protectionists, Peelites and some Radicals. Henceforth he became indispensable and uncontrollable. Shortly thereafter, he defended the rough-handling given to the visiting Austrian general, Haynau, whom the Radical press nicknamed 'General Hyena', by draymen protesting at what Palmerston called 'the barbarities committed by Haynau in Italy and Hungary'.[55] In 1851 his proposal to welcome

---

51. Machin, *Politics and the Churches*, pp. 196–228.
52. Prest, *Lord John Russell*, pp. 332–3, 338.   53. Ibid. p. 314.
54. Parry, *Rise and Fall*, p. 144.
55. Donald Southgate, *'The Most English Minister': The Policies and Politics of Palmerston* (London: Macmillan, 1966), pp. 283–4.

the Hungarian nationalist revolutionary, Kossuth, a further indication of his sympathies or pursuit of Radical approval, led to 'a
disagreeable altercation' between Russell and Palmerston, compounded by Palmerston's acceptance of a Radical petition denouncing the emperors of Austria and Russia as 'despots and assassins'.[56]
His unilateral approval of Louis Napoleon's *coup d'état* in France in
December 1851 finally led to his dismissal. To the relief of its
members, the government fell two months later on Palmerston's
'tit for tat' amendment to its militia bill.

The ministry of 1846–52 discredited both Russell and the Whigs,
partly because the tactic of centrism was at fault. As Palmerston was
to show between 1855 and 1865, the centre could be temporarily
occupied under favourable circumstances, but the centre is more
often the battleground of party politics. Both Peelites and Whigs
with their administrative concept of government saw the centre as
a means of making government independent of opinion and its
vexations, and accordingly independent of party. This was the logic
that moved the Whigs away from the Radicals and Irish, and led
Peel to ignore and then destroy his own party. Junction with the
equally autocratic but more imaginative and more capable Peelites
might have compensated the Whigs for the loss of the Radicals.
Without either Peelites or Radicals, the Whigs were becalmed.

Radicalism transformed

Finding a basis for concerted action with the Radicals was, if anything, even more difficult than combination with the sensitive
Peelites. Radicalism, both political and religious, transformed itself
in the 1840s. The largely metropolitan and intellectual Radicals who
had plagued the Whigs with demands for further parliamentary
reform in the 1830s had 'no public out of doors of sufficient influence to fall back upon', and had all but disappeared by 1841.[57] The
new tone of Radical agitation was set by the Anti-Corn Law League,
formed in 1839 from the Manchester Anti-Corn Law Association.
After a shaky start, by the end of 1843 the League had become what
The Times called 'a great fact . . . a new power . . . in the State'.[58]

---

56. Prest, *Lord John Russell*, pp. 334–5; Southgate, *'Most English Minister'*, p. 285.
57. Paul Adelman, *Victorian Radicalism: The Middle Class Experience* (London:
Longman, 1984), pp. 14–15.
58. Norman McCord, *The Anti-Corn Law League 1838–1846* (London: George Allen
& Unwin, 1958), p. 163.

Resting on the new wealth of industry, its organisation was impressive. As well as pamphlets and tracts issued by the ton, a weekly circular and from 1843 the *Economist*, the League sought to manipulate the key to power, the electorate, through the electoral registers.

It divided the country into twelve regions, each with its full-time paid lecturer-agent, including a Welsh speaker, who recruited members, collected subscriptions and organised the distribution of literature directly to electors. According to the League chairman, 'in every township, in every county where we have pretended to touch the register, we have either a local agent residing or we send a man to make a special enquiry from every voter'. Tracts were addressed and delivered personally to each elector. 'In that way we found every county voter in the kingdom.' The League, in consequence, built up 'an unequalled knowledge of the electoral scene throughout the country', far superior to that of the political parties.[59] It fought by-elections and secured the return of several of its members, including both Cobden and Bright, to parliament, and exploited the 40-shilling freehold qualification of the 1832 Reform Act to create voters in key constituencies by trading in property.

Its message won widespread support from Dissenting ministers, carefully orchestrated by the League, as a means of attacking the 'round-bellied bishops . . . the sleek, meek well-fed ecclesiastics of the State Church' whose dependence on the tithe gave them a vested interest in the Corn Laws,

> and therefore though famine should show its ghastly face in every corner of the land . . . though millions of the industrious poor should groan as if in the agonies of death and weep tears of blood – neither starvation, nor its frightful concomitants, would induce these holy men, who luxuriate in the embraces of the national harlot, to abandon one fraction of their livings.[60]

Despite Cobden's support for Graham's factory bill in 1843, and for the Maynooth grant in 1845, the League created a greater degree of moral unity than was usual in Radicalism. The repeal of the Corn Laws owed more to the Irish famine than to the League's agitation, but it appeared that its methods had been successful, and it was the appearance that led others to follow its example. Repeal briefly mended fences between the League and the Whigs, but for most of its existence the League was, as Cobden observed, 'at war to the knife with the Whig politicians, and they hate us as cordially as

---

59. Ibid. pp. 149–50.   60. Ibid. pp. 26–7.

the Tories and more thoroughly than they hate each other',[61] and
the breach soon reopened. The Radicals, particularly Dissenters
inspired by League methods and League success, moved on.

During the early 1840s polite Dissent took the same path, becoming aggressive Nonconformity as rational, Whiggish Unitarians
yielded leadership to provincial evangelicals.[62] The inadequacy of
Whig reforms left grievances simmering, especially that of church
rates where a series of legal cases provided the impetus for the
transformation of opposition into the general demand for 'the entire
separation of church and state'.[63] Edward Miall's decision to give up
his ministry for journalism, and the launching of the *Nonconformist*
under his editorship in 1841, was the first indication of the new
mood of Nonconformity; successful opposition to the education
provisions of Graham's factory bill of 1843 provided the confidence to form the Anti-State Church Association, modelled on the
Anti-Corn Law League, with the objective of disestablishment. The
transition from Dissent to Nonconformity was from a demand for
religious liberty to a demand for religious equality. Religious liberty
was in accordance with Whig principles, even if it proved difficult
to achieve; religious equality in the form of disestablishment was
not. The result was a widening gulf. Opposition to Peel's Maynooth
grant meant opposition to the Whigs by whose support it was carried. For many Nonconformists, as the *Eclectic Review* declared, 'The
time of our separation has come',[64] and preparations for a separate
party and electoral action were begun.

Whig education reform in 1847 confirmed Nonconformist hostility. A Dissenters' parliamentary committee chaired by the wealthy
Congregationalist businessman and philanthropist, Samuel Morley,
was set up to organise opposition to MPs who had voted for either
the Maynooth grant or the education grant of 1847.[65] Some forty-
six independent candidates stood, and twenty-six MPs in favour
of disestablishment were returned, as well as sixty more opposed
to further state endowment of religion.[66] As Sir Charles Wood,
the Whig chancellor of the exchequer, noted in March 1847, 'in
most of the large towns, the very best friends we have had, are the
persons now leading the anti-government education movement'.[67]
Radicalism had occupied the left of politics, clearly fighting a
Whig–Peelite 'centre' alliance, and in some places, like Halifax
where Miall and Ernest Jones fought together, cooperated with the

61. Ibid. p. 156.   62. Machin, *Politics and the Churches*, pp. 56–7, 165–6.
63. Ibid. p. 108.   64. Ibid. p. 176.   65. Ibid. pp. 183–6.
66. Ibid. pp. 189, 192.   67. Prest, *Lord John Russell*, p. 256.

respectable wing of the Chartists. They were defeated, as was Joseph Sturge, founder of the Complete Suffrage Union, at Leeds, by *ad hoc* central alliances of Whigs assisted by Conservatives.[68]

After 1847, although an independent Radical party remained a chimaera, the Whigs suffered a Radical onslaught on several fronts. In 1848, a budget deficit coincided with a French naval scare and the requirement to renew the income tax. Radical and protection-ist opposition panicked the government which withdrew its initial plan to extend and raise income tax and ultimately introduced four budget statements during the year, further destroying the Whig pos-ture of competent government. In May of the same year, a com-mittee of fifty-one MPs agreed on the 'little charter' – household suffrage, secret ballot, triennial parliaments and equal electoral districts – which was defeated in parliament, but aroused Russell's interest. In June he hinted at the possibility of further reform, abandoning his 'finality' stance of 1837, and in 1849 he sprang his wish to extend the franchise on a surprised and unwelcoming cabi-net. Russell, however, gradually wore down cabinet resistance, even if he secured no more than unwilling acquiescence. A bill was finally introduced in 1852, just before the government fell. Parliamentary reform was back on the agenda.

Russell acted alone in his efforts to restore some momentum to his faltering government. There was political logic in both a new reform bill and confrontation with the Pope. Chartist agitation culminating in the Kennington Common demonstration and a third mass petition in 1848, suggested the potential of mass support for the renewed Radical initiative on parliamentary reform. The eccle-siastical policy of the Durham letter, whilst expressing Russell's genuine Erastian concern for 'religious liberties and the civil rights of nations',[69] also offered political gains.[70] As Derby, who hoped to profit from the same sentiment, observed in 1851, 'even the most Radical towns . . . are . . . furiously anti-Papal'.[71] For the Whigs, however, the logic of appealing to the agitation for reform and to popular Protestantism with a view to gaining Radical support was inconsistent with centrism. It alienated the Peelites whom they sought to conciliate, and Palmerston without whom the government could not continue. Radicals and Peelites were not absolutely at opposite poles of the political spectrum; politic alignments were too

68. Machin, *Politics and the Churches*, pp. 190–1.
69. Prest, *Lord John Russell*, p. 320.
70. Machin, *Politics and the Churches*, p. 210.
71. Stewart, *Foundation of the Conservative Party*, p. 252.

confused to be susceptible of such simple bi-polar analysis. Both Radicals and Peelites wanted efficient, economical government which, with the exception of some patriotic radicals, entailed a cautious foreign policy. The difficulty was that a Whig government, on its record, lacked the ability to deliver the former, and whilst it included Palmerston, would not deliver the latter. Liberal politics remained fragmented.

Factionalism and the emergence of Palmerston

The Protectionist government under Derby (formerly Stanley) that replaced the Whigs in 1852 did not outlast the year despite limited success at the general election, and not only failed to recruit Peelite support but ensured that the Peelites would regard the Whigs with greater favour. Hitherto, protection kept Peelites and Protectionists apart, but in 1852 the Conservatives played the Protestant rather than the Protectionist card, and fought the election expecting to abandon protection after it. They did so, however, with a deliberately sectionalist and reactionary purpose. Exploiting 'the now awakened spirit of Protestantism' was a tactic to win 'the real battle of the Constitution which . . . is whether the preponderance in the legislative power is to rest with the land and those connected with it, or with the manufacturing interests of the country'.[72] This was to reopen the conflict behind the repeal of the Corn Laws. The leading Peelites were alienated by the general illiberalism of the government as much as its fading protectionism. Aberdeen and Graham were already inclined towards the Whigs, and Herbert and Newcastle also felt that 'upon the first proposition of a Stanley government the junction of parties would be completed'.[73]

During the election, the Conservatives attacked several Peelites, including Gladstone, on Protestant grounds, exploiting the vote on the Maynooth grant. As Maynooth revealed, the idiosyncratic high-church liberalism that characterised several leading Peelites, but especially Gladstone, distinguished them from the anti-Catholic Protestantism of the Conservatives as much as protection. After the election, Gladstone was still reluctant to separate from a Conservative party whose government he would not join, but he was almost alone amongst the Peelite leadership. Aberdeen summed up their

72. Ibid. p. 252.   73. Ibid. p. 251.

distaste for 'religious bigotry . . . more objectionable to me than
Protection itself . . . the conduct of the government is quite unprecedented, and their whole proceeding is the most dishonest I have
ever witnessed'.[74] Gladstone would not rejoin the Conservatives
alone, and his own alienation was accomplished by the debate on
Disraeli's budget. Its defeat was settled in advance by Whig–Peelite
negotiations for a successor ministry. The savagery of the Peelite
attack, Gladstone's response to Disraeli's jibes, 'his usually calm
features . . . livid and distorted with passion', and Conservative antipathy to Gladstone's supporters who 'prudently kept away' from
the Carlton Club where 'they could not have escaped insult', all
ensured that the breach would be bitter and final. Derby made
subsequent attempts to recruit Gladstone, and Gladstone still inclined to the Conservative party as late as 1859. Derby's overtures
came to nothing, and the party did not want him.

The Conservative government fell with the budget, to be succeeded by a Peelite–Whig coalition under Aberdeen. The desired
combination was at last in being. With Gladstone as chancellor of
the exchequer and including both Russell and Palmerston, the
ministry was nominally strong. Moreover the extension of the area
of disagreement with the Conservatives from the single question of
free trade to that of a general outlook, the liberalism of the government, afforded a basis for cohesion which might both transcend
internal disagreement on details and distinguish it from the opposition on issues of principle. There had been a significant realignment
during the ministerial crisis of 1851–2, which did contain, as the
queen hoped, the potential for 'a sound state of parties'. Beneath
the surface of the apparently formless factionalism of the 1850s,
when almost any political combination seemed possible, divisions
had, in fact, emerged.

This, however, is clearer in hindsight than it was to contemporary politicians, who either failed to recognise the significance
of the decisions made then, or were unwilling to accept them as
final because they felt uncomfortable with the consequences. In
refusing to join the Conservatives, either in 1852 or subsequently,
despite invitations to do so, Palmerston and the Peelites both threw
in their lot with the Liberal side of politics, and thus with Russell
and the Whigs. But personal rancour combined with genuine policy
disagreements to keep Liberalism divided, and thus to create the
impression that the Conservatives might recruit Liberal dissidents.

74. Ibid. p. 257.

Liberal disunity was central to the factionalism of the 1850s, and central to Liberal disunity was the position of Palmerston. His personal feud with Russell, exacerbated by Russell's restless ambition, was one source of tension. Peelite distrust of his foreign policy and its expense was another. Gladstone, in particular, not only disliked the church appointments made by Palmerston's government of 1855–8, but was outspoken in his criticism of both Palmerston's foreign adventures and the extravagance he discerned in the budgets of Sir George Cornewall Lewis, Palmerston's chancellor of the exchequer. Liberal politics thus took on the appearance of a game of musical chairs, in which the players, for various reasons, sought to avoid sitting down with Palmerston, or at least with Palmerston as prime minister. Palmerston eventually won, but it took the rest of the decade, and another minority Conservative government, before the politicians involved accepted Palmerston's supremacy, and 'a sound state of parties' could be realised.

The Aberdeen coalition that apparently promised so much was the first victim of this instability within Liberal politics. It was overshadowed almost from the first by the dispute between Russia and Turkey that became the Crimean war in 1854, and disrupted by personal rivalries. Russell believed that he had secured the reversion to the premiership which Aberdeen intended to vacate promptly, and became increasingly truculent when the worsening diplomatic situation and cabinet pressure kept Aberdeen in office. To occupy Russell, the government agreed to resume the question of parliamentary reform, but Russell's programme of lowering the borough franchise to £6 provoked Palmerston's resignation, although he quickly returned. Popularly interpreted as a protest against the government's indecisive handling of Russia, the resignation dissociated Palmerston from the drift into war. The outbreak of war in March 1854 obliged Russell to withdraw his reform bill, but not before he had secured a commitment to its reintroduction when circumstances permitted, and Palmerston in turn had declared that he could not support it.[75] The government was, like its predecessors, falling apart even before the demand for an inquiry into the conduct of the war by the veteran Radical MP, John Roebuck, brought it down in January 1855. Unable to secure support from either Palmerston or the Peelites, the Conservatives refused office, and the way was open for Palmerston who, almost alone from the coalition, had escaped with his reputation enhanced.

75. Prest, *Lord John Russell,* pp. 364–5.

Palmerston's government remained a coalition, since he was convinced that only a coalition could sustain 'a government strong enough to carry on its affairs with the support of Parliament' whilst parliamentary opinion remained so divided and party affiliations so weak.[76] He even secured the support of the Peelites, including Gladstone and Herbert, who were 'to all appearances very strongly bound by personal ties to Palmerston'.[77] Appearances were again deceptive. Palmerston's recognition that he had to let Roebuck's inquiry proceed provided the opportunity for their rapid withdrawal. The difficulty, as before, was Palmerston's conduct, or likely conduct, of foreign policy. As Palmerston told Gladstone, 'plainly and frankly, you distrust my views and intentions'.[78]

The swift ending of the Crimean war by negotiations left the Peelites looking slightly ridiculous but did not change either their basic distrust or their principled factionalism. The government was brought down in March 1857 by the combined votes of Peelites, Conservatives, Cobdenite Radicals and Russell on Cobden's motion condemning the bombardment of Canton, nominally in defence of British shipping. The ensuing election, virtually a referendum on Palmerston's policies, was a resounding endorsement for Palmerston and defeat for his opponents, but it produced no greater stability in parliament. Palmerston's determination not to alienate France led him to introduce a new conspiracy bill in 1858 when it appeared that Orsini had used British technology in his failed attempt to assassinate Napoleon III. He was again defeated on a Radical amendment, devised in consultation with Russell and Graham, and supported, as before, by Radicals, Peelites and a majority of the Conservatives. The Conservatives formed another minority government. A Liberal party and a 'sound state of parties' appeared as far away as ever.

Attitudes were nevertheless changing towards the issues that kept the Liberal sections apart. If only because they seemed in a permanent minority under the existing system, the Conservatives had a motive for raising again the question of parliamentary reform. Disraeli did so immediately after the 1857 election. Palmerston had by then indicated his own willingness to consider parliamentary reform by establishing a committee on the subject whilst in office which approved Russell's proposed £6 borough franchise, and then promising a bill once office was regained. In the constituencies,

76. Stewart, *Foundation of the Conservative Party*, p. 301.   77. Ibid. p. 298.
78. Donald Southgate, *The Passing of the Whigs* (London: Macmillan, 1962), p. 280.

John Bright, now Radical MP for Birmingham, campaigned violently, if unsuccessfully, to raise an agitation for household suffrage, equal electoral districts and the secret ballot during 1858; Gladstone concluded that no government could survive if it ignored parliamentary reform.[79] The Conservative reform bill of 1859, however, was too blatantly partisan in its proposals to increase landed influence in the counties. What Bright called a 'country gentleman's bill' was easily rejected on Russell's amendment in favour of extending the borough franchise which the Conservatives had left untouched.[80]

Defeated in the Commons, Derby dissolved parliament on the reform issue in April, but war in Italy, impending since the beginning of the year, broke out in the same month and rapidly overshadowed reform. The Conservatives gained twenty-six seats in the election, which still left them in a minority if the opposition could unite. Psychologically, it had already begun to do so. As early as 1846, Russell had declared his desire 'to secure a majority of Liberals', considering the Whigs as merely a section of a Liberal grouping.[81] Throughout the 1850s, senior politicians similarly regarded themselves as 'Liberals' in various ways. When the Peelites abruptly left Palmerston's first administration, Gladstone referred to 'the Liberal party' although he considered it 'dead'.[82] The Peelite, Newcastle, complained of the desire 'to crush all Liberals who are not Whigs',[83] whilst Sir Charles Wood, as a Whig, regretted the 'end of that fusion of all liberal bodies'.[84] In 1857 Granville, as another Whig, regarded the election as returning 'Government Liberals' as distinct from Radical Liberals; in 1858, those Radical Liberals themselves expressed 'the earnest wish . . . to see a Derby ministry formed . . . the effect of such a step being to unite every section of the Liberal party in opposition',[85] a prediction that finally proved accurate.

With Palmerston, despite reservations, and Bright prepared to accept reform on Russell's terms, reform was not quite the divisive issue of the recent past. Sympathy for Italian liberation was a cause that engaged liberal emotions, especially those of Gladstone and Russell, and together with the suspicion that the Conservative bias towards Austria would lead to war with France, offset distrust

---

79. Prest, *Lord John Russell*, p. 382.
80. Adelman, *Victorian Radicalism*, p. 35; Prest, *Lord John Russell*, p. 383.
81. Michael Bentley, *Politics Without Democracy 1815–1914* (London: Fontana, 1984), p. 141.
82. Southgate, '*Most English Minister*', p. 420.   83. Southgate, *Whigs*, p. 282.
84. Ibid. p. 283.   85. Stewart, *Foundation of the Conservative Party*, p. 319.

of Palmerston. The principal divisive issues of the previous decade were thus temporarily suspended whilst the natural desire of a majority to resume power was strengthened. A meeting of Whigs, Liberals, Radicals and Peelites at Willis's Rooms on 6 June 1859 concerted the overthrow of Derby's government; in so doing, although at the time they did not know it, or perhaps intend it, they put an end to the confusion in parliamentary politics that had existed since 1846, or even 1832. The personal rivalry between Russell and Palmerston was resolved in favour of the latter; Gladstone, whose antipathy to Palmerston Cornewall Lewis described in 1858 as 'a sort of mania',[86] finally committed himself to a Palmerston government; the Radicals were incorporated into a governmental alliance. Liberalism was on the path to organisation, and a two-party system re-emerged.

The problem with identifying the origin of the Liberal party derives from a number of factors. In one sense, Britain had had a two-party system since the Glorious Revolution of 1688. The Liberal party of the nineteenth century was, as Gladstone argued, a continuation of the Whig party of the eighteenth century, evolving to meet new circumstances. Regarded thus, the problem is reduced to identifying at which point in its evolution from the seventeenth-century soup, a distinctly new species of party emerged. That, in turn, depends on the definition of party used: the informal association described by Gorham, the disciplined unit that Peel required and modern politicians experience, or some intermediary state. The domination of liberal principles during the nineteenth century confuses the issue since the identification of a political grouping with those principles encourages the idea that a Liberal party actually existed. That, too, depends on the definition of party adopted. Liberalism itself, however, acquired new meanings, particularly as Radical ideas became more coherent and influential after the 1840s. The Whig tradition was an important component of Liberal ideology, and Whig leadership an important element in its political expression, but Whiggery did not represent the totality of Liberalism. When a Liberal party actually emerged turns not only on the definition of party, but on the definition of Liberalism.

Nevertheless, continuity does not exclude periods of chaos, a transition between one form and another. 1832–59, and indeed beyond 1859, was just such a period in the emergence of organised

---

86. E.D. Steele, *Palmerston and Liberalism 1855–1865* (Cambridge: Cambridge University Press, 1991), p. 115.

Liberalism. Liberal principles were predominant, but they exerted insufficient pressure either to compress the disparate Whigs, Radicals and Irish into a coherent whole, or to divide conservative Liberals and liberal Conservatives into two distinct political clusters. Only after 1846 did the Conservative Protectionists become identifiable as a distinctly illiberal political grouping; only in 1859 did the liberal Conservative Peelites acknowledge that their liberalism and their Conservatism were incompatible and that the former was more important; even after 1859, Palmerstonian and Whig centrism continued to blur the divide.

Ideology transcended political divisions and generated political fragmentation. MPs could not be dragooned. Nevertheless, as a result of Peel's demanding leadership and a clearer sense of what they were defending, the Conservatives were at least united enough to split. The self-styled Liberals more closely resembled a shoal of fish, a swirling mass forever changing shape and composition, fragmenting and recombining but never a single unit. They did not split because there was no party to split. In this amorphous quality lay both their strength and their weakness before 1859. In 1886 the Liberals did split, in a manner similar to the Conservatives in 1846 with approximately a third of the party sheering off, ultimately to be absorbed by the other side. By 1886 the Liberals had become recognisable as a party, as the culmination of a process begun, almost accidentally, in 1859.

CHAPTER TWO

Mid-Victorian Liberalism

Contemporaries were unimpressed with Palmerston's achievement in 1859. 'I do not think', wrote one member of the new government, 'that we shall be very long lived . . . after that I shall make my bow under any circumstances, for I am heartily sick of it.'[1] The coalition nature of the new administration was striking. Amongst the Whigs, Clarendon, who resumed the foreign secretaryship that he had held for much of the decade, called it 'a great bundle of sticks'[2]; Panmure, who had been secretary of state for war during Palmerston's administration of 1855–8 but was omitted from the new government, warned Palmerston of the difference between his old cabinet, 'composed of men well known to each other . . . having the same political aspirations', and his new cabinet which 'will contain sections of all different parties'.[3] For the Radicals, Cobden, who refused to join, noticed 'the union of all shades of opinion from the intense aristocratic exclusiveness . . . of . . . a large majority of the cabinet to the honest radicalism of Gibson, and the democracy of the Chancellor of the Exchequer [Gladstone]'.[4]

Palmerstonian centrism

Inclusiveness was the major reason for the government's survival and the emergence of the Liberal party as a reasonably coherent

1. E.D. Steele, *Palmerston and Liberalism 1855–1865* (Cambridge: Cambridge University Press, 1991), p. 87.
2. Norman Gash, *Aristocracy and People: Britain 1815–1865* (London: Arnold, 1979), p. 271.
3. Angus Hawkins, *Parliament, Party and the Art of Politics in Britain* (London: Macmillan, 1987), pp. 266–7.
4. Steele, *Palmerston and Liberalism*, p. 131.

force. The 'aristocratic exclusiveness' that Panmure defended and Cobden condemned had been a constant criticism of Whig governments. Together with the 'omission to consult the representatives of the large towns', it had aroused renewed protests from moderate and Palmerstonian backbenchers after Palmerston's fall in 1858. A meeting of 'industrial liberals' in May of that year 'to consider the present disorganised state of the party', was described by one of those present, W.E. Baxter of Montrose Burghs, as a 'protest against the constitution and policy of recent Whig governments'.[5] Under these circumstances, as Palmerston explained to another excluded Whig, Lord Ernest Bruce, it was essential 'to reconstruct the government upon a different principle, and . . . out of a larger range of political parties'.[6] The Radicals in any case insisted upon a meaningful representation in the cabinet, and concerted their claims with Russell who made his acceptance of the foreign office conditional on offers to Milner Gibson and Cobden, just as the Radicals insisted on the inclusion of Russell.[7] On Cobden's refusal, Clarendon's brother, C.P. Villiers, a veteran of the campaign against the Corn Laws, joined the cabinet alongside Gibson with several other Radicals in junior ministerial posts.

The effect was to neutralise much of their discontent. In describing Gibson later as 'the buffer to prevent us hitting his chief',[8] Cobden described the role of all the ministerial Radicals. Enthusiastic for office, they proclaimed their continuing commitment to 'advanced Liberalism', but in arguing the ministry's case made it acceptable to advanced opinion. Gladstone performed a similar role. He saw legislation, including budgets, as fulfilling political as well as administrative functions, and directed his budgets towards Radical opinion both in content and presentation. In 1860–1, it was Gladstone's presence in the cabinet, as well as that of Milner Gibson, that regained the allegiance of disaffected Radicals.[9] Much of the success of a Palmerstonian government that faced both left and right can be attributed to the effectiveness of Palmerston and Gladstone working in harness.

Like Russell, Gladstone was allowed to choose his own office, although Palmerston had an alternative chancellor in Cornewall Lewis, and was in a position to refuse. Gladstone resisted to the last,

5. Ibid. pp. 80–5.   6. Ibid. p. 94

7. Hawkins, *Parliament, Party*, pp. 258–9, 363, 272.

8. Steele, *Palmerston and Liberalism*, p. 131.

9. P.M. Gurowich, 'The continuation of war by other means: party and politics 1855–1865', *The Historical Journal* 27 (3) (1984), 617.

standing aloof from the Willis's Rooms meeting and voting with Derby's government in the confidence debate that overthrew it. But the election of 1857 had demonstrated to Gladstone both the popular support that Palmerston enjoyed, and that the Peelites had no political future in isolation.[10] Attributing national sympathy with Italy to 'the authority and zeal of Lord Palmerston and Lord John Russell' provided him with the opportunity he sought after thirteen years in a tributary to rejoin the political mainstream.[11] Failure to do so would, as he observed, leave him 'the one remaining Ishmael in the House of Commons', his career ended and his talents wasted.[12]

In 1859, Conservatives shared the general belief that the new Liberal government would be divided and brief. Derby thought 'it would be easy to get a majority against the present government'.[13] Significantly, he did not try. Palmerston was acceptable to Conservative opinion in parliament and in the country, where some Conservative associations declined to run candidates against Palmerstonian Liberals, and some candidates declared their general support for Palmerston.[14] Derby himself was more concerned that Palmerston should resist Radical pressure, 'in which case', as he wrote in 1857, 'I should feel it to be my duty . . . to give him any aid in my power.'[15] In 1860 he informed Palmerston that if his government were to disintegrate, 'the Conservative party would support . . . any administration which Viscount Palmerston might be able provisionally to make',[16] and in 1861 this arrangement was prolonged on condition that Palmerston did not reintroduce parliamentary reform or become involved in war against Austria, neither of which was by then on Palmerston's agenda.[17]

Behind Derby's offers lay the hope that by encouraging Palmerstonian restraint, a rift might develop within the government's ranks as Radicals grew restive.[18] 'Among Palmerstonians proper' there were, as Derby assumed, 'as strong Conservatives at heart as any in our ranks; and looking to Palmerston's increasing age and

10. John Morley, *The Life of William Ewart Gladstone*, vol. 1 (London: Macmillan, 1903), pp. 564–7; Steele, *Palmerston and Liberalism*, pp. 27, 112–15; Hawkins, *Parliament, Party*, pp. 71–2.

11. Steele, *Palmerston and Liberalism*, p. 116.

12. Morley, *Life of Gladstone*, vol. 1, p. 628; Hawkins, *Parliament, Party*, p. 272.

13. Hawkins, *Parliament, Party*, p. 268.

14. Steele, *Palmerston and Liberalism*, pp. 61, 137; Robert Stewart, *The Foundation of the Conservative Party 1830–1867* (London: Longman, 1978), pp. 316–18, 343–4.

15. Ibid. p. 316.   16. Ibid. p. 318; Steele, *Palmerston and Liberalism*, p. 160.

17. Stewart, *Foundation*, p. 318; Gurowich, 'Continuation', p. 625.

18. Gurowich, 'Continuation', pp. 623–5.

infirmities, the oftener these can be brought into the same lobby in opposition to Radical moves, the better for us'; but he was deceived by Palmerston's longevity and his ability to restrain or ignore his Radical fringe. Palmerston's position was further eased when Russell retired to the Lords in 1861, convinced by the loss of his bill of 1860 that reform had no future in conditions of parliamentary and public apathy.

After 1860, reform became virtually an open question. The proposal for a £6 borough franchise introduced periodically by the Leeds Radical, Edward Baines, permitted an expression of Liberal intent without precipitating divisive action. Radicalism was slowly burrowing its way into the Liberal fabric. By 1865, the cabinet, in Palmerston's absence through illness, decided to support Baines's reform motion, leaving Palmerston as the only cabinet minister who had not voted for it. Such progress was necessary to hold the governing coalition together. Brand, as chief whip, 'looking to the integrity of the Liberal party', urged support for Baines's proposal.[19] As Derby rightly predicted, when Palmerston died 'the Radicals will then push for extensive Parliamentary reform', although his other prediction, that the Whigs would then move to the Conservatives, anticipated events by twenty years.[20]

In turn, Palmerston could exploit the divisions his conservative approach created within the Conservative party. Palmerston's strength lay in his control of the central ground across party alignments, drawing support as required from either Conservatives or Radicals.[21] According to Lord Robert Cecil, the future Third Marquess of Salisbury and Conservative prime minister, every Conservative was in Palmerston's debt 'because he succeeded in doing that which it is most difficult and most salutary for a parliament to do – nothing'.[22] This was to underestimate not only what Gladstone was allowed to do, but Palmerston's own active foreign policy, and his even more active promotion of it through his carefully nurtured contacts with the press. The combination of calculated insults to foreign autocrats, public sympathy with foreign liberals and firm action against minor powers in defence of British interests which few, in Britain at least, distinguished from the interests of liberal civilisation and the progress of humanity, still caught the popular imagination and that of a sizeable group of patriotic Radicals.

19. Steele, *Palmerston and Liberalism*, p. 221.
20. Gurowich, 'Continuation', p. 627.   21. Ibid. p. 629.
22. Stewart, *Foundation*, pp. 310, 318.

Italian unification was the apotheosis of this policy. Reservations about French aggrandisement did not detract from genuine sympathy with 'the liberation of the Italian people from a foreign yoke' which Garibaldi's unexpected success in Naples made possible. Russell's dispatch of 27 October 1860 identified Britain with Italian unification when all the other major powers had withdrawn their representatives from Turin. The dispatch approved of the revolution of 'the people of Southern Italy', criticised the other powers for their censure of Piedmont and expressed British pleasure in 'the gratifying prospect of a people building up the edifice of their liberties and consolidating the work of their independence'. It was, claimed Russell, what the British, ever in the forefront of the march of progress, had themselves done, with similar outside assistance, in 1688.[23]

Subsequent efforts were less successful. Verbal support for the Polish revolt of 1863 and condemnation of Russia's 'barbarous' behaviour did not prevent Russia suppressing the Poles. Nor did bluff on behalf of Denmark prevent Bismarck invading Schleswig-Holstein in 1864. The government narrowly won the consequent vote of censure, but the episode marked the end of what the Radical W.E. Forster, echoing Conservative critics, called 'that meddling, dishonest system of apparent intervention . . . which is really non-intervention'.[24] The point, made by both Salisbury and Disraeli, that British foreign policy would have been more successfully conducted on the principles of Cobden and Bright, was not lost on either Radical, or on Gladstone. Whilst it lasted, Palmerstonian diplomacy successfully straddled the twin demands of the British public: support for liberal constitutionalism abroad but avoidance of war with a major power. The public, as Palmerston knew, liked to hear the lion roar in defence of liberalism, but did not want it to unsheath its suspiciously blunt claws.

Palmerston was favoured by circumstance. His success abroad, at least until 1860, was possible only because Britain was the leading naval power and the most dynamic economy at a time when potential rivals, with the occasional exception of France, were still struggling with the problems of unification and revolution. In domestic politics, the divisive issues of protection and Ireland which had overcome both Whigs and Tories in the 1840s were in temporary

23. John Prest, *Lord John Russell* (London: Macmillan, 1972), pp. 390–2; Donald Southgate, *'The Most English Minister': The Policies and Politics of Palmerston* (London: Macmillan, 1966), pp. 479–83.

24. Southgate, *'Most English Minister'*, p. 518.

abeyance. A return to prosperity by the early 1850s took much of the tension out of the political atmosphere, reducing both popular and agricultural discontent. After a sudden fall in 1851–2, wheat prices stabilised at around 50 shillings per quarter in peacetime.[25] Free trade did indeed appear to be a naturally or providentially ordained route to prosperity. 'We have committed ourselves to the general laws of Providence,' proclaimed *The Times* in 1852, 'and Providence now rewards us with a vista of social improvements, and unexpected blessings, which men had not dreamt of ten years ago.'[26] The Conservatives abandoned protection in the same year.

Relative prosperity also helped to reduce tension in post-famine Ireland, although the British government had done little to deserve tranquillity. 'We cannot feed the people', Russell told his lord lieu-tenant, Bessborough, in 1846,[27] and little effort had been made to do so. The Whigs, whatever their claims for administrative compe-tence, presided over arguably the most lethal famine in modern history, not excluding the third world. About one million people died as a direct result of the potato crop failures in the 1840s, and a further 2 million emigrated between 1846 and 1855.[28] Ireland was not pacified, still less reconciled, but it was temporarily silenced. Not until the Fenian outrages of the mid-1860s did it again intrude disruptively into mainland politics.

Because the party did not split, except for the reform crisis of 1866–7 which gave Derby his longest period as minority prime minister, the Whigs continued to dominate the Liberal party at the national level. Palmerston's administration of 1859 included '3 dukes, the brother of a fourth, 5 other peers or sons of peers, and 3 baronets of landed property'.[29] Gladstone, despite his reser-vations about the quality of the younger generation of Whigs which had been suspect since the mid-1840s, clung to the ideal of a service aristocracy, and displayed a similar preference for Whigs and aristocrats. Moreover, the Anglican landed establishment, of which they were the supreme examples, was well represented in the mid-Victorian parliamentary Liberal party. Of the 456 English Lib-eral MPs between 1859 and 1874, 114 were related to the peerage,

25. Gash, *Aristocracy and People*, p. 365.
26. Jonathan Parry, *The Rise and Fall of Liberal Government in Victorian Britain* (New Haven: Yale University Press, 1993), p. 168.
27. Prest, *Lord John Russell*, p. 241.
28. David Fitzpatrick, 'Flight from Famine' and Cormac O'Grada, 'The Great Famine and Today's Famines', in Cathal Poirteir (ed.), *The Great Irish Famine* (Dub-lin: Mercier Press, 1995), pp. 175, 248–50.
29. Stewart, *Foundation*, p. 317.

47 were patrons of livings, 122 were officers in the services or the militia, over half were large landowners, or gentlemen of leisure,[30] and the English MPs were 'overwhelmingly Anglican'.[31]

Few in number, their social prestige and political confidence allowed the Whigs to continue to exercise immense influence far beyond the twenty-three seats they controlled directly.[32] Many of the great Whig families were industrial as well as landed magnates; their piety gave them points of contact with industrialists and the Nonconformist conscience through a common impulse to philanthropy; their undogmatic approach to religion was that of moderate Anglican Liberals in the country. Though their role increasingly became one of conservatism from within, especially once Gladstone had assumed the leadership, the Whigs played an important part in reassuring moderate public opinion that sought gradual reform, but not major reconstruction.

Nonconformist Radicalism

The majority of Liberal, and even Radical, opinion was content with the gradual reform envisaged by the governing elite. Where it was extreme, Radicalism was divided. Baines was typical, a moderate in all respects but one, whose strong support for corn law repeal in the family paper, the *Leeds Mercury*, did not extend to sympathy with the attacks on the Whigs waged by Cobden and Bright. 'If he were not there [Yorkshire],' Cobden complained to Bright in 1848, 'I could undertake to rally the party tomorrow and in two years beat both the Tory and Whig aristocracy.'[33] Baines, however, valued the alliance between Leeds Radicalism and the local Whig gentry, and opposed on their behalf, if unsuccessfully, League efforts to open a registration campaign in the West Riding. Like the Leeds flax-spinner, John Marshall, first elected to parliament in 1826, he tended to regard the landed classes as 'natural leaders', at least whilst those leaders reciprocated the 'good understanding between country gentlemen and the towns'. From Halifax, the Liberal Conservative millowner, Edward Akroyd, like Cobden an Anglican, also warned against 'the Cobden and Bright party... Their object is to form a middle class administration in contradistinction to the

30. John Vincent, *The Formation of the British Liberal Party* (Harmondsworth: Penguin Books, 1972), pp. 46, 42, 41.
31. Ibid. p. 103.   32. Ibid. p. 62n.
33. Keith Robbins, *John Bright* (London: Routledge & Kegan Paul, 1979), p. 80.

aristocratic element which has hitherto predominated in the government of this country.'[34]

Yet because of the extremism of his Nonconformist commitment, Baines himself destroyed that good understanding. He came to national prominence in the Nonconformist opposition to Graham's factory bill in 1843, and opposed with equal vehemence the Whig Act of 1847. There was, he believed, 'no educational want that may not be supplied by the voluntary efforts of the people themselves'. To defeat the voluntaryists, Marshall successfully cooperated with the Conservatives in Leeds, Sir Charles Wood and Edwards joined forces in Halifax, and in 1848 the Whig magnate, Earl Fitzwilliam, supported the Tory, Denison, in the West Riding.[35] Cobden, who was personally committed to state education, attempted in 1848 to warn Baines off the divisive education issue, and found further fault with Nonconformist extremism in 1851 because their support for the ecclesiastical titles bill destroyed 'the principle of religious equality'.[36] Bright continued to denounce the Anglican establishment as strongly as anyone because of its political connections: it was an 'old political machine which has made a pretence of being a Christian Church',[37] an 'overgrown and monstrous abuse' that depended 'on the law and on the patronage of the squires'.[38] But he, too, was 'pretty tired of mixing up religion in any way with a scheme of school education', and in 1853 refused to lead a militant campaign for disestablishment.[39]

Militant Nonconformity was never leaderless; but without Cobden and Bright its leaders were second-rank figures at best. This made it easier to integrate within Liberalism because it remained disunited, yet harder because of its very diversity. Nonconformity was nevertheless vital to mid-Victorian Liberalism. With political divisions following denominational lines, Liberal superiority stemmed from the inequality of party identification between two groups, Anglicans and Nonconformists, of approximately equal size. Nonconformists voted Liberal in ratios of between 8 : 1 and 12 : 1 whilst Anglicans voted Conservative only between 2.5 : 1 and 4 : 1; put simply, there were far more Anglican Liberals than there were Nonconformist

34. Derek Fraser, 'Edward Baines', in Patricia Hollis (ed.), *Pressure from Without in Early Victorian England* (London: Arnold, 1974), pp. 188–93.

35. Ibid. pp. 193–9; Robbins, *John Bright*, p. 77.

36. John Morley, *The Life of Richard Cobden*, vol. 2 (London: Chapman & Hall, 1881), pp. 30, 96.

37. Robbins, *John Bright*, p. 95.

38. G.M. Trevelyan *The Life of John Bright* (London: Constable, 1925), p. 343.

39. Robbins, *John Bright*, pp. 60, 132.

Conservatives.[40] Liberal politics at the crucial local level revolved around the factories, chapels, kinship and commercial connections of the local Nonconformist elite. In Blackburn, Liberal leadership came from the Congregational chapels, especially the Pilkington Park Road chapel, 'the unofficial headquarters of Blackburn Liberalism',[41] which included among its members W.A. Abram, editor of the *Blackburn Times* and local Liberal party manager.[42] Religion, politics, journalism and factory ownership merged there in the Liberal interest, as they did in Hugh Mason's Albion chapel in Ashton, John Clough's chapel in Keighley[43] and the prestigious Horton Lane chapel in Bradford, the centre of Bradford's Radical community.

Jealous of their local power and independence, local activists were wary of interference from national bodies, even Nonconformist pressure groups.[44] Nonconformist agitation gained strength in the general religious revival of the 1850s. The Anti-State Church Association, which re-formed itself as the Liberation Society in 1853 to head the campaign for disestablishment, became 'an umbrella society for all Nonconformist causes',[45] and together with the United Kingdom Alliance (temperance) and the short-lived National Education League was the most important of a surfeit of leagues and societies within which Radicalism and political Nonconformity became virtually synonymous. Disestablishment was an avowedly political cause, primarily concerned, as the title 'Liberation Society' suggested, with liberty, a 'free' church, and 'free trade in religion'. Effective political intervention to sever the church–state connection, however, depended upon the willingness of members to ignore the claims of other issues, party loyalty and civic duty. A few, like Baines, were fanatical, believing that they 'must use their political influence according to the light God has given them . . . even if as a result of their actions a political party has to perish',[46] but, as in the West Riding, they alarmed the local constituency elites to the detriment of both Nonconformist and Liberal causes.

The relationship between Nonconformist pressure groups and the Liberal party moved in cycles. The Liberation Society, having

40. Jonathan Parry, *Democracy and Religion: Gladstone and the Liberal Party 1867–1875* (Cambridge: Cambridge University Press, 1986), p. 11.

41. Patrick Joyce, *Work, Society and Politics: The Culture of the Factory in Later Victorian England* (London: Methuen, 1982), p. 175.

42. Ibid. pp. 17–18, 204.   43. Ibid. pp. 175–6, 34.

44. D.A. Hamer, *The Politics of Electoral Pressure* (Brighton: Harvester, 1977), p. 129.

45. Ibid. p. 99.   46. Ibid. pp. 16, 117.

secured no recognition for what it regarded as its contribution to
Liberal success in the 1850s, particularly to the victory of 1857,
turned to militancy in the early 1860s. In 1861, Samuel Morley
advised against voting for any candidate who would not support the
abolition of church rates,[47] and in 1863 Edward Miall took this to
the logical conclusion of demanding 'an independent political party
. . . witholding our votes and our influence whatever may be the
consequences of our abstention to the Liberal party'.[48] But even
this contained ambiguities. Miall's independent party would 'gradually . . . but surely, absorb into itself the best elements of the Liberal
party', in effect becoming the Liberal party purged and transformed.
Miall also recognised 'the almost insuperable difficulty . . . in per-
suading those who sympathise with us in sentiment to stand by us
firmly in this kind of electoral situation'.

At conferences up and down the country, local opinion expressed
reservations. The Liberal millowner, Hugh Mason, objected strongly
to ending cooperation with the Liberal party. He was supported by
the influential preacher-politician and future MP of his own Ashton
chapel, J. Guinness Rogers, and the equally influential Congregationalist minister, R.W. Dale, from Birmingham.[49] Miall's strategy
had to be moderated, with increasing emphasis placed on working
within the Liberal party, and influencing the choice of candidate
during the selection procedure rather than confrontation afterwards. Like it or not, the Nonconformists needed the Liberal party
as much as it needed them. Intervention within the Liberal party
also worked. In the general election of 1865, the Society felt that
'almost all Liberal candidates were now satisfactory on the church
rates question', and that in seats targeted for opposition, 'the moral
influence of Liberal defeats . . . will be of a wholesome kind'.[50]

Temperance was less exclusively a Liberal party issue. In Liverpool, one third of the temperance movement was said to be
Anglican;[51] in Dundee, James Scrymgeour, the leading temperance
campaigner, was a Wesleyan and a Tory with access to churches of
many denominations. Nevertheless, he owed his livelihood to the
generosity of the dominant local Liberal elite.[52] The United Kingdom Alliance was thus more independent of the Liberal party, and
even opposed Samuel Morley, despite his eminence in Nonconformist and reforming circles, at the Bristol by-election of 1868, to

47. Ibid. p. 98.   48. Ibid. p. 104.   49. Ibid. pp. 106–10.
50. Ibid. pp. 112–15.   51. Ibid. p. 184.
52. William M. Walker, *Juteopolis: Dundee and its Textile Workers 1885–1923* (Edinburgh: Scottish Academic Press, 1979), pp. 334–5.

howls of Nonconformist anger. Its relationship with the party nevertheless followed a similar cyclical pattern. Between 1864 and 1871, it pursued a policy of impartiality, supporting candidates most favourable to temperance, although these were usually Liberal. In 1872 it was provoked into a militant strategy by the perceived inadequacies of the Liberal Licensing Act, with threats of independent candidates and abstentions. It returned to moderation before the 1874 election, with further outbursts of militancy in 1877–8, 1885 and 1896–1900.[53] Like the Liberation Society, the Alliance had delusions of forming an independent political party, but was enmeshed in similar ambiguities and divided loyalties.[54]

Particular issues confused attitudes further. R.W. Dale, the moderate opponent of Miall's militancy in the Liberation Society in 1863, was an advocate of independent action as a member of the National Education League in 1873[55]; by the mid-1870s he had reverted to his former moderation as the education issue declined. The long-term process was nevertheless one of steady incorporation of Nonconformist pressure-group activity into the Liberal party. Years before Gladstone made his celebrated remark that Nonconformity was the backbone of the Liberal party, Cobden recognised that 'the Liberal ranks of the middle class [were] almost exclusively filled by Dissenters', that Dissent was 'the soul' of the Liberal party, and Dissenters 'the very salt of Liberalism'.[56] Legislation to meet the grievances voiced by the Liberation Society, and the adoption of the moderate, 'local option', policy on temperance permitting ratepayers to opt for prohibition in their district, enhanced the identification of party and sects. The same process drove Liberal Anglicans and Liberal brewers into the Conservative camp, increasing the polarisation of parties.

Without middle-class, industrial Nonconformists, their leagues and their newspapers, the Liberal party would have lacked much of its support, money, energy and reforming commitment. Despite Palmerston's popularity which led to a net gain of twenty-three seats in 1857, the Whigs never fully recovered in the counties where the Conservatives held about two thirds of the seats throughout the 1850s.[57] Liberalism was increasingly an urban party, but not yet an

53. Hamer, *Politics of Electoral Pressure*, pp. 172–82, 210–14, 231–3, 239–67.
54. Ibid. pp. 27, 106, 181–3, 188–9, 201, 210, 214, 230, 259.
55. Paul Adelman, *Victorian Radicalism: The Middle Class Experience 1830–1914* (London: Longman, 1984), p. 85; Hamer, *Politics of Electoral Pressure*, pp. 123–4.
56. Morley, *Life of Cobden*, vol. 2, pp. 2, 21, 84, 146.
57. Stewart, *Foundation*, p. 340–1.

organised one. In 1868, central Liberal organisation was still largely in the hands of the chief whip, assisted by the Liberal Registration Association (subsequently the Liberal Central Association) and a political agent during elections. The central organisation, according to a Registration Association circular, as usual asking for money, offered 'valuable assistance' in the 'careful supervision of, and attention to, the Registration', but it went on 'in many of the principal constituencies care is taken of this most important matter by local societies, with which . . . it is not possible to interfere'. The central organisation existed to plug the gaps left by local neglect; it could not enforce a national programme, nor control the selection of candidates. On the contrary, the weakness of the central party and the power of the localities was such that the whips needed to preserve a strict impartiality in order to maintain the little influence they had.[58]

The great Nonconformist pressure groups could supply much of the national organisation that the Liberal party lacked, and, subject to local independence, integration between the national and local spheres through regional agents, touring lecturers, local branches and the network provided by congregational affiliations and family alliances. The Liberation Society had two agents in 1858, rising to thirteen by 1861, six of whom were in Wales.[59] After the model of the Anti-Corn Law League, each pressure group had a wealth of information on the social, denominational and political structure of individual constituencies, and could provide its own candidates. In particular, they were able to organise areas where local Liberalism was weak and there was little risk of treading on local toes. Wales was virtually organised for Liberalism by the Liberation Society when a tour by Edward Miall and the Congregationalist minister and Peace Society activist, Henry Richard, was accompanied by the establishment of electoral committees whose main achievement was to effect the registration of the Liberal vote.[60] The great expansion of the local press, most of it Liberal, after Gladstone's abolition of the stamp and paper duties, also provided a source of propaganda, effective by its very localism. In this respect there is much to be said for Vincent's conclusion that 'what was really new' about the Liberal party 'was not the slow adaptations of the Parliamentary

58. H.J. Hanham, *Elections and Party Management: Politics in the Time of Disraeli and Gladstone* (London: Longmans, 1969), pp. 349–356; Vincent, *Formation*, pp. 115–131.
59. Vincent, *Formation*, p. 107.
60. Hamer, *Politics of Electoral Pressure*, pp. 116, 196; Vincent, *Formation*, pp. 107–8.

party; but the adoption of that Parliamentary party by a rank and file'.[61] Nevertheless, it took many years before Nonconformists fully thought and acted as party Liberals rather than as Nonconformists seeking a political vehicle.

Free-trade Radicalism

Cobden regretted Baines's divisiveness on education precisely because he valued the role of Nonconformists within Liberalism. The ideological, or more accurately moral, link that bound Nonconformity with the economic liberalism expressed by Cobden and the Anti-Corn Law League was the individualism that lay at the root of both, and at the heart of Liberalism as a political creed. Cobden, an Anglican, attacked the establishment from the other side, the land rather than the church, with economic rather than sectarian arguments. For him, the logical continuation of the policies of the Anti-Corn Law League lay in cooperation with the Liverpool Financial Reform Association for 'fiscal reform and economy'.[62] He proposed also continuing the League's methods – registration and the creation of voters through the 40-shilling freehold qualification – within the existing electoral system, rather than campaigning for parliamentary reform. It would enfranchise the right sort of people, 'the teetotallers, nonconformist and rational Radicals who would constitute nine-tenths of our phalanx of 40 shilling freeholders'[63]; win the support of 'the influential money-givers in Manchester',[64] and, according to Cobden, double the electorate in seven years.[65]

The plan would circumvent the problem of redistribution, which was far more important in changing the nature of parliament than extending the franchise, and was generally 'the surest guarantee of our being able to break down the power of the aristocracy without an appeal to violence. A county or two quietly rescued from the landlords by this process will, when announced, do more to strike dismay into the camp of feudalism and inspire the people.'[66] Moreover, it appeared to offer the prospect of a direct attack on the land monopoly. 'The citadel of privilege is so terribly strong, owing to the concentrated masses of property in the hands of the comparatively

61. Vincent, *Formation*, p. 19.   62. Morley, *Life of Cobden*, vol. 2, pp. 23–4.
63. Ibid. pp. 52–3.
64. Ibid. pp. 40–2; Miles Taylor, *The Decline of British Radicalism 1847–1860* (Oxford: Oxford University Press, 1995), pp. 184–6.
65. Morley, *Life of Cobden*, vol. 2, p. 52.   66. Ibid. p. 102.

few that we cannot hope to assail it with success unless with the help of the propertied middle ranks of society and by raising up a portion of the working-class to become members of a propertied order.'[67] He found, however, that industrial property owners were interested neither in 40-shilling freeholders, nor in breaking up concentrations of property.[68] The Land Tenure Reform Association, dedicated to destroying the 'land monopoly' by abolishing primogeniture and entail and creating 'free trade in land' remained a minor arrow in the quiver of Radical organisations.

As a programme, the 40-shilling freeholder campaign faded quietly away by the early 1850s to be replaced by parliamentary reform, where the initiative passed to Bright. Cobden saw little future in agitating for further reform in view of the prevailing apathy and was, moreover, pessimistic about its effectiveness. Democracy was never an end in itself for either Cobden or the mainstream of mid-nineteenth-century Liberalism, but was valuable only as a possible means to a higher end, the liberation of the individual. Because rationality was an essential attribute of individuality, this meant in practice the liberation of the middle and upper-working classes, not the masses. Liberation entailed removing the aristocratic yoke, which in turn required curbing the government expenditure by which it was sustained. Radical attacks on Palmerston's foreign policy arose from a comprehensive critique in which the aristocratic doctrine of the balance of power abroad and aristocratic rule at home formed a single militarist system. 'You cannot comprehend at a thought', Bright argued,

> the sufferings which the theory of the balance of power has entailed upon this country. It . . . has loaded the nation with debt and with taxes, has sacrificed the lives of hundreds of thousands of Englishmen, has desolated the homes of millions of families, and has left us, as the great result of the profligate expenditure which it has caused, a doubled peerage at one end of the social scale and far more than a doubled pauperism at the other.[69]

The people's energies were 'perverted to a disastrous course, so far as *their* interests are concerned, by a ruling class which has reaped all the honours and emoluments, while the nation inherits the burdens and responsibilities'.[70] It operated as 'a gigantic system of out-door relief for the aristocracy of Great Britain'.[71]

67. Ibid. p. 53.   68. Ibid. pp. 97, 215.
69. Trevelyan, *Life of Bright*, pp. 333–4.
70. Morley, *Life of Cobden*, vol. 2, p. 133.   71. Trevelyan, *Life of Bright*, p. 274.

Free trade, in its widest interpretation, was the antithesis of aristo-cratic militarism. 'Free trade,' Cobden wrote in 1842, 'by perfecting the intercourse and securing the dependence of countries one upon another must inevitably snatch the power from governments to plunge their people into wars.'[72] Against Palmerstonian meddling, 'continually augmenting our standing armaments, and . . . oppress-ing and degrading the people with taxation',[73] Cobden and Bright pressed constantly for a formal policy of non-intervention and inter-national arbitration. They cooperated with those Nonconformist Radicals who opposed war on moral and religious grounds, but Cobden, as always, pressed the argument 'from politico-economical and financial considerations' not only for peace 'but also . . . a dimi-nution of our costly peace establishments'.[74] When the Peace Soci-ety switched the main focus of its attention from colonial to European affairs in the mid-1840s, it adopted Cobden's economic critique of European militarism and the appeal to the 'selfish inter-est' of economy over the moral influence of pacifism.[75]

Morality, nevertheless, underpinned this campaign just as it had the campaign against the Corn Laws. This was another key link with Nonconformity. For Cobden, 'it is this moral sentiment, more than the £.s.d. view of the matter, which impels me to undertake the advocacy of a reduction of our forces'.[76] Both Cobden and Bright believed in a retributive moral law 'written . . . for nations, and for nations great as this of which we are citizens. If nations reject and deride that moral law, there is a penalty which will inevit-ably follow.'[77]

> There is no permanent greatness to a nation except it be based upon morality. I do not care for military greatness or military renown . . . crowns, coronets, mitres, military display, the pomp of war, wide colonies, and a huge empire, are, in my view, all trifles light as air, and not worth considering, unless with them you can have a fair share of comfort, contentment and happiness among the great body of the people. Palaces, baronial castles, great halls, stately mansions, do not make a nation. *The nation in every country dwells in the cottage.*[78]

So, too, did the agricultural labourers. 'Dry bread is all they can get. The pigs have disappeared from their sties. They and their

72. Norman McCord, *The Anti-Corn Law League* (London: George Allen & Unwin, 1958), p. 32.
73. Morley, *Life of Cobden*, vol. 2, p. 8.   74. Ibid. pp. 144–5.
75. Taylor, *Decline*, pp. 173–9; Morley, *Life of Cobden*, vol. 2, pp. 67–71, 115.
76. Morley, *Life of Cobden*, vol. 2, p. 42.
77. Ibid. pp. 46, 56; Trevelyan, *Life of Bright*, p. 275.
78. Trevelyan, *Life of Bright*, pp. 274–5.

children are looking haggard and pale and ragged.'[79] But that, of course, was the point. With non-intervention, Britain would become a garden, 'every dwelling might be made of marble and every person who treads its soil might have been sufficiently educated'.[80]

Cobden was pessimistic in the 1850s because of the popularity of Palmerstonian policies, to which parliamentary reform was no answer. The people, he wrote to Bright,

> want information and instruction upon armaments, colonies, taxation and so forth. There is a fearful mass of prejudice and ignorance to dispel upon these subjects, and while these exist, you may get a reform of Parliament, but you will not get a reformed policy . . . there is as much clinging to colonies at the present moment amongst the middle class as among the aristocracy, and the working people are not wiser than the rest.[81]

In practice Cobden suspected the working classes to be considerably more prone to Tory blandishments, and totally unreliable. Bright was left to plough the democratic desert alone.

But Cobden had little more faith in the middle classes, even those who had supported the Anti-Corn Law League. Rather, as he told Bright, 'we have the labour of Hercules in hand to abate the power of the aristocracy and their allies, the snobs of the towns'.[82] In Manchester 'the great capitalists . . . form an aristocracy, individual members of which wield an influence over sometimes 2000 persons . . . The great capitalist class formed an excellent basis for the Anti-Corn Law movement, for they had inexhaustible purses, which they opened freely in a contest where not only their pecuniary interests but their pride as "an order" was at stake.' But 'now that their gross pocket question is settled' Manchester industrialists were 'a very unsound and to us a very unsafe body'.[83] In similar vein, Baines, he thought '*is aristocratic*'.[84] Even the criticism levelled at the government for its incompetent management of the Crimean war left Cobden rightly doubting whether 'it will so far raise the middle class in their own esteem as to induce them to venture on the task of self-government. They must be ruled by Lords.'[85]

Despite the support for Palmerston, however, the upsurge of urban self-assurance that came with renewed prosperity was necessary if liberalism was to succeed in counterbalancing the aristocratic

79. Morley, *Life of Cobden*, vol. 2, p. 179.   80. Robbins, *John Bright*, p. 105.
81. Morley, *Life of Cobden*, vol. 2, p. 39.   82. Ibid. pp. 57–8, 94.
83. Ibid. pp. 199, 211.   84. Fraser, 'Edward Baines', p. 185.
85. Morley, *Life of Cobden*, vol. 2, p. 166.

militarism that Cobden condemned with an alternative value system. The patriotic but Radical MP for Newcastle, Joseph Cowen, owner of the *Newcastle Chronicle* and local wirepuller, saw matters in a more optimistic light: 'Our towns are the backbone of the nation . . . They are carving out of raw materials the means of social elevation, amelioration and enjoyment . . . uniting in the bonds of amity long-estranged and oft-embattled lands, and binding all classes.' Towns represented modernity, 'that irresistible and victorious civilisation which has for its foundation industry and freedom – freedom of thought, of labour, of sale and exchange, which furnishes as complete a model of public and private prosperity and as stable a fabric of social happiness and national grandeur as the world has ever seen'. Cowen deliberately contrasted urban and rural civilisation, urban liberty and rural oppression. In his history, townsmen 'curbed the pretensions of the barons. . . . The noise of the workshops rose . . . and proclaimed the dawn of the day when trade asserted its independence, and industry claimed its rights.'[86] The role of the Liberal party was to complete this historic process by converting the claims of industry, and more especially industrial Nonconformity, into reality.

> The owner of 10,000 spindles confronted the lord of 10,000 acres; the one grasping the steam engine, the other the plough; each surrounded by an equal number of dependents, and bearing an equal share in the burdens and dangers of the state. Now the time has arrived when the shadow of injustice between such rivals could no longer be endured . . . Trade shall no longer pay a tribute to the soil.[87]

Changing the outlook of parliament by converting opinion, whether by creating freeholders, extending the franchise and/or redistributing seats, in order to reduce the power of the aristocracy, to prevent an aggressive foreign policy, to reduce taxation, to liberate income for investment and consumption, to provide employment and end poverty to secure the liberty and independence of the freeborn Englishman was a logical sequence which expressed the central rationale and values of mid-Victorian Liberalism. Free-trade Radicalism elaborated a set of political principles that were more distinctively Liberal than Whiggery and became an abiding theme, as did the opposition to military expenditure. Aided by the

86. Speech at Middlesbrough, October 1881, in B.I. Coleman, *The Idea of the City in Nineteenth Century Britain* (London: Routledge & Kegan Paul, 1973), p. 166–7.
87. McCord, *Anti-Corn Law League*, p. 25.

identification of Conservatism with the landed interest after 1846, it synthesised the many disparate elements of Liberalism into a common creed, and to a considerable extent, a political unity.

Palmerston succeeded in isolating the Cobdenite Radicals because his diplomacy was never as carelessly aggressive as Cobden believed, and expressed Britain's new, essentially urban, confidence at least as well as Cobdenite Radicalism. Palmerston recognised that the support he enjoyed depended on being able to keep out of major wars, and the need for low taxation in the longer term.[88] Well before the end of the administration, expenditure began to fall, although never as far as Gladstone wished, and 1865 saw another 'rough' cabinet on naval estimates.[89] Palmerston's retreat over the Schleswig-Holstein affair in 1864 was, according to Cobden, 'a revolution in our foreign policy', brought about by the overwhelming opinion of the country in favour of peace.[90] Bright believed 'the theory of the balance of power is pretty nearly dead and buried', which he attributed to 'years of preaching on foreign policy and non-intervention'.[91] But insofar as policy did change, it owed more to the replacement of Palmerston by Gladstone as Liberal leader. Gladstone gave the credit to Cobden, who

> showed that trade was not only a law of wealth, but a law of friend-ship, a law of kindness among nations; that every single transaction . . . was a transaction forming, as it were, one single thread in a web of concord woven between people and people. This is one of the ideas now made familiar to us; but permit me to remind you that this is a modern idea.[92]

Gladstonian Liberalism

As the chief exponent of that idea within the cabinet, Gladstone vigorously objected to Palmerston's proposed increases in defence spending to counter the threat from France. Together with his free-trade budgets, this endeared him to the Radicals, but in the short term he was bound to fail. Palmerston was determined that 'in the activity and scale of our defensive arrangements . . . we must

88. Steele, *Palmerston and Liberalism*, pp. 39, 210, 217.
89. Gash, *Aristocracy and People*, p. 277.
90. Morley, *Life of Cobden*, vol. 2, pp. 441–2.
91. Trevelyan, *Life of Bright*, pp. 333–4.
92. McCord, *Anti-Corn Law League*, p. 33.

not be overreached by financial economy', and with the country in the grip of an anti-French invasion scare he enjoyed the support of public and parliament alike. Graham warned Gladstone in 1860 that 'the will of the nation is in favour of military preparations quite regardless of expense . . . the attempt to struggle against it is in vain', and Argyll, another former Peelite, repeated the warning in 1861 when Gladstone again seemed on the verge of resignation.[93] Neither these warnings, nor Palmerston's of the 'evils and hazards' of resignation, were necessary.[94] Gladstone was well aware of the weakness of his position, and went to the brink, but never beyond. Despite his protests and threats of resignation, expenditure in 1861–2 was, much to the discontent of Cobden and Bright, the highest ever in peacetime.

Gladstone agreed with Cobden that war was inconsistent with previous French behaviour. Where Palmerston exuded distrust, Herbert feared 'a godless people who look upon war as a game', led by 'a gambler',[95] and Lewis 'a band of five hundred thousand robbers with a despot at their head',[96] Gladstone and Cobden saw the opportunity for reasonable negotiation calculated to remove misunderstandings. Gladstone's opposition to increased armaments derived not only from the expense, but from the belief, shared by Cobden and Bright, that they increased the likelihood of war, heightening international tension and conditioning public opinion to regard war as normal.[97] In the confrontation of 1859–60, his alternative to increased armaments was the Cobden–Chevalier commercial treaty to promote freer trade and thus harmony and understanding between the two nations. Its purpose was diplomatic, not economic. 'Neither you nor I', he wrote to Cobden, 'attach for the moment any superlative value to the Treaty for the sake of the extension of British trade . . . what I look to is the social good, the benefit to relations of the two countries and the effect on the peace of Europe.'[98] The cabinet and parliament accepted the treaty without enthusiasm on these terms, but not Gladstone's rationale. In adopting both Gladstone's treaty and Palmerston's fortifications, the government in 1860 pursued not a compromise but two parallel policies.

---

93. Steele, *Palmerston and Liberalism*, pp. 98–9, 106.
94. Morley, *Life of Gladstone*, vol. 2, pp. 45–6.   95. Ibid. p. 43.
96. Steele, *Palmerston and Liberalism*, p. 88.
97. Morley, *Life of Cobden*, p. 8; Morley, *Life of Gladstone*, vol. 2, p. 43.
98. H.C.G. Matthew, *Gladstone 1809–1874* (Oxford: Oxford University Press, 1988), p. 113.

In so doing, they endowed the Liberal party with two conflicting approaches to international tension, a fundamental fault-line in the Liberal party throughout its history. Successive crises tore the party apart between the rival protagonists of Palmerstonian realpolitik and the Cobdenite-Gladstonian moral order. At root, however, Palmerston's world of international anarchy was incompatible with the Liberalism which sought to establish the rule of law, moral and economic, in international as well as domestic affairs. Palmerstonians in various guises found themselves aligned with the Conservative party because they had no basis for disagreement. Because Palmerston was 'conservative' in domestic politics, the fault-line resembled a straightforward division between moderates and radicals, but the question of the approach to conflict was more complex. Belligerence was incompatible with Liberalism, but not with a particular strain of evangelical Radicalism, in which Britain became, in Bright's words, 'the knight-errant of the human race'.[99] Despite his generally Cobdenite views, Gladstone could be as susceptible to this as any fire-eating Radical.

Gladstone's desire to return to office in the late 1850s was prompted by his awareness of 'great things to do', especially in the completion of the free-trade fiscal system begun by Peel and continued in his own budget of 1853.[100] There was 'a policy going a-begging, the general policy that Sir Robert Peel in 1841 took office to support – the policy of peace abroad, of economy, of financial equilibrium, of steady resistance to abuses, and promotion of practical improvements at home'.[101] But this was also a deliberate political tactic.[102] The late 1850s revealed the restlessness of backbench Liberals, now joined by Radicals and Peelites, under Whig leadership. Gladstone's pursuit of causes embodied in 'big' bills gave the party a political role and a public identity that would rally supporters and provide a focus of unity. With Gladstone, the Liberal party became a party of movement and 'action', which encouraged adversarial politics, which in turn enhanced Liberal identity and unity.

Gladstone's budget of 1860 was conceived on these lines, as a 'big' bill. In February 1856, whilst out of office, he drew up a programme of fiscal and administrative reforms, the budgetary elements of which were elaborated in 1857 in the course of his

99. Robbins, *John Bright*, p. 105; Morley, *Life of Cobden*, vol. 2, p. 146.
100. Matthew, *Gladstone*, pp. 105–6, 109.
101. Morley, *Life of Gladstone*, vol. 1, p. 553.   102. Matthew, *Gladstone*, p. 114.

opposition to Lewis's budget: 'to lower indirect taxes when excessive in amount for the relief of the people and bearing in mind the reproductive power inherent in such operations – to simplify our fiscal system by concentrating its pressure on a few well-chosen articles of extended consumption and to conciliate support to the income tax by marking its temporary character'.[103]

Provision for the progressive reduction of income tax had been made in the budget of 1853, but was rendered impracticable by the Crimean war. Gladstone remained committed to its abolition until at least 1874, when this was the main proposal of his election address. But the objection was to a tax which bore on 'intelligence and skill', not to direct taxation itself, and the intention was always to replace it with another direct tax.[104] The purpose was social and political as well as economic. His budgets, as Gladstone stated in 1853, were not 'guided by any desire to set one class against another', but the reverse, to achieve a stable balance between the indirect taxes paid by the working classes and the direct taxes paid by the propertied that would be seen as fair by both.[105] Free trade, cheap government and low, fairly distributed taxes placed the government in a neutral position above any clash of economic interests and kept class out of politics. In practice, Gladstone was tied to the retention of income tax by his own non-fiscal objectives. He increased income tax in 1859 from the low level established by Disraeli in 1858, and raised it again in 1860 to provide revenue for Palmerston's defences, whilst still reducing the range of articles subject to indirect taxation to a minimum. This was one reason why he could, despite his protests, acquiesce in that expenditure. It was 'no small thing to get a cabinet to give up one and a half or two millions of revenue at a time when the public passion is for enormous expenditure'.[106]

Parliamentary approval of the budget relied heavily on the general support that Palmerston enjoyed.[107] Gladstone blamed his difficulties, and the rejection of the proposed repeal of the paper duties by the House of Lords, on the intrusion of Russell's reform bill,[108] but the repeal of the paper duties was the one item on which Palmerston made known his opposition. Despite Gladstone's anger, and support for action against the Lords from Russell and the Radicals, Palmerston also defused the potential constitutional conflict.

103. Ibid. pp. 106, 112, 125; Morley, *Life of Gladstone*, vol. 1, p. 559.
104. Matthew, *Gladstone*, p. 122.   105. Ibid. pp. 126–7.
106. Morley, *Life of Gladstone*, vol. 2, p. 22
107. Steele, *Palmerston and Liberalism*, pp. 103, 106.
108. Morley, *Life of Gladstone*, vol. 2, pp. 30–1.

Gladstone circumvented the Lords' opposition in 1861 by combining all his financial proposals in a single budget. The episode enhanced both Gladstone's growing radical reputation and the Liberal party's progressive image.

Gladstonian finance embodied a coherent social philosophy of reward for individual effort and equality of individual opportunity within the framework of social stability. 'In legislation of this kind,' Gladstone said of his 1860 budget, 'you are not forging mechanical supports and helps for men, nor endeavouring to do that for them which they ought to do for themselves; but you are enlarging their means without narrowing their freedom, you are giving value to their labour, you are appealing to their sense of responsibility, you are not impairing their temper of honourable self-dependence.'[109] The ethical underpinnings of Liberalism were as apparent in this as they were in its approach to foreign policy and overseas trade. It was assumed that the individual ought to look after himself, and that government and society ought positively to provide the conditions to make this possible, and negatively to place no impediments in the way, but that it should do no more.

Minimal government was implicit in the autonomous individual, and followed necessarily from neutral government and low taxation. But it was a relative term, a guideline and objective which mid-Victorians tried to qualify theoretically by the equally relative idea of 'expediency', as argued by Mill, or on grounds of religion or morality, 'for the sake of obviating social, moral or political evils' as Gladstone put it.[110] There was no 'abstract maxim as an inexorable rule' which determined the limits of legitimate government interference, nor could there be.[111] The steady but still extremely limited expansion of the Victorian state caused tensions in Liberal logic, but was contained by the moral elements within its overall intellectual framework for all but a minority of doctrinaires like Auberon Herbert or Wordsworth Donisthorpe who took Liberalism to the boundaries of anarchism.[112]

Economic opportunity and the liberation of enterprise allowed individuals to rise within narrow bounds, but mid-Victorian Liberalism was, in class terms, socially conservative. The permanent balance

---

109. Matthew, *Gladstone,* 116.
110. Michael Bentley, *The Climax of Liberal Politics: British Liberalism in Theory and Practice 1868–1918* (London: Arnold, 1987), p. 41; Matthew, *Gladstone,* p. 119.
111. Matthew, *Gladstone,* p. 118.
112. J.L. Finlay, *The English Origins of Social Credit* (Montreal: McGill-Queens University Press, 1972), pp. 19–20; Bentley, *Climax,* p. 45.

between direct and indirect taxation that Gladstone sought,[113] implied a similar permanence in the relationship of classes that the fiscal system was designed to reflect. Gladstone shared with Palmerston the belief that nothing could be done for the poor beyond the provisions of the poor law.[114] It was all the more important for the sake of social stability that government should be seen to be as fair and as efficient as possible in relieving burdens. Gladstone recommended his budget of 1860 as one which would 'win more and more for the Throne and for the institutions of our country the gratitude, the confidence and the love of a united people',[115] and criticised the supporters of high expenditure for their failure to 'apprehend any political changes, any alienation of the people from the Throne and laws, any disturbance of the relationship of classes, from . . . the increase of financial burdens'.[116] High expenditure was 'not only a pecuniary waste, but a great political, and above all, a great moral evil'.[117] Like Cobden, who feared 'a convulsion',[118] for Gladstone, retrenchment was a moral imperative to preserve the social fabric.

Liberalism and the working classes

Control of expenditure was also, despite Cobden's doubts, one argument for parliamentary reform. A wider electorate incorporating the skilled working classes might demand greater economy and lower taxation, and be less susceptible to Palmerstonian bluster. Gladstone's belief that the franchise should be related to taxation led to the £7 rental qualification of the Liberal government's reform bill of 1866, specifically to enfranchise 'the artisans and skilled labourers'.[119] By the 1860s, parliamentary reform had developed an inertia of its own that made incorporation of a section of the working classes a necessity if the political system was to retain credibility. Seen from within, the working class was fractured by a maze of minor differentials; seen from outside, as politicians saw it, the most obvious feature was the division between skilled workers in steady employment, relatively well-paid, literate, with a network of social,

113. Matthew, *Gladstone*, pp. 125–6.
114. Steele, *Palmerston and Liberalism*, 210.   115. Matthew, *Gladstone*, p. 116.
116. Steele, *Palmerston and Liberalism*, p. 98.
117. Morley, *Life of Gladstone*, vol. 2, p. 53.
118. Morley, *Life of Cobden*, vol. 2, p. 43.
119. Matthew, *Gladstone*, pp. 127–8, 133–4.

savings and trade institutions, and the residuum of the unskilled, casually employed and unemployed.[120]

The message pumped out to the working classes was of the identity of interests of all social classes. Workers were told that capitalists were 'glad to find the wages and advantages of labour may go on increasing', and they in turn should welcome 'the accumulation of fortunes' for 'without . . . accumulation of capital there never would be . . . increasing employment'.[121] Workers, like employers, had a stake in social and economic stability. In this 'union of class to class', Britain was a role-model for the world. 'In reforming your own fiscal and commercial system,' according to Gladstone, 'you have laid the foundations of similar reforms – slow perhaps but certain in their progress – through every country in the civilised world.'[122] For Palmerston, Britain held out a 'bright example of internal order and morality' which other nations would be 'unconsciously impelled to imitate'.[123] It was a message of self-congratulation in which the workers were invited to participate while recognising the contribution of their employers and rulers, and the necessity for continued collaboration.

Not all Liberals were prepared to take this line. Lowe's denunciation of the 'venality, ignorance, drunkenness and facility to be intimidated' of the lower orders[124] betrayed the real anxiety that underlay the forced assumption of working-class loyalty and moderation. The 'unity of classes' was itself an attempt to deny the existence of class, even while recognising it. Despite their radicalism, Cobden and Bright would have preferred to ignore both the reality and the language of class completely.[125] Closer contact could assuage some doubts. Gladstone's meetings with deputations of trade unionists convinced him of the safety of limited parliamentary reform, and further meetings that 'we have only to approach them in the right way, in order to find them thoroughly amenable to reason'.[126]

This was hardly a vote of confidence in the working classes, less so perhaps than his famous declaration in 1864 that any man 'not presumably incapacitated by some consideration of personal

---

120. Royden Harrison, *Before the Socialists: Studies in Labour and Politics 1861–1881* (London: Routledge & Kegan Paul, 1965), pp. 26–33.
121. Steele, *Palmerston and Liberalism*, pp. 36, 208.
122. Matthew, *Gladstone*, p. 116.
123. Steele, *Palmerston and Liberalism*, p. 26.
124. Trevelyan, *Life of Bright*, p. 352.
125. Steele, *Palmerston and Liberalism*, pp. 206, 228.
126. Matthew, *Gladstone*, pp. 131–2.

unfitness or of political danger, is morally entitled to come within the pale of the constitution', which caused such alarm as an apparent endorsement of universal suffrage. Gladstone admitted the error. His criteria for the exercise of the franchise 'self-command, self-control, respect for order, patience under suffering, confidence in the law, regard for superiors',[127] though class-referenced, were typically moral and personal rather than socio-economic. Based on individualist ideas, Liberalism lacked the intellectual framework to come fully to terms with class either as a concept or as a political reality, and its approach always had a degree of ambivalence.

Forced to think in class terms in the 1860s by the reform issue, the Liberal party split on the means to achieve an agreed objective: non-class politics. For reformers, enfranchisement of the skilled working classes was pre-emptive. As the moderately radical MP for Bradford, W.E. Forster, observed, 'if they are excluded as a class, and feared as a class, they will agitate as a class and demand admission as a class'.[128] For anti-reformers, enfranchisement would itself bring class into politics, and for the more alarmist, the threat of the redistribution of wealth from the 'haves' to the 'have-nots'.[129] Signs of division within the party were already apparent in the voting on Baines's motion in 1865.[130] The defeat of the Liberal reform bill in June 1866 through the desertion of some forty Whigs, Bright's 'cave of Adullam', threatened to return politics to the pattern of the 1850s, with the Liberals in disarray and the Conservative minority in office. Senior Liberals, including the chief whip, thought that the break-up of the party, the subject of speculation since the death of Palmerston in 1865, had finally occurred.[131]

Bright's campaign for household suffrage and his warnings of violence in the context of the agitation that followed the loss of the Liberal bill further alarmed Whigs and moderates. One result, a portent of things to come, was the loss of the Brecknock by-election in October 1866 when Lord Brecknock refused his help.[132] Opposition provided no springboard for unity as long as the reform debate lasted. In April 1867, Gladstone withdrew from the leadership in the Commons and left the party to its own devices. Yet the problem remained that of the 1850s: a recalcitrant fringe. It was large enough

127. Ibid. p. 139.   128. Steele, *Palmerston and Liberalism*, p. 222.
129. R. Taylor, *Lord Salisbury* (London: Allen Lane, 1975), p. 17; Maurice Cowling, *1867: Disraeli, Gladstone and Revolution: The Passing of the Second Reform Bill* (Cambridge: Cambridge University Press, 1967), p. 51.
130. Cowling, *1867*, p. 9.   131. Ibid. pp. 121–2, 129.
132. Ibid. pp. 123, 399.

to keep the party from office, but the main body was still intact, and the Liberal party recovered quickly enough once reform was out of the way. The debate of 1865–7 nevertheless marked a shift leftwards in the centre of gravity of the parliamentary party. Under Palmerston, the Whigs had been the centre with the Radicals semi-detached; after 1867, it was the Whigs who were semi-detached, uncomfortable and critical, whilst Bright, whom Palmerston had vetoed in 1859, joined the cabinet in 1868.

The 1867 Reform Act approximately doubled the electorate without realising the fears of Gladstone and Russell, still less those of the Adullamites and the Conservative right. It did, however, incorporate one aspect of 'class': in enfranchising urban house-holders subject to residence qualifications, it distinguished between the static, 'visible' working class and the mobile population.[133] Amongst the former, as Gladstone recognised at Bolton in 1864, the factory was an important instrument of socialisation and social control.[134] The deference associated with closed rural commu-nities where squire and parson exercised a form of 'social policing', was hardly less common in the boroughs. Derby, visiting Bury – a town with '40,000 inhabitants and a considerable trade' in 1867 – found 'an almost feudal respect for his family'.[135] For many workers, deference, whether real or feigned, went with the job. The middle classes dominated the industrial towns as employers, town-councillors, magistrates, owners of the local press and much else besides. They discriminated on the grounds of religion, moved children to schools of their own choosing, or building, insisted on temperance, supervised morals and expected their workers to attend their Sunday schools, churches or chapels. John Clough, the worsted manufacturer from Keighley, even banned all washing that spoiled the view.[136] It was expected that men would vote as their masters wished and that employers would use their 'legitimate influence' to this end. Influence merged seamlessly into intimida-tion so that, as the home secretary noted in 1869, 'Many a workman imagines intimidation that was never intended, but his fear is none the less real to himself.'[137]

Awareness of dependence underpinned deference, but many of the assumptions on which employer expectations were based were

133. Ross McKibbin, 'Why was there no Marxism in Great Britain?', *English His-torical Review* 99 (391) (1984), 304.
134. Steele, *Palmerston and Liberalism*, p. 36.
135. Joyce, *Work, Society and Politics*, p. 6.   136. Ibid. pp. 23, 173–4, 188.
137. Hanham, *Elections and Party Management*, p. 84.

shared by the workers themselves. If employers did not make their wishes known, workers made efforts to discover them, and themselves petitioned employers for the dismissal of other employees who did not vote the factory line. 'At a contested election in a Lancashire borough,' wrote W.A. Abram in 1868, 'one may see the entire body of workers at two rival factories pitted against each other, like hostile armies.'[138] Coercion, deference and the factory block-vote go some way towards explaining why sections of the new electorate accepted middle- and upper-class political leadership, and in consequence why those workers voted for one of the existing political parties. But working-class Radicals, subject to no such constraints, hostile to deference, and suspicious of middle-class leadership, were also fervent supporters of Gladstonian Liberalism. Thomas Burt, the Durham miners' leader, possessed sufficient influence of his own to induce Grey to stand down at Morpeth in his favour, but remained a loyal Liberal, as did Ben Pickard, founder and president of the Yorkshire Miners' Association.

Beyond the determinants of local urban politics lay the intellectual hegemony of Liberalism. The trade-union newspaper, the *Beehive*, accepted the argument pressed by Palmerston and Gladstone that capital formation was essential to working-class prosperity and that 'it would be wrong to drain from employers or capitalists more than they could afford to give. It would in the end be injurious to all.'[139] 'The true state of employers and employed,' wrote T.J. Dunning in an influential pamphlet in 1860, 'is that of amity . . . And the fact is that this state is for the most part their actual condition.'[140] As late as 1885, the working-class Lancashire writer, Ben Brierley, was still reiterating the same message of the union of classes at the launch of the *Cotton Factory Times*: 'the relationship of employers and employed is not merely a union of separate interests; but a recognition of the fact that both are identical'.[141] Deference was hardly needed; intellectually there was nowhere else for workers to go but with their employers.

Working-class Radicals were, like their middle-class associates, biblical Radicals, libertarians who shared the ideal of the independent workingman living in a free, self-governing community. They drew confidence from the economic and moral value of manual work and the Christian teaching of the moral superiority of the

138. Joyce, *Work, Society and Politics*, p. 201 and ch. 6 *passim*.
139. E.F. Biagini, 'British trade unions and popular political economy, 1860–1880', *The Historical Journal* 30 (4) (1987), 818.
140. Ibid. p. 834.   141. Joyce, *Work, Society and Politics*, p. 50.

poor. Radicals of all classes drew much of their inspiration from similar sources: a Protestant puritan tradition, whether evangelical Anglican or Nonconformist, that sustained individual liberty and tended, at least in terms of individual moral worth, towards egalitarianism; a historic tradition that looked back to a mythical past of the 'freeborn Englishman' robbed of his birth-right by the coming of Norman 'land-robbers' and of his freedom by the imposition of the 'Norman yoke', to Cromwell and the puritan revolution, the 'Glorious Revolution' of 1688–9, eighteenth-century rationalism and classical political economy.

There was a wide area of agreement between all sections of the Liberal party on basic principles. The long-standing Whig association with 'civil and religious liberty' and with the maxim, 'peace, economy and reform', concurred with propositions derived from working-class distrust of the state, Nonconformist grievances and free-trade economics. The educated elements of the working class acquired a conventional wisdom; as the self-educated trade-union activist, George Howell, observed, 'Adam Smith was the mainstay.'[142] Chapels developed positive cooperation as middle- and working-class leaders, frequently teetotallers and lay preachers, shared a common commitment to the good causes of Nonconformity. Gladstone became the 'people's chancellor' and the 'people's William' because the policies of free trade, a non-interventionist, neutral, minimal state, low taxation, low military expenditure, religious liberty and constitutional progress, a moralist foreign policy and avoidance of foreign entanglements represented, in large measure, the vision that the various sections of the Liberal party, but especially the radical section, had of Liberalism as a political creed.

The independence that began for working-class Radicals as a moral imperative extended into economic and political values, and translated in industrial society into collective self-help, trade unions, the extension of democracy and local self-government. It was at this point, the collective element in self-help, that working-class Radicalism began to differentiate itself from that of the middle classes, many of whom, including Cobden and Bright, were apprehensive of trade unions. With the exception of landed property, God-given, limited, monopolised and misused as a means of oppression not production, the working-class challenge was, and was recognised as being, directed at power not property. Working-class

142. Biagini, 'British trade unions', p. 831; McKibbin, 'Why was there no Marxism?', p. 322.

Radicals pursued political not social reform, promoting working-class candidates, campaigning for the secret ballot, legal status and employer recognition for trade unions, and democratic local government, which came to include self-government for Ireland.

The logic of Whig and middle-class Liberalism and the values they shared with working-class Radicalism led towards the incorporation that would realise this wider distribution of power. Gladstone's statement that any man not incapacitated should be enfranchised indicated the direction Liberalism, as doctrine, had to take. But neither Whigs nor middle-class Liberals shared the confidence in working-class capacity that the working classes had in themselves, or the values on which that confidence was based, once acknowledging moral worth translated to acknowledging political rights. In the disparity between the equal value of the individual as a moral being and the inequality of the individual as citizen lay the impetus for radical reform on which all could cooperate; from the disparity between social, political and moral values came the tensions between the Liberal elites and working-class Radicalism that could divide the party. In 1892, Isaac Holden, Bradford manufacturer, Nonconformist and Liberal, observed in tones reminiscent of Cobden that 'manufacture and commerce have made many plebeians rich. They should stay with the people. Alas! many have joined the nobles.'[143] The primary task of the mid-Victorian Liberal party was to prevent that choice arising.

143. Joyce, *Work, Society and Politics*, p. 1.

CHAPTER THREE

Gladstone, Whigs and Radicals

Gladstone's declaration after the Liberal victory in the general election of 1868 of his 'mission . . . to pacify Ireland' reflected the preparations he had made for the resumption of office at the head of a united Liberal party since 1866. For Gladstone, the paralysis induced by Adullamite disloyalty made the party unfit for 'great public purposes'. His inclination after the defeat of the Liberal reform bill had been for an election that would purge the party of what a supporter called 'all the rotten and effete elements . . . now associated with it'.[1] He publicly attacked the Adullamites, and consolidated the support of working-class and Nonconformist Radicals both in adopting a more democratic position on reform and in taking up the issues of church rates and Irish disestablishment. Proposed from opposition, but agreed with the Nonconformists beforehand, the church rates bill passed in 1868, as did resolutions on the Irish church, in a House of Commons still controlled by a Liberal majority, despite a Conservative government.

Reform: the ministry of 1868

Irish disestablishment was the 'big' measure that reunited the Liberal party in 1868 and brought Irish Catholicism back into the Liberal alliance from which it had strayed in the 1850s after the ecclesiastical titles bill. Fenian outrages and tenant-right agitation drew attention to the social problem in Ireland and led Gladstone initially to consider legislation on the land question, but disestablishment provided a less controversial rallying point for the Liberal

1. Maurice Cowling, *1867: Disraeli, Gladstone and Revolution: The Passing of the Second Reform Bill* (Cambridge: Cambridge University Press, 1967), pp. 105, 219.

party. Nevertheless, his programme of pacification was three-pronged from the start: 'there is the Church of Ireland, there is the land of Ireland, there is the education of Ireland . . . they are all so many branches . . . of what is called the Protestant ascendancy. . . . We therefore aim at the destruction of that system.'[2]

The disestablishment of the Irish church in 1869 was relatively uncontroversial. The most serious dispute arose over the amount to be allocated for the continued maintenance of the Anglican church, an issue of numbers not of principle which was resolved by negotiation with the church's Conservative defenders. In contrast, the Irish land bill brought the cabinet 'to the verge of dissolution'.[3] It involved interference with the rights of property, freedom of contract and the free market to which free traders objected on the grounds of economic doctrine and the Whigs as landowners. Gladstone sympathised with the intellectual objections and recognised the need to avoid legislation which might set a precedent for the mainland. Even then, his main constructive proposal, to extend to the rest of Ireland the customary tenure of Ulster which gave the tenant some security against arbitrary eviction and rent increases, went too far for his colleagues. The final bill did little more than give legislative recognition to Ulster tenant right and provide compensation for improvements and against arbitrary eviction in the rest of Ireland. The act went nowhere near meeting the demands of the Irish Tenants League for the '3Fs' – fair rents, fixity of tenure and free sale – each of which involved an infringement of the rights of property far beyond anything either Gladstone or the cabinet would contemplate in 1869–70.[4]

Irish identification with English Liberalism in 1868 was always conditional upon Gladstone's ability to deliver the 'justice for Ireland' that he appeared to promise. Gladstone enjoyed the support of the Catholic hierarchy during the election whilst disestablishment occupied centre stage, but this waned once disestablishment was passed. Meanwhile, both the movement for amnesty for Fenian prisoners and tenant-right agitation gathered pace in Ireland. The failure of the government to make significant concessions on either front began the dissolution of the connection with the Liberal party.

2. H.C.G. Matthew, *Gladstone 1809–1874* (Oxford: Oxford University Press, 1986), pp. 145–7.

3. Donald Southgate, *The Passing of the Whigs 1832–1886* (London: Macmillan, 1962), p. 343.

4. David Thornley, *Isaac Butt and Home Rule* (London: Macgibbon and Kee, 1964), pp. 79–82.

The Tipperary by-election in November, in which the Fenian prisoner O'Donovan Rossa was elected, indicated, and the Longford by-election in January confirmed, the extent of Irish alienation even before the disappointment of the Land Act.[5] In the wake of Gladstone's Irish legislation there emerged not a pacified Ireland but a more clearly defined Irish identity. The Tenant League programme of the '3Fs' received the backing of the Catholic hierarchy in March 1870, bringing together land and religion which, despite early Protestant involvement, formed the social basis of the Home Rule movement. Early in 1870, Gladstone was forced to yield to demands from his lord lieutenant, Spencer, and his chief secretary, Hartington, and introduce coercion.

The Irish were not alone in either their expectations or their disappointment. The Education Act of 1870, like the Irish Land Act, sought only to make good the deficiencies of the existing structure, not to carry out a thorough-going reform, and to do so as cheaply as possible. It provided for publicly funded schools to be run by locally and democratically elected school boards in areas where the existing voluntary provision was insufficient, but otherwise retained the voluntary structure with increased state aid. This, too, was a far cry from the National Education League's policy of a compulsory, national, state-aided, unsectarian education system, although in practice the League concentrated its opposition on Clause 25 which angered all Nonconformists by allowing school boards to use money from the rates to pay the fees of poor children attending voluntary schools. Over sixty Liberals opposed what they considered a Tory measure, and the bill finally passed with Conservative support,[6] whereupon the NEL took its cause to the country.

Its campaign, directed in its extreme form to the removal of the Liberal government and the purging of the party even at the cost of putting the Conservatives in, followed the usual Nonconformist pressure-group pattern, a national agitation through professional agents and lecturers backed by local branches, intervention in by-elections and threats of independent candidates. The League achieved a sort of success insofar as some constituencies like Shrewsbury, Plymouth and Bath where it acted were won by Conservatives;[7] by 1874, 300 of the 425 Liberal candidates were pledged to

5. Ibid. pp. 71–3.

6. J.L. Garvin, *The Life of Joseph Chamberlain*, vol. 1 (London: Macmillan, 1935), p. 172; Paul Adelman, *Victorian Radicalism: The Middle Class Experience 1830–1914* (London: Longman, 1984), pp. 80–1.

7. D.A. Hamer, *The Politics of Electoral Pressure* (Brighton: Harvester, 1977), pp. 126–35.

the repeal of Clause 25.[8] Gladstone, however, remained opposed to repeal,[9] and the much-vaunted Nonconformist revolt foundered, as earlier revolts had done, on the rock of local loyalty and the need to consider the wider aims of the party.

Much the same fate attended the United Kingdom Alliance's campaign against the Licensing Act of 1872 introduced by the home secretary, Henry Bruce, which militants considered only 'tinkering of the most imbecile kind'.[10] In the Preston by-election, the local Temperance Electoral Association supported the Liberal candidate despite his objections to UKA policy, and proposals to run independent candidates met the usual objections from the constituencies. By the 1874 election, the UKA had largely abandoned its militant stance, although it was still sufficiently independent of the Liberal party to support pro-temperance Conservatives, as at Grimsby, against hostile Liberals. The National Education League took advantage of the return of Bright, a strong opponent of Clause 25, to the cabinet in late 1873, to end its own revolt and return to the Liberal fold with a minimum of embarrassment.

At the other end of education, the admission of non-Anglicans to Oxford and Cambridge which the Lords had blocked in the 1830s was achieved without damage except to Gladstone's high Anglican scruples and Oxford loyalties. Further Liberal inroads on the privileges of the establishment caused wider distress. The extension of the principle of competitive entry into the civil service, first introduced in 1860, met sufficient opposition within the cabinet for it to become an open question, each minister deciding for himself whether to adopt the principle for his department. The seemingly innocuous proposal to abolish the purchase of army commissions, intended to produce a professional officer corps, caused outrage. As with the sale of offices in any *ancien régime*, purchase had built up a considerable vested interest and trade in what were regarded as the property of the purchasers. Compensation to allow the nation to 'buy back its own army from its own officers'[11] was not enough. Cardwell's army regulation bill was rejected by the Lords. The government was forced to abolish purchase by royal warrant, a procedure that appeared an arbitrary abuse of the royal prerogative in the light of the failure of legislation.

    8. Adelman, *Victorian Radicalism*, pp. 83–4.
    9. John Morley, *The Life of William Ewart Gladstone*, vol. 2 (London: Macmillan, 1903), p. 311.
    10. Brian Harrison, *Drink and the Victorians* (London: Faber, 1971), p. 273.
    11. Morley, *Life of Gladstone*, vol. 2, p. 361.

The introduction of the secret ballot in 1872, another stage in the liberation of the individual in one respect, was also a further attack on the 'legitimate influence' of the employer and landed classes. Gladstone was depressed that human failings made the secret ballot necessary, but there was too much evidence of those failings in the corruption and intimidation of the 1868 election for resistance to be further prolonged, except in the House of Lords. There, the bill of 1871 was rejected, and that of 1872 amended to make secrecy optional. Bright's view that 'there can be no better question . . . to go to a general election on than that of a real as AGAINST A SHAM BALLOT', was shared by the Lords, who gave way when the government threatened dissolution.[12] The form of the opposition to army reform and the secret ballot indicated the direction in which that Conservative opposition was evolving: the defence of property and its rights. Opposition to the government's licensing bills, especially the more far-reaching but abortive bill of 1871, was founded on the same principle: defence of the vested interest, or property, that licensees had in their licences. The government proposals to reintroduce restrictive licensing were condemned as confiscation, and Bruce himself as a 'communist'.[13]

During the long period of Liberal domination since 1846, the Conservative party had suffered from its identity as a sectional party of minority interests. The legislation of Gladstone's government gave it a new role, or a new guise for its old role, as the defender not just of landed property, but of property in general, into which the interests of specific types of property and privilege could be merged. Disraeli's attack on a government that 'harassed every trade, worried every profession and assailed or menaced every class, institution and species of property in the country',[14] struck at the weak point of post-Palmerstonian Liberalism. Moreover, the Conservatives also succeeded in identifying the defence of property with the defence of liberty. Liberal individualism, the right of the free rational individual to make his own choices, use his property how he wished, drink when and where he wished, was increasingly hijacked by Conservatism from the 1870s. The Liberty and Property Defence League formed in 1882 took its inspiration from the extreme liberal individualism of Donisthorpe. By 1914 property, individualism and liberty had become a staple Conservative doctrine, exemplified by Lord Hugh Cecil's *Conservatism* published in 1911.

12. Southgate, *Passing*, p. 351; Morley, *Life of Gladstone*, vol. 2, pp. 369–70.
13. Harrison, *Drink*, p. 267.   14. Morley, *Life of Gladstone*, vol. 2, p. 475.

In this form, Conservatism exploited a long-standing populist tradition. Bruce's proposals for inspectors paid for by the money raised in licence fees was damned as a threat to the liberties of the 'freeborn Englishman', creating a tension between liberty and party Liberalism which enhanced the credibility of Conservatism as the defender of traditional and peculiarly English freedoms. The old Tory Radical, J.R. Stephens, denounced such 'spies' as 'ready to pounce upon any man or society that the government of the day chooses to think is in opposition to it',[15] and the *Licensed Victuallers Guardian* described the relatively mild act of 1872 as 'at once revolutionary and despotic. It combines socialism with absolutism and the worst form of domestic tyranny.'[16] With this, sections of the working classes agreed. There was a class element in the Licensing Act, since regulation closed the pubs but not the clubs. In Cheltenham when the pubs were closed under the new regulations, frustrated drinkers surrounded the still-open clubs and forced them to close; there were similar events in Exeter, riots in Maidstone, Wolverhampton and Liverpool; Hugh Mason, paternalist employer and Liberal 'boss' of Ashton, found his house surrounded by a mob of 10–15,000 because of his notoriously puritanical views on temperance. The Ashton mob sang 'Rule Britannia', as did the mobs in Coventry and Oxford, emphasising the sentiment that 'Britons never shall be slaves'.[17] The combination of libertarianism and patriotism thus displayed explains a great deal about the difficulties that the Liberal party subsequently encountered in gaining mass support in an age of imperialism – especially as Disraeli, with Gladstone's connivance, appropriated the Palmerstonian inheritance of defence and empire for the Conservative party.

It was thus the more unfortunate that the government, through poor drafting, temporarily alienated the leadership of organised labour. Like the Irish and the Nonconformists, working-class Radicals had high expectations of the Liberal party in the first post-reform parliament. After his meetings with trade unionists, Gladstone had come round to the view that 'Trades' Unions were justifiable to a certain extent',[18] and the positive report of the Royal Commission on Trade Unions brought a substantial body of public opinion to the same point of view. Many employers had also reached this conclusion, and an increasing number of large employers favoured

15. Harrison, *Drink*, p. 267.   16. Ibid. p. 273.   17. Ibid. p. 276.
18. E. Biagini 'British trade unions and popular political economy 1860–1880', *The Historical Journal* 30 (4) (1987) p. 813.

union recognition and active cooperation. Most, like Bass, Brassey, Samuel Morley, Salt, Illingworth and Mundella, were not only Liberal in politics, but actively so. But pro-union employers also included the actively Conservative Hornby family in Blackburn and the dissident Whig, Elcho.[19] Equally, however, many employers were determined to resist trade unions and remain 'masters in their own house'. Significantly, the conflict turned on the question of power, not, in the first instance, on property or wealth. The Trade Union Act of 1871 provided security for union funds, but the Criminal Law Amendment Act, intended to allow strikes by protecting workers against charges of conspiracy, left trade unionists open to conspiracy charges under the common law, and removed such rights of peaceful picketing as had been provided by the Molestation of Workmen Act of 1850. Workers were soon penalised under the new legislation. Striking gasworkers were sentenced to twelve months' hard labour in 1872, and sixteen women at Chipping Norton were similarly sentenced to hard labour for intimidation in 1873.[20]

The government was slow to remedy the situation, and only considered further legislation late in 1873 amidst mounting trade-union discontent. The position was eventually rectified by Disraeli's government enacting in 1875 proposals already outlined by the Liberals. With the Conspiracy and Protection of Property Act and the Employers and Workmen Act, the unions were successfully incorporated within the legal system. George Howell, secretary to the parliamentary committee of the TUC, thought the legislation 'perfect', and the parliamentary committee itself believed union emancipation 'full and complete'.[21] Both were wrong.

Disintegration and defeat

By 1873, the Liberal government was clearly tottering. Its majority was sufficiently large to cope with the steady loss of by-elections, but these revealed the fundamental problem of reforming too little for its own supporters, and too much for the increasingly alarmed propertied classes. The parliamentary party disintegrated when

19. Royden Harrison, *Before the Socialists: Studies in Labour and Politics 1861–1881* (London: Routledge & Kegan Paul, 1965), pp. 37–9; Patrick Joyce, *Work, Society and Politics* (London: Methuen, 1982), pp. 60, 64–8, 79–82.
20. Henry Pelling, *A History of British Trade Unionism* (Harmondsworth Penguin Books, 1962), p. 74.
21. Matthew, *Gladstone*, pp. 213–14; Pelling, *British Trade Unionism*, p. 76.

Gladstone presented the last item of his tripartite pacification of Ireland, the Irish universities bill. Successive by-elections in Ireland and the declared attitude of the Catholic clergy made it clear that only denominational education would be acceptable[22]; equally public declarations by Hartington, who wanted to resign on the bill, made it clear that the Whigs would not agree to it. Gladstone's proposal for a 'neutral university', which the Nonconformists were prepared to support as the embodiment of secular education, left the Whigs uneasy and the Irish dissatisfied. Gladstone had few doubts, 'we know what we ought to give them whether they will take it or not',[23] but the government was caught, as so often in Irish affairs, between the Whig view that Ireland 'must be governed not according to Irish, but according to Imperial ideas',[24] and those Irish ideas. The bill was defeated on its second reading in March 1873 with thirty-eight Irish and nineteen Liberals in opposition and only sixteen Irish MPs in the government lobby. None of those survived the 1874 general election, and fifteen of them were removed by Home Rulers.[25]

This time, the Conservatives refused to form a minority government whilst the Liberals regrouped in opposition. The government was further damaged by scandals in the administration of the post office in July 1873. The chancellor of the exchequer, Robert Lowe, had to be removed from the treasury, prompting a cabinet reshuffle in which Gladstone again became chancellor despite the risk of a by-election in Greenwich where the government had just lost the other seat.[26] Throughout the year Gladstone sought an issue on which to dissolve with some chance of success, but there was, as he noted, 'no cause, no great public object on which the Liberal party are agreed and combined'.[27] Typically, Gladstone's gaze turned more and more towards finance where the government still had some reputation, and the party some degree of unity. Cardwell at the war office was let into Gladstone's secret plans for recovery 'based upon the abolition of the income tax and sugar duties with partial compensation from spirits and death duties'.[28] But the crucial word was 'partial'. The rest depended upon retrenchment and thus upon the unfortunate Cardwell, who was battered by demands for further

---

22. J.P. Parry, *Democracy and Religion: Gladstone and the Liberal Party 1867–1875* (Cambridge: Cambridge University Press, 1986), p. 359.

23. Matthew, *Gladstone*, p. 197.   24. Parry, *Democracy and Religion*, p. 364.

25. Matthew, *Gladstone*, pp. 197–201; Parry, *Democracy and Religion*, pp. 353–68.

26. Morley, *Life of Gladstone*, vol. 2, pp. 460–72.   27. Matthew, *Gladstone*, p. 224.

28. Morley, *Life of Gladstone*, vol. 2, p. 478.

reductions in military expenditure. Dissolution was precipitated by Cardwell's inability and unwillingness to find the required savings, by his threatened resignation, and Gladstone's fear of the complete disintegration of the cabinet on the issue. It was to become a familiar pattern in Gladstonian governments.

The intention to revise death duties and thus maintain the balance between direct and indirect taxation was omitted from Gladstone's election address when he sprang the election on an unprepared party in January 1874. With promises to abolish income tax and reduce local rates it appeared as a direct bid to reconcile the disaffected propertied classes. The rising Birmingham Radical, Joseph Chamberlain, described the address as 'the meanest public document that had ever . . . proceeded from a statesman of the first rank', and in general the politicised working class agreed with him.[29] Nevertheless, the defection of the party's Anglican, propertied wing was the key factor in its decline since 1870 and the main cause of defeat in 1874. The attack on the church, both by Liberal legislation and more forcefully by Radical Nonconformity, rendered the position of Anglican Liberal moderates increasingly difficult. Not only Whigs, but industrial employers of considerable local influence like Thompson and Ripley in Bradford, progressively distanced themselves from the party. In 1874, Ripley stood, and was elected, as a Conservative.[30] Gladstone himself believed that on the issues that divided the party, he sympathised with 'the advanced party', and the moderates saw nothing in the record of the recent government that would lead them to disagree. Rather they feared that he would be unwilling or unable to resist pressure for further advance and thus further damage the interests of the church and the influence and security of property.[31]

Propertied Liberals were well aware that such pressure was increasing upon both themselves and Gladstone. The democratisation of local party organisations following the Reform Act, even if still limited to some of the larger borough constituencies in northern England, Scotland and Wales, allowed Radicals to permeate local parties and secure Radical candidates. Whilst this made it easier for the pressure groups which constituted the spearhead of the 'advanced wing' to work within the party rather than confront it, it also frightened away local moderates and began a slow change in the nature of the party itself. The election of 1874 accelerated this

29. Matthew, *Gladstone*, pp. 222–3.
30. Parry, *Democracy and Religion*, pp. 395–6.
31. Ibid. p. 366; Southgate, *Passing*, p. 353.

process as Liberal losses were far greater in the counties and southern boroughs where moderates were strongest than in the northern English, Welsh and Scottish seats which were the heartland of Radicalism.[32]

Radicalism was also changing. In 1873 Joseph Chamberlain, Radical mayor of Birmingham and presiding genius of the National Education League, outlined his 'Radical programme' in the *Fortnightly Review*, incorporating the '4Fs': free schools, free land, free church, free labour. Clearly influenced by the Irish example, it similarly marked the beginning of the mingling of traditional sectarian demands with those of the dispossessed, and the gradual transition from denominational to social radicalism. Increasingly 'liberty' came to turn on the question of property, either in the Conservative version of the LPDL in which unfettered property rights were a pre-requisite of individual liberty, or in Chamberlain's doctrine of 'ransom', and subsequently that of 'New Liberalism' in which the property rights of the minority were to be restricted in the interests of the liberty of the majority.

Despite their earlier disaffection, the Radicals steadfastly proclaimed their loyalty to Gladstone in 1874, even if they did not fight with the same enthusiasm as in 1868. The one exception to this attachment was Ireland. There, working within the Liberal party ceased to be an option almost from the moment that Isaac Butt founded the Home Government Association in May 1870. Building on dissatisfaction with the 1870 Land Act, continued demands for tenant rights and for denominational education, the Home Rule movement grew steadily in strength, as revealed in successive by-election victories. By the general election of 1874, support for denominational education and Home Rule was almost essential in Catholic constituencies, and Liberals could promise neither. The Liberal party was not quite wiped out in Ireland in 1874, and Home Rule MPs still usually cooperated with the Liberal party, but the return of over fifty Home Rulers, however nominal,[33] marked the beginning of the end of the Liberal party in Ireland.

The increasing identification of the Liberal party with Nonconformity narrowed the party's base, and assisted the electoral recovery of the Conservative opposition. In 1874, Disraeli virtually annexed the Whig tradition of civil and religious liberty as well as

32. Parry, *Democracy and Religion*, pp. 393–9.
33. Thornley, *Butt and Home Rule*, pp. 195–204; Parry, *Democracy and Religion*, pp. 394–5.

the Palmerstonian tradition of strong defence to present the Conservative party as the true custodian of England's historic mission to 'guard civilisation alike from the withering blasts of atheism and from . . . sacerdotal usurpation . . . [T]he cause of civil liberty and religious freedom mainly depends upon the strength and stability of England.'[34] The Conservative party itself was becoming more 'liberal' in both doctrine and composition. It still defended the traditional institutions of the Crown, the church and the Lords, but it did so by presenting them as symbols of English liberty, guarantors of historic freedoms in an unfriendly world, not bastions of privilege in a 'landed constitution'. The landed classes were abandoned to the full force of the agricultural depression that began in the late 1870s, and attempts to return to protection were firmly rebuffed. The future lay with business Conservatives, converts from moderate Liberal Conservatism represented in the cabinet by W.H. Smith. This in turn forced the Liberal party to become more radical to retain a political identity.

Loss of the 1874 election surprised the party. Office, as the Conservative peer, Lord Malmesbury, observed in 1865, had become 'second nature' to the Whigs.[35] Nor should the defeat be exaggerated; the party won a majority of the popular vote, but throughout the mid-Victorian period the distribution of seats was such that the Liberals required well over half of the vote to hold even a slender majority.[36] The loss angered Gladstone, whose desire for 'an interval between parliament and the grave' at what he considered 'the close of my life' (he was sixty-five)[37] was both a personal reason for his wish to retire from the leadership, and a political weapon. To Gladstone, 'the habit of making a career by an open and constant active opposition to the bulk of the party and its leaders' had 'acquired a dangerous predominance among a portion of its members'.[38] Retirement was to 'school' the party, or in the view of Sir William Harcourt, solicitor general in 1873–4, to punish it.[39] Gladstone retreated to his tent to await the call of a party in need, always expressing his willingness to return if his 'aid should at any time be

---

34. W.F. Monypenny, and G.E. Buckle, *The Life of Benjamin Disraeli, Earl of Beaconsfield*, vol. v (London: John Murray, 1920), p. 268.

35. Cowling, *1867*, p. 80.

36. E.g. E.D. Steele, *Palmerston and Liberalism 1855–1865* (Cambridge: Cambridge University Press, 1991), p. 370 for 1852–65.

37. Morley, *Life of Gladstone*, vol. 2, p. 498.

38. Matthew, *Gladstone*, p. 205; Morley, *Life of Gladstone*, vol. 2, pp. 497–9.

39. T.A. Jenkins, *Gladstone, Whiggery and the Liberal Party* (Oxford: Oxford University Press, 1988), pp. 37–8, 42.

generally desired with a view to averting some great evil or procuring for the nation some great good'.[40] The next six years demonstrated Gladstone's acute sense of hearing and his keen eye for great evils. In so doing they also revealed that Gladstone was no mean exponent of that 'habit ... of constant active opposition' to the party leaders that he had so recently condemned.

Persuaded to stay on for the 1874 session, Gladstone finally made known his retirement in January 1875. His attendance had been infrequent, not least because on such issues as the repeal of Clause 25, Home Rule and the extension of the county franchise, when he was persuaded to stay away, his intervention would only have aggravated party disunity. His criticism of the Scottish patronage bill to abolish lay patronage in the Church of Scotland and his even stronger criticism of the public worship regulation bill against ritualism left the Whigs alarmed and confused.[41] 'What on earth he means on Church matters', commented Halifax, the former Sir Charles Wood, 'puzzles us all.'[42] An article on ritualism in the *Contemporary Review* closely followed by a pamphlet on the Vatican decrees condemning the doctrine of papal infallibility declared by the Vatican Council of 1870 left them yet more bemused.

In Gladstone's defence of spiritual freedom from lay discipline which affronted their fundamental Erastianism, the Whigs suspected, not without some justification, a willingness to consider disestablishment. Gladstone did not, as he noted, 'feel the dread of disestablishment'[43] and his actions, for the same reason as they alarmed the Whigs, encouraged the Nonconformists. Convinced that Gladstone would be 'driven by the force of logic and the pressure of events' to come out openly for disestablishment, the Nonconformists launched a new campaign as 'the next page in the Liberal programme'.[44] The fact that Gladstone's Vatican pamphlet distracted attention from disestablishment and that Gladstone thought it would assist party unity seemed to go unnoticed.

The divisions that had existed since 1870 were thus perpetuated into the new parliament, with Gladstone apparently confirming his leaning to the 'advanced wing'. The Whig leadership of Granville in the Lords and Hartington in the Commons that took over in

40. Morley, *Life of Gladstone*, vol. 2, p. 499.
41. Parry, *Democracy and Religion*, pp. 412–20; J.P. Rossi, 'The transformation of the British Liberal party: a study of the tactics of Liberal opposition', *Transactions of the American Philosophical Society*, 68 (8) (1978), 13–14; Jenkins, *Gladstone, Whiggery and the Liberal Party*, pp. 32–5.
42. Parry, *Democracy and Religion*, p. 422.
43. Morley, *Life of Gladstone*, vol. 2, p. 501.
44. Parry, *Democracy and Religion*, pp. 421–2.

January 1875 faced considerable difficulties both in restoring party unity and in handling Gladstone. The possibility nevertheless existed that Radical energy might burn itself out in a prolonged period of opposition, and Hartington was prepared to lead the party loosely as a group of semi-autonomous sections, each with its own leadership and organisation.[45] He was also prepared to make concessions, supporting the backbench bill to abolish Clause 25 in 1874,[46] was conciliatory on land law reform and announced his conversion to the extension of the county franchise and local government reform in 1877.[47] Left to themselves, the Whigs might have evolved a workable, if uneasy, relationship with the Radicals.

Gladstone and the politics of 'virtuous passion'

This, however, was to reckon without Gladstone. In his descent from High Toryism, Gladstone caught fire when he entered the atmosphere of Radicalism. Volatile in the causes he chose, his outlook nevertheless possessed an underlying unity. Freedom of opinion for the church, like self-determination for small nations, rested on his belief in the individual moral conscience which the church and the nation represented in institutional form. Neither required regulation by the state. Intolerant of opposition in politics, Gladstone paradoxically also epitomised the libertarian strand of Liberalism. The establishment of the church derived from the church's position as the repository of national morality, and nation and church had to be free to fulfil their particular mission with all the zeal at their command. Zeal in religion or politics was the last thing the Whigs desired; Gladstone, to their infinite disquiet, was zealous in all his causes.

His transition from the denominational politics of 1874 to the campaign against Turkish atrocities in Bulgaria in 1876, and thence to a generalised attack of 'Beaconsfieldism' (Disraeli became Earl of Beaconsfield in 1876), was thus only a shift from one issue to another in the same fundamental cause. Gladstonian liberalism in foreign affairs denied the bases of international rivalry upon which the policies of Palmerston and Disraeli rested. In 1856 Gladstone

45. Jenkins, *Gladstone, Whiggery and the Liberal Party*, pp. 45–7, 77–80; Parry, *Democracy and Religion*, p. 427.
46. Parry, *Democracy and Religion*, p. 412.
47. Rossi, 'Transformation', pp. 20, 57–8; Jenkins, *Gladstone, Whiggery and the Liberal Party*, pp. 77–8.

had been 'shocked . . . at the . . . shameful part which we seem to
be playing before the world', and in 1857 joined Cobden in condemning the coercion of China as an affront to

> natural justice . . . that justice which binds man to man, which is
> older than Christianity because it was in the world before Christian-
> ity, which is broader than Christianity because it extends to the world
> beyond Christianity; and which underlies Christianity because Chris-
> tianity itself appeals to it. . . . War taken at the best is a frightful
> scourge upon the human race, but because it is so, the wisdom of
> ages has surrounded it with strict laws and usages, and has required
> formalities to be observed which shall act as a curb upon the wild
> passions of man. . . . You have dispensed with all these precautions.[48]

Gladstone placed his faith in international law as a construct of
rationality and morality to regulate and reduce conflict, much as he
regarded the function of law in domestic society. Whilst Palmerston resolutely refused to submit to arbitration the dispute with the
USA over compensation for damage done by the warship, *Alabama*,
which had escaped from British yards through the dilatoriness of
the foreign office, Gladstone held fast to arbitration despite criticism, in the interests of international goodwill. His final resolution
of the long-running negotiations was a success for the principle of
arbitration and Liberal reasonableness in foreign affairs. But for
Liberal voters brought up in the Palmerstonian tradition, the payment of heavy compensation was more a national humiliation than
a triumph for civilisation.

For Gladstone, 'the sympathies of peoples with peoples, the sense
of a common sympathy between nations and the aspirations of
nations after freedom and independence are real political forces'.[49]
Here again, as in denominational politics, was the central distinction between 'nations' or 'peoples' and the 'state', or perhaps the
nation and the 'classes' who ruled the state. The Eastern question
was not one of regional power politics, but of 'peoples' seeking
liberation from an oppressive state, and it would be 'the populations
of these countries that will ultimately possess them',[50] not successor
states. In a world of nations, as Gladstone wrote in 1870 at the time
of the Franco-Prussian war, Britain's role was

> to found a moral empire upon the confidence of the several peoples.
> . . . The foremost among the nations will be that one, which by its

48. Morley, *Life of Gladstone*, vol. 1, p. 563.
49. Ibid. vol. 2, p. 561, quoting J.R. Green who had just met Gladstone.
50. Ibid. p. 567.

conduct shall gradually engender in the minds of the others a fixed belief that it is just. In the competition for this prize, the bounty of Providence has given us a place of vantage; and nothing save our own fault or folly can wrest it from our grasp.[51]

The acquisition of Cyprus was just such a folly because it reduced Britain's involvement in the Balkans to that of territorial acquisition, destroying 'the estimation of our moral standard of action, and consequently our moral position in the world'.[52] Britain, in Gladstone's vision, became not a state in a competitive state system, but a substitute for, or instrument of, God, dispensing justice and liberty to 'the 5,000,000 of Bulgarians, cowed and beaten down to the ground, hardly venturing to look upwards, even to their Father in heaven [who] have extended their hands to you'.[53]

The British tradition to which Gladstone appealed against Disraeli was 'a tradition not which disregards British interests, but which teaches you to seek the promotion of those interests in obeying the dictates of honour and justice'.[54] Its problem was its impracticality. At times Gladstone appeared to confuse the wish with the act, seeing in the Christian revolt in the Balkans 'the knell of Turkish tyranny in these provinces',[55] even though it was the Christians who were being massacred and the Turks who were doing the massacring. Gladstone also convinced himself that the 'new law of nations' in which he believed 'is gradually taking hold of the mind, and coming to sway the practice of the world; a law which recognises independence, which frowns on aggression, which favours the pacific, not the bloody settlement of disputes . . . above all which recognises, as a tribunal of paramount authority, the general judgement of civilised mankind'. This was an idealised fantasy of the Concert of Europe. Insofar as it still existed in the 1870s, its programme was written and conducted by Bismarck, and morality played little part in his orchestration of events. Even Gladstone recognised that Britain had 'no efficacious means of offering even the smallest practical contribution' to the relief of the suffering subjects of the Turk.[56]

It was not until the protest movement in Britain, particularly from outraged Nonconformists and High Churchmen, the very zealots that the Whigs distrusted, had become well-established, that Gladstone became involved. In it he rediscovered for 'the first time for a good many years, a virtuous passion' in politics. The publication of his pamphlet, *The Bulgarian Horrors and the Question of the*

---

51. Matthew, *Gladstone*, pp. 181–2.
52. Morley, *Life of Gladstone*, vol. 2, pp. 578–9.
53. Ibid. p. 567.   54. Ibid.   55. Ibid. p. 568.   56. Ibid.

East in September 1876 made him at once the principal figure in the agitation.[57] The effect was to divide the Liberal party once again along the basic fault-line in the Liberal approach to foreign policy. Despite Gladstone's protestations, his ardent involvement as an ex-prime minister and party leader in a moralist crusade in foreign affairs could be nothing other than a challenge to the leadership of Granville and Hartington, whose sympathies were substantially with the government and its pro-Turk, anti-Russian stance on the grounds of interest. Neither could accept Gladstone's demand for autonomy for the Christian states of the Turkish empire in the Balkans, still less Gladstone's apparent readiness to coerce the Turks that his demand for their expulsion 'bag and baggage' seemed to imply.

Whilst both sides tried to avoid confrontation, the party was, as Granville noted in October, 'very much divided'.[58] In December, with Gladstone the major speaker at a national conference on the eastern question, Hartington was convinced that if Gladstone went 'much further, nothing can prevent a break up of the Liberal party'.[59] But Gladstone himself was subject to conflicting desires. He resented the obligation to emerge from retirement that resulted from the inactivity of the official leadership, and steadfastly maintained that he was only 'a follower and not a leader in the Liberal party'. At the same time, he felt constrained to continue his agitation, and claimed that 'all the heart of the Liberal party' supported his position. As he ingenuously explained to Granville, he was only 'an outside workman, engaged in the preparation of materials which you and the party will probably have to manipulate and then to build into a structure',[60] apparently totally unaware that neither Granville nor the official party leadership wished to reconstruct the party from such materials. Both challenging and not challenging the leadership, he was hesitant in his actions and from time to time lapsed into silence.

In April 1877, frustration overcame Gladstone's caution towards open defiance. 'Now', he told Granville, the time had come 'for a substantive motion' by which he intended resolutions in parliament calling for the coercion of the Turks. Coming immediately after

57. Rossi, 'Transformation', p. 30; Jenkins, *Gladstone, Whiggery and the Liberal Party*, p. 56.
58. Jenkins, *Gladstone, Whiggery and the Liberal Party*, pp. 56–61, Rossi, 'Transformation', pp. 30–45.
59. Rossi, 'Transformation', pp. 45–8.
60. Jenkins, *Gladstone, Whiggery and the Liberal Party*, p. 57.

the outbreak of war between Russia and Turkey which made such a policy irrelevant, appeared to justify the government's anti-Russian approach, and reawakened a powerful undercurrent of anti-Russian sentiment, the timing was curious. But if Gladstone believed that its very irrelevance would enable the leadership to support a symbolic gesture, he miscalculated.[61] Hartington treated Gladstone's resolutions as a direct challenge, and supported by his colleagues decided to oppose them directly. He also threatened to resign if a majority of the party supported Gladstone.[62] Fear of complete disruption of the party was sufficient to force a compromise. Gladstone toned down his resolutions, the leadership withdrew its opposition and the party went, with the Radicals furious at Gladstone's retreat, to its inevitable miserable defeat in the Commons. The indiscipline that Gladstone condemned in 1874 and fomented thereafter was strengthened by the clear evidence that the party now had two policies proposed by two leaders.

As if to reinforce the duality that had emerged as a result of his campaign, Gladstone agreed to address the newly formed National Liberal Federation in Birmingham at the end of May. Created by Chamberlain, the NLF was an organisational innovation designed to give radicalism a stronger base within the Liberal party after the failure of the National Education League and the collapse of the disestablishment campaign of 1874–5. The aim was to capture the party from below by democratising local constituency associations and uniting them into a national federation whose influence the leadership would be unable to resist. Implicit in its formation was the coming of modern party discipline, imposed upon leaders as well as followers. Individual Whigs might survive, but only by imitating Chamberlain and working with their local associations. The Whigs as Whigs would disappear, as would that freedom of action that Gladstone saw as indispensable to his style of leadership. Hartington treated the NLF as another threat to his leadership, and sharply rejected Chamberlain's invitations to address meetings in both 1878 and 1879.

In practice, the sectional identity of the NLF and its avowedly factional purpose reduced its effectiveness. Local associations in other major cities resented its claims and the attempted domination of Chamberlain and Birmingham. Whigs and moderates refused to be 'led by the new Birmingham school',[63] and challenging

---

61. Ibid. pp. 60–1.   62. Ibid. pp. 61–2; Rossi, 'Transformation', pp. 51–4.
63. Jenkins, *Gladstone, Whiggery and the Liberal Party*, p. 72.

Gladstone was out of the question. After the split of 1886, although occasionally troublesome, the NLF was effectively captured from above. Radicals, especially working-class radicals, were forced to look elsewhere. The stifling of the NLF was one minor factor in the emergence of independent Labour in the 1890s. In the 1870s it was one more weapon in the Liberal party's internal struggle.

The popularity of Disraeli's successful brinksmanship and their own divisions left the Liberals effectively paralysed as an opposition. In January 1878 the decision to oppose Disraeli's demand for emergency credit taken at a bitter meeting ended in a fiasco. Rumours that the Russians were already besieging Constantinople allowed the official leadership to withdraw their opposition, a position in which they felt more comfortable and which they maintained even when the rumours were revealed as false. In the vote, 103 Liberals opposed the government, 10 supported it and the remainder took the new official line of abstention. At the committee stage, 113, including Gladstone, opposed the government in defiance of the leadership.[64]

An ill-advised amendment in April against Disraeli's precautionary proposal to call out the reserves moved by Sir Wilfrid Lawson after the leadership had decided not to act, drew only fifty-four votes whilst the leadership again took refuge in abstention and twenty-five Liberals voted with the government.[65] Gladstone supported Lawson on the grounds that he had 'a higher duty than that of party allegiance'.[66] The party achieved greater unity in opposing the movement of Indian troops to Malta, but the leadership only acted because the alternative was further independent Radical action, and within a week Gladstone and Hartington were again on opposite sides. In July, Disraeli returned from the Congress of Berlin bringing peace with honour and the acquisition of Cyprus, 'a new Asiatic empire' as Gladstone contemptuously called it. The country supported the government, Hartington himself saw little to criticise, and many in the Liberal party saw even less.[67]

Liberal unity on foreign affairs was re-established with a speed and ease which made clear the disruptive impact of Gladstone's agitation on the Eastern question. Wars in South Africa and Afghanistan, defeat by the Zulus at Isandhlwana and the massacre of the

---

64. Ibid. pp. 65–6.   65. Ibid. p. 71.

66. Rossi, 'Transformation', p. 70; Jenkins, *Gladstone, Whiggery and the Liberal Party*, p. 66.

67. Jenkins, *Gladstone, Whiggery and the Liberal Party*, p. 67; Rossi, 'Transformation', p. 75.

British garrison at Kabul in September 1878 after early successes broke the jingo spell. Liberal reaction to these wars was initially similar to that on the Eastern question, with Hartington cautious and Gladstone and the Radicals critical. But when the government attributed the Afghan war to the weakness of previous Liberal policy for which the Whigs had been responsible, the Whig reaction left Hartington in danger of being left behind by his own party. The attack on government policy in December 1878 produced much greater unity than Hartington expected, and allowed him subsequently to adopt a more active opposition which consolidated the conciliatory moves he had made in domestic policy the preceding year. The real loser appeared to be Gladstone, who was associated with a minority of some sixty Radicals attempting to sustain a policy almost devoid of popular support. In the spring of 1878 anti-Russian jingo mobs burned Gladstone in effigy and stoned his house. Nor could Gladstone rally the full strength of Radicalism. Bright and the peace societies sympathised with the morality of his agitation, but not its militancy, whilst Russophobe Radicals like Joseph Cowen actively supported the government. Gladstonian agitation also produced a reaction from a section of the Whigs who were rumoured to be about to secede and form an independent party of 'Palmerstonian Whigs'. By February 1878, George Goschen, first lord of the admiralty in Gladstone's previous government, but on the far right of the party and already adrift from Hartington after the latter's endorsement of county-franchise reform, thought secession inevitable because Gladstone had pushed Hartington too far towards Radicalism.[68]

This was one factor which determined Hartington to keep his distance from Chamberlain. Throughout 1877–8 Hartington tried to maintain contact with the Radicals while fearing a breakaway from the right. But with Gladstone's campaign drawing off Radical enthusiasm towards foreign policy while offering nothing on the domestic front, Radicals like Chamberlain whose interests were primarily domestic were not in a strong position to make demands. The Radical programme, such as it was, laid emphasis on electoral and local-government reform which Hartington had already accepted, and Chamberlain had no power to threaten a split on the left to counterbalance Goschen's threat from the right. His invitations and Hartington's abrupt refusals to address the NLF clearly revealed Chamberlain as the supplicant. Moreover, any Liberal

---

68. Jenkins, *Gladstone, Whiggery and the Liberal Party*, pp. 73–4.

cabinet under Whig leadership would need to conciliate Radical support; Gladstone, with his reputation for Radicalism, could and would ignore it, but needed to conciliate Whigs and moderates. Under these circumstances, Chamberlain showed increasing willingness to come to terms with Hartington's leadership for the sake of unity on a common programme of moderate domestic reform.

During 1879, Hartington was in an increasingly strong position in the struggle for control of the party. His moderation rallied the majority behind him and Chamberlain's section of the Radicals inclined to his leadership by default. Gladstone, unacceptable to the Whig right, looked an unlikely figure to restore the party's fortunes by recovering those moderates whose defection in 1874 had been the primary cause of the party's defeat. That the moderates were still the main problem was revealed by the difficulty in finding candidates for county constituencies, where, late in 1879, forty-nine divisions still remained unfilled. During 1879, without Gladstone, the Liberal recovery allowed the leaders to revise their estimates of the election results progressively upwards from a Conservative majority of twenty in August to a Liberal majority of thirty to forty-five by the end of October.[69]

Midlothian and the triumph of Gladstone

Gladstone's candidature for Midlothian, arranged early in 1879 to provide the platform for a major campaign with the maximum of publicity, disrupted the reunification of the party under Hartington. His aim of keeping old issues 'alive and warm . . . to join on the proceedings of 1876–9 by a continuous process to the dissolution',[70] in practice kept 'alive and warm' the very issues on which the Liberals were most divided. The first Midlothian campaign of November–December 1879 increased tensions within the party by reawakening Radical doubts about his commitment to domestic reform and hardened Whig doubts about his long-term intentions. Despite his denials, the campaign looked like a renewed bid for the leadership, and Hartington again almost resigned.[71] Success would, by implication, condemn the cautious policy of the Whig leadership and make Gladstone dominant over his colleagues in any future

---

69. Ibid. p. 104.   70. Morley, *Life of Gladstone*, vol. 2, p. 587.
71. Rossi, 'Transformation', pp. 100, 105–6; Bernard Holland, *The Life of Spencer Compton, Eighth Duke of Devonshire* (London: Longman, 1911), pp. 259–61.

Liberal government. Halifax even argued that defeat in the next election might be profitable to the Whigs because it would solve 'the Gladstone difficulty',[72] especially since the Whigs, who sympathised with Disraeli's policy until 1878, did not envisage its reversal in the event of Liberal electoral success.

Briefly, electoral defeat did appear a possible outcome which could be laid at Gladstone's door. The relatively poor performance of the party in the early months of 1880 was attributed by many to the alienation of moderates by Gladstone's campaign. Yet this raised a new difficulty, the prospect that the Irish would hold the balance of power in the new parliament. Relations between official Liberalism and the Irish were increasingly strained and in 1877 Hartington wished to sever the formal connection.[73] On the eve of the election, the *Manchester Guardian* was still predicting only a narrow Liberal majority and a hung parliament.[74] With the Radicals, twenty-nine of whom voted for Redmond's motion on Irish distress, holding consultations with the Irish, the Whigs feared a Liberal government willing to make concessions on Home Rule and land reform.[75] Gladstone himself was willing to consider an agreement with the Irish on the basis of reformed local government which he saw as a necessary pre-condition for the further reform of Irish land tenure.[76] Whig fears of a Gladstone–Radical–Irish deal prompted Hartington's warning that participants in such deals would lose more than they gained, and was a major element in the belief of Liberal moderates that Gladstone was not safe.

The Whig position was nevertheless incongruous, virtually hoping for the electoral defeat of the party to which they not only belonged, but which they led. Granville, almost echoing Halifax, saw more merit in a Conservative minority government relying on outside Whig support than an outright Liberal victory. In consequence, apart from the domestic reforms wrung from them by Radical pressure, the Whigs had little of a distinctive Liberal position to offer. The moderate Liberalism of which they were the spokesmen was still close to moderate Conservatism, and still underpinned centrism. During the Balkan crisis, both Whigs and moderate Conservatives were alarmed by Disraeli's brinksmanship, and Carnarvon and Derby resigned from Disraeli's government because of it. But both groups accepted the government's definition of British

72. Jenkins, *Gladstone, Whiggery and the Liberal Party*, p. 111.
73. Rossi, 'Transformation', p. 66.
74. Jenkins, *Gladstone, Whiggery and the Liberal Party*, pp. 114–21.
75. Ibid. p. 116.   76. Ibid. pp. 122–3.

interests, and Disraeli's success before 1878 gave them little scope to challenge him.

By default, Gladstone's condemnation of the government set the agenda for the 1880 election campaign, established the Liberals' claim to office, and when it succeeded, made Gladstone indispensable. His Midlothian campaigns were theatrical performances, designed to appeal beyond parliament directly to the electorate and to the superior morality that Gladstone now discerned in the masses, against the corrupt and corrupting influence of the elite. As such, it was, as Gladstone intended it to be, the culmination of the agitation of 1876–9, expounding from a position of greater strength and with greater vigour than had been possible during his dispute with Palmerston, the virtues of morality in foreign policy.

What made Gladstone's moralism effective was not its application to foreign policy in isolation, but the impact of foreign policy on Britain herself. As a result of an adventurous foreign policy, Disraeli's government was obliged to bring in three successive unbalanced budgets and increase income tax. For Gladstone, as for Cobden, this was axiomatic, as were the broader consequences of high taxation, poor trade, depression and unemployment. The depression began, on cue, in 1879. Distress was aggravated by a series of poor harvests, and it was not difficult for Gladstone to make the necessary connections for his audiences. Flouting the laws of political economy and good government brought its own retribution on an immoral government and an immoral people. In that respect, the laws of political economy were themselves guarantors of morality in politics. Cobden had died in 1865, but the Liberalism he had systematised lived on.

Gladstone's unofficial campaign gave the Liberal party the best of both worlds in 1880. While Gladstone rallied Nonconformist enthusiasm in what he and most others believed was his last election, Hartington and Granville were reassuringly safe figures at the head of the party. The party was also surprisingly well organised despite its recent divisions and more seats were fought than in any previous election,[77] another indication of the growing polarisation of politics. Nevertheless, the results also revealed a growing reliance upon the Celtic fringe.[78] Many victories were won by narrow majorities. Twenty-nine seats were held by fewer than 100 votes, and the drift of the suburbs to Conservatism, first evident in

77. Rossi, 'Transformation', p. 108.
78. Michael Bentley, *Politics Without Democracy* (London: Fontana, 1984), p. 231.

1868, proceeded unhindered.[79] In Ireland, the Home Rulers also continued their onward march, although the scale of the Liberal victory temporarily delayed the fulfilment of Whig anxieties. Ultimately, the Liberal victory owed less to Chamberlain's organisation, Hartington's moderation or Gladstone's passion than to the depression, for which the government was blamed. Insofar as Gladstone was necessary to make the connection, this, rather than his denunciation of government immorality abroad, was his major contribution to victory.

The election was nevertheless regarded as a one-man victory, and all Hartington's early advantages crumbled to nothing. Gladstone had been recalled by the nation over the heads of his party. He was not only able to resume the leadership, but to oblige Granville and Hartington to invite him to do so, confirming their subordination. His return once again reduced the Whigs from their central position to that of a section of the party. Their dependence on Gladstone was accentuated by the abiding fear that without him the party might fall into the hands of a Radical–Irish alliance and that if they opposed him, he might throw his immense influence behind such an alliance. As long as Gladstone remained, both Whigs and Radicals had no choice but to compete for his approval, leaving him free to pursue his own line and play them off against each other. Gladstone's predominance retarded the long-term development of the party. His apparent ability to get the voters to the polls served as a substitute for grassroots constituency organisation, prevented the emergence of alternative leaders, precluded the development of party policy by debate, and relieved the factions of the need to reconcile their differences by compromise.

As prime minister after 1880, he called few cabinets and was inclined to confront them with ready-made policies disguised as hypotheses. He saw little need to attend to the long-term future of the party since he had returned with a negative, or at best restorative, programme. Once he had undone the damage caused by Disraeli, he envisaged returning to retirement. In office after 1880, Gladstone was paradoxically the factor which at once held the party together and yet destabilised it. The long period of opposition had resolved none of the underlying problems of Liberal disunity. They were obscured and to a degree circumvented by the complexity of Gladstone's outlook, Whig flexibility, the diversity of Radical opinion and Chamberlain's inability to arouse or comprehend

79. Rossi, 'Transformation', p. 121.

enthusiasm which limited his effectiveness as a Radical leader. Gladstone regarded popular morality as a control over government action, not a substitute for administration by an elite. He thus provided a continuing role for the Whigs as administrators if they did not challenge him on policy. The Whigs in turn were prepared, reluctantly and within limits, to bend on policy in order to remain in contact with the Liberal party. The alternatives were marginalisation or Conservatism.

Whig flexibility also provided scope for a degree of understanding with the Radicals of their respective roles. Like Gladstone, the Whigs saw no point in acting before the time was ripe, when further resistance would leave them isolated. Unlike Gladstone, they regarded their function not as one of bringing issues to fruition, but of providing the frosty blast of criticism that might blight development. That attitude was an open invitation to Radicals to warm up the political atmosphere. The activities of Nonconformist pressure groups and the National Liberal Federation were the natural consequence of the political approach of the Liberal elite. The NLF was also one factor in propelling Chamberlain into the cabinet in 1880, only four years after his election as an MP.

Chamberlainite Radicalism added a new element to both Liberal politics and Liberal factionalism. He saw, perhaps too clearly, that in politics as in business the logical end of competition is monopoly, and showed few signs of understanding, still less of sharing, traditional Liberal views on the potential harmony of competing interests in either domestic or international politics. He shared with the Whigs a common language of power, uncomplicated by morality, which facilitated alliances of convenience such as that emerging in the late 1870s. Chamberlain and the Whigs understood each other even when they disagreed; neither fully understood Gladstone. Chamberlain's ideas for the use of power were nevertheless anathema both to Gladstone and the Whigs. Even his early campaign for the '4Fs', though heavily influenced by its sectarian origins, involved the use of state power to regulate private interests to achieve social harmony. In providing a positive radical role for the state he foreshadowed aspects of 'New Liberalism' and the political practice of Lloyd George, especially in his 'unauthorised programme' of 1883–5.

The complexities of Liberal disintegration after 1873 lay in this three-fold disagreement between Gladstone, the Whigs and Chamberlain about the source and use of power. For Gladstone, power rested in moral opinion, for the Whigs in educated opinion and for

Chamberlain in organised opinion. Their views on the use of power, and thus on the nature of the Liberal party, reflected these different views of its source. Gladstone sought to emancipate the moral individual and nation from the state, Chamberlain to reform society through the state, and the Whigs simply to govern, leaving emancipation to an ill-defined social process. These divisions permitted a variety of alignments according to the issues in dispute and the likely political advantage. The problem for the new Liberal government was to retain all groups within the Liberal party despite their differing views of Liberalism and the purpose of that party. Its position was not eased by the discrepancy between the outlook of its dominant leader and the international realities created by the actions of other powers, and the presence of a substantial third party of Irish Home Rulers dedicated to the disruption of the political system.

CHAPTER FOUR

The Complications of Ireland and Empire

Because opposition had resolved none of the outstanding differences within the Liberal party, the administration of 1880–5 was marred by frequent disputes and constant threats of resignation. Almost all of the cabinet threatened to resign, or in Gladstone's case retire, at some point, and usually more than once. Gladstone's constant reiteration of his intention to retire led to a jockeying for position by the Whigs and Radicals, each with an eye to the post-Gladstonian situation, which led them to take up positions which would rally their respective supporters for the anticipated showdown. Paradoxically, this disunity made Gladstone's continued presence necessary as the arbiter between the sections, and thus prolonged uncertainty and disunity. In 1883, the cabinet had to recall Gladstone from holiday to resolve the dispute that had arisen over Irish policy in his brief absence. Both Gladstone and the party at large grew to believe that he was indispensable, yet both were waiting for the eventual departure.

Despite Gladstone's restorative election campaign, the Liberals entered office in 1880 with an outline domestic programme, the reform of the county franchise and local government on which Whigs and Radicals had agreed in the late 1870s. Franchise reform, requiring an immediate general election, was postponed, but local-government reform, the creation of county and district councils with revenue-raising powers and financial responsibility became a major issue after the election. It accorded with Gladstone's long-standing desire to reform local finance and remove the nagging problem of the rates.[1] But although the first local government bill

---

1. H.C.G. Matthew (ed.), *The Gladstone Diaries*, vol. X (Oxford: Oxford University Press, 1990), pp. xcviii–xcix.

was drafted in 1881, and a succession of bills for the English counties, London and Ireland followed, the government failed to pass a single measure. Local government fell victim to a combination of the pressure of other business, especially foreign affairs and Ireland, and the effectiveness of Irish obstruction. Considering the 'legislative subjects before us for the chief work of the next Session – such as Land, suffrage, local Government' in September 1880, Gladstone found them all driven out of mind by 'the gravity of the Candahar affair', and this was to become a frequent refrain.[2] The years 1880–4 provided no 'solid meal . . . for the Liberal lions' that Chamberlain felt necessary 'if they are to be kept from rending one another', and rend one another they did.[3]

Problems of empire

Ending Disraeli's little wars caused few difficulties. British troops were rapidly withdrawn from Afghanistan, although the new regime established there existed with British guarantees of its security, and control of its foreign policy. The Zulu war was never likely to be more than a diversion, and as Gladstone observed, the Boers 'are perhaps better qualified to solve the Zulu question'.[4] The more awkward problem was the Boers themselves, who in December 1880 rose against Disraeli's annexation of the Transvaal. In an application of Liberal reasonableness in foreign policy, Gladstone ignored the unexpected and unimportant defeat at Majuba and abandoned annexation. As in Afghanistan, Britain retained control of foreign policy by the conventions of Pretoria (1881) and London (1884).

Reducing government expenditure proved to be a greater, and ultimately an insoluble, problem. Expenditure in 1881 was almost £85 million and in 1885 topped £100 million. That this was still low taking into account the rise in taxable revenue, did not lessen the adverse political impact on a government that leaned heavily on its reputation for sound finance. Gladstone had become chancellor of the exchequer as well as prime minister in 1880 with precisely this in mind.[5] Nor were the overseas complications of 'Beaconsfieldism' fully resolved. Neither Afghanistan nor the Dutch republics in South Africa were fully independent. Both existed under

2. D.A. Hamer, *Liberal Politics in the Age of Gladstone and Rosebery* (Oxford: Oxford University Press, 1972), p. 86.
3. Ibid. p. 86.   4. Matthew, *Gladstone Diaries*, vol. X, p. lxxxviii.
5. Ibid. pp. xcv–xcviii, xxx.

British 'suzerainty', a concept Gladstone had devised during the Eastern-question debates to resolve the problem of local Christian self-government without precipitating the complete breakdown of the Turkish empire.[6] The value of the concept lay in its lack of definition. It was 'elastic',[7] meaning whatever the contracting parties wanted it to mean. It left Britain half involved, the source of future entanglements and future Liberal divisions.

Gladstone's confusion and cabinet disagreements led to the semi-solution of 'suzerainty' becoming in practice Liberal policy towards imperial problems, whether this was an attempt to reduce involvement, as in Ireland, or an obligation to move from partial to full involvement, as in Egypt. The central quandary continued unresolved until the end of the century as the party successively struggled with the problems of the Sudan, Uganda and again the Boer republics. For the ministry of 1880–5, the main problems were Egypt and Ireland. By 1880, Britain already had some responsibility for Egyptian financial stability following Disraeli's purchase of Suez canal shares and the Anglo-French dual control of 1876–9. Gladstone complained at the time that this would lead to 'a new African empire',[8] but subsequently forgot his own prophecy. As a result, the government was taken by surprise by the sudden eruption of Egyptian protest.

Gladstone's response was conditioned by the need to maintain 'all established rights in Egypt, whether they be those of the Sultan, those of the Khedive, those of the people of Egypt or those of the foreign bondholders'.[9] Riots in Alexandria in June 1882 led to British bombardment, Bright's resignation and ultimately military intervention. Involvement created a succession of disagreements within the cabinet as Hartington argued for the recognition of long-term occupation as a necessity, Gladstone that occupation was temporary, and the Cobdenite Radicals that the occupation should never have taken place and withdrawal should be immediate. Despite the arguments, by September 1882 Britain had secured control of a largely unwanted Egypt from which the Liberals were unable to escape.

Moreover, by occupying Egypt Britain incurred responsibilities that dragged her further south. The defeat of the Khedive's army by Mahdist rebels in the autumn of 1883 extended the Egyptian imbroglio into the Sudan. In January 1884, the cabinet decided on

---

6. Ibid. 1986 vol. IX, pp. xxxiv, xliv–xlvii; vol. X, p. lxxxvii.
7. Ibid. vol. IX, p. xlvii.   8. Ibid. p. lxxiv.   9. Ibid. p. lxix.

evacuation of the Sudan and compelled the Khedive to accept this decision, but unwisely chose the Christian militant, General Gordon, for the task, while still disagreeing about what exactly that task was. Gordon, moreover, was employed by the Khedive, by whom he was made governor of the Sudan, and was widely suspected of having his own view of the purpose of his mission. The government, paralysed by its conflicting opinions and Gladstone's personal interest in Egyptian finance, relegated discussion of Gordon's situation to 'five minutes at the fag-end of business'.[10] Gladstone regarded the Mahdi as a genuine nationalist, and the Sudan as a 'people . . . struggling rightly to be free',[11] a view which conveniently coincided with his desperate wish to avoid involvement. On this assessment, Gordon was deliberately remaining in Khartoum to commit the government to reconquest and permanent occupation. Chamberlain shared Gladstone's suspicion of Gordon's motives but supported swift military action to rescue him; Hartington wanted to mount a major expedition which led to not unfounded suspicions that he sympathised with the expansionist motives attributed to Gordon. Thus, although the government decided on intervention in April 1884, it was only in August, again by threatening resignation, that Hartington got his way.

By then it was too late. Khartoum fell, Gordon perished, and with him the reputation of a government held responsible for the death of a popular hero and the abandonment of the territory for which he died. News of the fall of Khartoum in February 1885 led Gladstone to retire to bed with 'overaction of the bowels' and to consider resignation, which the majority of the government favoured, after the government won the vote of censure by only fourteen votes.[12] The government's indecision during the Sudanese emergency arose from genuine disagreement within the cabinet, but it was aggravated by the sheer weight of distractions elsewhere. 'This day, for the first time in my recollection,' Gladstone noted on 2 August 1884, 'there were *three* crises for us running high tide at once: Egypt, Gordon and franchise.'[13]

The crises continued to multiply, each one fuelling division within the government. In September, Boer annexation of Bechuanaland following the movement of settlers into the area created another minor crisis in South Africa; German colonial expansion in the

10. Richard Jay, *Joseph Chamberlain: A Political Study* (Oxford: Oxford University Press, 1981), p. 83.
11. Matthew, *Gladstone Diaries*, vol. IX, p. lxxviii.   12. Ibid. pp. lxxxii–lxxxiii.
13. Ibid. vol. X, p. cvii.

Pacific and Africa led to criticism of government weakness both at home and in Australia, and early in 1885 Russian expansion to the Afghan frontier led to a potentially serious border dispute. This very multiplicity allowed the government a means of escape. Gladstone exploited the confrontation with Russia to secure approval for withdrawal from the Sudan because the troops might be needed elsewhere. The Russian dispute was resolved by negotiation, as, with some difficulty, was the difference with France over Egyptian finances, whilst a military expedition removed the Boers from Bechuanaland at the price of adding another protectorate to the empire. It was, nevertheless, desperate stuff, policy made on the hoof by a government that had no clear policies on the handling of imperial power, and whose basic philosophy provided only contradictory indications.

The problem of Ireland

Despite the length of the occupation, Ireland presented similar problems to those of empire. Ireland formed no part of the 'call' that had brought Gladstone back into active politics in 1876, but it became the greatest difficulty that the Liberal government faced. The emergence of the Land League in October 1879, the increase in evictions and concerted, widespread disorder in Ireland under the impact of the agricultural depression, demonstrated the failure of the earlier Land Act. Together with the assumption of the leadership of the Irish Home Rule party by Parnell this marked a new, more critical, and for the Liberals even more divisive, stage in the evolution of the Irish problem. Parnell's position as president of the Land League effectively united agrarian and nationalist discontent, and in British politics made the Irish Parliamentary Party the focus of both. For Gladstone, at least, Ireland rapidly came to dominate other issues, even the dismantling of the legacy of Beaconsfieldism. 'Spoke on the Transvaal,' he noted in 1881, 'but I am too full of Ireland to be *free* in anything else.'[14] Throughout the life of the government, he worked within the logic of his own argument that all of Ireland's needs could be met within the framework of the Union, but he did so with diminishing conviction. Failure led ineluctably towards an acceptance of Home Rule.

Both the nature of the problem and Liberal discord dictated a two-pronged approach of coercion and concession, the former to

14. Ibid. p. cxvi.

satisfy the Whigs and lead them reluctantly to accept concession, the latter to satisfy the Radicals and lead them reluctantly to accept coercion. But it was also a well-worn technique of suppressing agitation by force whilst removing its support by reform, which might also in this case separate the agrarian and nationalist issues. Coercion was introduced early in 1881 to placate restive Whigs who saw forbearance in Ireland as 'mawkish sentiment . . . by talking weak twaddle . . . we shall in a short time have civil war in Ireland'.[15] But in order to placate the Radicals, coercion was to last for one year only, thereby ensuring further controversy in the near future. Already, Hartington and Forster on one side, Chamberlain, Bright and Dilke on the other, had threatened resignation on this issue.[16] The danger of Whig revolt was indicated by the fate of the compensation for disturbances bill of 1880, a temporary measure expiring at the end of 1881 that was designed to give some protection to poorer tenants evicted for non-payment of rent if that non-payment had been due to the harvest failures of the previous two years. Concern for the rights of property led twenty-one Liberals to vote against the second reading in the Commons, and a majority of Liberal peers to join the Conservatives in rejecting it in the House of Lords.[17]

The central question of Irish land reform was political, the restoration of order within a Liberal framework, not the economic problems of Irish land tenure. For the cabinet this meant simply determining how little the Irish would accept, given that neither Gladstone nor the Whigs wanted to give them anything at all. Gladstone's respect for property and rights of contract made him more sympathetic to the Whig position than the Whigs realised. It was only with great reluctance, following the report of the Bessborough Commission on the Irish land question that favoured the '3Fs', and further evidence of Irish demands, that he accepted that moderate reform would be insufficient and that he must concede the '3Fs'.[18] The Whigs with even greater reluctance came to the same conclusion. Even then, Gladstone's acceptance of the '3Fs' was hesitant, obscure and temporary. He still maintained that ideally freedom of contract was more beneficial to Ireland,[19] but conceded, with the young Whig, H.R. Brand, that when dealing

15. T.A. Jenkins, *Gladstone, Whiggery and the Liberal Party* (Oxford: Oxford University Press, 1988), p. 154n.
16. Jay, *Chamberlain*, p. 52.
17. Jenkins, *Gladstone, Whiggery and the Liberal Party*, p. 149.
18. Matthew, *Gladstone Diaries*, vol. IX, p. lxxviii; vol. X, p. cxiii.
19. Ibid. vol. X, pp. cxv, cxvi.

with Irish land, it was necessary 'to throw political economy to the winds'.[20]

Whig rebellion was limited by awareness that premature defection might throw Gladstone into the Radical camp or result in a Radical Liberal party on Gladstone's retirement. Nevertheless, two hostile Whig amendments to the land bill objecting to state interference in property rights drew support from thirty-four and twenty-five Liberals respectively.[21] Argyll, who had resigned in April 1881, subsequently condemned 'the mischievous tendencies of Gladstone's leadership, and . . . the utter instability he is imparting to all the fundamental principles of government',[22] and voiced his fear of 'the inclined plane on which we are now all standing – the letting go of all that has hitherto been understood as sound Liberal principles'.[23] In this he spoke for the Whigs at large.

For Gladstone, too, the Irish Land Act of 1881 with its Land Commission and land courts to fix rents was a considerable concession of principle to the necessities of the Irish situation. Land courts were 'a form of centralisation, referring to public authority what ought to be transacted by a private individual'.[24] As became clearer in the following three years, this was a fundamental distinction between his and Chamberlain's Radicalism. Chamberlain and Dilke had both threatened resignation against the weakness of Gladstone's initial proposals simply to modify the 1870 Irish Land Act.[25] The political advantage of their pro-tenant stance lay in the continuing potential of a Radical–Irish alliance, which Chamberlain sought until his quarrel with Parnell in 1885. The extension of state interference with private property and the breach of the principles of free trade in this 'exceptional' Irish legislation left Chamberlain unperturbed. As he said in 1885, 'I am not afraid of the three F's in England, Scotland or Ireland.'[26]

At least the Land Act was relatively effective. Combined with the arrest of the leading figures in the Land League, and finally in October 1881 of Parnell himself, it undermined the Land League, which could not denounce the Act without harming the cause of those whom it claimed to serve. Eight days after the arrest of Parnell, the Land League itself was proscribed when it tried to protest against the arrests by launching a 'no rent' campaign. This

20. Jenkins, *Gladstone, Whiggery and the Liberal Party*, p. 171.
21. Ibid. pp. 156–9.   22. Ibid. p. 161.   23. Ibid. p. 162.
24. Matthew, *Gladstone Diaries*, vol. X, p. cxvi.   25. Jay, *Chamberlain*, pp. 54–5.
26. J.L. Garvin, *The Life of Joseph Chamberlain*, vol. 1 (London: Macmillan, 1935), p. 553.

situation, however, suited neither Parnell, who saw his position in Ireland waning as he languished in Kilmainham prison, nor Gladstone who recognised only too clearly that he had achieved a suspension of hostilities, not a settlement. Moreover, the greater the illusion of calm in Ireland, the greater would be the pressure from the Radicals not to renew coercion when it lapsed in the autumn of 1882.

Whig fears of Radical intentions had some justification. In the spring of 1882, negotiations between Chamberlain and Parnell via Captain O'Shea resulted in Parnell's release. The 'Kilmainham treaty', as the deal was labelled once Parnell's offer to cooperate with the Liberal party 'in forwarding Liberal principles' became public, was at best a vague understanding in which Parnell agreed to assist the working of the law in Ireland in return for his release and a satisfactory solution to the problem of tenants in arrears with their rent. In practice, the 'no rent' campaign was already in difficulties, and the government was committed to dealing with the question of rent arrears at Gladstone's insistence, as a refinement of the Land Act.[27] The agreement suited both parties. Parnell could return with the status of martyr, and Gladstone again had someone to negotiate with. It was, in his words, 'a golden moment'.[28] As is the nature of golden moments, satisfaction was brief.

The 'treaty' brought about Forster's resignation as Irish chief secretary which the Radicals had been seeking for some months; within days, his replacement, Hartington's brother, Lord Frederick Cavendish, and T.H. Burke, a Dublin Castle official, were murdered in Phoenix Park, Dublin. Ironically, this temporarily settled Whig fears. After what had appeared to be a Radical triumph both in the context of Irish policy and the cabinet contest for Gladstone's support, the government had to respond with extensive coercion. The new Crimes Act was to last for three years, removing the danger of Radical subversion and limiting if not ending the possibility of a Gladstone–Parnell agreement conducted by and for the benefit of Chamberlain and the Radicals. Until 1885 the Whigs could lend their support to 'vigorous administration' in Ireland, and on the basis that Ireland was a special case support the arrears bill introduced by Gladstone on 15 May.[29] Firm action on Egypt, and Gladstone's acceptance of compromise, under pressure from

27. Jenkins, *Gladstone, Whiggery and the Liberal Party*, pp. 165–6.
28. Matthew, *Gladstone Diaries*, vol. X, p. cxxi.
29. Jenkins, *Gladstone, Whiggery and the Liberal Party*, pp. 165–70; Matthew, *Gladstone Diaries*, vol. X, pp. cxx–cxxi.

Hartington, on franchise and redistribution at the end of 1883, also eased Whig anxieties.

Ireland, however, could not be accommodated within what Liberals, especially Whiggish Liberals, considered the 'fundamental principles of government'. Liberals were either forced into coercive policies which brought to a head the inherent conflict between Liberalism and the executive functions of government, or ameliorative measures which contradicted Liberal ideas on property and political economy. For Gladstone, semi-permanent coercion, or oppression, in Ireland would corrupt British government as oppression in the Balkans had corrupted the Turks, and was similarly doomed to failure, 'for if we are at war with a nation, we cannot win'.[30] The ameliorative measures of the Liberal government were always hastily conceived with a political purpose because the party failed to grasp the reality of Irish conditions and demands. Not surprisingly, Ireland divided the party. This in turn complicated the treatment of Irish problems by entangling policy in the struggle for power within the party.

Parliamentary reform and social politics

By late 1882, frustrated at the failure of Radicalism to make any headway in the first two years of the government, Chamberlain was seeking 'a new departure in constructive radicalism'.[31] 'The politics of the future,' he wrote in January 1883, 'are social politics.'[32] Chamberlain was not alone in reacting to rising social discontent under the impact of economic depression. The publication of Andrew Mearns' *The Bitter Cry of Outcast London* in 1883 led John Morley, Chamberlain's erstwhile Radical ally in the press and from 1883 MP for Newcastle, to investigate the situation in his constituency and conclude that there was also an 'outcast Newcastle'. Dilke did the same in London and as president of the local government board set up a royal commission on the housing of the working classes.

Popular discontent was already the subject of agitation. The visit of the American land reformer, Henry George, to Britain in 1881, and the publication of his *Progress and Poverty* led to widespread discussion of his radical ideas for land taxation both in Britain and in Ireland. Morley found London workers 'full of the ideas of Henry George', and the Land Reform Union began an

---

30. Matthew, *Gladstone Diaries*, vol. X, p. cxix.   31. Jay, *Chamberlain*, p. 71.
32. Ibid. p. 74.

active campaign to convert grassroots Liberalism to some form of land nationalisation.[33] George's critique of the 'land monopoly', by which landowners who had usurped the land from the people were able to siphon off for their own use the increase in land values that accompanied social progress and economic development, and his proposal for a tax equivalent to the total value of the land in the name of justice, found a ready audience amongst Radicals and workingmen already familiar with the concept of the 'unearned increment' and a history that told of expropriation. His ideas, and those of the Land Nationalisation Society, made steady progress within the Liberal party. 'Socialism', in the vague contemporary sense, was, as Chamberlain remarked, 'in the air',[34] and threatened radicalism from the left.

The Radical response was a series of articles in the *Fortnightly Review* in the autumn and winter of 1883–4. The programme was interventionist in arguing social responsibility for the poor and giving the state some role in undertaking that responsibility, but for the most part it was a restatement of traditional Radical democracy which had always had a social dimension. It thus combined Nonconformist policies of disestablishment and free education with newer demands for democratic local government, the payment of MPs and land and housing reform to be paid for from graduated taxation. Whig fears that 'the way is being paved for a new party on Gladstone's retirement' were premature in 1883.[35] Social politics might be the politics of the future, but that future lay on the other side of a successful Reform Act, when the extended franchise would, in Radical expectations, ensure their predominance, especially if the Irish aligned themselves with Radical causes. For the present, Chamberlain had no choice but to continue within a Gladstonian Liberal party. In December 1882 Gladstone indicated his determination to prolong his leadership by handing over the exchequer to Childers and bringing Dilke into the cabinet as president of the local government board to reduce his personal burden.

The political debate nevertheless remained as frustratingly barren as ever. The reform of London government foundered in contention, and local government reform lapsed. Chamberlain did, however, secure an undertaking that the promised reform of the franchise would finally be dealt with in 1884, which in turn meant that Gladstone would have to reconcile the Whigs. He could only

33. Michael Barker, *Gladstone and Radicalism: The Reconstruction of the Liberal Party in Britain 1885–94* (Brighton: Harvester, 1975), pp. 7–8.
34. Jay, *Chamberlain*, p. 71.   35. Ibid. p. 71.

do so by abandoning his plan, which Chamberlain supported, to deal with the franchise alone, and leave redistribution to a later date, perhaps after his retirement. Gladstone's concerns were personal and political: his age and failing health, and the complexity of redistribution which might threaten the fragile unity of the party. Chamberlain's reasoning was more tactical, and turned on the expectation that a subsequent parliament elected on a wider franchise would be more radical in composition. Hartington consistently opposed both the separation of the two aspects of reform, and the extension of franchise reform to Ireland on the same terms as the rest of the country, and accompanied his opposition with the usual threats of resignation. By December 1883 he had been worn down, and agreed to support the extension of the franchise both in Great Britain and Ireland on condition that Gladstone outlined a redistribution scheme in introducing franchise reform, and agreed to stay on to pass redistribution in the next session, thus thwarting both Gladstone's desire to escape, and Chamberlain's pursuit of political advantage.

The internal Liberal dispute proved unnecessary. Whilst franchise reform proved to be the 'big bill' which held the Liberal party together and secured Irish support, franchise without redistribution proved too much for the Conservative party which rejected it in the Lords in July 1884. The Radicals, not entirely restrained by Gladstone, relished the summer and autumn confrontation with the Lords; Gladstone, assisted by Dilke, quietly negotiated a redistribution compromise with Salisbury which once again left the Radicals without a cause. The Reform Act of 1884 extended the borough franchise to the counties, providing household not manhood suffrage, which, together with the long period of residence required and the complex registration requirements for lodgers, left Britain well short of democracy. Parliamentary reform in 1867 and 1884 reflected the continuing Victorian fear of the 'residuum', the poor and mobile, in favour of stationary respectability, and in so doing excluded some 40 per cent of the adult male population from participation in politics.[36]

Redistribution created single-member constituencies on a population basis throughout the country with the exception of cities between 50,000 and 150,000 which retained their double-member constituencies. Instructions to the boundary commissioners to take

---

36. Neal Blewett, 'The franchise in the United Kingdom 1885–1914', *Past and Present* 32 (1965), 27; Duncan Tanner, *Political Change and the Labour Party 1900–1918* (Cambridge: Cambridge University Press, 1990), p. 102.

account of the interests of the population in creating constituencies helped to separate rural from urban and middle- from working-class areas, both to the benefit of the Conservative party which could henceforth reap the advantages of 'villa Toryism' grouped in suburban islands of Conservatism. In contrast, the great reduction in the number of two-member constituencies exacerbated Liberal electoral and factional problems by preventing the party running a Whig and a Radical in harness.[37]

The passage of reform was a mixed blessing in other, more immediate, ways. Reform was the only major domestic achievement of a ministry beset by problems and no longer able, as the slender majority on the Gordon vote indicated, to mobilise its supporters. The passage of reform relieved the Irish of the need to keep the government in power and removed the last bond holding the disparate Liberal majority together. For the Radicals, the Reform Act, which Chamberlain described as 'the greatest revolution this country has undergone',[38] appeared to bring entry into the promised land of a post-Gladstonian party in which a powerful Radical section, reinforced by the constituency organisations and a popular mandate, would control the party. By 1885, both Dilke and Chamberlain, albeit in common with several of their cabinet colleagues, were looking for a way out of a government which was going nowhere. Chamberlain's speeches in January 1885, drawing on the social policies of the existing *Radical Programme*, were both a premature launch of the Radical election campaign and a pre-emptive bid for control. The attitude to the rights of property, which in the case of land Chamberlain described as only 'a trust . . . limited by the supreme necessities of the nation',[39] differentiated the Radical position, not only from the Whigs, but also from Gladstone who condemned what he called 'construction' in familiar words, 'taking into the hands of the state the business of the individual man'.[40]

Chamberlain's language and imagery were those of popular Radicalism, drawing on the Bible, which he specifically cited to defend himself against his critics,[41] and the myth of lost rights and stolen land. In 1883 he described Salisbury as 'the spokesman of a

37. James Cornford, 'The transformation of Conservatism in the late nineteenth century', *Victorian Studies* 7 (1) (1963), 52–8; Matthew, *Gladstone Diaries*, vol. X, p. cviii.

38. Garvin, *Life of Chamberlain*, vol. 1, p. 532.   39. Ibid. p. 556.

40. John Morley, *The Life of William Ewart Gladstone*, vol. 3 (London: Macmillan, 1903), p. 173.

41. Peter Fraser, *Joseph Chamberlain: Radicalism and Empire 1868–1914* (London: Cassell, 1966), p. 51.

class . . . who toil not neither do they spin, whose fortunes originated by grants made in times gone by for the services which courtiers render kings and have since grown and increased while they have slept'.[42] His history traced the evolution of property from a time when 'every man [had] a right to a part of the land of his birth' to a system of 'private ownership' in which some land at least had been 'wrongfully appropriated'. The system 'has been so sanctioned by law that it might be very difficult and perhaps impossible to reverse it. But then I ask what ransom will property pay for the security which it enjoys?'[43]

The programme, while considerably less inflammatory than the language, did envisage clear interference with the rights of property in the social interest. Reformed and democratised local government was to possess compulsory powers to purchase land 'at a fair value for public purposes', which included the provision of allotments and smallholdings, the '3 acres and a cow' policy of Chamberlain's lieutenant, Jesse Collings. By attempting to halt, and even reverse, the movement from the countryside to the towns, this proposal was one intended solution to urban overcrowding and high rents. More directly, Chamberlain also proposed compulsory powers for urban local government to force landlords to improve slum housing, and the taxation of the 'unearned increment' in land values to finance slum clearance without charging the ratepayer. Proposed by Mill in the 1860s,[44] the taxation of the 'unearned increment' had good Liberal credentials, as did the differentiation between earned and unearned income which resembled Gladstone's wish to replace income tax. The terrifying doctrine of 'ransom', subsequently rephrased into the hardly less frightening concept of 'insurance', both of which suggested the transfer of property by the menace of mass revolt, transformed itself into graduated taxation. This was more controversial, especially in its social and political implications. Gladstone in particular believed that graduated taxation would lead to 'that source of all evils, discord between class and class' as well as harming the workers by discouraging the accumulation of capital which was the source of economic growth,[45] although Chamberlain claimed in 1885 that Gladstone had changed his mind.[46]

42. Garvin, *Life of Chamberlain*, vol. 1, p. 392.   43. Ibid. pp. 549, 556.
44. Jay, *Chamberlain*, p. 76.
45. E.D. Steele, *Palmerston and Liberalism 1855–1865* (Cambridge: Cambridge University Press, 1991), p. 34.
46. Bernard Holland, *The Life of Spencer Compton, Eighth Duke of Devonshire*, vol. 2 (London: Longmans, 1911), p. 72.

Chamberlain's proposals were framed in those class terms which Gladstone deplored, the opportunity of the Radicals in politics being also the opportunity of the 'toilers and spinners' who 'for the first time . . . will have a majority of votes and the control, if they desire it, of the Government of the country'.[47] But his purpose was primarily pre-emptive, to act before the absence of reform threw the new democracy towards more extreme solutions, and thus to avoid the development of class politics. His programme required only a further extension of the steadily expanding responsibilities of the Victorian state, and was a natural development of the 'municipal socialism' he had practised in Birmingham in the 1870s. It permitted, but did not oblige, local authorities to use compulsory powers. Gladstone disliked Chamberlain's version of liberalism, but would accept compulsion although he preferred to 'try freedom first'.[48]

The real issue was the responsible use of property by individual owners, and a recognition that 'property has obligations as well as rights'.[49] Chamberlain himself maintained that his policy was really a defence of property, 'putting the rights of property on the only firm and defensible basis . . . the danger to property lies in its abuse'.[50] But this was the crucial point. Chamberlain did question the existing distribution of property and in that sense the right of property itself on the grounds of natural rights, history and efficiency. In so doing he challenged the foundations of the mid-Victorian Liberal edifice reared on individualism. The 'eternal laws of supply and demand . . . the necessity of freedom of contract . . . the sanctity of every right of property' including the right of abuse as well as use, were for Chamberlain 'the convenient cant of selfish wealth'. Instead, he proclaimed 'the death knell of the laissez-faire system . . . the intervention . . . of the State on behalf of the weak against the strong, in the interests of labour against capital, of want and misery against cant and ease'.[51]

This was Argyll's inclined plane. If freedom of contract and the rights of property were not sacrosanct, there was no necessary stopping point between Chamberlain's 'socialism' and more extreme versions. The outcry of 'selfish wealth' against Chamberlain between 1883 and 1885 arose in a context of 'property' already alarmed by the example of Ireland, the agitation in England and the extension of the franchise, from which the Radicals expected and moderates

47. Garvin, *Life of Chamberlain*, vol. 1, p. 548.
48. Holland, *Life of Devonshire*, vol. 2, p. 92.
49. Garvin, *Life of Chamberlain*, vo. 1, p. 549.   50. Fraser, *Chamberlain*, p. 51.
51. Jay, *Chamberlain*, p. 112.

feared so much. Victorian politicians were well aware that property was a legal construct and that political democracy was potentially the high road to social democracy. Salisbury, in his role as spokesman for the non-spinning classes, had warned as early as 1867 that democracy could lead to the use of taxation 'as an instrument of plunder',[52] and Wemyss (formerly Elcho) that 'the central question' of parliamentary reform was 'one of property'.[53] It was the Radicals' misfortune that such fears were not limited to the landed aristocracy.

Cross-currents: Ireland and social reform

Although Chamberlain resisted Gladstone's suggestion that he tone his speeches down, and hinted as usual at resignation, he did, in effect, suspend the campaign at the end of January. The death of Gordon required a brief closing of ranks in self-preservation, but unity perished in the debate on the renewal of Irish coercion. With the Irish vote in British constituencies at stake, both Gladstone and the Radicals hoped that the Home Rulers could still be attached to the Liberal party. Spencer's proposals for the renewal of limited coercion softened by land purchase or local government reform, were met by Chamberlain's more ambitious proposal for an Irish Central Board and coercion restricted to one year only. If agreed, local government reform along these lines would form the basis of Liberal legislation in the next parliament, thereby achieving the object of binding the Irish to the Liberals for the election. Chamberlain envisaged a Board with extensive powers, dealing not only with routine administrative matters like the Poor Law and public works, but education and the controversial land question. In Chamberlain's mind the Board was almost a subordinate legislature, 'altogether independent of English government influence', with powers of taxation in Ireland for strictly Irish purposes, that might deflect the demand for a separate Irish parliament.

As such, it was too much for Parnell, who envisaged a much more restricted role for the Central Board, precisely so that it would not distract from the agitation for full Home Rule. It was also too much for the Whigs. Chamberlain presented a much-reduced scheme to the cabinet, but despite Gladstone's strong support, the

52. Robert Taylor, *Lord Salisbury* (London: Allen Lane, 1975), p. 17.
53. E. Bristow, 'The Liberty and Property Defence League and individualism', *The Historical Journal* 18 (4) (1975), 763.

cabinet narrowly rejected it on 9 May. Nevertheless, the Radicals had, as Gladstone commented, 'a winning position'. They had finally engineered a situation in which they had the support of Gladstone against the Whigs.[54] Perhaps aware of the implications of this for his own position, Gladstone, who on other occasions had simply ignored cabinet decisions, or postponed them until he got his way, accepted the rejection of the Irish Central Board scheme with only private protests.

Publicly, Gladstone was still determined on retirement once the issues of reform and redistribution were concluded, as they were on 21 May. Moreover, he was engulfed in a tidal wave of resignations on disparate issues. The Radicals were hinting at resignation on both Ireland and the increase in indirect taxation in Childers's budget; Childers himself threatened resignation because of Radical objections; Hartington and Selborne, the lord chancellor, had already offered their resignations over the withdrawal from the Sudan, and Gladstone's proposal of a land purchase scheme to ease coercion in the absence of any local government reform led to the resignations of Dilke, Chamberlain and Shaw-Lefevre. On 8 June the government was defeated on a Conservative amendment to the budget, and finally escaped office amidst the, by now, usual relief.

Defeat was primarily the result of the Liberal malaise; over seventy Liberals did not vote in the crucial division.[55] But an Irish–Conservative combination created the majority, and when Salisbury's 'caretaker' ministry decided not to renew coercion, the way was open to more substantial cooperation that culminated in Parnell's advice to Irish electors in mainland constituencies in November to vote Conservative in the coming election. Irish rapprochement with the Conservatives, and Parnell's pursuit of a hung parliament to exploit the apparent competition between the two major parties, ended Chamberlain's hopes of a Radical–Irish alliance for the election and in the new parliament. Chamberlain learned of his misapprehension in July, abandoned his new policy to extend the Central Board scheme to National Councils for each component of the United Kingdom, and broke with Parnell with some bitterness.[56]

The issue of Ireland cut across the political debate on social policy on which Chamberlain launched a national campaign. With

54. Jay, *Chamberlain*, pp. 105–7.   55. Matthew, *Gladstone Diaries*, vol. X, p. cxxv.
56. Jenkins, *Gladstone, Whiggery and the Liberal Party*, pp. 252–3; Garvin, *Life of Chamberlain*, vol. 2, pp. 3–30; Jay, *Chamberlain*, pp. 108–10.

Gladstone ill and recuperating in Norway, this campaign set the agenda for the late summer. Chamberlain still assumed that Gladstone would retire, an outcome that appeared the more likely because of his illness, and dismissed out of hand the possibility of a hung parliament with the Irish holding the balance. In Gladstone's absence, the public speeches of his heirs apparent gave the appearance of Liberal factions more intent on fighting each other than the Conservatives, Hartington defending landowners and the rights of property, Chamberlain calling Hartington a 'Rip Van Winkle' out of touch with Liberal opinion, a jibe which rankled.[57] Yet this was only half of the story. Chamberlain was in broad agreement with Hartington in resisting Parnell's claim to independence,[58] and in the run-up to the election was anxious to avoid a party split. He would work with Hartington, whom he thought would 'yield, grumbling as usual, but still yielding',[59] but not with Goschen and the more right-wing Whigs.[60] By November, with Gladstone's return to politics and his interest in Ireland known, 'Rip Van Winkle' was singled out as one who 'is entitled to the fullest and most respectful consideration for anything he may have to say'.[61]

Likewise Hartington, when he learned early in August of Chamberlain's breach with Parnell, saw the advantage of not alienating Chamberlain completely despite their differences on social policy. After Chamberlain's public attack on Parnell at Warrington on 8 September, he advised Goschen to moderate his criticisms of Chamberlain and to concentrate upon Parnell and Home Rule.[62] Despite his attack on Chamberlain at Waterfoot on 29 August, Hartington was prepared to consider Chamberlain's proposals for compulsory land purchase on an experimental basis. His main objection was the gulf 'between the general declarations of what has to be done and the measures he proposes' which would give rise to vague and unrealised expectations.[63] Throughout the campaign he avoided complete rejection of radical proposals, for, as he explained to the queen, they were not 'revolutionary', although 'some of them are open to question on the ground of expediency'.[64]

Gladstone's return to active politics in September brought a new factor into the situation. Both Chamberlain and Hartington were

57. Garvin, *Life of Chamberlain*, vol. 2, p. 103.   58. Jay, *Chamberlain*, p. 114.

59. Jenkins, *Gladstone, Whiggery and the Liberal Party*, p. 210.

60. Jay, *Chamberlain*, p. 114; Barker, *Gladstone and Radicalism*, pp. 18–19; Garvin, *Life of Chamberlain*, vol. 2, p. 102.

61. Jenkins, *Gladstone, Whiggery and the Liberal Party*, p. 217.   62. Ibid. p. 253.

63. Holland, *Life of Devonshire*, vol. 2, p. 72.

64. Jenkins, *Gladstone, Whiggery and the Liberal Party*, pp. 215–16.

obliged to welcome this, reinforced as it was by Gladstone's threat
not just to retire if unwanted, but to speak out on 'the difficulties
arising from divergencies'.[65] Gladstone's intervention restored the
factional conflict to its position before the government's resignation
in June. Whatever might have been the possibilities of an accommodation between Chamberlain and Hartington in his absence, his
presence transferred that necessity to one of seeking Gladstone's
approval. Gladstone, however, had returned because of the unfin-
ished business of Ireland, not 'to fight merely the battle of the
Whigs and Radicals', and maintained his right to retire if no Irish
crisis arose.[66] His precise intentions were, and could only be, unclear, since they depended on the outcome of the election which
alone would reveal what the Irish demanded and the political power
they had to insist upon those demands. But whilst most of the party
concluded that any demands beyond extensive local government
were impossible, the collapse of the Central Board scheme and
Conservative intrigues with the Irish convinced Gladstone that they
would have to be met. Early in August, having confirmed that Central
Boards were dead, he told Hartington that 'a separate legislature in
some form or other will have to be considered. Resistance to any
further demands for separation, and equal treatment with England
and Scotland,' was no longer 'a practical policy'.[67]

Gladstone's immediate task was to maintain party unity into that
election without tying himself to any particular policy. His election
manifesto contained no concessions to Chamberlain, virtually ignoring the issues raised by his campaign. Hartington took heart from
it as leaning 'to the side of moderation'[68]; Chamberlain acknowledged that it was 'a slap in the face to us', but recognised the need
to work within it, and convinced himself that it put forward only a
minimum programme which did not preclude adoption of his key
proposals. As he explained to Dilke, 'extra powers to Local Authorities are hinted at, revision of taxation in favour of the working
classes is distinctly implied, and Free Schools are not finally dis-
approved'. Gladstone, he believed, was 'squeezable'.[69]

To stay in touch with Gladstone, Chamberlain steadily back-
pedalled on his unauthorised campaign from refusal in September

65, Holland, *Life of Devonshire*, vol. 2, p. 87; Jenkins, *Gladstone, Whiggery and the Liberal Party*, pp. 254–5.

66. Jenkins, *Gladstone, Whiggery and the Liberal Party*, pp. 241–2.

67. Ibid. p. 243; Holland, *Life of Compton*, vol. 2, pp. 77–8.

68. Holland, *Life of Devonshire*, vol. 2, p. 73.

69. Garvin, *Life of Chamberlain*, vol. 2, p. 96; Barker, *Gladstone and Radicalism*, pp. 20–4.

to join any government 'on the narrow basis of the programme now presented'[70] to virtual acceptance of Gladstone's manifesto by November. His retreat was influenced by the difficulties which the campaign increasingly encountered, not only because it was clearly alienating moderate Liberals in large numbers, but because, in trying to meet objections, Chamberlain also alienated Nonconformist opinion.[71] Under these circumstances, with Gladstone dangling an as yet unspecified radical initiative on Ireland which Chamberlain assumed would be local government reform, an understanding with Gladstone which might recreate the alignment of May and isolate the Whigs had distinct advantages.

For Hartington, the problem was the reverse of Chamberlain's. While urging Gladstone to speak out strongly against Chamberlain's social proposals and defy Parnell, he desperately tried to pin Gladstone down on Ireland. Gladstone's manifesto contained nothing 'alarming' on Ireland, in itself, but after their meeting in August, Hartington could 'read between the lines'.[72] Neither Hartington nor Chamberlain were deceived by Gladstone's tactics. Labouchere's leak to Chamberlain of Gladstone's indirect discussions with the Irish and 'that he is disposed to grant the fullest Home Rule etc.' merely confirmed Chamberlain's suspicions 'as to the intentions of our great chief'.[73] Chamberlain nevertheless dismissed Gladstone's 'instinct . . . that Ireland may shoulder aside everything else',[74] and its implication that in Ireland Gladstone had found 'a policy . . . which would unite us all and which would necessarily throw into the background those minor points of difference about the schools and smallholdings'.[75] In this Chamberlain was wrong. In Ireland Gladstone had found a policy which reasserted his leadership of the party, and pushed aside not only other 'minor points of difference', but Chamberlain's pretensions to define the policy of the future and in effect make himself the next leader of the party.

Gladstone secured the outward semblance of pre-election unity because his own indefinite position made his argument that nothing would be clear until after the election incontrovertible. Beyond that, his plans relied on an independent Liberal majority which would allow the Liberals to take office without a policy on Ireland and give Gladstone time to educate his party and the country. It

70. Garvin, *Life of Chamberlain*, vol. 2, pp. 97, 101, 108; Morley, *Life of Gladstone*, vol. 3, pp. 224–5; Jay, *Chamberlain*, pp. 116–17.

71. Barker, *Gladstone and Radicalism*, pp. 26–35.   72. Ibid. pp. 73, 77–8.

73. Garvin, *Life of Chamberlain*, vol. 2, p. 118.   74. Ibid. p. 113.

75. Jay, *Chamberlain*, pp. 118–19.

was a legitimate expectation, since everyone from the chief whip to the Whigs, as well as Chamberlain, predicted such an outcome.[76] The election would show whether there was or was not 'the fixed desire of a nation, clearly and constitutionally expressed' for self-government. On the 'leverage' that this provided, Gladstone hoped to overcome the opposition of Chamberlain and Hartington in his own party, and then that of the House of Lords. It was another fine expression of Liberal expectations of reasonableness, but it was a slender lever with which to bring about what Gladstone recognised would be 'a mighty heave in the body politic'.[77]

The election result clearly demonstrated the Irish desire for self-government. The Parnellites won eighty-five seats in Ireland and one in England, the Liberals were eliminated in Ireland, and the Conservatives won eighteen seats in Ulster. It was a disaster for Chamberlain, who was widely held responsible for heavy Liberal losses in the boroughs,[78] and to that extent reinforced the moderates. But in leaving the Parnellites holding the balance in a hung parliament, the result was a disaster for the Liberal party as a whole. After the election, the Irish were in a position to ensure that Gladstone's inclination became Gladstone's policy, but left him no time to educate his party or assert his authority, and tarnished all his future actions with the stain of the unscrupulous pursuit of power.

Home Rule and division

Briefly, Gladstone still aspired to conceal Liberal divisions, encouraging the Conservative government to deal with the Irish problem on terms which would facilitate his independent support. But Salisbury made no proposals on Home Rule and had none to make. The revelation of Gladstone's conversion to Home Rule on 17 December, the 'Hawarden kite', removed what little room for manoeuvre Gladstone had left, and the Liberal party began to polarise around the issue of Home Rule, which Hartington condemned outright on 21 December. Although he wanted an absolute majority, the result also strengthened Gladstone's hand in other respects. The Irish, although condemned to permanent third-party status in what had become a three-party system, were sufficiently numerous, unified,

---

76. Jenkins, *Gladstone, Whiggery and the Liberal Party*, pp. 244, 258.
77. Morley, *Life of Gladstone*, vol. 3, p. 240.   78. Jay, *Chamberlain*, p. 119.

electorally secure and obstructive to threaten permanent political instability in Britain and permanent violent disorder in Ireland. By removing the Irish from Westminster and leaving the Irish responsible for their own domestic government, Home Rule resolved both problems in a liberal way. The alternative was draconian regulation of parliamentary debate and permanent military rule in Ireland which Chamberlain had already likened to the Russian occupation of Poland. It is an interesting reflection on their liberalism that in the final analysis Chamberlain and Hartington were prepared for this; Gladstone was not.

Once it became clear that the Irish would shift their support from the Conservatives to the Liberals, Gladstone acted to remove Salisbury's government, using Collings's '3 acres and a cow' amendment to do so on 26 January without revealing his hand on Ireland. He formed his government on a policy not of Home Rule but of the examination of Home Rule, which admitted the possibility that after examination, Home Rule might not be adopted. Hartington agreed to give Gladstone 'a fair trial', and Chamberlain joined the cabinet on this basis. In neither case, however, did this indicate a willingness to accept Home Rule if the enquiry found in its favour.

Hartington's position was simple. He had little sympathy with Irish 'rebels', wanted law and order maintained in Ireland and the rights of landowners protected. He had consistently opposed Home Rule since Butt raised the issue, and equally consistently supported coercion, with or without remedial legislation; he had objected to the extension of franchise reform to Ireland and opposed Chamberlain's Central Boards scheme. Subsequently he voted to keep the Conservatives in office in January 1886, refused to join Gladstone's government and voted against the Home Rule bill in April 1886. His one positive suggestion in January 1886 was to expel the Irish MPs from parliament 'for our sake not theirs', and govern Ireland as a 'subject province'. 'He could not tell and did not much care' what the Irish thought of the idea,[79] but he would not concede Home Rule, and there was no reason for Gladstone to believe that he would.

Tactically he had to tread carefully. As long as the possibility existed that Gladstone might abandon Home Rule and do a deal with Chamberlain, he had to avoid precipitate action which might undermine his position in the Liberal party. The emergence of three-party politics destroyed the Whig position by confronting them

---

79. Jenkins, *Gladstone, Whiggery and the Liberal Party*, pp. 269–70.

with two independent radical demands which could not be simultaneously resisted. As so often, but particularly since the mid-1870s, the Whigs found themselves in the strange position of hoping for the defeat of the party to which they belonged in order to give independent support to a weak Conservative government, thus controlling both Liberal Radicalism and Conservative reaction. In 1886, however, a large Liberal majority would have strengthened Chamberlainite Radicalism, whilst a hung parliament strengthened the Irish. Their room for manoeuvre had ended.

In party-political terms, leaving aside the merits of the policy, Gladstone's decision to proceed with Home Rule in 1886 amounted to a choice between the Irish and the majority of the Whigs for whom Hartington spoke. His choice of the Irish may not have been wise. As others realised, the value of the Irish alliance was temporary, since the passage of Home Rule would probably mean the removal of the Irish from the House of Commons. But it was consistent with Gladstone's progressive disillusionment with the Whig aristocracy since 1866. He had contemplated a purge then, and in 1886 still thought that a purge on Home Rule, which was certain to include the Whigs, would be beneficial to the party. As he wrote to Hartington, one of the main causes for the advance of 'modern Radicalism' was 'the gradual disintegration of the Liberal aristocracy'.[80] He had a case. Even Hartington asked in October 1885, 'Where are the Whigs? . . . if I thought that there was any possibility of a united Liberal party again being formed I should be disgusted at the want of support I have received.'[81]

Chamberlain's position was more complex. On the principle of Irish reform, he was prepared to give 'the widest possible self-government' for Ireland 'consistent with maintaining the unity of the Empire',[82] which included powers of what he called 'taxation'. His theme was that the solution to the Irish problem was either National Councils, including a separate body for Ulster, or complete separation. Anything else was a half-way house which would leave the Irish dissatisfied and lead ultimately to separation. Chamberlain's claim to prefer complete separation to a nominal union[83] has to be seen in this context. In January 1886 he worked out the implications of 'complete separation' suggesting that Ireland might become a 'protected state' in which Britain's only responsibility would be to protect Ireland against foreign aggression as much for

80. Holland, *Life of Devonshire*, vol. 2, p. 91.   81. Ibid. pp. 73–4.
82. Jay, *Chamberlain*, p. 108.   83. Ibid. p. 123.

the sake of Britain as Ireland.[84] Like Hartington's 'subject province' proposal, it was a deliberate absurdity, a warning of the ultimate destination of Home Rule, to pressurise the party back towards the National Councils which represented Chamberlain's bottom line on Irish constitutional reform.[85]

Policy, however, was always occluded by tactics. Chamberlain and Gladstone were manoeuvring for support in a party which desperately wanted the restoration of unity, each trying to make the other appear responsible for disruption rather than to find genuine points of compromise. Chamberlain produced schemes for constitutional reform off the top of his head, like the application of the American constitution he outlined to Labouchere in December 1885,[86] the federal Home Rule scheme he proposed in the Commons in April 1886,[87] or the use of the Canadian constitution as a model in June.[88] Having abandoned his own proposals in the summer of 1885, he did not want to think again about Ireland, and resented its intrusion into what had been a party debate on social policy on which he hoped to lead in the near future.

For the sake of that future he had to appear conciliatory and positive, and to distinguish his position from the Whigs whose co-operation with the Conservatives was deeply unpopular in Radical circles. His tactics were founded on the belief that Gladstone would carry neither the Liberal party nor the country with him on Home Rule, that the 'party must go to smash and the Tories come in', and that 'after a few years those of us who remain will be able to pick up the pieces'.[89] Ireland was an unwelcome interlude, but it was only an interlude. This was a reasonable calculation given that Gladstone had returned to politics solely to deal with the Irish crisis, and at seventy-seven might be expected to retire when he failed. It was a calculation that the Whigs also made, looking forward to the reconstruction of the party in opposition under Hartington's leadership once Gladstone had failed.[90] It was a miscalculation.

The cabinet enquiry into Home Rule proceeded without consultation. Chamberlain focused his objections to Gladstonian Home Rule on the removal of Irish MPs from the House of Commons. Their retention, on which he insisted, was only a prelude to a series

84. Garvin, *Life of Chamberlain*, vol. 2, p. 161; Jenkins, *Gladstone, Whiggery and the Liberal Party*, p. 274n.
85. Jay, *Chamberlain*, p. 124.   86. Garvin, *Life of Chamberlain*, vol. 2, p. 145.
87. Jay, *Chamberlain*, p. 124.   88. Garvin, *Life of Chamberlain*, vol. 2, p. 248.
89. Ibid. p. 240.
90. Jenkins, *Gladstone, Whiggery and the Liberal Party*, pp. 280–1.

of consequential changes that he thought retention would entail, the ultimate object of which was 'the complete subordination of the Irish Assemblies to the Imperial parliament'.[91] Because Gladstone was also obliged to appear conciliatory, there were a number of occasions between Chamberlain's resignation in March and the final defeat of the Home Rule bill in June when compromise appeared possible. Chamberlain, however, would not move from his basic position that a separate Irish legislature was impossible so that 'surrender' had to come from Gladstone. Even apart from Gladstone's desire to meet what he considered Ireland's legitimate demand for self-government, meeting Chamberlain's terms meant losing the support of the Irish, acknowledging Chamberlain's supremacy, and retiring in favour of Chamberlain and his vision of Liberalism. Forced to choose between Chamberlain and Parnell, a Gladstonian or a Chamberlainite Liberal party, and the leadership or retirement, Gladstone rebuffed Chamberlain.

The intrigues from September 1885 to June 1886 thus came to nothing. Despite the subtle manoeuvrings for advantage and the more or less genuine attempts at compromise, each of the three major protagonists occupied substantially the same position on Irish government at the end that they had held at the beginning. The final outcome, in which the Radical, Chamberlain, and the Whig, Hartington, combined against Gladstone to reject his Irish policy only appears strange and unpredictable if a fixity of purpose is attributed to Gladstone, but denied to them, their frequently restated objections to Home Rule ignored, and the replacement of social politics by Home Rule as the central issue disregarded. Otherwise, although Chamberlain above all did not wish it, it was a position that had been as carefully prepared as any other, and as likely a denouement. Even that section of the party that remained with Gladstone had little enthusiasm for Home Rule on its merits, and did so out of party loyalty, and fear of or respect for Gladstone himself.[92] If this indicated the extent to which the Nonconformists had become party Liberals by the mid-1880s, it also tied these most Protestant of Protestants to an unholy alliance with Irish Catholics. General antipathy apart, their views on denominational education were diametrically opposed. Nor was the cabinet enthusiastic. 'It is not as if any of us thought it a good thing in itself, or beneficial either to Ireland or England', the future leader of the party, Sir

---

91. Garvin, *Life of Chamberlain*, vol. 2, p. 222.
92. Jenkins, *Gladstone, Whiggery and the Liberal Party*, p. 288.

Henry Campbell-Bannerman, wrote. 'We regard Home Rule only as a dangerous and damaging *pis aller.*'[93]

Liberalism and the Liberal party in 1886

In June 1886, ninety-three Liberals, including both Chamberlain and Hartington, voted against Home Rule to defeat Gladstone's government; in the general election in July, the Gladstonian Liberals were decisively defeated by the combined Conservative and Liberal 'Unionists' working together in an electoral alliance. The Home Rule schism and the election destroyed the mid-Victorian Liberal hegemony. Until then, whilst the Liberal party in parliament had broken up with alarming frequency, the electorate had steadfastly re-elected Liberals for another try at government. After 1886, the Liberals were relegated to twenty years of opposition, broken only by the weak minority government of 1892–5, and formed a majority government only once more before their decline into third-party status in the 1920s. The election saw the Conservatives recover their county losses of 1885 and continue their progress in the suburbs. 'Unionism' proved a potent cry in Devon and Cornwall where the strength of Nonconformity masked the anti-Catholic and imperialist disposition of the predominant Methodists, and where the ethnic vote was influential, especially western Scotland and Lancashire. Liberalism was forced back on a shrunken traditional Liberal heartland of northern England and the Celtic fringe.

The Liberal coalition created in Lichfield House and Willis's Rooms was crumbling into its component sections. The Irish, always loosely attached, had gone with Butt's Home Government Association; 1886 saw the departure of the Whigs. The proportion of the party from the 'aristocratic-landowning' section declined from over 40 per cent that it had maintained from Palmerston's days until the early 1880s, to 31.4 per cent in 1885 to only 8.1 per cent in 1892, which left county Liberalism leaderless.[94] With the loss of the Whigs, the Liberals lost the reassurance they gave to the moderates, and the bulk of the moderates themselves. Moderate alienation was not just the product of Irish policy. The extension of the franchise and Chamberlain's response to it played their part, as the election of 1885 revealed. But Home Rule, with its apparent disregard for

93. Ibid. p. 289.
94. Ibid. pp. 225–6, 291; Michael Bentley, *The Climax of Liberal Politics* (London: Arnold, 1987), p. 28.

the security of Irish landowners, Irish Protestants and the empire at large, was a further indication that the Liberal party was no longer 'safe'.

The loss of the Whigs turned the slow transition of the Liberals into a middle-class, Nonconformist party into an abrupt transformation, although the remaining Whigs still disproportionately filled the party's upper echelons. Electorally, the alienation of the moderates left the party increasingly dependent upon the working classes, which raised the question of the role the working classes were to play in the Liberal party in the future. Two trade unionists had become MPs in 1874, but there were still only eleven 'Lib-Labs' in 1885.[95] Nevertheless, far from being the prelude to the rise of Labour and the decline of the Liberal party, the extension of the franchise was also a lifeline for the Liberals. How long it could keep the party afloat depended on the handling of the integration of the working-class electorate, and the interaction between this and the recovery of the moderate vote. A middle-class party resting on working-class votes was no more, or less, absurd than an aristocratic party resting on middle-class votes, a practice that served the Liberal party well in the middle fifty years of the nineteenth century. Its successful operation required continuing evolution and, if the precedent was followed, would ultimately entail the shedding of a section of the middle classes.

With sectional electoral support, both socially and geographically, Liberal credibility as a national party transcending class and regional interests was also thrown into question. After 1886, their policy appeared avowedly sectional, and of little direct interest to the majority of mainland Britain except for the damage it might do to the 'integrity of the empire'. Gladstone's determination after the election to continue 'to meet the wants and wishes of Ireland' limited the degree to which other causes could benefit from the radicalisation of the party that resulted, by default, from the defection of the Whigs. In particular it limited its ability to meet the wants and wishes of its working-class supporters.

The loss of Chamberlain, the outstanding Radical of the 1880s and self-appointed spokesman of the poor, was significant in removing the one figure who might confront Gladstone directly. But Chamberlain could not compete with Gladstone in the 1880s in either prestige or policy. Gladstone had acquired the popular stature of a

95. Henry Pelling, *A History of British Trade Unionism* (Harmondsworth: Penguin Books, 1963), pp. 75, 105–6.

heroic, almost biblical, figure, whose libertarian and liberationist principles founded in morality and embodied in free trade and the minimal, neutral state expressed the outlook of popular Radicalism far more than Chamberlain's interventionist materialism. Chamberlain, as Gladstone observed, had no 'incandescence'.

Chamberlain's positive attitude to the use of power was in some respects the antithesis of Liberalism as popularly understood and embodied in the mid-Victorian Liberal party. His desire for 'strong government' led him to criticise as inefficient 'a system of government originally contrived to check the action of kings and Ministers which meddles, therefore, far too much with the Executive of the country'.[96] But it was precisely these forms and traditions of parliament which Gladstone venerated and which, as guarantors of 'the hardly-won liberties of the people', gave legitimacy to its laws in the eyes of popular Radicalism.[97] Chamberlain's critique of parliament and elevation of the material over the moral anticipated Rosebery's Liberal Imperialist campaign for 'national efficiency' at the turn of the century, Lloyd George's outlook both before and after the war, and even Oswald Mosley's Fascist condemnation of parliamentary procedures in both argument and phrasing.

The same qualifications applied to Chamberlain's conception of the action of local government. As Radical mayor of Birmingham between 1873 and 1876 he achieved great things. But the provision of new sewers, an extended and safer gas supply, street lighting, clean water, a rebuilt town centre, libraries and public parks were achieved by ruthless methods which took little account of free debate or individual consciences. Decisions were railroaded through, and the system managed by what Chamberlain himself called his 'despotic authority'. It was possible because Chamberlain reorganised the local Liberal Association, purged the old leadership and gained popular backing for his programme, but it came close to that tyranny of the majority manipulated by an oligarchy that made mid-Victorian liberals so wary of democracy.

Chamberlain's methods made the epithet 'Jacobin' applied by his critics peculiarly appropriate, but once he departed from the traditional assumption that there was little that could be done for the poor, the positive use of power followed. In an urbanised, industrialised society, a state that intervened, provided and regulated was perhaps the only way to create the economic security and

96. Garvin, *Life of Chamberlain*, vol. 2, p. 191.
97. Ross McKibbin, 'Why was there no Marxism in Great Britain?', *English Historical Review* 99 (391) (1984), 313–14.

independence that Liberals believed was essential to real liberty. But like 'New Liberalism' which in some of its aspects followed a similar path, the strong state raised in even more acute form the question of the control of power, and thus the extent to which the political system was to provide for the involvement of the working classes. In this context, Chamberlain's proposal for the payment of MPs was one means of securing a semblance of participatory self-government under new conditions.

Chamberlain's programme was never this systematic and in no way provided a new theory of Liberalism in a mass industrialised society. It indicated a possible line of development for the Liberal party, but one which required a fundamental shift in the laissez-faire values that underpinned mid-Victorian Liberalism. This was far from happening in the 1880s. The borough losses in 1885 revealed the limited appeal of the programme, and the election of 1886 the limits of Chamberlain's own prestige; he returned to parliament with only a dozen or so adherents. Chamberlain's defection, far from damaging the Liberal party by diverting it from the high road of social radicalism into an Irish bog, may well have saved it from abandoning its liberalism.

CHAPTER FIVE

Conservatism, Labour and the First Downfall of the Liberal Party

Far from demoralising the party, schism and defeat in 1886 produced a rather desperate euphoria as the party claimed to have rediscovered the unity and sense of purpose lost in the discord of 1880–5.[1] The feeling rested on acceptance of the Gladstonian view that the party was 'an instrument for the attainment of great ends' and a union of 'common convictions'.[2] This ideological conception of 'party' allowed the split of 1886 to be regarded as the product of a fundamental difference of principle, so that the party became, in the words of Robert Spence Watson, soon to become president of the NLF, 'better and stronger for its recent purge'.[3] Moreover, this instrumental view of the party's role sustained the Liberal claim to be a national party even when it did not enjoy the support of the nation. Unlike the sectional objectives of the Conservatives, Labour and most obviously, the Irish, it embodied what the nation desired, or ought to desire. The pursuit of 'great ends' conferred sanctity on the party despite its minority status, or even, as martyrs who had forsaken power for the public good, because of that minority status. On this basis the Liberals could, with an aura of superiority that infuriated their opponents, continue to believe that they were a national party long after they had become an embattled minority.

In reality, the Liberal party was itself becoming sectional. The most obvious evidence of this was the growing importance of the politics of the Celtic fringe, which followed from increased electoral dependence. The prominence of Irish issues in the parliament of 1880–5 and the adoption of Home Rule were followed by Gladstone's decision in 1889 that he should at last support Scottish

1. D.A. Hamer, *Liberal Politics in the Age of Gladstone and Rosebery* (Oxford: Oxford University Press, 1972), pp. 124–6.
2. Ibid. pp. 122–3. 3. Ibid. pp. 125–6.

disestablishment, and the emergence, almost by default, of Welsh disestablishment as the next reform to follow Home Rule. The causes of Celtic nationalism were the most natural development of Midlothian Radicalism, and had the advantage of simplicity. They were supported within the party by relatively coherent regional blocs, and being regionally specific they carried no implications for reform in Great Britain as a whole, where the party was undecided.

Intellectual renewal, political frustration

In the late 1880s there were signs that despite the loss of Chamberlain, the party had retained an element of social Radicalism in its outlook. Morley, who had broken with Chamberlain because of the 'socialism' of his unauthorised proposals, spoke during 1888 and 1889 on slum housing, high rents, old-age poverty, low wages, national insurance against sickness, malnourished schoolchildren, and raised the question of the public provision of school meals. It was, however, a brief foray into social politics, and expressed the outlook less of Morley than that of a band of younger Liberals grouped around the respected backbencher, Arthur Acland, which included the rising figures of Asquith, Haldane and Sir Edward Grey, who briefly hoped that Morley might provide a lead on social Radicalism.[4] Another member of the group, L.A. Atherley-Jones, gave the title 'New Liberalism' to this advocacy of interventionist social reform to distinguish it from the 'old Liberalism' of Nonconformist Radicalism.

New Liberalism was a response to the same pressures that provoked Chamberlain's 'unauthorised programme', the manifest failure of 'laissez-faire' and in particular the continued existence of poverty, malnutrition, poor housing and lack of education revealed by successive studies from the 1880s onwards. The response sprang from the ethical tradition of Liberalism, but an ethical tradition that had, for the new generation of Liberals influenced by Darwinian ideas, been severed from its religious roots[5] and refounded in rationality. The fusion of rationality and ethical behaviour created reciprocal obligations: on the individual to pursue the 'social' or 'common' good which constituted rational behaviour for a social

---

4. Peter Clarke, *Liberals and Social Democrats* (Cambridge: Cambridge University Press, 1978), p. 24; Michael Barker, *Gladstone and Radicalism* (Brighton: Harvester, 1975), pp. 175–86.

5. Clarke, *Liberals and Social Democrats*, pp. 12–14, 18–22.

being; on society to enable the rational individual to pursue his ethical ends through the instrumentality of the state. New Liberalism went beyond Chamberlain in its concept of community, abandoning the traditional view that individual liberty was achieved against society and the state in favour of the achievement of liberty through society and the state. In so doing it avoided the need to aggregate individual interests to discover a majority, and resolved the problem of the tyranny of the majority that resulted from Chamberlain's utilitarian appeal to the greatest happiness of the greatest number. The tension between the individual and society of mid-nineteenth-century Liberalism, and explicit in the idea of the minimal state, was internalised within the individual himself.

New Liberals found a scientific basis for their arguments in biology which had, by the late nineteenth century, replaced mathematics and physics as the fashionable intellectual infrastructure. The concept of society as an organism in which individuals resembled cells reinforced the argument that individual liberty was secured only within and through society, and individual interests were inseparable from, but subservient rather than identical to, the good of the whole. The requirements of the social good provided a means to test the merits of state intervention which transcended the doctrine of expediency, and meant that rather than each case being judged on its merits, reforms could be initiated according to an overarching formula.[6] The same concept also overcame objections to the taxation of one class to benefit another. By extending the application of the idea of the 'unearned increment' from the land to all property which could only exist in a social environment, New Liberalism evolved the concept of 'social property'.[7] It justified both differentiated and graduated taxation since society was only reclaiming its own for its own use. 'All expenditure', wrote Herbert Samuel in *Liberalism*, published in 1902, 'which succeeds in improving the part benefits, not that part alone, but the whole community, and this is why all sections may justly be called upon to share the cost of measures which in their direct and immediate application touch only the well-being of the poorer.'[8] Hobson's theory of underconsumption provided the intellectual foundations for the

6. Michael Freeden, *The New Liberalism: An Ideology of Social Reform* (Oxford: Oxford University Press, 1978), p. 159.

7. See the report of Hobson's paper on individual and state property in Michael Freeden (ed.), *Minutes of the Rainbow Circle 1894–1924*, Camden 4th Series Royal Historical Society, 1989, p. 37.

8. Freeden, *New Liberalism*, p. 126.

redistribution of income that welfare accomplished, preventing the accumulation of savings looking for an outlet not available at home, creating an enlarged domestic market, and eliminating the need for imperial expansion.[9] 'Ransom' was legitimised.

On this basis, New Liberalism produced policies that transformed Liberal Radicalism. The right to work and a minimum 'living wage' were merely the beginning of society's responsibilities in the name of justice.[10] By 1912, the Liberal MP, Russell Rea, was considering free heating, lighting and feeding of children as well as minimum housing.[11] The social control of municipal services, the nationalisation of railways and mines, and, Hobson argued, all energy resources, followed from a vision of society in which all aspects were integrated. Railways, for example, affected, amongst other things, land policy, urban and housing policy, labour mobility and unemployment[12]; the field for radical action was almost limitless. New Liberalism, while it retained contact with sympathetic MPs, developed through the 1890s outside the official party, in debating societies, lecture tours, and above all the press, in books, the fortnightly and monthly journals, specialised newspapers like the *Progressive Review*, the *Speaker* and its successor, the *Nation*, and the more radical Liberal dailies. As an ongoing debate, its advocates did not agree on all details, nor was there an agreed programme, but it publicised new radical priorities and provided a new language of reform which gradually changed the perceptions of political argument. How far the politicians understood the conceptual framework of the language they borrowed, or where New Liberalism might lead, was another matter.

In the early 1890s the Liberal party was not even listening. 'Official Liberalism', as Atherley Jones noted, 'is completely out of touch with the aspirations and aims of modern Liberal thought.'[13] This was certainly true of Morley, who retreated when he came up against the vested interests of the friendly societies, the rival priorities of Ireland, and the indifference or hostility of his colleagues.[14] By the late 1880s, official Liberalism had an old-fashioned air, still focused on Nonconformist issues, temperance, disestablishment and the sectarian aspects of education, rather than grappling with the problem of liberty in an industrial society. Home Rule provided Gladstone with a means to bring a much-needed order to Liberal politics, but at the expense of innovation. With the argument that 'Home Rule

---

9. Ibid. pp. 130–1.   10. Ibid. pp. 88, 131, 163, 210, 215, 217, 235.
11. Ibid. p. 150.   12. Ibid. pp. 150, 221.   13. Ibid. p. 146.
14. Barker, *Gladstone and Radicalism*, pp. 175–86.

blocks the way', the consideration of potentially divisive reforms could be postponed indefinitely. Nothing could be done in other directions, Gladstone argued, until the 'Irish obstruction' was removed.[15] In following Gladstone in 1886, the Liberal party became his prisoners.

This did not, however, prevent the re-emergence of grassroots sectionalism in the National Liberal Federation which was only briefly restrained by the Home Rule commitment. In 1887 and 1888, whilst endorsing traditional Liberal causes, it acknowledged the official line; but in 1889, with the list of reforms steadily growing, the annual conference dropped the reference to the overriding importance of Ireland and its prohibitive role.[16] The already weakening hold of Home Rule was broken in 1890 by Nonconformist outrage at the revelation of Parnell's adultery with O'Shea's wife, Kitty. The campaign against Parnell reflected Nonconformist resentment at the hijacking of the party for Home Rule and a move to recapture it for Nonconformity. Their threatened revolt forced Gladstone to insist on the removal of Parnell from the Irish leadership as a condition for the continuation of the alliance.[17]

In the immediate aftermath of the Parnell scandal, the pressures for some extension of the Liberal programme beyond Home Rule were too great to be contained, and the leadership scoured the attic for neglected causes, but not new ones. Even Gladstone considered the possibilities, alighting on 'one man one vote' and registration reform which the former home secretary and chancellor of the exchequer, Sir William Harcourt, found 'not inspiriting' and Morley 'not by itself adequate'. Harcourt saw more mileage in temperance on which Gladstone was unreliable, whilst Morley seized on rural reform and the emancipation of the village labourer.[18] But a leadership raid on accumulated nostrums, especially one of such diversity, was unlikely to provide a domestic programme to enthuse the party as a united body. Gladstone did not care, and whilst he remained, the others did not count.

With similar insouciance, Gladstone accepted the conference resolutions en bloc at the NLF conference in Newcastle in 1891, establishing no priorities beyond Home Rule, and adding nothing constructive of his own. The so-called 'Newcastle programme'

---

15. Hamer, *Liberal Politics*, pp. 126–33.   16. Ibid: pp. 137–8.

17. John Kent, 'Hugh Price Hughes and the Nonconformist conscience', in G.V. Bennett and J.D. Walsh (eds), *Essays in Modern English Church History* (London: Black, 1966), pp. 189–94.

18. Barker, *Gladstone and Radicalism*, pp. 205–17, 258–60.

tied the party after its victory in the 1892 general election to an impossible range of reforms. Harcourt, who resumed his place at the exchequer in the Liberal government of 1892–5, casually listed for Gladstone's benefit, the items for the first session of the new parliament – '(1) Temperance and Local Option; (2) Village Councils with control of schools; (3) Registration Reforms and One man one Vote; (4) Payment of Members; (5) Welsh Disestablishment' – as the only way 'of holding together our majority . . . the very *minimum* of what we should bring forward and . . . only a fraction of what you pledged us to at Newcastle'.[19] Collectively, the new government had no clearer idea of priorities than the party at large.

Plans to 'address ourselves to those subjects of Liberal legislation which would be both *concise* and telling, in the various divisions of Great Britain',[20] foundered as dependence on Irish support ensured that Home Rule occupied a fruitless first session. Without a clear majority the government was powerless against the Conservative-dominated House of Lords which proceeded to wreck Liberal legislation without fear of retribution. Home Rule was overwhelmingly rejected, to be followed by the abandonment of the employers' liability bill and the forced acceptance of amendments to the parish councils bill which severely restricted the new councils' powers. Emasculated or not, it was the only major piece of legislation that the Liberals managed to carry in three miserable years.

Liberal Imperialism

The government was distracted from the outset by the revival of dissension on imperialism. Egypt remained the poisoned chalice. As foreign secretary, Rosebery ignored Gladstonian principles in favour of continuity of policy from the outgoing Conservatives. Dispute broke out between Rosebery on the one hand and Gladstone, Harcourt and Morley, who had also resumed his former office of secretary for Ireland, on the other as early as September 1892 over the annexation of Uganda and control of the Nile. For the Gladstone faction, since the ultimate aim of policy remained the evacuation of Egypt, further expansion in north or east Africa was illogical and unacceptable. For Rosebery, who regarded Egypt as a long-term

---

19. Peter Stansky, *Ambitions and Strategies* (Oxford: Oxford University Press, 1964), p. 2.
20. Barker, *Gladstone and Radicalism*, pp. 260–1.

commitment much as Hartington had done, expansion was a necessity. The dispute was fuelled in January 1893 by the request from Lord Cromer, the consul-general in Egypt, for more troops which Rosebery supported and Gladstone opposed. Compromise on this, and prevarication, in the form of Sir Gerald Portal's investigative mission to Uganda, resolved nothing. Rosebery, despite his isolation in the cabinet, had his way, and Uganda became a British protectorate in 1894.

Heightened international tension which resulted from imperial confrontation and the growing rapprochement of Russia and France, also lay behind the naval estimates crisis of December 1893–March 1894 that led to Gladstone's final resignation. The issue was depressingly familiar, Gladstone's habitual objection to increased expenditure, especially arms expenditure, placing him in conflict with defence ministers. The novel element lay in the willingness of his colleagues to endure Gladstone's threat to 'reserve active liberty of action',[21] and with a combination of apprehension and relief, watch him resign. Even then, Gladstone could not accept the finality of his retirement, and hinted at another diversion on which he might continue to lead: the powers of the House of Lords. He remained almost until his death in 1898 a brooding presence over his successors.

By prolonging the uncertainty over his eventual resignation for three months, Gladstone created the ideal conditions for intrigue in an already divided cabinet. Although rooted in a genuine disagreement over imperial policy, the personal element in the bitter quarrel between Harcourt and Rosebery that blighted the Liberal party for the rest of the decade was greatly aggravated by the contest for the succession. Harcourt finally accepted Rosebery's leadership of the party, with himself as chancellor of the exchequer and leader in the House of Commons, on condition that he was given access to foreign office dispatches in time to intervene, an indication of the distrust that prevailed.[22] The restraint was largely ignored both by Rosebery and the foreign office. Harcourt was only belatedly informed of the Anglo-Congolese Treaty of April 1894 designed to keep France out of the Nile valley, and not consulted on the Grey declaration of March 1895 warning France off with the threat of war.[23]

Dissension was further increased by Rosebery's criticism of the graduated death duties in Harcourt's budget of 1894, an instalment

21. Ibid. p. 21.   22. Ibid. pp. 64, 94.   23. Ibid. pp. 110–21.

of Gladstonian fiscal radicalism transferring direct taxation from productive to unproductive sources. Rosebery made two basic criticisms: the power of property that would be offended, 'an enormous and insidious force [which] influences innumerable employees and dependents . . . its mere panic is power', and the danger of 'a horizontal division of parties, in which the Liberal party would rest on nothing but a working-class support'. Harcourt in reply echoed Chamberlain and foreshadowed Lloyd George, dismissing the alienation of 'those who find themselves deprived of monopolies which they ought never to have possessed and privileges which enrich them at the expense of their poorer fellows', and blaming the party itself for any failure to secure mass support. The 'desire to avert the "cleavage of classes" . . . is natural, but you are too late. The "horizontal division of parties" was certain to come as a consequence of Household Suffrage. The thin end of the wedge was inserted and the cleavage is expanding more and more every day', an argument that Rosebery considered 'nonsense' in view of the balance of classes achieved by the Conservatives.[24] By September, although still chancellor and leader in the House of Commons, Harcourt was referring to himself as 'not a supporter of the present government', and the rival leaders were not on speaking terms.[25]

Behind Gladstone's resignation and the Rosebery–Harcourt dispute lay two fundamental questions, the solution of which was fundamental to the Liberal party's long-term future: its policy on imperialism and its relationship to the working and middle classes. To the party's detriment, the divided and embittered state of the leadership precluded the discussion of either. Instead, as Home Rule, which Rosebery had welcomed in 1886 as giving order to 'a flabby, disconnected majority', lost its cohesive qualities, Rosebery sought another unifying principle of the same order, which he found, as Gladstone had done, in the reform of the House of Lords. But whilst Home Rule as a policy was progressive in the framework of Midlothian Radicalism, the Lords were merely an impediment to progress, which, if removed, left the party's post-Gladstonian future no more clearly defined. Moreover, as a unifying principle, it failed. The party went into the 1895 general election with neither the will to seek, nor the means to achieve, unity. Its last days were overshadowed by the fear that Gladstone might return from retirement to denounce its major measure of the 1895 session, Welsh

24. Robert Rhodes James, *Rosebery* (London: Weidenfeld & Nicolson, 1963), pp. 343–5.
25. Stansky, *Ambitions and Strategies*, pp. 142–3.

disestablishment, and once again it escaped office with relief. Rosebery fought the election on Lords reform; Harcourt fought, and lost, on temperance, Morley on Home Rule, whilst the bulk of the party focused on Welsh disestablishment. Despite a reasonable showing in the popular vote, and an adverse swing of only some 4.5 per cent,[26] the election was a rout. The party was so demoralised, and consequently impoverished, that it left 124 seats uncontested, and only 177 Liberals were returned.

Opposition removed the last pressure on the Liberal leadership to preserve some semblance of unity and responsibility. In 1896, Rosebery seized the opportunity provided by Gladstone's condemnation of the Armenian massacres to resign. Even more than Gladstone's resignation in 1894, this was disingenuous, a retreat which left open the possibility of his recall, should 'some unsuspected crisis' make this desirable.[27] Harcourt, whose succession to the party leadership would merely have accentuated division, had to be content with the *de facto* leadership conferred by his status as leader in the House of Commons. In 1898, he too announced his retirement from the Liberal front bench, shortly followed by Morley, with whom the withdrawal had been concerted. These retirements were also retreats into a position of political independence, the better to wage the factional war.

Their action was precipitated by Kitchener's reconquest of the Sudan, and the subsequent confrontation with the French at Fashoda in September. In October, Rosebery not only spoke out in support of reoccupation, but claimed it as Liberal policy. The future leaders of Liberal Imperialism, Grey, Asquith, Haldane and H.H. Fowler, the former secretary of state for India, lined up behind him in the following months. Morley fired the first retaliatory shot in the 'little England' campaign to resist this 'Jingo invasion of the Liberal party'[28] in his resignation speech at Brechin in January 1899, and the second in February in a parliamentary motion criticising the government's Sudanese policy. Some thirteen Liberals voted with the government, and the party began to fall apart on imperialism. The process was completed by the outbreak of war in South Africa.

Increasing tension between Britain and the Boer republics in South Africa during the summer and autumn of 1899 was matched by increasing polarisation amongst the Liberals into pro-Boer and

---

26. Ibid. p. 178.
27. James, *Rosebery*, p. 402; The Marquess of Crewe, *Lord Rosebery* (London: John Murray, 1931), vol. 2, p. 559.
28. Stansky, *Ambitions and Strategies*, p. 273.

Liberal Imperialist groups which the new party leader, Sir Henry Campbell-Bannerman, was powerless to prevent. In June, the 'Liberal Forwards', a ginger group of radicals, established the Transvaal Committee to agitate against war, and despite the outbreak of war following the Boer ultimatum in October, the anti-war movement gathered strength through a series of *ad hoc* organisations from the moderate South Africa Conciliation Committee to W.T. Stead's virulent Stop-the-War movement which condemned all Liberals as 'dumb dogs'.[29] Between 1899 and 1902, pro-Boer MPs, together with the Irish who saw in the Transvaal a fellow victim of British oppression, proposed a series of resolutions in Parliament which made little difference to events in South Africa or government policy, but publicised and widened the divisions within the Liberal party.

On the other side, the Liberal Imperial Council, under the chairmanship of Lord Brassey, broke with Campbell-Bannerman in November 1900. For the first year of the war at least, Campbell-Bannerman, whose personal sympathies lay broadly with the pro-Boers, attempted to hold a central position between the two factions, condemning the government's pre-war diplomacy as provocative in common with the pro-Boers, but accepting the need to fight a war that had begun and the policy of annexation, both of which were essential to the Liberal Imperialists. His efforts met with little success, and the centre itself became no more than a faction. In the division on Sir Wilfrid Lawson's motion in July 1900 to reduce the colonial office vote, the party split neatly three ways, the Radicals supporting Lawson, the Imperialists voting with the government, the centre following Campbell-Bannerman into abstention.

The Liberal party faced the general election of 1900 opposing an apparently successful government in wartime, and accused of sympathising with the enemy. Yet despite a shortage of money, great difficulty in finding candidates and the government cry that 'every seat lost to the Government is a seat gained to the Boers', the Liberals in fact fared remarkably well, even improving slightly on their 1895 performance by winning 184 seats. During the 1890s the Liberals were reduced to the core of their hard-line support, but the election results of 1895 and 1900 revealed that support was still substantial. Comparison with the 1906 election, which performed a similar reductionist exercise on the Unionists, leaving them with

29. Arthur Davey, *The British Pro-Boers 1877–1902* (Cape Town: Tafelberg, 1978), pp. 74–87.

157 seats from which they recovered to dominate politics in the twentieth century, suggests that the Liberal party at the end of the nineteenth century was still reasonably healthy in the country, whatever the antics of the leadership.

The unexpected continuation of the war by Boer guerrillas, whilst it damaged the government in the long term, temporarily continued and deepened Liberal disunity. Campbell-Bannerman's denunciation in June 1901 of the 'methods of barbarism', the concentration camps and farm burnings by which the British army confronted guerrilla warfare, provoked an open split with the Liberal Imperialists. He secured a vote of confidence from the party at a meeting at the Reform Club on 9 July, but only by turning imperialism into an open question. His speech produced a dramatic response from Rosebery, who appeared to believe that the 'unsuspected crisis' he awaited had at last arisen.

Rosebery had been looking to reconstruct the Liberal party since 1895. Prior to the election, he had already condemned the 'worn out and effete Newcastle programme'.[30] After it, he attributed defeat to 'a more general and deeply rooted cause – Mr G,'s general programme since 1880'.[31] It was impossible 'for the Liberal party to remain nailed to the innumerable political propositions lightly accepted by Mr. Gladstone for the promotion of his Irish policy. The party needs to make a new start, and to shed much of this.'[32] It had become 'all legs and wings, a daddy long-legs fluttering among a thousand flames; it had to be consumed in order that something more sane, more consistent, and more coherent could take its place'.[33] In 1901, he denounced the Reform Club compromise in favour of a complete split because of a 'fundamental and incurable antagonism of principle with regard to the Empire'. On 19 July he raised the wider question of the party's new start and 'clean slate', and threatened that if the Liberal party did not reform, he might well become the rallying point of a new party.[34] His new approach involved the abandonment of Gladstonian idealism in overseas policy, which he described as a vain 'attempt to carry into international policy the spirit of the Gospel itself', in favour of his own policy of active imperialism.[35]

At his request the Liberal Imperial Council was transformed into the Liberal (Imperial) League, with a projected fund of £10,000

30. Stansky, *Ambitions and Strategies*, p. 172.
31. Ibid. p. 180; James, *Rosebery*, p. 385.
32. Crewe, *Lord Rosebery*, vol. 2, pp. 522–3.   33. James, *Rosebery*, p. 386.
34. Crewe, *Lord Rosebery*, vol. 2, p. 570.   35. James, *Rosebery*, pp. 411–12.

to run its own candidates,[36] and in a widely publicised speech at Chesterfield on 16 December he closed the debate on South Africa, arguing strongly in favour of a negotiated peace, but extended the debate on the Liberal party's future. The theme of his speech was the abandonment of Home Rule, the clean slate and the doctrine of 'efficiency', which he discussed primarily in terms of the parliamentary and administrative system, widely agreed to be responsible for an incompetent conduct of the war. The speech evoked enthusiasm among Liberal Imperialists who saw in it the lead they had been calling for since Rosebery's tactical retirement, which Haldane had rightly described as 'only the beginning of the battle'.[37] Early in the 1890s, the imperialists amongst those 'New Liberals' disillusioned by Morley had turned to the glamorous figure of Rosebery, then acquiring a reputation as a social reformer and friend of the working classes through his work as chairman of the newly formed LCC and his settlement of the miners' dispute in 1893.

Both the connection with London progressivism and with the Fabian socialist, Sidney Webb, were sustained through the 1890s, and it was Webb who set out the intellectual position of Liberal Imperialism in his article 'Lord Rosebery's escape from Houndsditch' in 1899. Liberal Imperialism condemned Gladstonian individualism both at home and abroad, and conversely linked imperial expansion with social reform as forms of state intervention resting on a common principle. Social reform was necessary for imperial survival, for, as Rosebery argued, 'in the rookeries and slums which still survive an imperial race cannot be reared'.[38] His condemnation of old 'shibboleths' and 'fly-blown phylacteries', and Fowler's more explicit denunciation of 'the dry biscuit of an old political economy',[39] appeared to herald the end of the association of Liberalism with the minimal state.

The effectiveness of the Chesterfield speech lay in its avoidance of aggressive imperialism in favour of negotiation, and its appeal to those who sought renewal at home. When the Liberal League was formed in February 1902, Webb wanted 'a dozen opposition planning committees', to work out the details of that 'real programme

36. Alan Sykes, *Tariff Reform in British Politics* (Oxford: Oxford University Press, 1979), pp. 18–19.

37. James, *Rosebery*, p. 397.

38. Bernard Semmel, *Imperialism and Social Reform* (London: Allen and Unwin, 1960), p. 62.

39. H.C.G. Matthew, *The Liberal Imperialists* (Oxford: Oxford University Press, 1973), p. 137.

of social reforms' that he and Haldane been discussing throughout the summer of 1901 and intermittently for the past decade or more.[40] Even so committed a pro-Boer as Lloyd George openly praised Rosebery's intervention.[41] In theory, Liberal Imperialism overcame the problem of the 'cleavage of classes', integrating the working classes through social reform, whilst reconciling the middle classes through the concept of national efficiency which made reform at home the logical consequence of Britain's imperial mission. The new Liberal party would be a 'national party' both in the accepted Liberal sense of looking 'at the interests of the community from the point of view of the community as a whole',[42] and in the breadth of its support.

In February 1902, Rosebery announced his 'definite separation' from Campbell-Bannerman, but after the formation of the Liberal League he made little effort to liaise with his principal supporters and launched no sustained campaign. His talents, as Grey observed, made him 'conspicuous in the crowd, a head taller than it; people keep looking and admiring, no one else can stand so tall, but those who are quite close see that his feet aren't upon the ground'.[43] 'Definite separation' also went too far for those with political ambitions or Nonconformist priorities. Asquith, although a vice-president of the League, had no intention of separating himself from the Liberal party,[44] and even Sir Robert Perks, the League treasurer but also a leading Wesleyan Methodist, argued that they should 'make it plain that we are, and mean to remain, Liberals'.[45]

Orthodox Liberals questioned whether Rosebery's social imperialism was 'liberal' at all. 'All that he said about the clean slate and efficiency', Campbell-Bannerman wrote of the Chesterfield speech, 'was an affront to Liberalism and was pure claptrap. . . . It is not unfavourable to the chance of unity in the war and peace issue; but ominous of every horror in general politics',[46] a view not surprisingly endorsed by Harcourt. Liberal Imperialism reversed traditional priorities, as when Asquith considered social reform 'not as a moral question . . . but as a question of social and imperial efficiency' in

40. Ibid. p. 68.

41. Martin Pugh, *Lloyd George* (London: Longman, 1988), pp. 25–6.

42. Sykes, *Tariff Reform*, p. 20.

43. G.M. Trevelyan, *Grey of Fallodon* (London: Longmans, 1937), pp. 79–80; James, *Rosebery*, p. 426.

44. Roy Jenkins, *Asquith* (London: Collins, 1964), p. 133.

45. Sykes, *Tariff Reform*, p. 23.

46. J.A. Spender, *The Life of the Right Hon. Sir Henry Campbell-Bannerman, GCB*, vol 2. (Sevenoaks: Hodder and Stoughton, n.d.), p. 14.

July 1901.[47] Efficiency, as Campbell-Bannerman understood, was not a policy, but a respectable cloak for the pursuit of power. It involved making 'the condition of our national fitness equal to the demands of our empire – administrative, parliamentary, commercial, educational, physical, moral, naval and military fitness'.[48] The empire was to be governed and extended; the working classes were to be housed and educated, made sober, thrifty and hardworking as an essential component of an imperial race capable of sustaining imperial burdens. Liberty did not enter into these calculations at all.

Liberal Imperialism and the doctrine of efficiency proved a dead end for New Liberalism, as it was for Liberalism as a whole. Rosebery's phoenix was not a new post-Gladstonian Liberal party, but an attempt to reconstruct the pre-Gladstonian one. In shedding his 'Gladstonian chains ... to start with a *tabula rasa*',[49] he wanted to restore 'the Liberal party to what it was in richness, variety and strength before 1886',[50] and in May 1899 made a veiled appeal to the Liberal Unionists to return to the party to merge 'the old Liberal spirit with the new Imperial spirit'.[51] For that reason alone, the programme to bring about 'efficiency' had to remain vague. The social basis of the Liberal League reinforced the moderate identity of Rosebery's Liberal Imperialism. Perks proposed 'an individualistic social programme', preferred 'wealthy young Liberals' to Rosebery's suggestion of sponsored candidates, scorned ordinary subscriptions and based the League's finances on the contributions of a few extremely wealthy men. One such, the engineering magnate, Weetman Pearson, explained that the League was essential to the party 'if it is once more to include the men of weight and substance who have been alienated from it in recent years'.[52] Another, Sir Charles Tennant, Asquith's new father-in-law, was, according to Asquith's son, Raymond, 'possessed by an almost maniacal hatred of trade unions and all their works'.[53]

Such support left little scope for adventures in what Perks described as the 'communistic' ideas of Sidney Webb, or indeed new policy initiatives of any kind. The new Liberal party that would contain 'all the elements which existed before 1886' meant above all the return of the Whigs and moderates, and the recreation of

47. Matthew, *Liberal Imperialists*, pp. 71–2.   48. Ibid. p. 141.
49. James, *Rosebery*, p. 392.   50. Crewe, *Lord Rosebery*, vol. 2, p. 523.
51. James, *Rosebery*, p. 408.   52. Sykes, *Tariff Reform*, p. 22.
53. John Jolliffe, *Raymond Asquith: Life and Letters* (London: Century, 1987), p. 33.

the old Palmerstonian coalition of the centre. Effectively this would, as in Palmerston's last years, neutralise the party politics with which Rosebery was so ill at ease, and allow administrative experts to deal with problems that were in Rosebery's view 'becoming too large for parties to deal with'.[54] Despite Rosebery's criticism of the party system, however, Liberal Imperialism remained part of a debate about the nature and future of the Liberal party, not about the transformation of party politics. Following the precedent of those earlier 'moderates', the Whigs, whose centrism they shared, the moderates of the Liberal League sought in a reconstruction of parties a refuge from the anxieties created by Radicalism and the 'cleavage of classes' while still remaining, in some sense, Liberals.

The emergence of Labour

Public disorder and rising labour militancy lent substance to moderate fears. The unemployed rioted in London in 1886 after a demonstration organised by the Social Democratic Federation got out of hand, and there were further demonstrations in 1887. With socialist assistance, trade unionism developed amongst un-skilled workers pursuing what the young socialist engineer, Tom Mann, called 'the true Unionist policy of *aggression*'.[55] The effects were more visible in the provinces than in the relatively orderly London strikes of the gasworkers, matchgirls and dockers whose success owed much to the public sympathy for the conditions their protests exposed. In Leeds, troops were required to protect black-legs from gasworkers, in Hull to protect them from seamen, and in Scotland from miners. At Featherstone colliery in Yorkshire two men were shot by beleaguered troops when, according to the home secretary, Asquith, 'the complete destruction of the colliery was imminent'.[56] The spread of militancy to the older unions revealed still more clearly the impact of the depression, and the degree to which the mid-century consensus had depended upon the feeling of prosperity. The miners found their wages tied to declining prices; the boot and shoe operatives and the engineers were hit by mecha-nisation which threatened their craft status; employers were pres-sured by the attempt to maintain competitiveness and profitability.

54. James, *Rosebery*, p. 403.
55. Henry Pelling, *A History of British Trade Unionism* (Harmondsworth: Penguin Books, 1963), p. 94.
56. Jenkins, *Asquith*, p. 68.

Structural change, the replacement of small family firms by larger impersonal combines, removed personal contact between employers and workers, aggravated the decline in industrial relations, and undermined the material base upon which mid-Victorian Liberalism transcended class conflict.

Confrontation in the form of labour strikes and employer lockouts became a familiar part of the industrial scene, produced initially more by changing conditions and economic pressures than any fundamental change in the outlook of the unions. Ben Pickard, who remained staunchly Lib-Lab and continued to use his great influence on behalf of the Liberal party,[57] brought most of the local miners' unions together in the Miners Federation of Great Britain in 1889 in support of the eight-hour day and a minimum wage. Attempts to prevent wage cuts nevertheless led to confrontation, and a lengthy lockout from July to November 1893. William Inskip, general secretary of the National Union of Boot and Shoe Operatives, Liberal municipal councillor in Leicester and committed Lib-Lab, could not avoid industrial confrontation and the boot and shoe lockout of 1895. The relatively stable conditions and formal negotiating structure of the cotton industry did not prevent the cotton spinners' lockout of 1892–3, nor the historic moderation of the engineers in the protracted engineers' lockout of 1897–8.

Lockouts were a testimony to the militancy of the employers as much as that of the unions. Under economic pressure, as one employer observed, 'Humanity must make room for iron.'[58] The use of blacklegs, support for the National Association of Free Labour, the formation of aggressive employers' federations to counter union organisation and in 1898 of the Employers' Parliamentary Council to counter TUC lobbying, all indicated an increased determination to confront the unions. Most effectively of all, employers challenged the unions in the courts. By 1901, when the Lords handed down the Taff Vale judgement rendering unions liable for losses incurred as a result of strike action, the position that the unions thought they had secured between 1869 and 1875 had been completely undermined. The Blackburn weavers case (1901) confirmed that, in the view of the courts, unions did not even have the right of peaceful picketing.

A small body of socialist activists, assisted by rank-and-file apathy on political issues, gave the union movement a more radical tone

57. David Howell, *British Workers and the Independent Labour Party* (Manchester: Manchester University Press, 1983), pp. 19–20.
58. Ibid. p. 95.

than was justified by the attitude of most union leaders or the majority of union members. The adoption of a socialist objective by the TUC in 1893 and by the boot and shoe operatives in 1894 nevertheless marked a weakening of Lib-Lab influences and collaborationist trade unionism, and explained why employers felt they had to resist 'extreme Socialistic doctrines encroaching upon the individual rights of manufacturers'.[59] Herein lay one of the prime reasons for the shift of middle-class opinion. 'The intermediates,' Chamberlain wrote in 1894, 'the men who hold the balance of elections – are disgusted and frightened . . . frightened at the prospects of confiscation which are in the air and found expression at the Trade Union Congress the other day.'[60] The Conservative leadership shared these exaggerated fears. Writing to W.H. Smith, leader of the House of Commons in 1889, Salisbury described 'a state of bloodless civil war. . . . To loot somebody or something is the common object under a thick varnish of pious phrases', and Smith, himself a middle-class recruit to Conservatism, agreed not only with Salisbury, but also with Harcourt: 'The extension of the suffrage . . . has made the extreme Radicals masters of the liberal party, and men support a policy now from which they would have shrunk with horror ten years ago.'[61]

It was an analysis with which many Liberals sympathised. As Perks observed, speaking for the wealthy Nonconformists he represented, 'One of the reasons why Toryism has got hold of the middle classes and the artisans is that as these classes have prospered and acquired their houses, they have inclined to the Conservative party because they dread the doctrines which Sidney Webb thinks would prove so popular.'[62] Nonconformity, the section of the middle class most solidly Liberal in mid-century, revealed the transfer of allegiance most clearly. The gradual secularisation of society undermined chapel solidarity, and class affiliations began to supersede those of religion. The removal of many immediate Nonconformist grievances by the mid-1870s facilitated their integration into the lower echelons of an 'establishment' from which they had once felt excluded. By the 1890s, the Nonconformist preference for the Liberal party had fallen sharply. They were, according to one minister in 1892, 'a large section of the middle class, which

---

59. Ibid. p. 102.
60. Kenneth Young, *Arthur James Balfour* (London: G. Bell & Sons, 1963), p. 167; Peter Fraser, *Joseph Chamberlain: Radicalism and Empire* (London: Cassell, 1966), p. 152.
61. Sykes, *Tariff Reform*, p. 12.   62. Ibid. p. 22.

has hitherto been Liberal, but in which are many whose minds are exercised about socialist tendencies'. 'Trade Unionism and the present position of the Labour Question' were 'driving thousands into the Conservative camp'.[63]

Labour militancy created difficulties in the pursuit of working-class support by a party which sought to be 'classless', but within the still largely undifferentiated left there was room for cautious accommodation between organised labour and the Liberals on questions of labour policy like the eight-hour-day which divided trade unionist from trade unionist as much as trade unionist from Liberal.[64] Labour representation was the key issue, because it was so often raised, not always accurately, in terms of independent representation. In the 1892 general election Keir Hardie, John Burns and Havelock Wilson were returned as independent Labour candidates, and in January 1893, Hardie chaired the foundation conference of the Independent Labour Party at Bradford. The Liberal party was well aware of the demand for increased working-class participation in politics. At Newcastle in 1891 Gladstone argued that 'it ought to be a great effort of the Liberal party to extend the labour representation in parliament',[65] and Schnadhorst as secretary of the NLF sought to place such candidates in vacant constituencies. Labour candidates were allowed a free hand on labour questions provided they agreed to support the Liberal programme, in particular Home Rule. This was true even of 'independent' candidates. Both Burns and Hardie were given a free run by the Liberals in 1892.[66]

Nevertheless there were severe limitations on the Liberal party's commitment to this enterprise. The party willed the end, but failed to provide the means. Harcourt noted when proposing the programme for 1892 'that in my experience at the Election, the "Payment of Members" is the one thing the Labour Party attach much value to'.[67] It was a logical forward move in the process of integration from the extension of the franchise, a relatively cheap political change but one that was essential if ever working-class representation was to become a reality in any numbers. The Liberals were

63. D.W. Bebbington, 'Nonconformity and electoral sociology', *The Historical Journal* 27 (3) (1984), 640–7, 652–5.

64. Pelling, *British Trade Unionism*, p. 106.

65. Kenneth O. Morgan, *The Age of Lloyd George* (London: George Allen Unwin, 1978), p. 114.

66. Barker, *Gladstone and Radicalism*, pp. 134–8, 145–54.

67. Stansky, *Ambitions and Strategies*, p. 2.

not thinking of large numbers of working-class MPs, but only of a specialised section of the party of perhaps forty or fifty.[68] This was not incompatible with the limited ambitions of the Independent Labour Party, which did not include government. The Liberal problem was that whatever the intentions of its central organisation, it too often failed to overcome the resistance of its predominantly middle-class constituency associations to working-class candidates. Schnadhorst had no success in trying to place such candidates in vacant constituencies in 1890–1, he had to overcome local resistance to give Hardie a free run in West Ham in 1892, and failed in his attempt to do the same for Havelock Wilson in Middlesbrough, although Wilson still won. The party had only twenty-five labour candidates in 1892, and after the election labour representation had made no advance on the number of working-class MPs elected in 1886.[69]

The Labour party had its roots in such local difficulties. Leading figures like Keir Hardie, who founded the Scottish Labour Party after his rejection in East Lanark, Ramsay MacDonald, rejected in Southampton, and Arthur Henderson, rejected in Newcastle, all initially sought nomination as Liberals.[70] As MacDonald complained, the Liberals 'kicked us out and slammed the door in our faces'.[71] George Lansbury, another potential Liberal candidate, broke with the Liberal party when the NLF refused to discuss the eight-hour day.[72] According to MacDonald, writing after his experience of Liberal–Labour rivalry in the Attercliffe by-election in 1894, would-be Labour candidates were experiencing similar problems 'in scores of other constituencies throughout the country', in Mid-Lanark, in Newcastle, where the local Liberals were 'scouring the face of the earth for a capitalist to oppose the nominee of the Trades Council', in 'Wigan . . . Huddersfield, Bradford, Manchester, Bolton, South Shields, Glasgow and elsewhere'.[73]

As a result, there was a gradual movement of opinion within organised labour towards independent candidates. It was very much a generational change. Ben Pickard intervened against the ILP in by-elections in Attercliffe in 1894 and Barnsley in 1897 and solidly maintained the Lib-Lab stance of the Yorkshire Miners' Association. His death left a vacuum in Yorkshire mining politics which

---

68. Barker, *Gladstone and Radicalism*, p. 135.   69. Ibid. pp. 133–5.
70. Ibid. p. 132.
71. David Marquand, *Ramsay MacDonald* (London: Cape, 1977), pp. 35–8.
72. Barker, *Gladstone and Radicalism*, pp. 136, 145–6.
73. Marquand, *Ramsay MacDonald*, p. 36.

finally permitted limited ILP infiltration.[74] The Lancashire Miners'
Federation turned towards independent representation after Sam
Woods, a successful Liberal candidate in Ince in 1892 and Walthamstow in 1897, failed to gain the Dewsbury nomination in 1901.[75]
William Inskip was unable to accept the socialist objective of the
National Union of Boot and Shoe Operatives, and resigned as the
union's parliamentary candidate. By 1900, the union's nominee,
T.F. Richards, was a socialist and member of the ILP.[76] Lib-Labs
were forced on to the defensive as activists pointed to Liberal indifference or identification with employers in the bitter confronta-
tions of the 1890s. In 1899, the TUC conference, pressed by the
ILP and ILP members within the trade union movement, endorsed
a resolution from the Amalgamated Society of Railway Servants
to convene a conference of labour and socialist organisations on
labour representation. From its meeting in 1900 came the Labour
Representation Committee. The Committee was an umbrella organisation not a political party, but it served a vital purpose in giving
an institutional unity to those who, for whatever reason, stood as
Labour candidates.

For the majority, even of activists and ILP members, 'independence' did not necessarily mean socialism, and often meant no more
than direct representation. Its advocates were inconsistent, or did
not bother with fine distinctions. T.F. Richards, the militant scourge
of Lib-Labs in NUBSO, assiduously sought Liberal assistance once
he had been adopted as 'independent' Labour candidate for West
Wolverhampton. His action was endorsed by his union despite its
nominal commitment to both socialism and independence.[77] Socialism, or complete isolation from any other party, were assertions
of working-class identity and working-class frustration, but they were
not essentials. Indeed, trade unionists were often suspicious of
socialists, especially outsiders. What was essential was that the interests of labour should be represented in parliament by working men.
It was this that the Liberal party was so signally failing to provide
when its local selection committees rejected labour candidates.

For Labour activists, the Liberal party had chosen its side in
the 'cleavage of classes'. MacDonald predicted that ultimately the
barriers between the Liberal and Conservative parties would dissolve, 'and the political battle will be fought out by the "interests"
on the one side and the wage-earners on the other'.[78] Correct in its

74. Howell, *British Workers*, p. 19–24.   75. Ibid. pp. 30–1.
76. Ibid. pp. 98–106.   77. Ibid. pp. 107–8.
78. Marquand, *Ramsay MacDonald*, p. 37.

long-term analysis, the forecast suggested a future for the Liberal party along the lines that Rosebery pursued, and made the Conservative party as much or more of a threat than Labour to the continued existence of the Liberal party as a political institution. Macdonald, however, wrote off Liberalism and the Lib-Lab position too easily, underestimating both the strength of the Lib-Lab outlook within industrial Labour and the capacity of the Liberal party to adapt. It was the ILP that had to compromise to secure trade-union support for candidates who were often no more than nominally 'independent'. In the general election of 1900, despite an electorate with a working-class majority, independent Labour secured only 1.8 per cent of the vote, and two seats. One of those elected, Richard Bell, quickly adopted a Lib-Lab stance, and by 1904 was intervening in the Norwich by-election on behalf of the Liberal and against the LRC candidate.[79]

Nor, despite the apprehension which favoured Conservatism, were the middle classes yet lost to Liberalism. Liberal weakness after 1886 was the product of the abstention of former supporters as much as a decided transfer of allegiance.[80] Moreover, part of the defection of middle-class Nonconformists arose from objections to specific policies, especially Home Rule and the Irish alliance. Anti-Catholicism remained sufficiently strong for entire chapel communities to desert, especially Methodists. This was a testimony to the continuing strength of their Nonconformity, rather than its erosion by secularisation and class feeling.[81] Their political affiliation was volatile, conditioned by immediate political issues, the attitude of the parties, their competence and their unity. Around the turn of the century, the political future was peculiarly unclear. Neither the Liberal nor the Conservative party had clarified their response to the new situation created by the claims of industrial and political labour. Independent Labour did not yet threaten the Liberal position, and there were changes that a Liberal government might make in the electoral system to minimise the threat, such as the introduction of the alternative vote. The Conservative party had not yet secured an unshakeable hold on the middle classes. The Liberal party was still able, as the recovery between 1902 and 1906 demonstrated, to transcend the feared 'cleavage of classes' that threatened its *raison d'être* as a classless agent of the national interest.

79. Howell, *British Workers*, pp. 79–80.
80. Neal Blewett, *The Peers, the Parties and the People* (London: Macmillan, 1972), pp. 20–3.
81. Bebbington, 'Nonconformity', pp. 647–52.

Liberal revival

The success of mid-Victorian Liberalism and late-Victorian Conservatism alike depended upon a combination of opposition disunity
and calculated moderation to retain the centre vote. The Liberal
recovery between 1902 and 1905 followed this pattern. The Conservatives recreated their mid-Victorian image of the incompetent,
divided party of privilege and wealth, the protagonist of financiers,
brewers, landlords and the church at the expense of the nation. In
so doing, they rekindled old Victorian passions and enabled the
Liberal party to rebuild its mid-Victorian alliance for one last time.
As the party which took the credit for apparent success in South
Africa in 1900, the Conservatives took the blame for the brutality
and inefficiency of the prolonged guerrilla war which followed.
The shadow of South Africa haunted the government to the advantage of the Liberals right up to the general election of 1906.

Boer maltreatment of British miners in the Transvaal had been
one of the primary justifications for the war, with the prospect of
a post-war South Africa providing employment and settlement for
British migrants. In the event, the mines were rapidly reopened
to restore the South African economy, and the labour shortage met
by the importation of indentured Chinese workers, herded into
barracks and subjected to corporal punishment. 'Chinese slavery'
affronted Liberal humanitarianism, alarmed organised labour and
added force to the view that imperialism was inseparable from exploitation and Conservatism inseparable from vested capitalist interests. The war and its aftermath stripped imperialism of its glamour
and turned attention inwards to the contemplation of an industrial
and imperial nation in decline. Revelation of the high proportion
of army volunteers from the large towns rejected as physically unfit
appeared to confirm the alarming findings of Booth and Rowntree,
whose investigations suggested that up to 30 per cent of the urban
population was too poor to maintain basic standards of nutrition
and health. Cross-party though it often was, the social-imperialist
link between domestic poverty and overseas performance gave all
Liberals a common interest in the 'condition of England' question.
The Liberal Imperialists either drifted back towards the centre of
the party, or found themselves stranded.

Moreover, if the Liberal party chose to take it up, the 'condition
of England' question was a Liberal issue, as Conservative attempts
to confront it within the confines of Conservative prejudices and
priorities rapidly revealed. Balfour's education bill of 1902 was

prompted by the need to introduce efficiency into the education system, and to rectify the anomalous position of secondary education created by the 'Cockerton judgement' of 1899–1901 which determined that the secondary education provided by the school boards, responsible for elementary education, was unlawful. But it was also a response to the party-political cry from Conservative benches to rescue the increasingly impoverished but largely Anglican voluntary schools. As an attempt to promote efficient administration by abolishing school boards and placing education under a local authority committee, it was supported by a few Liberals who, like the Webbs and Haldane, placed efficiency before sectarianism. But the abolition of the school boards, and above all the proposal to provide rate aid for denominational voluntary schools, reawakened Nonconformist fury.

Sectarian rivalry did not destroy the Education Act, despite a rate strike by Nonconformists in the more embittered parts of Wales, but it reunified the Liberal party and reinvigorated its grass roots almost overnight. Apparently ardent Liberal Imperialists like Perks surrendered their imperialism to their Nonconformity and rejoined the mainstream. The party leadership, ready to seize on an issue that would pull the party together, was swept along by the tide of Nonconformist anger. Reinforced by the Conservative Licensing Act of 1904 which infuriated temperance reformers by providing compensation for surrendered licences, their outrage flowed with undiminished force into the election campaign at the end of 1905. As in the past, Nonconformist commitment and organisation also made good deficiencies in the Liberal party's own organisation, especially in London, where Liberal organisation had been crumbling. Whereas in 1900 Herbert Gladstone, as Liberal chief whip, had bewailed both the shortage of candidates and funds, between 1902 and 1906 at by-elections and in the general election, Nonconformists came out as Liberal candidates to win seats regarded as hopeless, with funds more than adequate to meet their expenses.[82]

The Liberal party had little choice but to rally to the Nonconformist cause, even if opposition to the Education Act was something of an embarrassment to a party whose former leader had so recently proclaimed the policy of efficiency, and even to the middle-class Nonconformists themselves. No such reservations impeded the party's response to Joseph Chamberlain's tariff reform campaign.

---

82. Stephen Koss, *Nonconformity in Modern British Politics* (London: Batsford, 1975), pp. 72–3.

Intended to unify the empire and protect British industries, jobs and wages whilst capitalising electorally on imperialist and social-imperialist sentiment, his proposals for preferential tariffs on imported foodstuffs and a general tariff on manufactured goods not only split the Unionist party into feuding factions of tariff reformers and Unionist free traders, but attacked the very heart of Liberalism. Defending free trade was, according to Ripon, who was old enough to have held office under Palmerston, 'the greatest political struggle even of my long political life. . . . Everything else sinks into insignificance. . . . We must be prepared to unite with anyone who will help and part company with anyone who will not.'[83]

It was on this basis that the Liberal leadership rebuilt the hegemonic Liberal alliance of the mid-Victorian years. Already assured of the committed support of Nonconformity provided there was no backsliding on the education issue, negotiations between Herbert Gladstone, the Liberal chief whip and Ramsay MacDonald, secretary of the LRC, secured Labour endorsement of Liberalism at the price of giving LRC candidates a free run in selected constituencies in most of which Liberal candidates had little chance. The Gladstone–MacDonald pact, like the arrangements with Nonconformity, made good specific Liberal deficiencies in important areas. Sectarian politics cut across class fears and allowed the party to regain middle-class support that had been lost for the past twenty years; the alliance with Labour allowed a class appeal that undermined working-class Conservatism in its areas of strength, and correspondingly of Liberal weakness, especially Lancashire. Similar negotiations with the dissident Unionist free traders foundered on the sectarian issue, but some individual free-trade Unionists did transfer allegiance on the fiscal issue, including Winston Churchill, Devonshire, formerly Hartington, and J. St. Loe Strachey. Strachey as editor of the weekly *Spectator*, and Devonshire by his reputation for sensible moderation, were influential figures, and both advised voters to vote Liberal in 1906. Negotiations were successful with the Irish, now a more disciplined body whose leader, John Redmond, agreed to the demotion of Home Rule in the forthcoming election in return for a 'step-by-step' approach to Irish self-government.

Ironically, Ireland completed the reunification of the Liberal party. The 'step-by-step' policy announced by Campbell-Bannerman at Stirling in 1905 was promptly denounced by Rosebery, who remained unaware of the difference between his 'clean slate' and the

83. Sykes, *Tariff Reform*, p. 64.

smudged doodlings of his nominal lieutenants whose agreement Campbell-Bannerman secured beforehand. Rosebery was left in aggrieved isolation. Like Rosebery, Balfour misread the situation, and wrongly sensing another Liberal split on Ireland resigned so that Liberal disunity would widen before the election. The error allowed Campbell-Bannerman to overcome the reservations of the leading Liberal Imperialists in the Commons, Asquith, Haldane and Grey, who had earlier agreed between themselves only to serve if Campbell-Bannerman went to the Lords, by arguing that the defence of free trade overshadowed all other issues and necessitated a united front. Asquith showed little hesitation in becoming chancellor of the exchequer and heir apparent, but only prolonged negotiation lured Grey into the cabinet as foreign secretary.

Supported by Labour, the Irish, and reinvigorated Nonconformity, endorsed by leading Whigs, Campbell-Bannerman led both a united party and a reconstructed coalition into the 1906 election against a divided and demoralised Conservative party. The situation allowed him to fight a largely negative campaign, without promises that might arouse moderate fears. Taken as a whole, the Conservative government's policies, past and proposed, appeared as a reassertion of privilege at its most arrogant and opposition was infused with a common sense of injustice that gave a moral tone to even the most materialist issue. Flogging and brutality in an empire generally regarded as a civilising mission, 'the church on the rates', proposals for tariffs that appeared to protect landowners at the expense of the food of the poor and to threaten the competitive position of industry, working-class institutions stripped of their legal protection by an exclusive and unelected House of Lords, all denied the values of even the most moderate Liberalism as well as the accepted canons of economics. Between 1900 and 1906, Conservatism lost the grip it had been acquiring on the political centre which returned to a Liberal party that defended traditional Liberal values. In January 1906 the party won a landslide victory and an independent majority for the first time since 1880 and the last time in its history.

CHAPTER SIX

Welfare, Finance and Freedom

The 1906 election was a disaster for the Conservative party. In the wake of its overwhelming defeat, Sir John Gorst, architect of the Conservative victory of 1874 that initiated the late-nineteenth-century revival, predicted that 'the old Conservative party has gone forever and . . . hereafter the Liberal and Labour parties will divide the supremacy in the state'.[1] The opening months of the 1906 parliament saw a triumphant reassertion of Liberal values: the commitment to free trade was overwhelmingly reaffirmed by 474 votes to 98; Milner, lately high commissioner in South Africa, was censured for his endorsement of 'Chinese slavery' and Liberal principles on empire re-established by the grant of responsible government to the Transvaal. From the first, however, the Liberal domestic programme ran into serious difficulties. That programme reflected the nature of the Liberal majority and the debts the party had incurred. Trade union demands were met by the Trades Disputes Act which restored the privileged position that the legal decisions of the 1890s had removed, and by the extension of employers' liability in a further Workmen's Compensation Act. The former was a Labour measure adopted by Campbell-Bannerman who threw over the proposals of his own law officers, W.S. Robson and J. Lawson Walton. Both major parties viewed the political arrival of organised Labour with some concern, and Balfour deliberately avoided confrontation by allowing labour and social reform legislation to pass unhindered through the Conservative-dominated House of Lords.

No such delicacy was shown towards the major measure of the 1906 session, the education bill with which the government

---

1. José F. Harris and Cameron Hazlehurst, 'Campbell-Bannerman as prime minister', *History* 55 (185) (1970), 375.

attempted to meet the grievances of the Nonconformists, some 200 of whom were nominally ranged behind Perks in the Non-conformist Parliamentary Council although only 70 or 80 were active.[2] Balfour had decided in 1906 that the Unionist party should still control 'whether in power or in Opposition, the destinies of this great empire',[3] and the education bill was so badly mauled by the Lords that it had to be abandoned. Unlike labour legislation, the quarrel between church and chapel was a familiar nineteenth-century battlefield where the Lords and the Unionist party rightly felt secure. Further attempts to legislate on education in 1907 and 1908 were abandoned when no compromise could be found between the feuding denominations. Attempts to deal with licens-ing were no more successful. The bill promised in 1907 was never introduced, and that of 1908 was rejected by an unrepentant upper house.

Social reform: the renewal of Liberalism

Apart from labour legislation, the Liberals' main successes were in the field of social reform. This was regarded, not always correctly, as a 'labour' issue by both major parties, and was thus partially exempt from the Lords' veto, but the reforms did not amount to a committed, coherent or distinctive Liberal policy. The eight-hour day for coal miners, so hotly debated in the early 1890s, was finally achieved in 1908, a year later than initially promised and too late to dissuade the Miners Federation of Great Britain from trans-ferring its considerable support to the Labour party. The provision of school meals, proposed by the Unionist-appointed Interdepart-mental Committee on Physical Deterioration in the wake of the Boer war, was enacted as a result of a Labour initiative and was only permissive. The inclusion of school medical inspection in the Education (Administrative Provisions) Act of 1907 stemmed from the efficiency-minded permanent secretary at the board of education, Sir Robert Morant. The government itself, battered by Unionist opposition and the Lords veto, was tentative even on social reform. The Children Act of 1908, setting up juvenile courts and provid-ing safeguards for children at home was, despite its innovations,

2. Stephen Koss, *Nonconformity in Modern British Politics* (London: Batsford, 1975), pp. 77–8.
3. Roy Jenkins, *Mr Balfour's Poodle* (London: Heinemann, 1954), pp. 18–19.

presented defensively as a consolidating measure to avoid parliamentary confrontation.[4]

The most important social reform of Campbell-Bannerman's ministry came through the exchequer. Asquith met the expectation of reduced military expenditure in 1906, and subsequently not only reduced tea and sugar duties but secured a healthy surplus which allowed him to set aside the money for old-age pensions in 1907, and introduce them in 1908 on what he believed was a sound financial basis. Old-age pensions were hardly a controversial innovation by 1907, and indeed Asquith regarded their coming as inevitable, but their realisation had been bedevilled by conflicting interests, disputes between contributory and non-contributory systems and concern about the expense. Abandoning the contradictions of a contributory insurance system that would be affordable to the working classes, acceptable to the friendly societies and immediate in application by adopting a simple non-contributory system paid from general taxation cut the gordian knot, but at some financial risk.

The budget of 1907 found the money required by increasing the incidence of death duties and differentiating between earned and unearned income for income-tax purposes. New Liberals, who were coming close to describing the government's record as a 'failure', took heart from Asquith's 'brilliant budget' which was claimed to typify 'New Liberal finance', even if it did not rest on Hobson's argument that all high incomes were substantially socially rather than individually earned and could be taxed as 'social property'. In such arguments, and in the extension of Asquith's modest steps towards higher direct taxation on the rich, lay the way forward for a Liberal party apparently moving from traditional Radicalism to 'social democracy'. To meet the challenge, Balfour re-orientated tariff reform towards domestic rather than imperial politics during 1907, emphasising its revenue-raising capacity as the alternative to Liberal 'socialism'. As it became clear that Asquith had greatly underestimated the costs of old-age pensions, so the controversial component of 'social politics' increasingly revolved around the alternative policies of direct and indirect taxation.

During 1907 and 1908, as a result of the activities of the Lords and its own lack of enterprise, the government had little positive domestic legislation to show for three years in office, despite its huge majority. Rather, it was coming to resemble the previous

4. Bernard Wasserstein, *Herbert Samuel: A Political Life* (Oxford: Oxford University Press, 1992), p. 107.

Liberal administration of 1892–5, when the Liberal pessimists spoke of 'ploughing the sands' and Liberal optimists of 'filling the cup', sending measures to the Lords for rejection until public resentment had reached sufficient heights to overflow into an anti-Lords campaign. The difficulty in 1908, as in 1895, was that in the judicious exercise of their powers, the Lords had not spilled a drop. In June 1907, Campbell-Bannerman easily carried a resolution that the powers of the Lords should be restricted so that 'within the limits of a single Parliament the final decision of the Commons shall prevail',[5] but the government had not yet proposed the measures that would provoke a popular outcry.

The steady loss of by-elections from the autumn of 1906, accelerated by the short but deep recession from 1907–9, suggested the reverse, that the government was faltering badly. The resurgence of tariff reform as a dynamic response to the economic downturn sharpened Liberal and popular awareness that the party was becalmed, and in danger of being left behind. Labour gains, though fewer than those of the Unionists, were even more dramatic because of Labour's recent arrival as a parliamentary force. Pete Curran's victory in a three-cornered contest at Jarrow seemed to demonstrate that Labour no longer needed a Liberal alliance; Victor Grayson's in Colne Valley that an avowed socialist lacking official Labour endorsement could nevertheless take a formerly safe Liberal seat. Both victories were the result of protest votes, and both seats were regained in the general elections of 1910, but in the midst of a sharp depression with rising unemployment and increasing demands for revenue to meet the costs of social reform, by-election defeats suggested the decline of working-class support and the force of Unionist criticism of free trade both as an economic and a fiscal policy. Both boded ill for a Liberal government frustrated but apparently rendered impotent by the selective obstruction of the Lords.

The Cabinet reshuffle that followed Campbell-Bannerman's resignation in April 1908 accentuated the importance of 'social politics', most obviously by the promotion of Lloyd George to the exchequer and Churchill to Lloyd George's old post at the board of trade. Ambitious newcomers with careers to make, Lloyd George and Churchill brought to the Liberal government a combative dynamism that the government had hitherto lacked. Neither was

5. John Wilson, *CB: A Life of Sir Henry Campbell-Bannerman* (London: Constable, 1973), p. 563.

constrained by the intellectual baggage of traditional Liberalism. Rather, as Reginald McKenna, nominally Lloyd George's ministerial colleague, observed privately to Balfour over dinner, 'you disagree with us, but you can understand our principles. Lloyd George doesn't understand them and we can't make him.'[6] Churchill showed a greater understanding of the ideas of the New Liberalism, if not the old. His letter to the *Nation* in March 1908 on 'the untrodden field in politics' expounded the idea of the 'minimum standard', and in December he sent Asquith an outline programme to realise such a policy, under-pinning 'the existing voluntary agencies by a comprehensive system – necessarily at a lower level – of state action'. The first three of his 'steps' – '1. Labour Exchanges and Unemployed Insurance; 2. National Infirmity Insurance etc: 3. Special Expansive State Industries – Afforestation – Roads:'[7] – formed a central part of the Liberal social programme of the next three years.

Like Lloyd George, who saw in the old-age-pensions legislation that he took over from Asquith a measure 'that appealed straight to the people' and would 'help to stop this electoral rot',[8] Churchill saw social reform not only as desirable in itself, but as a policy which would revive the flagging fortunes of the party. During 1908, Churchill and Lloyd George were thinking on similar, if unoriginal, lines about insurance schemes to protect the working, respectable poor against the impact of temporary unemployment. In the debate on the old-age-pensions bill, Lloyd George stressed that this was an 'incomplete' solution which not only did not deal with 'all the unmerited destitution in the country' but left untouched what he saw as 'the worst part of that problem', the 'young man who is broken down and who has a wife and family to maintain' so that 'the suffering is increased and multiplied'.[9] Churchill in turn recommended to Asquith that they should 'thrust a big slice of Bismarckianism over the whole underside of our industrial system'.[10]

The celebrated 'people's budget' of 1909 was thus a response to specific fiscal requirements and was shaped more by political than economic calculations. By extending the principle of differentiation and attempting to tax socially created wealth, the budget appealed in particular to New Liberals. Yet it was not an ideological budget.

6. Austen Chamberlain, *Politics from Inside* (London: Cassell, 1936), p. 87.

7. Randolph S. Churchill, *Winston S. Churchill: Companion Volume* vol. 2:2 (London: Heinemann, 1969), p. 863.

8. Bentley B. Gilbert, *David Lloyd George: A Political Life* (London: Batsford, 1987), p. 337.

9. Ibid. p. 339.   10. Churchill, *Churchill*, p. 863.

As Hobson recognised, 'no conscious theory of taxation but sheer political necessity has driven the Liberal party along the road which many of its members treat [*sic* ?tread] reluctantly'.[11] It would have been rash to expect otherwise with Lloyd George at the exchequer. His failure to secure a reduction in either Haldane's army estimates or McKenna's navy estimates, together with Asquith's under-estimation of the real cost of old-age pensions created a serious deficit for the coming year, aggravated by the decline in the yield in indirect taxes as a result of the trade depression. The party was in the doldrums, losing by-elections to the left and the right, unable to pass its major measures and devoid of new policy initiatives. Despite the desire of both Asquith and Lloyd George as chancellors to meet the cost of social reform by reductions elsewhere, most notably in defence, the Liberal party had in practice shifted from the Gladstonian tradition to become a party of interventionist rather than minimal government, and in consequence of expenditure rather than retrenchment.

The 1909 budget marked another, long, stride in this long-term adjustment. Lloyd George sought not simply to balance the books for the coming year, but to produce a surplus for several years to provide for further measures of social reform. These included the labour exchanges which Churchill introduced in 1909, and the far more extensive national insurance proposals currently under consideration. As such, the budget was designed explicitly to meet the challenge of tariff reform, and demonstrate that, contrary to tariff-reform assertions, social reform could be financed within the free-trade system. At the same time the budget served as a possible vehicle for circumventing the House of Lords, especially by increasing licensing and spirit duties to achieve the temperance objectives thwarted by the rejection of the government's licensing bills. Lloyd George was in fact delighted rather than 'disturbed by the fate of the Licensing Bill . . . as he was looking forward to taxing the trade',[12] a shrewd reaction since much of his extra revenue came from that source rather than his innovative and controversial taxes on land. These, however, had a broader social purpose, providing a mechanism by which it was hoped to force undeveloped land on to the market and ease the urban housing problem.

Land taxation, which Asquith had initially investigated, also rallied a powerful section of the left, the Land Values Group, which

---

11. Peter Clarke, *Liberals and Social Democrats* (Cambridge: Cambridge University Press 1978), p. 115.

12. Lord Riddell, *More Pages from My Diary* (London: Country Life, 1934), p. 10.

included some 280 Liberal and Labour MPs, over 240 of whom had signed a petition presented by Wedgwood in November 1908 in favour of land values taxation.[13] They represented the steady expansion of a Liberal tradition that went back to Henry George's campaigns of the 1880s and Chamberlain's unauthorised campaign, and in a more general sense to the attacks of Cobden and Bright on the landed aristocracy. The land, as Hobhouse argued in 1907, was 'the true battleground for a struggle with the Lords'. The budget's land taxes, 20 per cent on the 'unearned increment' charged when the land changed hands, and 1/2d. in the £ on the capital value of undeveloped land, were minor in their immediate application, but opened the way for land valuation and a thoroughgoing onslaught on the 'land monopoly'. In this respect the budget was the culmination of almost a century of Liberal confrontation with 'feudalism' in both its constitutional and its social aspects, and was likely to provoke the Lords into extreme action, even though Lloyd George 'ridiculed the rumour that the Peers would or could interfere with the Budget'.[14]

Increases in income tax and death duties were similarly politically shaped. The Liberals were well aware of the dangers of increasing the already heavily taxed lower middle classes, and the budget of 1909 was carefully framed to protect incomes of less than £2000 a year. Instead, graduation, with an increase in the top rate from 1/– to 1/2d. and a super-tax of 6d. on incomes over £5000, attempted to shift the burden to the rich as part of the broader objective of redistributing taxation from the poorer to the richer, from indirect to direct taxation, from earned to unearned incomes and from productive to what was considered unproductive wealth. Political considerations also militated against overtly increasing the tax burden on the working classes. Asquith had in 1907 reduced tea and sugar duties as taxes on working-class necessities; Lloyd George, seeking more revenue from indirect taxation, increased beer and tobacco duties as luxury taxes.

The incorporation of elements of social reform, and the pursuit of finance for further social reform, moved Liberal policies towards the area where the Lords had shown the greatest reluctance to intervene, and opened the way for legislative progress that had been so lacking in the previous two years. At the same time, as a budget that made possible 'implacable warfare against poverty and

13. Bruce K. Murray, *The People's Budget* (Oxford: Oxford University Press, 1980), pp. 46–7, 102.
14. Riddell, *More Pages*, p. 10.

squalidness',[15] it was intended to make a direct appeal to the working classes. Insofar as he still wished to retain traditional Liberal supporters from the middle classes, Lloyd George looked to traditional Liberal causes. As he told Robertson Nicoll, influential editor of the Nonconformist *British Weekly*, it was up to Nonconformity to bring the middle classes into the Liberal fold.[16] The budget sustained the moral coalition that was Liberalism and avoided explicit class confrontation by singling out so-called 'unearned' and 'unproductive' wealth, rather than reproductive capital. The confusion of the constitutional position of the House of Lords with the economic and social position of the landlord, and the special place that landed 'feudalism' occupied in Liberal demonology, simplified the appeal to traditional Liberalism, which grew stronger as the possibility of rejection became more likely during the summer of 1909.

Lloyd George's speeches against the Lords at Limehouse and Newcastle in the summer of 1909 were thus populist, emphasising the democratic aspects of the 'people's budget', in a 'peers versus the people' campaign. At Newcastle in October he echoed less poetically Chamberlain's 'lilies of the field' speech, asking whether the opinion of '500 men, ordinary men chosen accidentally from among the unemployed' should override the judgement of the electorate: 'who ordained that the few should have the land of Britain as a perquisite; who made 10,000 people owners of the soil, and the rest of us trespassers in the land of our birth?'[17] This was still historic, biblical Radicalism in the tradition of John Ball, not, despite Unionist allegations, class warfare. Unionist criticism of the budget as 'socialism' enhanced its left-wing image, but reduced the positive side of Unionist policy to arguments against the taxation of wealth and capital, accentuating the image of the Conservatives as the party of wealth, privilege and property.

The budget was a resounding success in meeting its immediate objectives. Politically, the Liberal party was revitalised; whatever the Lords did, the budget, as a direct attack on their constitutional, social and economic supremacy, appeared to open up both the immediate and longer-term future for Liberalism. Rejection in November 1909 offered an election against a traditional enemy with new weapons and the moral conviction that in their exclusive

15. Murray, *People's Budget*, p. 120.   16. Ibid. p. 238.
17. Herbert Du Parcq, *Life of David Lloyd George*, vol. 4 (London: Caxton Publishing Company, n.d.), p. 696.

selfishness the Lords had overstepped the mark and flouted constitutional conventions. Despite its limitations and Hobson's own
coolness, New Liberals linked it directly to Hobsonian doctrine.[18]
New Liberal enthusiasm was as much combative as ideological. The
Nation had throughout 1908 stressed the importance of fiscal means
to further progressive policies. After three years of domination by
the Lords, met with ineffectual resolutions and speeches without
action, it was the sense that the Liberal government had bitten the
bullet and that Liberalism was once again moving that heartened
progressive opinion most. Although the Liberal chief whip, J.A.
Pease, was unwilling to make further concessions on seats, Lloyd
George was reassured by both Keir Hardie and Ramsay MacDonald,
and the Labour party rallied to the 'progressive alliance' and support of the budget. Moreover, the budget was also a fiscal success.
Lloyd George succeeded in gaining his surplus not simply for a
year, but for several years; not until 1914 was he again obliged to
go looking for money.

Social reform: political complications

Nevertheless, success was not achieved without some cost. The
majority of the cabinet regarded the budget with deep suspicion,
and only accepted it, with some modifications, for lack of any alternative. The gloomy feeling that Liberalism had nowhere to go lurked
constantly throughout the last Liberal administrations, even at the
highest levels. Within the parliamentary party, there was a substantial body of opinion that believed that in any case, the budget was
steering the party in the wrong direction. Throughout the summer,
as the budget was under discussion, there were rumblings of a
backbench revolt of 'moderate' Liberal MPs which the whips had
some difficulty in containing, and only then by summoning special
meetings to argue the budget's case. Just as the budget moved the
party in the direction of newer Liberalism, so the revolt against it
represented doubts not merely about the budget but about the
whole trend of party policy. The core of the opposition was the
rump of the Liberal League, led, inconstantly as always, by Rosebery.
Negotiations between disaffected Liberals and equally disaffected
Unionist free traders had begun even before the introduction of
the budget for the formation of a new self-styled 'moderate' Centre

18. Clarke, *Liberals and Social Democrats*, p. 115.

Party in opposition to both Liberal 'socialism' and Conservative 'protection'. Ultimately only two MPs, both with brewing interests, voted against the third reading of the 1909 budget, but an exceptional number of Liberal 'moderates', including Perks, retired at the general election of January 1910, and one, Harold Cox, appropriately secretary of the diehard non-interventionist Cobden Club, stood as an anti-budget independent.

In the general election of January 1910 which followed from the Lords' rejection of the budget, the Liberals lost the south-east and the suburbs, but retained the Celtic fringe, the industrial north and London. Contemporaries and historians alike have interpreted this regional distribution of the major parties in class terms, and in those terms, the Liberals were ceasing to be the party of the middle classes, but crucially without becoming the sole party of the working classes. It had been clear for some time that competition between Liberal and Labour could give victory to the Unionists on a minority vote, the latest example being the Bermondsey by-election in October 1909.[19] Working together, Liberal and Labour reinforced each other. Within the still severely restricted franchise of the pre-war period, the two parties combined could bring out the skilled working- and lower-middle-class vote for a common cause. Allied with Celtic nationalism, itself not without a tinge of class identity in Scotland and Wales, this was sufficient to give the Liberals a narrow victory in both of the elections of 1910, January and December.

It was, however, a narrow victory which destroyed the Liberal party's independent majority, the last it ever enjoyed, and left the government reliant, as in 1886 and 1892, on Irish votes. Relations between the government and the Irish party had steadily deteriorated since the end of 1906, with Irish dissatisfaction being responsible for the withdrawal of the government's Irish councils bill in 1907 and Redmond's refusal to advise Irish electors to support Churchill in the north-west Manchester by-election in 1908.[20] The spirit duties of the 1909 budget antagonised the Irish still further, and a minority broke completely with the Liberals and followed Healy and O'Brien into open opposition. Only the certainty that the Liberal party would deliver Home Rule could keep the Irish loyal and induce them to support the 1909 budget. This, in turn, ensured that the Liberals would finally confront the House of Lords.

19. Murray, *People's Budget*, p. 207.
20. Peter Rowland, *The Last Liberal Governments*, vol. 1 (London: Barrie & Rockliff, 1968), pp. 140, 154–5.

The government's position at the start of 1910 was extremely difficult, though no more difficult than that of the opposition. Despite Liberal assertions during the election that they would not take office without guarantees for the passage of future legislation, the king refused such guarantees without a second election. Moreover, insofar as the election of January 1910 had been a referendum on the budget forced by the Lords, and the Irish party was opposed to the budget, then the election had, in fact, returned an anti-budget majority. Only the priorities of the Irish, which placed Home Rule above all else, kept the Liberals in power. Negotiations with the Irish ended with an agreement that the government would introduce its policy to remove the Lords' absolute veto as a resolution to be embodied in legislation after the passage of the budget. On this basis, the Irish swallowed their reservations, and the budget of 1909 was finally passed in April 1910.

Confrontation with the Lords and the second general election was delayed by the death of Edward VII and the general desire to spare his successor, George V, the awkwardness of royal intervention in a constitutional crisis at the start of his reign. The ensuing constitutional conference of four leading figures from the Unionist and Liberal parties met throughout the summer without resolving the crisis. Home Rule, on which no compromise was possible, lurked behind all discussion of Lords' reform and compelled confrontation between the major parties. The Unionist claim that the government still held power only because of a 'corrupt bargain' with the Irish that distorted the verdict of the January election contained an element of truth, and added to the bitterness that characterised politics in the pre-war years. It was, nevertheless, an inevitable consequence of the emergence of a multi-party system from the disintegration of the mid-Victorian Liberal coalition. For all that the multi-party system usually functioned in a two-party manner, the independent Liberal majority of 1906–10 was the aberration after 1885, and the Liberal party was rarely able to determine its own priorities, or even its own policies.

It was an indication of both Lloyd George's detachment from traditional Liberalism and his executive approach to politics that was to become more apparent during the war that, as the conference faltered, he proposed a coalition of the two major parties to circumvent both the deadlock between them and the Irish stranglehold on British politics. His memorandum of August 1910 emphasised the urgent need to tackle major deficiencies in British society that would otherwise fall foul of party-political conflict, by-passing the most controversial issues, and suggesting a royal commission on tariff reform with the implication of action if the commission reported favourably. The proposed coalition, however, was directed not only against the Irish, but against the more extreme sections of the major parties, and Balfour rejected the idea out of hand, not only because of its own intrinsic difficulty, but for the sake of party unity. On the Liberal side not only Churchill, who was no less unconventional than Lloyd George, but Asquith's closest colleagues, Crewe and Grey, saw merits in the scheme – as, according to Lloyd George, did Asquith, even though he was to be relegated to the Lords. The interest shown by leading Liberals was another indication of the degree to which the Liberal party had become dependent upon its non-traditional and even illiberal elements. Thus Crewe thought the party had 'got not far from the end of our tether as regards the carrying of large reforms' and Grey foresaw 'the break-up of the Liberal party and a time of political instability, perhaps of chaos' if the conference failed, as it did.[21]

Lloyd George saw the future somewhat differently, but no more optimistically. As he told the newspaper magnate, Lord Riddell, in 1912, 'I have two alternatives to propose – the first is to form a coalition, settle the old outstanding questions, including Home Rule, and govern the country on middle lines acceptable to both parties, but providing measures of moderate social reform. The other is to formulate and carry through an advanced land and social reform policy.'[22] Coalition was not an isolated response to the special circumstances of 1910, but a central element in Lloyd George's political thinking well before the outbreak of war. The radical alternative would move the Liberal party dramatically in the direction of 'liberal socialism', and in electoral terms require much greater cooperation with the Labour party, and reciprocally, the abandonment of the suburbs and the great majority of the middle classes. Few, it seemed, saw much future for the Liberal party as it was.

For the immediate future, Lloyd George proceeded with the planned instalment of moderate social reform, compulsory national insurance, introduced in 1911. The general election of December 1910 that followed the break-up of the constitutional conference confirmed the result of the previous January and left the Liberals in power with Irish support. But despite the bitterness that surrounded the passage of the Parliament Act limiting the Lords to a

21. Alan Sykes, *Tariff Reform in British Politics 1903–13* (Oxford: Oxford University Press, 1979), p. 230.
22. Riddell, *More Pages*, p. 77.

suspensory veto with the threat of Home Rule to follow, party disagreement over the insurance bill was limited. For health insurance, the bill required contributions of 4d., 3d. and 2d. weekly from the employee, the employer and the state covering all workmen earning below £160 p.a., recorded by stamps on insurance cards. This '9d. for 4d.' as Lloyd George proclaimed it, would entitle insured workers to 10/– weekly for thirteen weeks and 5/– weekly for a further thirteen weeks, together with medical treatment from doctors employed by the approved societies. There were reduced contributions and benefits for employed women, and the option of joining the scheme for better-paid workers who would, however, have to make up the employer's contribution. The scheme was administered by local health authorities, supervised by a national insurance commission.

Unemployment insurance was considerably more limited, applying only to specific trades liable to seasonal fluctuation: in particular, building, shipbuilding and engineering. Contributions were 2.5d. weekly from employee and employer, and 1d. from the state, entitling the unemployed worker to 7/– (6/– in the building trades) per week for fifteen weeks. Administration was through the labour exchanges which, Churchill claimed, provided a character test since application there indicated a willingness to work.[23] The principle of insurance was not contentious in the party-political sense, but rather the reverse. Austen Chamberlain, as shadow chancellor of the exchequer, thought the unemployment provisions 'hazardous, tentative, incomplete and probably bad', but the sickness scheme was 'a good one' and he envied Lloyd George his opportunity.[24] As with old-age pensions, the difficulty lay in squaring the various interests, an area where Lloyd George's talents as an extra-parliamentary fixer came into their own. Compulsory national insurance affected not only the friendly societies, but the doctors and the industrial insurance companies which provided mainly burial benefits. The friendly societies were brought into discussions as early as 1908 and proved amenable to involvement in the state scheme which promised to rescue them from financial disaster as the population steadily aged. The British Medical Association also succumbed to Lloyd George's blandishments, encouraged by the financial pressures upon doctors and hospitals that followed from those of the friendly societies.

23. Rowland, *Last Liberal Governments*, vol. 2, p. 34; Clarke, *Liberals and Social Democrats*, p. 122.
24. Austen Chamberlain, *Politics from Inside*, pp. 336, 338.

The industrial insurance companies had to be bought off. Lloyd George was forced to abandon pensions for widows and orphans which had been a central feature of his plans from the beginning, and to allow the companies to participate in the scheme as 'approved societies' without fundamental alteration to their commercial structure. Much though he disliked the concession, it was not important to him: he regarded insurance as a 'temporary expedient' and, fully imbued with new liberalism, anticipated the day when the 'State will acknowledge a full responsibility in the matter of making provision for sickness, breakdown and unemployment. . . . Gradually the obligation of the State to find labour or sustenance will be realised and honourably interpreted. Insurance will then be unnecessary.'[25] In reality, the National Insurance Act of 1911 was to be the high point of Liberal social legislation. Together with old-age pensions, Asquith felt that the two insurance schemes 'form the largest and most beneficial measure of social reform yet achieved in any country'.[26]

The intended beneficiaries were less convinced. Although non-contributory old-age pensions were widely, although not universally, welcomed, the National Insurance Act was a serious electoral liability. Its passage coincided with the pre-war nadir of the Liberal party between November 1911 and August 1912,[27] but its effect was still being felt much later. It played a prominent role in the loss of Newmarket in May 1913,[28] in G.P. Gooch's defeat at Reading in November 1913, and in both Masterman's defeats in 1914: Bethnal Green in February and Ipswich in April.[29] 'Called to see Masterman,' Riddell recorded in his diary on 24 May, 'he said he should never have been asked to fight Ipswich. Defeat was certain from the first. . . . The result was chiefly due to the Insurance Act.'[30] The problem was the contributory nature of the Act, and more generally the question of compulsory deductions from wages which brought into particularly sharp focus the ambivalent relationship between welfare reform and individual liberty, independence and responsibility.

Social reform: the context

State intervention on the Edwardian scale evoked various responses. All sections of opinion, including the Labour party, made the

25. Rowland, *Last Liberal Governments*, vol. 2, p. 29.   26. Ibid. p. .32.

27. Peter Clarke, 'The electoral position of the Liberal and Labour parties 1910–1914', *English Historical Review* 90 (357) (1975), 833.

28. Ian Packer, 'Lloyd George and the land campaign', in Judith Loades (ed.), *The Life and Times of David Lloyd George* (Bangor: Headstart History, 1991), p. 150.

29. Gilbert, *Lloyd George*, vol. 2, pp. 64, 86.   30. Riddell, *More Pages*, p. 213.

familiar distinction between the 'respectable' poor of honest, sober, thrifty, industrious working men who might, through no fault of their own, be in temporary difficulties, and the 'idle and worthless' residuum. *The Times* in 1906 warned of the slippery slope of ever-extending state welfare which would undermine individual responsibility and create a nation of state dependents. As it rightly pointed out, the logic of the arguments for the provision of school meals led to the provision of clothing, housing and any further necessities that would remove impediments to learning until society grew to expect state provision.[31] The majority report of the Royal Commission on the Poor Law in 1909 attributed the increase in aged paupers since 1900 to the emergence of just such a dependency culture, 'the general feeling that the state is able and willing to make provision and even lavish provision for parents whose sons fail to support them', and required the restoration of filial and family responsibility.[32] In the same vein, the Liberal Old Age Pensions Act of 1908 was means tested on a sliding scale between £21 and £31 10/– annual income and attempted to distinguish between the deserving and undeserving poor by excluding those in receipt of poor relief on or after 1 January 1908, and those who had not attempted to provide for themselves and their families.[33]

Working-class opinion was also often sceptical. The *Cotton Factory Times* was

> anything but enamoured of this growing tendency to enact laws governing the private concerns of workmen. The people who have much done for them gradually lose their backbone ... the result is that the habit of leaning on a support grows stronger until in time there will be no individual strength left. ... If workmen want to insure let them do it themselves. If they wish to provide for their old age, the proper course is to save part of their wages. ... The workman's duty is to combine and see to it that he gets his full share of the produce of his labour, and let him do his own saving if he wishes.[34]

Acceptable reforms were those which empowered the trade unions, such as the Trade Disputes Act. Opposition to national insurance

31. Donald Read, *Documents from Edwardian England* (London: Harrap, 1973), p. 226.

32. D. Collins, 'The introduction of old age pensions into Great Britain', *The Historical Journal* 8 (2) (1965), 249.

33. Ibid. pp. 258–9.

34. Pat Thane, 'The working class and state "Welfare" in Britain 1880–1914', *The Historical Journal* 27 (4) (1984) pp. 885–6.

arose because it removed the worker's control over, and reduced, his disposable income, threatened thereby to make it impossible to continue his trade-union contributions, duplicated one of the unions' main functions, and placed the administration in the hands of outsiders, employers and the state.

Similar objections were levelled against regulatory legislation such as school medical inspection and the 'children's charter', which applied middle-class standards and were enforced by instruments of middle-class oppression: health visitors and police. There was a bitter awareness that such intrusive regulation was applied only to the working classes whilst the middle classes were left alone.[35] 'Man', the Foresters maintained, 'is a responsible being. To rob him of his responsibility is to degrade him.'[36] The Children's Act, intended to make the parent 'more responsible for the wrongdoing of his child' and to protect children in the home, was attacked from one side as the imposition of middle-class standards on families with working-class incomes, and from the other as 'grandmotherly legislation' which reduced individual responsibility and undermined national morality. Both sides were in effect arguing for the same thing; working-class independence entailed working-class responsibility, and vice versa.[37] In addition, employers were concerned about the cost of social reform, and many, led by the Employers' Parliamentary Association, were broadly opposed on economic grounds.[38]

Nevertheless, the majority of Edwardians of all shades of opinion were broadly committed to state intervention. Labour organisations, the TUC, trades councils, the ILP and to lesser extent the cooperative movement advocated low-cost housing, free compulsory education, school meals, old-age pensions, poor-law reform, the eight-hour day, the abolition of 'sweating', minimum wages, health reforms and action to reduce unemployment. Socialists added nationalisation, but this set them apart from the labourism of the majority of the Labour movement, which was wary of both state control and of socialists, and looked to local government as a safer instrument of interventionist progress. The Labour party supported the Liberal party in its reform programme, including the National Insurance Act which divided both the party and the broader Labour

---

35. Ibid. pp. 893–5; Stephen Reynolds, *Seems So: A Working Class View of Politics* (London: Macmillan, 1911), *passim.*

36. Thane, 'Working class and state "welfare"', p. 880.

37. Wasserstein, *Samuel,* pp. 102–8; Reynolds, *Seems So,* pp. 30–9.

38. Roy Hay, 'Employers and social policy in Britain: the evolution of welfare legislation, 1905–14', *Social History* 4 (1977) p. 440.

movement, and went beyond the government in its proposals for the 'right to work'.

Employers in varying degrees supported improved technical education, old-age pensions, labour exchanges, health, and unemployment insurance, although this last was sometimes regarded as aiding indiscipline.[39] They were well aware of the social-control implications of social reform, and the positive function that welfare served in attaching the working class to the capitalist system, providing incentives for the 'deserving' poor and identifying the worthless for 'the sternest measures'. Compulsory evening classes would provide technical education to increase efficiency, but they would also reduce idlers on street corners and inculcate discipline.[40] Labour exchanges, regarded as registries of available labour, could be used to recruit strike-breakers and, if linked to identity cards and work records, which insurance cards threatened to become, acted both as instruments of control and a means of distinguishing those seeking work from the 'worthless', docile workers from 'troublemakers'.[41] State welfare schemes also had the advantage, as labour leaders suspected, of transferring some elements of labour costs from the employer to the state. The extension of employers' liabilities under the Workmen's Compensation Act, which included industrial diseases as well as accidents, made health insurance to which workers contributed extremely attractive, especially if, as in the German example, insurance funded compensation claims.[42]

Conservatives, whilst divided, were no less committed to aspects of state intervention. Tariff reform was the most obvious example of this, but the provision of school meals, school medical inspection and old-age pensions all had Unionist as well as Liberal pedigrees; Milner, as a social-imperialist, shared the concern about juvenile employment that prompted the Education (Choice of Employment) Act of 1910, and although his solution, compulsory military service, was unacceptable to the generality of either Liberals or Conservatives, it struck a chord with his fellow *étatiste*, Lloyd George, who expressed himself privately in favour of national service well before the war.[43] The Unionist party generally welcomed the national insurance bill, and cooperated in the passage of the Miners' Minimum Wages Act. Even a moderate like the fourth Marquess of Salisbury was prepared to consider minimum wages in key industries in return

39. Ibid. pp. 451, 453.   40. Ibid. p. 440 n. 31.
41. Ibid. p. 450; Thane, 'Working class and state "welfare"', p. 898.
42. Hay, 'Employers', pp. 448, 452.
43. Riddell, *More Pages*, pp. 94, 104, 140.

for no-strike agreements, whilst the semi-official Unionist Social Reform Committee produced a variety of reports on poor-law reform, education and housing between 1912 and 1914. Liberal intervention had points of contact with the Unionist party, and particularly its social-imperialist wing. It was this, and the radical authoritarian aspects of New Liberal theory, that gave some degree of reality to Lloyd George's coalition schemes before the war, and the continuation of his wartime coalition after it.

State intervention remained divisive and contentious. The nature, scale, financing and control of interventionist reform were all areas of actual and potential controversy, but the divisions in opinion were not along strict class or party lines. Once they moved into the area of social and economic legislation, all political parties had to tread a narrow line to satisfy the coalition of interests that they sought to represent. As a party that sought to be classless, but relied heavily on working-class votes, the Liberals faced the greatest problems in implementing welfare reform, but they also had the greatest opportunity. Conservatism could exploit class politics to build up a solid core of support amongst property-owners, but the middle classes made up only 25–30 per cent of the electorate.[44] The working classes that made up the other 70–75 per cent were divided by a myriad of distinctions and differentials that emerged most strongly when the state intervened in welfare and industrial questions. Their reactions demonstrated how spurious was the belief that labour was a social or political entity that the Labour party might represent, and thus how reform required more than a sectionalist, materialist appeal if it was to gain general assent. Liberalism with its moral and universalist nucleus had the potential to provide this.

Social reform: the coercive potential

The Liberal problem with labour and interventionist reform lay in its incomprehension of the defensive conservatism of the working classes, their way of life and their mistrust of interference. Having failed to incorporate labour, it remained a party of middle-class outsiders, leaving it open to the accusation that in extending state intervention it was more interested in expanding social control over the working classes than creating opportunities. Keir Hardie

44. Duncan Tanner, *Political Change and the Labour Party* (Cambridge: Cambridge University Press, 1990), p. 119.

regarded both Asquith and Haldane as 'cold-blooded reactionaries of the most dangerous type'[45]; A.G. Gardiner, Liberal editor of the *Daily News*, was more correct when he noted simply that Asquith's 'roots are less deep in the democratic soil', but the suspicion was not groundless. Neither Lloyd George nor Churchill was particularly interested in individual liberty or had much confidence in the working classes' ability to use it.[46] The *Nation* in 1908 believed that 'no pure workman's party can go very far. Middle class brains and training are indispensable to it.'[47] Even the most Radical elements of the Liberal party in its most Radical phase remained elitist.

In moving towards social democracy, Liberalism ceased to aspire to a pluralist liberal democracy. Instead, New Liberalism reinforced the ever-present elitism of the liberal outlook. 'Poverty' in the hands of Rowntree, whose study of York, *Poverty: A Study of Town Life* (1901) greatly influenced the Edwardian attitude to deprivation, was an abstraction expressed in statistics, not a way of life to be endured by ordinary men and women. New Liberalism did indeed seek 'increased material welfare for those who labour with their hands', but it did so 'not that they may seize upon a few more coarse enjoyments but that they may enter upon a purer and higher life'.[48] 'The state', Herbert Samuel told the progressive intellectuals of the Rainbow Circle, 'exists to promote the best life of its members rather than their happiness, if by "happiness" we mean their pleasure as judged at the moment by themselves.'[49] Their concept of the minimum level of welfare went beyond mere subsistence to include 'ample opportunities of recreation', but the idea of 'art, music, travel, education, social intercourse',[50] whilst it might include brass bands and choral singing, was unlikely to extend to working-class whippets or proletarian pigeons.

In 1911, when he had been a leading exponent of welfare reform for three years, Churchill rather belatedly asked Riddell what the masses were interested in. 'I said "Earning their living and football." I told him about the immense sales of the football editions and the great interest in pigeon racing. I mentioned that on some Saturdays in the summer £2,000,000 worth of birds were in the air.

45. Wilson, *Campbell-Bannerman*, p. 506.   46. Riddell, *More Pages*, p. 132.
47. Clarke, *Liberals and Social Democrats*, p. 140.
48. Peter Weiler, *The New Liberalism: Liberal Social Theory in Great Britain 1889–1914* (London: Garland, 1982), p. 35.
49. Michael Freeden (ed.), *Minutes of the Rainbow Circle 1894–1924* Camden 4th Series Royal Historical Society (1989) p. 88.
50. Michael Freeden, *The New Liberalism: An Ideology of Social Reform* (Oxford: Oxford University Press, 1978), p. 71.

He said, "I must tell the Prime Minister about the pigeons."' Riddell also had to disabuse him of the likelihood that the working classes would want to be rehoused from their slums in 'fine blocks of dwellings with central cooking and heating, swimming baths etc. . . . I responded "I think most people prefer a comfortable little house of their own. They don't like being herded together, nor do they like interference and dictation." '[51] As C.F.G. Masterman noted, 'All that the poor want . . . is to be left alone.' But as he also noted, 'Many who are conscious that the poor want to be left alone are not convinced that they ought to be left alone.'[52]

Even to this best-intentioned of Liberals, working-class culture remained hidden, alien and somewhat dangerous. In *The Condition of England*, Masterman wrote of 'the city Crowd' with its 'note of menace . . . the evidence of possibilities of violence in its wayward-ness, its caprice, its always incalculable mettle and temper' and 'more than the menace, the overwhelming impression . . . of inepti-tude; a kind of life grotesque and meaningless'. He contrasted this aggregated personality with those of its component individuals, in whom 'is resistance, courage, aspiration, a persistence which carries through the daily task with some energy and some enjoyment . . . immediately the mass of separate persons has become welded into the aggregate, this note of distinction vanishes. Humanity has become the Mob.'[53] His image of 'the "City type"' as 'a new race hitherto unreckoned and of incalculable action', prone to 'hooli-ganism, and a certain fickle excitability of temper',[54] expressed a rejection both of urban man and the environment that created him.

Rowntree, another member of Lloyd George's 'brains trust' in the years before the war, similarly lamented the physical and moral deterioration that occurred through urbanisation. 'The town dweller . . . suffers from living too quickly and living in a crowd. His opinions are the opinions of the crowd – and a crowd is easily swayed.'[55] Both he and Masterman looked fondly back to an 'Eng-land of the past . . . an England of reserved silent men, dispersed in small towns, villages and country homes . . . reared amidst the fresh air and quieting influences of the life of the fields'.[56] Liberalism

51. Riddell, *More Pages*, p. 22.
52. C.F.G. Masterman, *The Condition of England* (London: Methuen, 1911 edn), pp. 101–2.
53. Ibid. pp. 105–6.
54. C.F.G. Masterman 'Heart of Empire', in Read, *Documents*, p. 23.
55. B.S. Rowntree, and May Kendall, 'How the labourer lives: a study of the rural labour problem', in ibid. p. 22.
56. Masterman in ibid. p. 23.

never fully came to grips with the mass culture of urbanised, indus-trialised Britain. Industrial towns, once sources of pride to Victorian Radicals and industrialists, became objects of fear from which to escape, their remaining inhabitants resembling the Morlocks who emerged from their caverns to prey upon the surface-dwelling Eloi in H.G. Wells's parable, *The Time Machine.*

New Liberal intellectuals elaborated this distrust of the masses into a theory of government that became, despite its name and intentions, actually or potentially authoritarian. As the embodiment of the 'common good', the state had the right and the responsibil-ity to intervene to prevent oppression, whether of one individual by another, or of one class by another. 'The first condition of univer-sal freedom', as L.T. Hobhouse noted in his New Liberal textbook, *Liberalism*, published in 1911, 'is a measure of universal restraint' through the impartial operation of the law.[57] In this thinking, the state acted as a referee between competing interests, including economic interests whether of trade unions or employers or both, for the benefit of society as a whole.[58]

By incorporating a social and economic dimension lacking in traditional Liberalism, New Liberal interventionism did, as New Liberals argued, extend liberty. But New Liberalism went further than this, deriving from its organic concept of society the right of the state to intervene to regulate individual behaviour, despite the wishes of the individual, for the benefit of both the individual him-self and the social whole of which he was a part. New Liberalism subordinated the individual to social development no less thor-oughly than social-imperialism subordinated him to the pursuit of national power. 'A right', according to Hobhouse, 'is nothing but what the good of society makes it. . . . If therefore any right to any form of property or freedom no longer serves a good social purpose, it must go.'[59] Compulsory national insurance was an instalment in forcing people to be free.

This rejection of the rights of the individual against the state followed from the internalisation of the tension between liberty and oppression. In striving to encourage the 'higher', socially motivated, and therefore rational and free, aspect of individual character, and to repress individual selfishness, New Liberals sought

---

57. L.T. Hobhouse, *Liberalism* (1911; 1964 edn Oxford: Oxford University Press), p. 17.
58. David Powell, 'The New Liberalism and the rise of Labour 1886–1906', *The Historical Journal* 29 (2) (1986), 384.
59. Clarke, *Liberals and Social Democrats*, p. 27.

in legislation the same ends as the Whigs, the transformation of character itself by creating conditions in which the individual was required to be socially virtuous. Liberty was redefined as the opportunity to become. What the individual was to become was what society decided was 'a good social purpose', but the individual could not disagree with that without being irrational. Liberation meant not freeing the individual as he was, with all his faults, but in transforming the individual into someone else.

The horrors of New Liberalism were less apparent in its measures to assist the rationally capable to play their part in the fulfilment of the social purpose through interventionist welfare reform, than in proposals to deal with those whose capacity was in doubt, or for whom there was no social role. Beveridge, Churchill's adviser on unemployment, accepted that ideally the industrial system should find 'room . . . for everyone who desired to enter [and] in which everyone who did find a place should obtain average earnings'. But not only would 'those men who through general defects . . . must become the acknowledged dependents of the state' lose 'all citizen rights – including not only the franchise but civil freedom and fatherhood', but 'those . . . who may be born personally efficient, but in excess of the number for whom the country can provide' would face the choice of 'loss of independence by entering a public institution, emigration, or immediate starvation'. This was not the elimination of those who could not meet a test of 'industrial efficiency', but the elimination of those who, although efficient in themselves, were not efficient in serving society's ends as defined by the state.[60]

Because the 'social' or 'common' good, and the 'social', 'common' or 'general' will rested, like the Whig vision of good legislation, on an assumed objective ethical standard, their realisation might be against the apparent interests not only of some individuals, efficient or inefficient, but a majority. 'The interests of every man', according to Hobhouse, 'are no doubt in the end bound up with the welfare of the whole community . . . but the direct and calculable benefit of the majority may by no means coincide with the ultimate good of society as a whole',[61] at which point the majority was repressed. In evading the tyranny of the majority, New Liberalism contained the potential for the tyranny of the minority. Elitism was the necessary result of defining liberty qualitatively. New Liberals and their moderately socialist associates like Ramsay MacDonald constantly

60. Freeden, *New Liberalism*, pp. 184–5.   61. Ibid. p. 14.

reasserted their commitment to democracy and the individual while the ideas they elaborated redefined both to the point where they faded into insubstantial shadows.

The New Liberal ideal of the state as an objective ethical construct standing above politics fell foul of the reality that state intervention was part of the political process. In the political game, the state was not the referee, but the ball for which the rival teams competed. The theory might be classless, but the reality could not avoid entanglement in class issues. Libertarian critiques of welfare reform, Stephen Reynolds's *Seems So* and Hilaire Belloc's *The Servile State*, built their arguments around the imposition of middle-class standards upon working-class communities. Belloc stressed the servile implications of compulsory insurance, whereby workers were provided with material benefits, but paid for this with the loss of their liberty, the right to control their own earnings which were not even extracted by state officials, but by their employers who were themselves exempt, and with the loss of their insurance benefits if they were dismissed for misconduct. What the worker wanted, as Reynolds argued, was economic, not social, reform, an increase in wages that preserved choice. Riddell and the Board of Trade's chief industrial negotiator, Sir George Askwith, also understood this. 'I asked him [Askwith]', Riddell recorded, 'whether he did not think the people were determined upon more wages to spend in their own way, and that doles would not satisfy them. He answered, "Yes."'[62]

Welfare reform was not a simple way to revive the Liberal party from its late-nineteenth-century doldrums, despite the successes after 1908. It was fraught with political complications and dangers and bedevilled by elitism. The Liberal party had not escaped the middle-class outlook of the 1890s, and its attitudes to labour whether in welfare reform or local politics remained a combination of condescension and apprehension. In some areas where the local challenge from Labour became significant, local Liberals sought arrangements with local Conservatives, or fought as Independents which often amounted to the same thing. Equally, however, New Liberalism could revitalise local parties. Nor was it necessarily an intellectual trap which destined the Liberal party to be the harbinger of the 'servile state' in conflict with its libertarian past and working-class culture. Greater radicalism, rather than less, offered an alternative, in which the solution to unemployment was neither

62. Riddell, *More Pages*, p. 41.

relief nor insurance, but the 'right to work', and the solution to poverty was not 'state alms' but higher wages which would allow workers to make their own provision for illness and old age.[63] There were signs immediately before the war that despite all its other distractions, Liberalism was heading in this direction.

63. Thane, 'Working class and state "welfare"', p. 880.

CHAPTER SEVEN

Rumours of a Strange Death

Trouble with the legislative expression of New Liberalism and the potential direction of its theories was but one aspect of the problems that appeared to face Liberalism in the years immediately before the First World War. It seemed that the whole character of society was changing as passion and violence replaced the rationalism and consensus that were believed to epitomise liberal England. The campaign for women's suffrage, prosecuted for years by the National Union of Women's Suffrage Societies with that decorum and ineffectuality that were expected of women, was transformed by the aggression of the Women's Social and Political Union. A wave of industrial unrest tinged with syndicalist revolutionary rhetoric, in which troops were encamped in city centres and workers killed, led sober politicians to reach for their revolvers.[1] The Home Rule bill produced a search for greater firepower still, gun-running, an army 'mutiny' and unprecedented support for unconstitutional violence by a Conservative party that once prided itself on constitutionalism and respect for the law.

Contemporaries were bemused. 'The worker', according to H.G. Wells, 'is beginning now to strike for unprecedented ends – against the system, against the fundamental conditions of labour, to strike for no defined ends at all . . . the new-fashioned strike is far less of a haggle, far more of a display of temper.'[2] Suffragette outbreaks were attributed to 'the physiological psychology of woman . . . her periodically recurring phases of hypersensitiveness, unreasonableness and loss of sense of proportion . . . there is mixed up with the

---

1. Austen Chamberlain, *Politics from Inside* (London: Cassell, 1936), p. 444.
2. H.G. Wells, 'What the worker wants', in Donald Read, *Documents from Edwardian England* (London: Harrap, 1912), p. 274.

woman's movement much mental disorder'.[3] Violence in Ireland was much more predictable, although for Liberals perhaps no less easy to understand. The problems of gender, class and nationalism that Georgian Liberalism faced were exacerbated by the Liberal tendency to define rationalism in male, middle-class, English terms. For the government, obliged to maintain order, there was the additional complication of reconciling repressive action with the framework of Liberal attitudes and beliefs. Too much would destroy its Liberal credentials, too little would call into doubt its capacity to govern.

Militant unrest: women and workers

Ironically, much of the militancy between 1911 and 1914 resulted from the frustration of expectations aroused by the first majority Liberal government since 1885 and the dramatic arrival of Labour as a parliamentary force. By 1910, anomalies in the franchise, both male and female, remained unreformed, Home Rule seemed as remote as ever, and, despite the Trades Disputes Act, trade unions battled ineffectively for recognition and against declining real wages in an adverse economic climate. There were tactical difficulties with each of the manifestations of violence that affected both the short- and medium-term future of the party with an election due to be held at the latest by the end of 1915; but political action could, at least in some cases, remove the grievance and the agitation it engendered.

Women's suffrage complicated the question of franchise reform, partly because of the nature of the WSPU's demand for the limited enfranchisement of property-owning women which was expected to reinforce Conservatism, partly because the cabinet was divided. Most significantly, Asquith was strongly opposed in principle. By 1910, pressure had led to the formation of a cross-party 'conciliation committee' and a 'conciliation bill' which proposed the vote for women householders in order to attract the support of pro-suffrage Conservatives without alienating Liberals. In this it failed. Lloyd George thought the bill 'spells disaster to Liberalism'[4] because of its Conservative bias. Even so, the bill secured a substantial majority

3. Sir A.E. Wright, 'The unexpurgated case against woman's suffrage', in ibid. pp. 286–7.
4. David Morgan, *Suffragists and Liberals* (Oxford: Blackwell, 1975), p. 82.

when reintroduced in 1911, and obliged the government, which had thus far avoided the issue, to promise limited time for discussion in 1912 and produce its own alternative.

The government's franchise and registration bill of 1912 proposed manhood suffrage and ostensibly remedied the deficiencies of nineteenth-century reform legislation, simplifying the registration rules and abolishing plural voting which in December 1910 had given the Conservatives some thirty seats.[5] In effect, and probably in intent, it also torpedoed the conciliation bill. The government overcame Liberal divisions, and in particular Asquith's scruples, by promising to allow amendment of the bill to enfranchise women on similarly democratic terms. Seen as an impossibilist tactic to confound the conciliationists since it would create an electorate with a majority of women, the bill was greeted with hostility by the major suffrage organisations and a renewal of militant violence. It was, nevertheless, a skilful ploy. Despite the majority opinion in the Commons for women's suffrage, the party nature of the government's reform bill was likely to divide the House on party lines. However, the speaker's ruling against a women's suffrage amendment rendered such tactics unnecessary. The government withdrew the bill and in 1913 introduced a short bill abolishing plural voting, which had been its primary consideration since the Lords vetoed such a bill in 1906.

By 1914, it was clear that whilst the militant suffrage movement had moved the issue to centre stage, it had not brought the government to its knees, and that continued and intensified violence was having the opposite effect of alienating support. In surviving without acting, the Liberals may be considered successful. But as a party of reform, survival by denying reform was a repudiation of the party's political purpose. The responsibility for this lay almost exclusively with Asquith. The majority of Liberal MPs were in favour; the other leading anti-suffragists, notably Loreburn, the lord chancellor, and Lewis Harcourt, the colonial secretary, were not essential to the government's survival, and the suggested higher age qualification for women removed the potential female majority in the electorate. There were, as Asquith himself virtually confessed in 1914 to a delegation of Sylvia Pankhurst's East End Suffrage Federation, no insuperable reasons except his own prejudice for opposing the democratic enfranchisement of women.

---

5. Duncan Tanner, *Political Change and the Liberal Party* (Cambridge: Cambridge University Press, 1990), p. 450.

There was some risk in resistance. Alienation of moderate suffragists led to their active cooperation with Labour. By 1913 the NUWSS had quadrupled its membership since 1909, and was ready to oppose anti-suffragist Liberals in 156 constituencies.[6] Even the Women's Liberal Federation resolved in 1912 that unless the franchise bill included women's suffrage, amicable relations with the party might become impossible.[7] The maintenance of order led to some dangerously illiberal practices. From 1909, suffragettes responded to imprisonment with hunger strikes, the government with force-feeding, and in 1913 the 'Cat and Mouse' Act which provided for the re-arrest of prisoners released on grounds of ill-health once their health was restored. Moreover, a Conservative victory in 1915 might lead to the passage of the conciliation bill and the vote for pro-Conservative propertied women. The franchise question, both male and female, could not be indefinitely postponed.

Labour unrest after 1910 created the same twin problems of executive action and party policy. The party had not come to terms with a trade union movement which had trebled in membership between 1888 and 1910, and almost doubled again to 4.1 million between 1910 and 1914. After 1910, economic recovery offered an opportunity to reverse a decade or more of falling real wages. Whilst fully fledged syndicalism remained a fringe belief, the strikes of the pre-war years contained an insurgent 'proto-syndicalist mood' which questioned the political as well as the industrial system.[8] To that extent, the labour unrest, which in the peak year of 1912 led to the loss of 41 million working days, was a challenge to the Labour and Conservative parties and the established trade union leadership as well as to the Liberal party. Nevertheless, as the government of the day the Liberals bore the opprobrium when troops were ordered in, and especially when workers were injured or killed, as they were in Tonypandy, Liverpool, Llanelli and Dublin. As the party of 'New Liberalism', there was the additional risk of acquiring the image of the party of class-based 'social control'.

Whilst strikes were widespread in many industries, government intervention was most visible in the major strikes by coal miners, seamen, dockers and railway workers which threatened national security and the distribution of food supplies. Moves towards union

---

6. Morgan, *Suffragists and Liberals*, p. 125.   7. Ibid. pp. 103–4.
8. Bob Holton, *British Syndicalism 1900–1914* (London: Pluto Press, 1976), p. 207; Van Gore, 'Rank and file dissent', in Chris Wrigley (ed.), *A History of British Industrial Relations 1875–1914* (Brighton: Harvester, 1982), p. 69.

consolidation, especially the formation of the Transport Workers Federation and the National Union of Railwaymen; the national character of strikes and strikers' demands; developing inter-union cooperation, most evident in negotiations for a 'triple alliance' between railwaymen, miners and dockers, and frequent sympathy strikes in industries related by trade or locality, brought a new dimension to the scale of labour unrest. The counter-militancy frequently shown by employers in their refusal to negotiate and their resort to blacklegs also aggravated both the violence and the government's dilemma. Direct ministerial intervention offered a short-term solution, and both the rail and London dock strikes were ended in this way in 1911, but in neither case were the basic issues resolved.

Under pressure from the king and the public alike to do something, the government institutionalised this informal brokerage by extending the conciliation structure within the Board of Trade established by the Conciliation Act of 1896. By 1911, the Board had built up a considerable expertise in industrial mediation and gained recognition from trade-union leaders. The establishment of a separate industrial relations department under the experienced George Askwith, and a new industrial council to mediate under his chairmanship, marked a new stage in the evolution of the state as industrial referee. However, the procedure was purely voluntary, and the more radical trade unionists of 1910–14 regarded Board officials with some justification as a 'capitalist set', and the conciliation procedure in general as inimical to the interests of the working classes. Moreover, delegating the problem of labour unrest to civil servants did not sideline the issue politically. The government was obliged to intervene with minimum-wage legislation to end the national coal strike of March 1912, to establish a remarkably ineffectual cabinet committee on industrial unrest in April, and to consider legislation again in the summer to resolve the London dock strike. It was spared this only by the collapse of the strike in the face of the unbending opposition of the employers led by the prominent Liberal, Lord Devonport.

For the Liberal party, industrial conciliation was crucial as a specific application of the policy of the incorporation of the working classes, which was also the object of welfare reform. Liberalism could not accommodate confrontation beyond narrow limits; a 'classless' party required a 'classless' society. The view from below could be different. Despite Liberal aspirations, conciliation could not be dissociated from class antagonism. Syndicalists borrowed heavily from Belloc's 'servile state' analysis of welfare Liberalism, combining the repression of direct action by the police and military with the sapping of independence by welfare legislation into a single state conspiracy to break the trade union movement in the interests of employers.[9] It drew strength from deeper working-class traditions, particularly their libertarian culture. New Liberalism in either its social or industrial forms ran directly up against not coherent class consciousness, but a generalised cultural awareness. True syndicalists were a small minority, unable ever to mount a serious challenge to the official union leadership. But whilst official trade unionism, including the leaders of the triple alliance of 1913, respected Askwith and the conciliation system, they also thought in class and confrontational terms, seeking to use the power of the state to reinforce their own bargaining position against recalcitrant employers, not because they had become servants of a putative classless state.[10]

They were, in any case, under pressure from their followers. The extension of government patronage,[11] the bureaucratisation of trade unions and the incorporation of trade union officials into the state machinery by conciliation created a rift between officials and the rank and file, and distrust of the entire process. The unrest of 1910–14 was marked by unofficial action which union officials not only had difficulty controlling, but of which they were often the first targets. Rank-and-file discontent demonstrated the limits of incorporation as a policy to contain labour, and of the state functioning as a referee.[12] Nor were union radicals without cause. Industrial conciliation boards dominated by middle-class professionals, and decisions made by a middle-class magistracy who applied the criteria of middle-class economics and defended profitability, ensured that awards made through the conciliation procedure were usually less than the unions concerned might have gained by confrontation and direct bargaining without state intervention. The Conciliation Act was, the ILP argued, 'the most effective device by which the trade union movement [had] been humbugged by the dominant class'.[13]

9. Holton, *British Syndicalism*, pp. 137–8, 182–3.

10. Roger Davidson, 'Government administration', in Wrigley, *Industrial Relations*, pp. 171–2.

11. G.R. Searle, *Corruption in British Politics* (Oxford: Oxford University Press, 1987), pp. 227–9.

12. Van Gore, 'Rank and file', pp. 46–70; Holton, *British Syndicalism*, pp. 32–4.

13. Davidson, 'Government administration', pp. 169–71; Van Gore, 'Rank and file', p. 51.

Libertarians, from the Italian anarchist Malatesta on the far left to W.J. Sanderson on the far right, saw in labour unrest the desperate defence of liberal England against a dictatorial government. It was a critical phase in the evolution of the relationship between Liberal party and liberal country. Communal libertarianism had to adjust to the increasingly national scale of society and the enlarged role of the state. Although expressed as a concern for wage rates, conditions, and union recognition, labour unrest was part of a continuing struggle for control that had to become political because the industrial and social structure was ultimately maintained politically. Participation in, or the capture of, the state became essential to the preservation of liberty. Insofar as the Liberals were failing before the First World War, they were failing politically simply because social reform and industrial conflict could not be divorced from politics.[14]

Women and working-class men did not seek reform from above, and had few policy proposals that distinguished them from Liberalism. They sought representation, a presence in parliament to defend their own interests rather than have them interpreted by outsiders. Yet the Liberal party not only denied the vote to women, it was still, as in the 1890s, reluctant to run workers as Liberal candidates, and almost as reluctant to facilitate the return of working-class MPs in any guise. Like the suffragette movement, the labour unrest of 1910–14 was an attempt to coerce the government in the absence of meaningful parliamentary representation. Unlike the suffragette movement, in certain crucial respects it succeeded. In observing that the Coal Mines (Minimum Wage) Act 'may be the knell of the old Liberal party',[15] Lloyd George appreciated the declining autonomy of an unrepresentative parliament and the longer-term significance of government regulation of industry.

Home Rule and Irish militancy

The reintroduction of a Home Rule bill for Ireland also represented the successful coercion of parliament. Liberals believed Home Rule to be a vote loser, but after the elections of 1910 had little choice but to reaffirm their determination to proceed with Home Rule to secure Irish acquiescence in Lloyd George's budget. Morley

---

14. Holton, *British Syndicalism*, pp. 35–6, 137, 176–8.
15. Lord Riddell, *More Pages from My Diary*, (London: Country Life, 1934), p. 49.

was virtually the last representative of Gladstonian commitment in a cabinet which largely shared Asquith's scepticism. The party in parliament and in the constituencies resumed the burden in a mood of dutiful resignation to redeem a pledge given, and to remove an issue which again 'blocked the way', but with little sympathy for the passions which inspired either Irish nationalism or Ulster resistance. Ultimately, Home Rule was to be comprehended within mainland politics, and the governing factor was always its impact on the mainland electorate.

Consequently, the government gave little thought to the drafting of the Home Rule bill that it eventually introduced in April 1912, which closely followed that of 1893 except in the complex financial provisions devised by Samuel. In particular, it made no concessions to Ulster separatism, ignoring both Ulster's violent reaction and the Conservative party's endorsement of Ulster militancy. This was largely, though not entirely, the product of cabinet myopia. Churchill, Lloyd George and Birrell, the Irish secretary, all took Ulster opposition seriously. Lloyd George and Churchill formally proposed the exclusion of Ulster in February 1912 before the introduction of the bill, but the cabinet rejected this course in favour of subsequent amendment if, as Asquith expected, it became necessary as a result either of new evidence or 'the pressure of British opinion'.[16]

Asquith's policy of 'wait and see' had behind it the rationale that if Nationalists and Ulstermen were ever to be brought to compromise, it would only be when faced with the civil-war alternative. But in so doing the government let pass the opportunity to attempt to impose a settlement. An amendment to exclude the four clearly Protestant Ulster counties proposed by the Liberal imperialist backbencher, Thomas Agar-Robartes, was thus rejected in June 1912, despite cabinet divisions. Home Rule for all Ireland was passed by the Commons for the first time in January 1913. The amendment nevertheless revealed serious rifts within the party. As long as the outcome appeared to be the coercion of Ulster, protests came from Liberals sympathetic to Ulster. Agar-Robartes spoke for south-western Liberalism where Methodist hostility to Catholicism remained a potent force. Nonconformists in northern England had similar reservations, as did federalists in Scotland. As the likelihood of concession became greater, so did the danger of rebellion from the other wing of the party, eager to assert Liberal determination

16. Peter Rowland, *The Last Liberal Governments*, vol. 2 (London: Barrie & Jenkins, 1971), p. 163; Patricia Jalland, *The Liberals and Ireland* (Brighton: Harvester, 1980), pp. 58–67.

to fulfil its obligations, afraid of the electoral liability of Home Rule, and opposed to compromise with the Unionist enemy, especially under duress of dubious legality.[17]

By the autumn of 1913, however, the government was wavering as it finally began to realise that violent resistance in Ulster was not just a possibility, but a virtual certainty. Tactically, it had placed itself in a weak position as a result of the failure to take decisive action during 1912. Under the provisions of the Parliament Act, the bill could only be modified during its first parliamentary circuit; after January 1913 the government needed Unionist consent if special provision was to be made for Ulster. The options now left were a negotiated compromise or the forcible coercion of Ulster. Pressure from the king and intrigue by Churchill led to a series of secret talks between Asquith and Bonar Law, and subsequently Asquith and Carson, which provided Asquith with some information on the Unionist position, but were otherwise fruitless. Bonar Law did promise in October 1913 to abide by the results of an election and abandon Ulster if the Liberals won, but this reaffirmation of Unionist policy and constitutional propriety was itself of uncertain value since Bonar Law could not necessarily control his more militant followers even amongst English Conservatives.

Thus far, events had fallen out as Asquith claimed to have expected: 'that in the end we should probably have to make some sort of bargain about Ulster as the price of Home Rule. But I have never doubted that, as a matter of tactics and policy, we were right to launch our Bill on its present lines.'[18] The Liberals, however, still did not have a compromise to propose, nor, after January, the power to enforce acceptance of it. Lloyd George solved the first problem in November by reviving his proposal of February 1912 for the temporary exclusion of Ulster with automatic inclusion in Home Rule Ireland after a number of years. The policy would, as Lloyd George stressed, 'make it impossible for Ulster to take up arms, or if they did, put us in a strong position with British public opinion when we came to suppress it'.[19] Support for this proposal on 13 November marked the defeat of the protagonists of the original bill and Home Rule for all Ireland.

Redmond's reiteration of Nationalist objections to exclusion, and his belief that compromise proposals should only be made at the last minute, nevertheless reinforced Asquith in further delay before

17. Jalland, *Liberals and Ireland*, pp. 87–92, 124–5.
18. Rowland, *Last Liberal Governments*, vol. 2, p. 219.
19. Jalland, *Liberals and Ireland*, p. 167.

announcing the new policy.[20] In the meantime, the government stepped up the pressure on both sides by prohibiting arms imports into Ireland and ruling out a general election before Home Rule passed. Asquith's third meeting with Bonar Law in December was accordingly unproductive, as was his subsequent meeting with Carson. Both rejected Asquith's proposal of 'veiled exclusion': Ulster representation in a Dublin parliament with the right to contract out of its legislation.[21] Convinced that the Liberals had nothing further to offer, Carson went off to Ulster to rally the faithful, whilst the Unionists considered amending the Army Annual Act in the Lords, a desperate gamble which might re-focus opinion on the coercion of Ulster. Like Lloyd George, Bonar Law realised that compromise proposals, even as little as 'veiled exclusion', would appear to 'a good many people . . . so reasonable that Ulster would not be justified in resisting, and that it would settle the Irish question'.[22]

Whether 'veiled exclusion' was a time-wasting device or a serious threat as Bonar Law feared, the government was, as the cabinets of November 1913 implicitly recognised, committed to some form of Ulster exclusion. The rejection of 'veiled exclusion' left only the Lloyd George scheme, which its author proposed again on 16 February. This formed the basis of Asquith's offer of an amending bill to come into force at the same time as Home Rule itself, which would allow any Ulster county by majority vote to opt out for six years, with automatic inclusion at the end of that period. Rejected by Carson as merely 'a stay of execution', the opposition counter-proposal of a United Kingdom referendum attempted to prevent the government seizing the moral high-ground in the struggle for public support. Despite promises to the Irish Nationalists, Asquith was still prepared to revise his terms, offering Bonar Law on 19 March the exclusion of six Ulster counties with a plebiscite after six years on continuing the exclusion.[23]

It was too late. Opposition willingness to make concessions rested on an awareness that a cornered government might use the army to coerce Ulster. Asquith believed as early as September 1913 in 'the certainty of tumult and riot, and more than the possibility of bloodshed', and both Haldane and Birrell advised pre-emptive military moves at that time to 'overawe the rebels' and prevent such bloodshed. Nevertheless, nothing was done.[24] Incensed by the

---

20. Ibid. p. 176.   21. Rowland, *Last Liberal Governments*, vol. 2, pp. 288–90.
22. Ibid. p. 293.   23. Jalland, *Liberals and Ireland*, pp. 196–206.
24. Ibid. pp. 140, 162, 208.

rejection of a compromise believed to be fair and realistic, the government, and especially the advocates of the compromise, Churchill and Lloyd George, abruptly faced this necessity. Troop movements were ordered for 20 March to secure arms depots and barracks; the result was the 'Curragh mutiny'. Confused orders to Sir Arthur Paget, the commanding officer in Ireland, allowing officers with family connections in Ulster to remain behind, and for the removal rather than the arrest and court martial of other officers who refused to act, were confusedly presented by Paget as the beginning of coercive operations against Ulster in which officers had a choice of participation or resignation. Brigadier Hubert Gough and the majority of his cavalry officers at the Curragh opted for resignation. The government thus found itself negotiating with the disaffected officers of its own army, which ultimately resulted in a written promise to Gough, signed by Seely, the war minister, and Sir John French, chief of the imperial general staff, that the government would not use the army to impose Home Rule upon Ulster.

The 'Curragh mutiny' itself was a minor set-back but it occurred amidst widespread fears for the strain that coercion might impose on the army's loyalty. Bonar Law warned Asquith of a possible military refusal at their first secret meeting at the end of October 1913, and the king also believed that many officers would resign.[25] After the mutiny, French conjured up the vision of the army collapsing throughout the empire,[26] and Asquith himself believed that 'if we were to order a march upon Ulster . . . about half the officers in the Army . . . would strike'.[27] Labour unrest had reached the army, and the government had lost, or believed itself to have lost, the power to coerce. It was forced to reconsider, and oblige its Nationalist allies to reconsider, the permanent rather than the temporary exclusion of Ulster.

Moreover, the accusation of a government plot to coerce Ulster removed the moral high-ground that the government had occupied with its proposals of 9 March. Some of the damage was undone by the revelation of UVF gun-running from Germany in April, which re-established the issue of Ulster extremism in the ongoing poker game for the hearts and minds of the electorate. Negotiations therefore continued. Much had also been achieved. By the summer of 1914 the Unionists had come to accept the principle of Home Rule for Catholic Ireland, the Nationalists less clearly that exclusion would

---

25. Rowland, *Last Liberal Governments*, vol. 2, p. 291.   26. Ibid. p. 319.
27. Jalland, *Liberals and Ireland*, p. 239.

have to be provided for Protestant Ireland. Lloyd George noted towards the end of May, and Asquith in June, that the contentious issue was now the area to be excluded.[28] Neither private talks, nor the Buckingham Palace conference in late July, could resolve this, but although still sufficient to provoke violence, it was a matter of detail. Disagreement, even between the two Irish parties, was limited to Tyrone, and to a much lesser extent Fermanagh, where Asquith thought an arrangement possible.[29] This was relatively unimportant from a party-political point of view. Conflict between Irish extremists over such an apparently insignificant issue would do no harm, and could be helpful to the extent of revealing to an electorate well tired of Ireland the intolerance of those with whom the government had to deal. Boundary disputes could be handed over to a boundary commission, and the political problem shunted. In electoral terms, the Liberals might consider that they had circumvented the Irish bog with some success, despite frequent mismanagement.

Home Rule and Ulster resistance were part of the wider problem that confronted Liberalism after 1910; a problem that was never simply a question of lawlessness, but of social structure and elite government. Rioting workers, women who broke windows, Ulster-men who armed, all found themselves powerless within the existing power structure, and apparently unable to make themselves heard by working within it. This was not, however, a new phenomenon, a 'strange death of Liberal England', but the usual ritual of political change, whereby reform was conceded after frequently violent extra-parliamentary agitation. Between 1910 and 1914, the Liberal party thus found itself forced to consider concessions to women, to workers and to Ulster, as governments in the past had considered the extension of the franchise, labour legislation and Irish self-government. The conservative quietism of the majority of the ministry, Asquith's preoccupation with tactics, and Churchill's move to the admiralty left the party dangerously reliant on Lloyd George for new initiatives, even on Ireland.

Lloyd George and the land campaign

Lloyd George's personal reputation had faded since 1910 with the unpopularity of national insurance and his involvement in the Marconi scandal. His purchase of shares at pre-market prices in the

28. Rowland, *Last Liberal Governments*, vol. 2, pp. 339, 344.   29. Ibid. p. 344.

American Marconi company at a time when the government was awarding a contract to the English Marconi company led to allegations of ministerial corruption. Nevertheless he retained Asquith's confidence and his influence in an unimaginative cabinet. Together with the New Liberal intellectuals, he also had more than enough ideas to sustain the party as a party of action. No sooner was the National Insurance Act passed than speculation surrounded Lloyd George's next progressive move. The result was the land campaign, a logical extension of the 1909 budget campaign, if not of the budget itself.

Between mid-February and late March 1912, Lloyd George, hitherto sceptical, changed his mind on the possibilities of legislative minimum wages as a result of the coal strike.[30] He was accordingly more responsive to a memorandum presented to the cabinet committee on labour unrest in May from a group of New Liberals, proposing a general policy of minimum wages beginning with agriculture and transport, reform of local taxation and 'connected with this . . . the problems of housing and the acquisition of land'.[31] Thus inspired, Lloyd George sketched out a programme that followed precedents already well established by Irish legislation and the Trade Boards Act, of land courts to determine both agricultural wages and farmers' rents so that the burden of any wage increases would fall on the landowner. Simultaneously, he established an unofficial land enquiry committee to gather information. At this point, and for some time to come, Lloyd George's thinking was still largely rural, and typically insouciant. In January 1913, he saw no need 'to formulate a scheme of reforms, but the evils of the existing conditions should be explained and enforced, and out of the discussions thus raised a scheme of reform could gradually be evolved'.[32] Ultimately, the land enquiry committee's rural report, supposedly ready for the printers in April, was not published until October, some days after the campaign was officially launched at Bedford.

Lloyd George's Bedford speech was necessarily vague, but it achieved the desired effect of arousing interest. His second speech at Swindon went further, announcing a ministry of land, a board of land commissioners, a minimum wage for labourers, and houses

30. Ian Packer, 'Lloyd George and the land campaign', in Judith Loades (ed.), *The Life and Times of David Lloyd George* (Bangor: Headstart History, 1991), p. 146; Lord Riddell, *More Pages*, pp. 38, 47–9.

31. Bentley B. Gilbert, *David Lloyd George: A Political Life*, vol. 2 (London: Batsford, 1992), p. 58.

32. Trevor Wilson (ed.), *The Political Diaries of C.P. Scott* (London: Collins, 1970), p. 69.

financed by money in the national insurance fund. Lloyd George had grasped early on that the key to the housing problem was wages, since only greater income would enable low-paid workers to afford the higher rents of improved housing.[33] He was, however, still thinking in rural terms. The urban worker, as the miners' leader, Vernon Hartshorn, explained to Riddell, 'wants something for himself',[34] a point driven home by the Reading by-election defeat.[35] The Land Enquiry Committee, headed by Rowntree, clearly understood this point if Lloyd George did not. Its urban report, which finally emerged in April 1914, stressed the housing problem and proposed that local authorities should be responsible for housing provision. To this end it recommended central grants to local authorities under central supervision, and simplified procedures for municipalities to purchase land compulsorily, together with the regulation of leases and minimum wages which again had in mind the need of workers to afford economic rents.[36] The derating of improvements, to levy rates upon the site value of the land alone instead of on the value of the land and its improvements (usually buildings), for which the land valuation incorporated in the 1909 budget was essential, together with compulsory purchase by municipalities, had already been proposed in memoranda of August and October 1913,[37] and Lloyd George himself mentioned derating in his Bedford speech.

What the government lacked was bills refining ideas into legislative proposals; what Lloyd George lacked, apart from the ability to handle detail, was time. Asquith, whose hopes of escape from the Irish imbroglio by a general election in 1913 had been dashed by the Marconi scandal, was now considering an election in the summer of 1914. This was curious, since plural voting would not be abolished before May 1915,[38] but it put Lloyd George's hitherto leisurely progress with land reform under acute pressure. Lloyd George's attempt to meet a new time-scale led him to cram the fiscal side of his land reforms into the budget of 1914. There, land reform merged, as Lloyd George in his elastic way intended, with the reform of local government finance on which he had established a departmental committee early in 1912. He proposed site value rating and the derating of improvements to encourage land

33. Ibid. p. 69.   34. Lord Riddell, *More Pages*, p. 75.
35. Gilbert, *Lloyd George*, vol. 2, p. 64.   36. Packer, 'Lloyd George', pp. 148–9.
37. Bentley B. Gilbert, 'David Lloyd George: the reform of British landholding and the budget of 1914', *The Historical Journal* 21 (1) (1978), 124.
38. Tanner, *Political Change*, p. 320.

sales and building, and large grants from central government to ease the severe financial difficulties of local authorities that followed from their increased responsibilities under previous legislation and which would be exacerbated by the budget's derating proposals.[39] The money was to come from higher income tax, super-tax and death duties. The problem was timing. Derating was impossible until the land valuation was complete, which would not be before 1915, but the grants, even the provisional grants to tide local authorities over until April 1915, were tied to the implementation of derating.[40] The government, as Captain Pretyman, veteran of the campaign against the 1909 land taxes pointed out, thus proposed to raise revenue by increased taxation to meet expenditure which parliament had not approved, and which could not be used for the purpose for which it was raised.[41]

It was this constitutional impropriety, and the sheer size of the tax rises, which caused trouble. The cabinet had been barely consulted, and as in 1909, 'moderate' or 'Gladstonian' Liberals took offence. A deputation met Asquith on 15 June, and its members subsequently expressed their objections in a letter to *The Times* on the 18th which Asquith, the key figure, thought 'a very able document, and as to most of its arguments there is no real answer.'[42] Confronted by the threat of a hostile amendment supported by some forty or fifty of its own backbenchers, which a leading rebel, Richard Holt, described as a 'combined remonstrance by businessmen and some survivors of the Cobden-Bright school of thought against the ill-considered and socialistic tendencies of the Government finance',[43] the government gave way. The land clauses covering derating and grants were dropped forthwith, and income tax reduced to 1/3d. Labour and Radical MPs in turn abstained to protest against the reduction of the income tax. The budget, as Riddell noted on 12 July, 'has been a fiasco'. However, he also noted that Lloyd George was 'in excellent spirits and full of fight'.[44]

The budget was a set-back for the land campaign and for the Liberal party. It reflected not only Lloyd George's carelessness, but the many pressures that both Lloyd George himself and the

39. Rowland, *Last Liberal Governments*, vol. 2, p. 325; Gilbert, *Lloyd George*, vol. 2, p. 83.

40. Gilbert, 'Reform of British landholding', p. 132.

41. Ibid. p. 133; Gilbert, *Lloyd George*, vol. 2, pp. 84–5.

42. Gilbert, *Lloyd George*, vol. 2, pp. 88–90.

43. Michael Bentley, *The Liberal Mind 1914–1929* (Cambridge: Cambridge University Press, 1977), p. 15.

44. Lord Riddell, *More Pages*, p. 218.

government were under. Some, though not the bulk, of the additional revenue the chancellor sought to raise was to meet the increased naval estimates brought forward by Churchill which had occasioned a protracted dispute in which both had offered to resign. The compromise exacted by Asquith still left the prospect of a further dispute the following year. Preoccupied by Ireland, the cabinet had also given little thought and less assent to the policies so vaguely sketched by Lloyd George, and was initially, with the possible exception of Grey, unenthusiastic at best. In May, after Lloyd George's budget speech, Rowntree complained that the campaigners had so far received no guidance on the urban minimum wage, the building of houses, or even the outline of rating reforms, without which they could not hope to appeal to the urban workers.[45] The land campaign under the guidance of the Central Land and Housing Council set up by the new chief whip, Percy Illingworth, was nevertheless substantial, even if still predominantly rural. In January 1914 it had sent out 150 voluntary and 80 full-time speakers, and by May had distributed 1.5 million leaflets. Despite the budget débâcle it was stepped up in May–June, as if the government was preparing for an autumn campaign. More significantly, the leadership began to grapple with the urban problem. In July, Asquith finally approved the urban minimum wage, by which time the cabinet had agreed to most of the proposals in the urban report.[46]

A month later, the outbreak of war swept aside the land campaign, Ulster rebellion, and militant suffragism, and transformed the context of labour unrest. On the eve of war, the Liberals, both as a party and as a government, faced serious problems. Irish negotiations had broken down and diehards in the Unionist party, convinced that the army would not coerce Ulster, were encouraging Carson to declare an Ulster provisional government.[47] Further industrial unrest was almost certain in 1915, as was suffragette militancy. Whatever the fate of the land campaign, the financial difficulties of over-burdened local authorities required prompt action, and combined with the requirements of the navy made significant reduction in taxation impossible. Social Radicalism and high taxation were alienating yet more moderate Liberals, to add to the defections of 1909–10. Masterman's defeat in Ipswich drew attention not only to the unpopularity of Home Rule with Nonconformists and the

45. Rowland, *Last Liberal Governments*, vol. 2, pp. 324–5; Gilbert, 'Reform of British landholding', pp. 134–5.

46. Packer, 'Lloyd George', pp. 150–1.   47. Gilbert, *Lloyd George*, vol. 2, p. 105.

National Insurance Act with workers, but severe defects in Liberal constituency organisation. Most urgent of all was the need to reaffirm the progressive alliance with Labour.

Liberalism on the eve of war

Despite its problems, there was no clear indication in 1914 that the Liberal party would lose a general election in 1915, nor that, whether it won or lost such an election, it would be defunct within a decade. Both Labour and Conservatism posed threats to Liberal success but both parties also faced difficulties at least as serious as those faced by the Liberals. Labour had won only forty-two seats in December 1910, just two of them against Liberal opposition and in both cases without Unionist competition.[48] Moreover, fifteen of those seats were sponsored by the MFGB, and were thus the product of the transfer of that union's allegiance from Liberal to Labour in 1909.[49] Affiliation of the union did not mean a transfer of the loyalties of its members, large numbers of whom continued to vote Liberal as they had done in the past.[50] Instead, affiliation to the Labour party led to factionalism within the MFGB and damaged both the union and the Labour party. In August 1913 the *Labour Leader* claimed that 'the Labour Party would be a great deal stronger without five, at least, of the miners' members', a remark which illustrates yet another Labour weakness, the internal rift between socialists and Lib-Lab reformists, the mining MPs being decidedly in the latter camp.

Nor did by-elections between 1910 and 1914 suggest that Labour was about to make a dramatic breakthrough. The party came third in all fourteen three-cornered contests in that period, even though these were in industrial constituencies where Labour had established a foothold.[51] Rather, apart from a very small number of constituencies, Labour relied upon Liberal acquiescence to hold even the few seats it had. There is a case, made even by contemporary Labour supporters, that Labour was actually declining after 1910,[52] despite slight progress at the municipal level where the ward, as a

48. Peter Clarke, 'The electoral position of the Liberal and Labour parties, 1910–1914', *English Historical Review* 90 (367) (1975), 828–9.

49. Roy Douglas, 'Labour in decline', in K.D. Brown, *Essays in Anti-Labour History* (London: Macmillan, 1974), p. 113.

50. Clarke, 'Electoral position', p. 831.   51. Ibid. p. 831.

52. Ibid. p. 832; Douglas, 'Labour in decline', *passim*; Neal Blewett, *The Peers, the Parties and the People* (London: Macmillan, 1972), pp. 389–95.

smaller electoral unit, permitted such minority-party expansion more easily. If the party was expanding, it was doing so slowly and erratically. The crucial factor remained that although Labour frequently drew on Liberal traditions, especially a secularised version of Nonconformist values, the two parties usually did best in areas that were spatially distinct.[53] Labour was, as Austen Chamberlain noted, as much a challenge to Conservatism as to Liberalism.[54] In terms of government, it was not yet much of a challenge to either.

Labour's best hope of further expansion, and even survival, lay in threatening the Liberal party within the Progressive Alliance negotiated in 1903. The Conservatives won six of the fourteen three-cornered contests between 1910 and 1914 on a minority vote because of the Liberal–Labour clash. In 1914 Labour appeared to have plans for confrontation, and had prepared a list of 117 candidates with the prospect of reaching perhaps 150–170, but jostling for advantage was inherent in Lib-Lab understanding. Labour had neither the financial nor the union backing for such action, nor the capacity to withstand Liberal retaliation.[55] Labour was not freed from the shackles of the Osborne judgement which outlawed the political levy until 1913, and even then unions were obliged to ballot their members and keep the political fund separate from the union's general funds.

Moreover, even after a favourable vote, rank-and-file members were extremely reluctant to pay up. The introduction of the payment of members as part of a deal to secure Labour support for national insurance eased one aspect of the financial problem, but electorally Labour could never do more than ensure a Conservative victory, a potentially suicidal course of action. The future of a Labour party that handed the working classes over to the mercies of a party that was contemplating, among other things, the abolition of the payment of MPs and the revision of the Trades Disputes Act of 1906 was likely to be bleak, as Labour politicians were only too well aware. Labour, even at its most confrontational, could not win a general election in 1915; it could expand slightly with Liberal acquiescence; it could lose heavily.

In 1915, the Conservative party had ground to make up before it began to challenge for office since the abolition of the plural vote would cost it some thirty seats. It was also still seriously divided, having failed to heal the rift over tariff reform that had been so

53. Tanner, *Political Change, passim.*
54. Austen Chamberlain, *Politics from Inside*, p. 198.
55. Tanner, *Political Change*, pp. 325–37.

damaging in 1906 and 1910. Bonar Law's Edinburgh programme of tariffs on manufactured goods but not on foodstuffs was patched together in January 1913 to hold the party together after a Lancashire revolt against the abandonment of the referendum on tariff reform promised by Balfour in 1910. It was a compromise, and as the bitterness surrounding the Kendal by-election revealed, tariff-reform tolerance was stretched to the limits.[56]

Conservative fiscal policy provoked outrage from the farming community, normally the bastion of Conservatism, which the promise of rating relief in November 1913 failed to satisfy. The party did not expect the farmers to vote Liberal, despite the allure of Liberal proposals for land-tenure reform, but it did fear abstention. 'The present strength of [the] party', as the former chief whip, Sir Alexander Acland Hood, noted in 1912, 'comes largely from the agricultural districts.' To this, the National Farmers Union pointedly added that over 80 seats were held by the Conservatives with majorities under 500.[57] Fears for rural constituencies were aggravated by a complete failure to counter the land campaign, despite several specialist committees set up to formulate a policy.[58] All the information reaching the central office and the leadership suggested that the campaign was succeeding in the Conservative heartland of the southern and south-western counties.[59] Efforts to exploit the unpopularity of the National Insurance Act did not extend to the framing of an alternative policy, and the party similarly failed to agree a policy on industrial unrest. As the party chairman, Steel-Maitland, observed, 'We cannot outbid the Liberals or Socialists [but] if we cannot outbid, we ought to show them that we sympathise.' Showing sympathy was hardly a substitute for a policy, and in any case, as Steel-Maitland added, 'this is just what we do not do'.[60]

The Conservative problem was that it was still, as it had been throughout the Edwardian period, split between a dynamic, organised, radical wing of interventionist tariff reformers and a conservative wing of squires and businessmen. In 1914, the former, encouraged by Steel-Maitland and working through the USRC, was still committed to the full programme of tariffs on food as well as manufactured imports, and proposed wages boards and minimum wages for both agriculture and industry, and housing reform and rating relief, both assisted by exchequer grants. In many respects

56. E.H.H. Green, *The Crisis of Conservatism* (London: Routledge, 1995), pp. 274–80.

57. Ibid. pp. 280–4, 290.   58. Ibid pp. 292–3.   59. Ibid p. 290.

60. Ibid. p. 305.

close to the Liberal interventionist programme, it differed on the usual grounds of finance, relying on the income from tariffs and the upturn in the economy that tariffs were expected to bring, rather than higher direct taxes. The existence and radicalism of this wing of Conservatism remained, with the authoritarian elements of New Liberalism, the latent foundation for coalition.

In 1914, however, the Conservative party was more inclined to reaction, considering with some favour not a progressive appeal to labour, but restrictions on the powers of trade unions and on working-class representation.[61] Attempts to divert attention from mainland politics to the Home Rule controversy proved unavailing. Concentration on Ulster involved the abandonment of both the principle of union and the southern Irish Unionists; encouragement of illegal resistance by Ulster risked a backlash against those seen as responsible for violence from a British electorate already tired of Ireland and its intransigence. Division paralysed the Conservative party in all directions. On the eve of war the Conservative party was, in the view of its most recent historian, 'in a mess . . . it was unsure of its future strategy or even its future'.[62]

Conservative confusion reduced the risk of Liberal losses to the right of those moderate Gladstonians who disliked interventionist Liberalism and its cost, but who would find it difficult to support a Conservative party still committed to tariffs. The land campaign appeared to be succeeding exactly where the Liberals had the best chance of success. With Labour constraining the party in industrial seats and Conservatism in control of the suburbs, Liberalism could not hope for substantial gains in urban areas, although the combination of housing reform and reduced rates had some resonance there amongst both working and middle classes. In rural areas, where the party had lost heavily in 1910, there were seats to be regained and won. The land campaign, by focusing on landowners and their misuse of land, 'idle land in the hands of idle men',[63] recreated the cross-class appeal of the 1909 campaign as an attack not on wealth, but on an unproductive surplus. 'The land scheme', as Riddell noted, 'is a shrewd political move. While it deals with present day economic troubles, it is framed to appeal to the Liberal politician who is not prepared to attack the commercial classes, but will rejoice in attacking the pockets and privileges of his traditional

61. Alan Sykes, *Tariff Reform in British Politics* (Oxford: Oxford University Press, 1979), pp. 259, 261–2.
62. Green, *Crisis of Conservatism*, pp. 304, 268.
63. Gilbert, *Lloyd George*, vol. 2, p. 55.

bugbears and enemies, the squires and the ground landlords.'[64] Conservative party organisers agreed.

The joker in the potential 1915 pack was Ireland, which still sent forty-two MPs to Westminster under the provisions of the Home Rule Act. The identification of the Conservative party with Ulster extremism and the subversion of the Nationalist ideal of a united Ireland suggested that the Irish MPs might still split on religious lines, and that the Nationalists would cooperate with the Liberals. On the other hand, Irish affinities on education, licensing and protection lay with the Conservatives; the politics of the post-Home Rule Irish party were accordingly unpredictable. Irish politics also spilled over to the mainland, where in 1910 the Liberals were believed to have won some twenty seats in England and nineteen in Scotland because the Irish Catholic vote was mobilised in their favour by the United Irish League.[65] As the party that passed Home Rule, the Liberals might legitimately expect, at least in 1915, to retain the majority of that support. It was nevertheless volatile, especially on the issue of education; this was the downside of Liberal identification with Nonconformity. Ominously, in 1909 when the Liberal–Irish alliance was under strain, T.P. O'Connor spoke of the difficulty of resisting 'the trend for our people to vote for the Tory',[66] as if Irish support for Liberalism was unnatural on all grounds except Home Rule.

Nevertheless, in comparison with its rivals, the Liberal party was not in bad shape in 1914. Nor was the longer-term outlook necessarily bleak. The minimum wage and its role in facilitating housing reform indicated the policy's real potential as a means for New Liberalism and the Liberal party to escape the servile state analysis. In this respect, the Trades Boards Act, which the *Nation* deemed 'in embryo the boldest and most far-reaching of all the social reforms which separate modern constructive Liberalism from the older policy that bore that name',[67] was of greater significance than national insurance, even though the latter, in first Conservative and then Labour hands, became the basis of the future welfare state. Minimum wages, as a real national minimum rather than as state regulation of wages, allowed scope for differentials, yet enhanced economic freedom by restoring the worker's control over his increased income. Unpopular insurance might then become, as

64. Ibid. pp. 58–9.   65. Blewett, *Peers, Parties and People*, p. 351.
66. Ibid. p. 59.
67. Peter Clarke, *Liberals and Social Democrats* (Cambridge: Cambridge University Press, 1978), p. 115.

Lloyd George intended, merely a temporary expedient. Everything depended on how minimum-wage legislation operated, and equally significantly, whether it could be enforced. Elitist arrogance was still the party's Achilles heel. New Liberal intellectuals still thought of government for, rather than in cooperation with, the working classes. Even Lloyd George, who should have known better, had little time for either trade unions or their leaders.[68]

Two things might damage Liberalism: in the short term, the collapse of the Progressive Alliance and confrontation with Labour which would permit a Conservative victory on a minority vote; in the longer term, the still unresolved problem of the representation of the working classes by the working classes. Liberalism needed to convert the electoral alliance of 1903 and the working relationship in parliament into a more permanent coalition, in effect to institutionalise that coalition as the mid-Victorian party had done, and on which its success as a party was based. Lloyd George was sympathetic to Labour demands, thought, typically, of a quasi-coalition by finding room for Ramsay MacDonald in the cabinet as a Labour member,[69] and treated Liberal and Labour as two sides of progressivism in his speech at Criccieth on 2 June 1914.[70] The alternative vote, discussed but rejected during consideration of the 1912 franchise bill,[71] offered a way forward for progressivism that circumvented negotiations with Labour. There were opportunities in an open future which the outbreak of war closed down.

Liberalism and the demands of war

War had always threatened the integrity of the Liberal party through its challenge to Liberal values, even in the days of Palmerston. At the beginning of August 1914, with anti-war radicalism still substantial on the left of the party and Lloyd George as its potential leader, it appeared as if the party might suffer an immediate split. Lloyd George and several other ministers were reluctantly considering resignation when the German invasion of Belgium and Grey's

68. Chris Wrigley, 'Lloyd George and the Labour Movement after 1922', in Loades, *Life and Times of Lloyd George*, p. 51; Gilbert, *Lloyd George*, vol. 2, p. 56.
69. David Marquand, *Ramsay MacDonald* (London: Cape, 1977), pp. 141–3, 150–1, 159–60.
70. Rowland, *Last Liberal Governments*, vol. 2, p. 341.
71. Martin Pugh, *Electoral Reform in War and Peace 1906–1918* (London: Routledge & Kegan Paul, 1978), p. 15.

defence of his diplomacy which the invasion appeared to justify restored cabinet unity, with only three minor resignations. Home Rule was passed but implementation was deferred until the end of the war; Irish Nationalists, Ulster Loyalists and the Conservative party rallied behind the war effort in a party truce, shortly followed by an industrial truce announced by Labour. The government was strengthened by Kitchener's assumption of the war office, and with a few exceptions not only Labour MPs and trade-union leaders but the fervent socialists of the British Socialist party became staunch patriots in an outburst of national support for a war expected to be brief and victorious. The dissident Liberal and Labour minorities found themselves united in impotent isolation.

Nevertheless Liberals in general, whether in government, parliament or the constituencies, accepted the war with reluctance, and with a desire to compromise their ideals as little as possible. Emergency measures were few. To Liberals, economic liberalism remained the route to efficiency, the usual commercial sources best for the procurement of military supplies. Moreover, the expectation of a short war weighed against excessive disruption of normal business procedures, and in a war fought to defend 'civilisation' against 'Prussian militarism', conscription was barely imaginable as an alternative to voluntary recruitment. Liberals were nevertheless caught up in its momentum. Lord Bryce, a noted Liberal intellectual, former Irish secretary and ambassador to Washington, chaired a committee of inquiry into German atrocities in Belgium even though impartial evidence was impossible to obtain; Masterman threw himself into the work of government propaganda. Sir Robert Hudson of the NLF became chairman of the Joint War Finance Committee, Sir Jesse Herbert worked with the Parliamentary Recruiting Committee,[72] and local leaders and Nonconformist clergy up and down the country held patriotic meetings and encouraged recruiting.

Patriotic fervour was a Conservative not a Liberal disposition and Liberals who adopted it only enhanced the appeal of Conservatism. Those who took the unpopular stance of opposing the war against their own government were drawn towards Labour, whilst those who embraced the war with reluctance lapsed into quietism. Intellectually and organisationally, Liberalism had nothing to contribute to war, or 'the war', except to protest against its excesses. Liberal convictions and grassroots Liberal organisation both withered, whilst

72. Chris Cook, *A Short History of the Liberal Party 1900–1976* (London: Macmillan, 1976), p. 64.

Conservatism and Labour, which rested on the unions and found residual unity in its class mission, both acquired a greater sense of purpose. The limitations of fighting a major war on Liberal principles also became rapidly visible as the western front became bloodily entrenched. The government faced the disappointed expectations of the public, the criticism of the press, and increasingly of a backbench Liberal 'ginger' group that became in 1916 the Liberal War Committee, all demanding greater energy in the prosecution of the war irrespective of the military possibilities. The hastily improvised Dardenelles assault of March–April 1915, muddled both in conception and execution, arose largely from the political need to provide signs of action and an easy victory. Instead, the ensuing débâcle contributed further to the government's growing reputation for slackness and incompetence.

The real damage done by the 'ginger' group, and its Unionist counterpart, the Unionist Business Committee formed in January 1915, lay in the very vagueness of their demands. In condemning government inefficiency and inactivity, Liberal and Unionist critics alike threw responsibility upon the government for the failure to achieve the decisive breakthrough on the western front that the army maintained was possible. Munitions were at the heart of this. Voluntary recruitment took skilled men away from essential occupations, and by the end of 1914 munitions firms were already complaining of the shortage of skilled labour. In the absence of a national munitions policy and control over the allocation of raw materials and manpower, the government could do little. But the government was also divided on interventionist regulation and hampered by overlapping departmental responsibilities which set Lloyd George at the treasury against Kitchener at the war office. The problem was compounded by its implications for labour relations. The war disrupted the peacetime economy, leading to labour shortages in war-related industries, unemployment in others, and sharp price rises in basic commodities. Class tensions were exacerbated by exhortations to sacrifice largely directed towards the working class by a middle and upper class that seemed to have foregone few of its own pleasures. A short but disruptive strike by engineers on the Clyde in February 1915 for higher wages to compensate for the rise in prices demonstrated the rapid alienation of labour at the shop-floor level and the increased power it gained from war.

'Dilution', allowing unskilled workers and women to undertake work formerly reserved for skilled men, also had political ramifications. In March 1915 negotiations supervised by a treasury committee on production under Sir George Askwith resulted in a 'shells and fuses' agreement whereby the unions accepted 'dilution' in the engineering industry for the duration of the war. Subsequently, the government took control of the engineering industry under the emergency provisions of the Defence of the Realm Act, and in the 'treasury agreement' the unions accepted compulsory arbitration and dilution in return for control of excess wartime profits. By November 1915, the government had also regulated the pithead price of coal and house rents, and was being driven into economic regulation irrespective of its principles and in the absence of a coherent policy. Politically, demands for greater energy in waging war came down to support for Lloyd George's style of interventionism to the detriment of the ministers who opposed him and the disrepute of the government as a whole. Whether in peacetime or wartime, Lloyd George was a committed interventionist; orthodox Liberals were not. The treasury agreement, capped by Asquith's agreement to make Lloyd George chairman of a munitions of war committee, marked the triumph of Lloyd George and his conception of Liberalism over his opponents.

Lloyd George's moves to regulate munitions production in March 1915 were one side of a wider crisis in the politics of munitions which came to a head with the failure of the Allied spring offensive at Neuve Chapelle and Aubers Ridge. The failure was attributed by the army, and thence by politicians critical of the government, to the shortage of shells, the diversion of resources to the Dardenelles, malingering workers, and general government incompetence, which embraced both the Dardenelles and malingerers. Asquith's complacency in denying the shell shortage on 20 April despite widespread knowledge of the shortage amongst MPs, and criticism of munitions workers by Lloyd George,[73] encouraged such opinions; Bonar Law's willingness to accept Asquith's statement incensed the backbench pressure groups.[74]

Against this background, the resignation in May of the first lord of the admiralty, Admiral Fisher, over the Dardenelles fiasco created a crisis of both parliamentary and public confidence which threatened to engulf not only the Liberal government, but also the Conservative leadership which, in the eyes of the increasingly influential Unionist Business Committee came close to complicity

---

73. Trevor Wilson, *The Myriad Faces of War* (Oxford: Polity Press, 1986), p. 196.
74. Ibid. p. 199.

in the government's sins. Reconstruction of the government seemed to both Asquith and Bonar Law preferable to a renewal of party controversy and an election which might jeopardise both Bonar Law's leadership and Asquith's party. The result was a hastily and secretly agreed coalition which created consternation amongst Liberals, who still saw the Conservatives as the traditional enemy and had not realised, or preferred not to recognise, that the political changes caused by the war already left the Liberal government dependent upon Conservative goodwill.

Liberals still dominated the major cabinet offices in the coalition which Asquith announced on 26 May 1915, with Lloyd George in the key office of minister of munitions, McKenna replacing him at the treasury. Bonar Law took the relatively unimportant office of colonial secretary. Churchill, heavily implicated in the Dardenelles fiasco, was replaced by Balfour at the admiralty and Haldane sacrificed to a highly selective anti-German hysteria that overlooked Milner's strong German connections, and left Von Donop, despite his name, in his sensitive position at the war office. Haldane was the scapegoat, not only for the failures of the government in wartime, but for its Liberal past. If the outbreak of war proved Grey right to many previously suspicious Liberals, Britain's apparent lack of preparation for war and consequent lack of success could be attributed to Liberalism itself. Right-wing Conservatives had constantly preached suspicion of Germany, military preparedness, conscription, the threat from foreign goods and foreign aliens, and the importance of the empire. The image of Liberalism was the antithesis of this, free-trading, cosmopolitan, anti-imperialist and neglectful of defence. The war and its dismal early months appeared to prove the Conservatives right, the Liberals wrong. Liberalism was ineffectual sentimentality.

Coalition nevertheless changed little. The major issue remained the injection of drive into the war effort. This, in turn, meant increased governmental interference and regulation, on which the political battle-lines were already drawn up, although the problem shifted during the summer of 1915 from munitions to men. The institutional problems also remained. Both the cabinet and the War Council (renamed the Dardenelles Committee) were too large, the former debated again what the latter proposed, and the nonchalant figure of Asquith presided over both. Dynamism, or its appearance, was, as before, provided by Lloyd George. In his first speech as minister of munitions on June 3 he announced his support for military conscription, and his readiness to adopt industrial conscription.[75] The Munitions of War Act of July 1915, embodying the treasury agreement, did just this in a mild form, introducing 'leaving certificates' that prevented munitions workers moving to other employment without the employer's approval.

In the same speech Lloyd George also noted the vanishing of party politics, anticipated a reconstruction of parties, and implied his own preference for coalitionism.[76] His pursuit of 'a properly disciplined nation'[77] moved him closer to the social-imperialists associated with the Conservative party. Riddell noted in November that 'L.G. is gradually shedding the Radical Party. . . . He finds his supporters amongst the Conservatives.'[78] Lloyd George was becoming the chief architect of the destruction of Liberal values, not least because he spoke as a nominal Liberal. Liberal doubts about his Liberalism were in turn becoming more widespread,[79] but the reasons were those which had led some Liberals to doubt his grasp of such principles before the war. The new ministry of munitions became the embodiment of Lloyd George's view of the need for the organisation and leadership of the people from above, even if this entailed cutting corners with democracy and liberty.

Conscription, of which Lloyd George increasingly became the advocate, hit at the very essence of Liberalism in its removal of individual liberty. The last six months of 1915 saw the Liberal party at war with itself, as Lloyd George, his backbench supporters and the Conservative party pressed Asquith, the non-interventionist ministers and the majority of the party to introduce it. Despite their opposition in principle, the need for flexibility to respond to wartime emergencies obliged the anti-conscriptionists to base their arguments on the ultimately untenable position that voluntary recruiting had not been exhausted. The Liberal position thus became one of negation, delaying conscription whilst admitting that it might become necessary. In so doing, Asquith merely reinforced the image that both he and the Liberal party had already acquired, of being insufficiently committed to the war and dilatory in its conduct. The 'Derby scheme' by which unmarried men would be asked to pledge their willingness to serve if required was a political expedient to deflect a cabinet crisis in October 1915 in which

75. John Grigg, *Lloyd George from Peace to War* (Berkeley: University of California Press, 1985), p. 263.

76. Ibid. p. 264.   77. Wilson, *Myriad Faces*, pp. 211, 215.

78. Lord Riddell, *Lord Riddell's War Diary* (London: Ivor Nicholson & Watson, 1933), p. 136.

79. Wilson, *Myriad Faces*, pp. 211–12, 208.

ministers from all sides, including Lloyd George, most Conservatives, Asquith himself, McKenna and Runciman all threatened to
resign.[80] By the end of 1915, Lloyd George was openly condemning
the government for 'too little, too late', and his resignation was
again widely rumoured.

Asquith accepted, when announcing the Derby scheme, that unmarried men would have to be conscripted if that scheme failed,[81]
and this was enacted in January 1916, provoking the resignation of
the home secretary, Sir John Simon. McKenna and Runciman,
however, abandoned their objections, and Grey also remained after
threatening resignation.[82] Conscription for married men followed
in May with Liberals, including Asquith, blaming Lloyd George for
the betrayal of both principles and colleagues. 1916 was a year of
disaster for Liberalism. The war went badly on all fronts, culminating in the abandonment of the costly and futile Somme offensive
in November. The exclusion of Ireland from conscription legislation
following the Easter Rising in April demonstrated the tenuous hold
that Britain had on Irish loyalties. The severity of the subsequent
repression undermined what remained of British authority in Ireland
and more significantly, that of the Liberals' allies, Redmond and
the constitutional Irish Parliamentary Party. Irish sentiment began
to swing rapidly towards Sinn Fein. A compromise Home Rule
settlement, negotiated by Lloyd George between Redmond and
Carson, based on the immediate implementation of Home Rule
with Ulster exclusion, foundered on the rock of backbench Conservatism, despite being recommended by Bonar Law.

The government was losing all authority. The coalition was subject, as Asquith's Liberal government had been, to constant criticism from its nominal supporters. In addition to Simon's resignation
in January, Carson had resigned in October 1915 nominally over
the failure of the Allies to support Serbia, but really because of a
more general estrangement from his colleagues; Selborne resigned
over Ireland in June 1916. The cabinet was riven by dissension, and
survived primarily because the range of issues on which it disagreed
prevented the emergence of a single group with sufficient stability
and authority to provide an alternative. The resulting indecision,
combined with departmental incompetence, focused discontent
increasingly on the structure of government itself.

80. John Turner, *British Politics and the Great War* (New Haven: Yale University
Press, 1992), pp. 68–72.
81. Wilson, *Myriad Faces*, p. 213.   82. Ibid. pp. 213–14.

By November 1916, Lloyd George and Bonar Law, who desperately needed to reassert his authority over his party after its revolt in the 'Nigeria' debate on the disposition of confiscated German property, had agreed to demand reconstruction in the form of a small war committee which would include themselves but exclude the discredited Asquith. They were abetted by Carson, a leading 'Nigeria' mutineer whose reputation on the Conservative backbenches had been enhanced by his willingness to criticise his former colleagues. The demand was backed, at first tacitly and then explicitly, by the threat of Lloyd George's resignation with the implication that Bonar Law and the Conservative members of the coalition would follow him out. Asquith, after initial resistance, appeared to concede to this demand which would have left him as prime minister in overall charge of the government, but on 4 December he reversed his earlier agreement and reiterated his conviction that the prime minister must be the chairman of any such committee. Since the main objective was to sideline Asquith, compromise became impossible.

Asquith, perhaps believing on the basis of the coalition's experience that no one else could form a government, did not wait for further negotiations, but resigned on 5 December. He miscalculated. Lloyd George succeeded where Bonar Law failed, and became prime minister on 7 December 1916. His cabinet was dominated by Conservatives, not least because most senior Liberals preferred to follow Asquith into what Asquith called 'organised support', but which was, for the most part, embittered but disorganised opposition. The split between Asquith and Lloyd George was one more stage in the disruption of the party which had begun with the war itself. The pressures of war set active interventionists like Lloyd George on a different course from that of reluctant warriors like Asquith, accentuating the pre-war differences in outlook. Frequently aligned with the howling chorus of Conservative critics of the government, in wartime Lloyd George revealed his distance from the values of traditional Liberalism to show his other face, that of the pre-war coalitionist. His faith in the capacity of central government, if staffed by the right men, whether politicians like himself and Bonar Law or the businessmen whom he recruited to wartime administration, was fundamentally at odds with belief in either inexorable economic laws or, indeed, any laws.

Lloyd George was not the only Liberal minister to stray wilfully from the path of righteousness. McKenna's budget of 1915 not only made large increases in direct taxation, but imposed substantial tariffs on 'luxury' items. McKenna's desire to fund at least some of the war from income rather than loans, to spread the burden on to the rich who could pay, and to distinguish between essentials and luxuries, could all be seen as 'liberal' in a redistributive sense, but the deviation from free trade could not be disguised. Nor could that of the Paris Resolutions of 1916, negotiated by Runciman and introduced in the Commons by Asquith, which sought to ensure that post-war Germany would never again recover her economic power by excluding her from international trade. The strict Gladstonian, Francis Hirst, in his history of free trade, found the wartime period 'disheartening to those who put their trust in the sincerity and fidelity of party leaders. . . . No wonder that the rank and file of Liberal electors . . . have been a little sore ever since', but it was McKenna's budget that drew this criticism, not the war-time practices of Lloyd George.[83]

Nevertheless the sense that Lloyd George was not a Liberal, his cooperation with the Conservative critics of the conduct of the war in pressing for conscription, his reputation for unscrupulous ambition, furthered by his close contact with, and exploitation of, the press, led to the view in the Asquithian section of the party that Lloyd George was a traitor who had conspired with the political enemy to unseat Asquith for his own ends. Such a gloss on Lloyd George's political activities between 1914 and 1916, which placed the split of 1916 in a particular explanatory context, created a mythology that had a political importance independent of the events themselves. Political parties tend to recover from splits, even as serious as that of the Conservatives in 1846 and the Liberals in 1886. The split of 1916, nevertheless, differed in kind from that over Home Rule. In 1886, there had been one unchallengeable leader to whom the party might rally. After 1916 there were two men who might call officially upon the loyalty of the party, a leader who was no longer prime minister, and a prime minister who was not leader of the party. Both could be respected or despised for their individual virtues and vices. Loyalty itself was divisive.

By becoming prime minister, Lloyd George gained the potential to distort the nature of Liberalism itself. The heightened role that war gave to the state, and the debasement of orthodox Liberalism in the minds of its self-styled protagonists, pushed Liberalism back towards a servile state. According to the highly orthodox

83. F.W. Hirst, *From Adam Smith to Philip Snowden: A History of Free Trade* (London: T. Fisher Unwin, 1925), pp. 61–3.

Liberal newspaper, the *Westminster Gazette,* there were 'no limits on the claims of the state to the service of its individual citizens in a struggle in which its honour and it may be its existence is at stake'.[84] Lloyd George only removed these sentiments from their wartime context and limitations.

Here again, the crisis of 1916 differed from that of 1886. Home Rule was a reassertion of libertarianism; Chamberlain, who had just sounded 'the death-knell of laissez-faire', was banished to cooperation with the Conservatives, together with his social-imperialist ideas. Lloyd George, who was, like many others, well aware of the similarities between his career and Chamberlain's was, as Riddell noticed, 'going the same road as Chamberlain'.[85] Like Chamberlain, his understanding of Liberalism was one that discarded libertarianism in favour of coercive intervention and was accordingly in conflict with the party's, and the country's, understanding of what the creed and the party stood for. But in 1916 Lloyd George was not going into exile, but into power. The fate of the party was not sealed in 1916, although recovery would be more difficult than in the past. Much still depended upon Asquith, and even more rested with the reaction of Liberals themselves. Lloyd George could propose, but he could not dispose.

84. Michael Freeden, *Liberalism Divided* (Oxford: Oxford University Press, 1986), p. 20.
85. Riddell, *War Diary,* p. 137.

CHAPTER EIGHT

Lloyd George and Coalitionism

The triumph of Lloyd George was not followed by the triumph of British arms. There was some success in the Middle East, but this could not offset retreat in the Balkans, the defeat of Italy and above all the failure of the summer offensive on the western front where the third battle of Ypres, better known as Passchendaele, was another unsuccessful bloodbath. Russia's withdrawal from the war following internal collapse and revolution would be more than compensated by America's entry in April 1917, but apart from the availability of American credits to ease an increasingly desperate financial situation, the full advantages of American participation would not be felt for some time. In the meantime, Germany was free to reinforce the western front.

At home, the pressures of war drove the government into ever more rigorous intervention. In the face of shortages of all kinds, even essential industries were combed for men, the mines, railways, shipping and food production came under government control, rents and prices were regulated and rationing introduced for all essential supplies. Below the small war cabinet, the government functioned as a complex of regulatory offices, new ministries staffed by a-political businessmen reflecting, as the creation of the ministry of munitions had done, the priorities of the war rather than any ideological impulse to collectivism.[1] Apart from the politically sensitive ministry of labour which remained in the hands of political Labour, 'businessmen of push and go' were recruited to both old and new ministries. With the cabinet advised by a permanent cabinet secretariat, and the 'garden suburb', so-called because Lloyd

---

1. Kenneth O. Morgan, *Consensus and Disunity: The Lloyd George Coalition Government 1918–1922* (Oxford: Oxford University Press, 1989), p. 16.

George's personal advisers were housed in huts in St James's Park, acting as a prime minister's office, the Lloyd George coalition operated as an executive in a largely non-political environment.

Coalitionism and the general election of 1918

Despite Lloyd George's frustration at the compromises he had to make to conciliate the sections of the House of Commons,[2] his government had little trouble in comparison with its predecessor. Conservative backbenchers were noticeably less critical of a government that included so many Conservatives; Asquith refused to lead the saving remnant of the Liberal party in a policy of opposition, and Labour, both parliamentary and trade union, made the right protest noises whenever the government threatened the interests of workers, but remained astutely patriotic in practice. Arthur Henderson did resign over the government refusal to allow Labour delegates to attend an international socialist conference in Stockholm, but he was replaced by another Labour MP, G.N. Barnes. Given the popular mood, evident in 1915 when C.B. Stanton as an unofficial patriotic candidate, albeit supported by secret Conservative funds,[3] defeated James Winstone, the Labour candidate, in Keir Hardie's old seat of Merthyr Tydfil, any other response by Labour was political suicide. Industrial labour recognised similar constraints, reinforced by the government's powers of conscription if it overstepped the very tight limits of patriotic tolerance.

The relative lack of opposition was also partly the product of two years of war itself. The central issues of principle had been resolved under the Asquith coalition, and resolved in favour of government regulation, almost irrespective of the consequences for the liberty of the individual. The popular response to wartime problems was to demand government action, as in the demand for rationing that followed food shortages and the poor distribution of essential supplies. Rationing grew from local initiatives to a national system by 1918. Popular discontent during 1917, as the government established its interventionist machinery, was high enough to cause some alarm. Lord Lansdowne's letter of November 1917 proposing a negotiated peace reflected Liberal as well as Conservative fears that

2. Lord Riddell, *Lord Riddell's War Diary* (London: Ivor Nicholson & Watson, 1933), p. 317.
3. Barry M. Doyle, 'Who paid the price of patriotism? The funding of Charles Stanton during the Merthyr boroughs by-election of 1915', *The English Historical Review* 109 (434) (1994), 1215–22.

continued war would threaten the breakdown of the domestic social order.[4] Lloyd George, however, had already ruled out any conclusion but a German surrender, and in that at least he could rely on the full backing of public opinion.

The adversity that had had such weakening effects on Asquith's government thus tended to have the opposite effect, rallying the nation and stifling dissent. The press blamed the generals rather than the government for the slaughter of Passchendaele, and Ludendorf's surprise offensive in March 1918, which raised fears of defeat, was met by an upsurge of national unity. It also precipitated the only serious political crisis the coalition faced in wartime, the Maurice debate of 9 May 1918. In a letter to *The Times*, General Maurice, the former head of military intelligence, challenged the figures on troop numbers in France, in effect alleging that the government had starved the army of men and was largely responsible for the military crisis. Asquith, albeit half-heartedly, pressed the issue to a division in which ninety-eight Liberals voted against the government.

The Liberals had been divided before, in March 1917 on the question of protection for the Indian cotton industry, and in April 1918 on the application of conscription to Ireland. But the Maurice debate was the only occasion on which Asquith provided a lead and the official Liberal whips acted as tellers against the government. It marked the growing separation of the two wings of the party since the split of 1916, and led the Liberal Coalitionists to crystallise their hitherto amorphous position. The nucleus of a distinctive Coalitionist grouping was formed on 17 May.[5] It was not an entirely unpremeditated move. According to Addison, the minister of reconstruction, he and other leading Liberal Coalitionists were discussing an election programme in January.[6]

Lloyd George had certainly lost faith in the future of the Liberal party by then, and was intermittently considering a separate organisation. As Riddell reported his thinking in January 1918, the old Liberal party was

> a thing of the past [which] cannot be galvanised into life. He doubts the success of the great efforts now being made by the Liberal

4. Trevor Wilson, *The Myriad Faces of War* (Oxford: Polity Press, 1986), pp. 760–1; John Turner, *British Politics and the Great War* (New Haven: Yale University Press, 1992), pp. 248–52.

5. Morgan, *Consensus and Disunity*, p. 28.

6. Roy Douglas, *The History of the Liberal Party 1895–1970* (London: Sidgwick & Jackson, 1971), p. 113.

organisation, who are very busy indeed in all directions. He thinks that it may come to a fight between him and Henderson, and that all Parties including Labour will be split and reconstituted.[7]

In March, Lloyd George again discussed 'combination' with the Conservatives, and questioned Riddell about the prospect of a general election which, as Riddell pointed out, would require his own candidates. Apparently the key Conservative leaders, Bonar Law and Balfour, were in favour of combination,[8] and Lloyd George's interest in an election was possibly stimulated by the knowledge that Sir George Younger, the Conservative party chairman, thought an election essential if the coalition was to continue into peacetime.[9]

For most of 1918, however, it was anticipated that the war would continue well into the following year, and that the election would take place in wartime. Lloyd George negotiated on two fronts. In September, through Lord Murray (formerly Elibank), he proposed that Asquith should join a reconstructed government with a share in government appointments, on a programme that included Home Rule for Ireland excluding Ulster, the introduction of conscription to Ireland and an immediate election. Asquith refused, and Murray felt that he had 'been present at the obsequies of the Liberal party as I knew it'.[10] This was premature, but Lloyd George's belief that the old Liberal party was beyond resurrection suggests that such negotiations were a safeguard against the failure of more important negotiations with the Conservatives.

On 12 July, a meeting of Coalition Liberals considered the election programme, and the next day, Guest, their chief whip, urged Lloyd George to discuss both a programme and candidates with the Conservatives. Both sides wavered, with Bonar Law still concerned in early October that an alliance might split the Conservatives. Nevertheless, by the end of the month, Guest was able to confirm to Lloyd George that both the programme and the allocation of candidates had been agreed, with 150 seats reserved for the Lloyd George Liberals. The approved candidates, ultimately 374 Conservatives, 159 Liberals,[11] and others from minor parties, were sent a letter of support jointly signed by Bonar Law and Lloyd George which Asquith contemptuously termed, 'the coupon'.

7. Riddell, *War Diary*, p. 309.   8. Ibid. p. 317.
9. Douglas, *Liberal Party*, p. 113.   10. Ibid. pp. 117–18.
11. Trevor Wilson, *The Downfall of the Liberal Party 1914–1935* (London: Collins, 1966), p. 157; Martin Pugh, *The Making of Modern British Politics 1867–1939* (Oxford: Blackwell, 1993), p. 177, gives the Conservative figure as 374.

It was not, however, a wartime election. The defeat of Ludendorf's offensive in July was followed by the unexpectedly rapid collapse of Germany and an armistice on 11 November. Crucially, political attitudes did not readjust. Both Unionists and Coalition Liberals approved the joint programme on 12 November; the election was called for 14 December in a confused political situation. The coalition manifesto was in many respects radical in its proposals: a League of Nations to prevent further war; the settlement of returned soldiers on the land, a 'comprehensive' attack on inadequate housing, 'larger opportunities in education', 'improved material conditions and the prevention of degrading standards of employment' to promote social harmony; the gradual development of self-government for India and Home Rule for Ireland within the empire but excluding Ulster; somewhat vague proposals to 'promote the unity and development of the empire', which included imperial preference as far as this could be achieved without new taxes on food or raw materials; protection for British industry against unfair competition and dumping, and as a final sop to Conservative opinion, reform of the House of Lords.[12]

In commending the agreed programme to Liberals on 12 November, Lloyd George stressed the radical elements in 'a magnificent Liberal speech'.[13] Asquith approved the speech as an expression of Liberal policy which would not harm the unity of the Liberal party,[14] and Massingham, editor of the radical *Nation*, even concluded that Lloyd George aimed 'to displace the Asquithian Liberals with a radical party of which he is the head. . . . As for Toryism it is plainly doomed.' H.A.L. Fisher, the president of the Board of Education, somewhat naively, but perhaps in character for an academic who had briefly wandered into politics, thought the speech designed to promote Liberal reunion, and was apparently unaware of the 'coupon' negotiations, as was Massingham.[15] The programme nevertheless aroused Liberal misgivings. Fisher found the social programme 'sketchy', and with Edwin Montagu, the secretary of state for India, and Churchill protested against the concessions made to the Conservatives on fiscal policy.[16] The speech of 12 November was designed to win hesistant Liberals to the idea of coalition by emphasising the programme of post-war reconstruction, but the

---

12. Kenneth O. Morgan, *The Age of Lloyd George* (London: Arnold, 1978), pp. 192–3.

13. Wilson, *Downfall*, p. 136.   14. Ibid. pp. 138, 166.   15. Ibid. p. 152.

16. Morgan, *Age of Lloyd George*, pp. 189–91.

commitment was there to emphasise, and Fisher himself drew up the final coalition manifesto.

Such a commitment could, however, be given a conservative twist. In commending the programme to his Unionist audience, Bonar Law stressed the need for the coalition as an antidote to revolutionary change, and read a letter from Lloyd George which concentrated upon fiscal policy, Ireland and Welsh disestablishment and considered social reconstruction in social-imperialist terms, 'the imperative need of improving the physical condition of the citizens of this country through better housing, better wages and better working conditions . . . because the well-being of all the people is the foundation upon which alone can be built the prosperity, the security, and the greatness both of the United Kingdom and of the Empire'.[17] The Liberal and Conservative glosses of the same programme were nevertheless consistent. Whilst many Conservative backbenchers continued to distrust Lloyd George, and many Coalitionist Liberals still hoped for Liberal reunion, the coalition leadership had developed a mutual respect and common outlook which allowed Bonar Law to consider Lloyd George as a future leader of the Conservative party.[18] In the immediate post-war situation, neither 'conservative' Conservatives nor 'liberal' Liberal Coalitionists dared challenge their respective leaders or their programme, although the coupon arrangements were undermined in some localities.

The election campaign was perforce predominantly anti-Labour. Labour voted overwhelmingly to leave the coalition on 14 November and fight independently. Henderson had been preparing the party for this since his resignation in August 1917, and at one point envisaged as many as 500 candidates.[19] The eventual total of 388 still meant that, for the first time, Labour was nominally making a bid for office. No general election had been held since December 1910, and the war had transformed the position of both political and industrial labour. Office gave the party experience, confidence and some respectability, without deepening the split between pacifists and patriots. Workers in general, and trade unions in particular, gained a hitherto unknown importance. Wartime shortages and government regulation, both of which were seen to discriminate

17. John Ramsden (ed.), *Real Old Tory Politics: The Political Diaries of Sir Robert Sanders, Lord Bayford 1910–1935* (London: The Historians Press, 1984), p. 115.

18. Morgan, *Consensus*, p. 31.

19. Trevor Wilson (ed.), *The Political Diaries of C.P. Scott 1911–1928* (London: Collins, 1970), p. 320.

against the working classes, aggravated class feeling and left militancy bubbling below, and often through, the surface of patriotic unity. The government carefully supported trade-union officials against shop-floor resentment in an acceleration of pre-war incorporation, which in turn enhanced the status of trade unionism. Membership increased from 4.5 to 6.5 million, whilst the unions lost much of their earlier suspicion of political involvement.[20]

In contrast to its impact on Liberalism, the war did not threaten Labour's fundamental purpose or philosophy, but rather enhanced it. The patriotic sacrifice of workers at home and in the trenches allowed it to capture the moral high-ground in defending workers against the more oppressive and unjust aspects of state intervention, and against the apparent lack of sacrifice on the part of the rich. As the *Herald* observed, 'money spent on luxury cannot be spent on the war, neither can it be spent on providing the necessities of life for the poor'. In this context, the proposed capital levy and the campaign against profiteering could be presented not as rapacious socialism, but simply justice which the state was failing to provide.

Unlike the Liberals, Labour understood the defensive mentality of the working classes and the defensive role of trade unions. As one Labour organiser wrote, 'it is for us to drive home that we are the only people who can be looked to for protection'.[21] The War Emergency Workers National Committee kept alive the commitment to working-class interests, expanded contacts with Labour in the localities in parallel with the extending tentacles of government, and facilitated cooperation between the various opinions within the party in wartime. In particular MacDonald and Henderson continued to work together, especially during the last year of the war, in preparation for the election and the new party constitution. There were tensions. Increased class consciousness intensified trade-union opposition to middle-class socialists, an opposition which found expression both in the TUC and during the ratification of the 1918 constitution; but it was never enough to sustain a separate 'patriotic labour' organisation resting on union resentment. The breakaway National Democratic Party was only a rump, and only eighteen NDP candidates were given the coalition 'coupon' in 1918. The Labour party constitution of 1918 made concessions to the

20. Ross MacKibbin, *The Evolution of the Labour Party 1910–1924* (Oxford: Oxford University Press, 1974), p. 105.

21. Duncan Tanner, *Political Change and the Labour Party 1900–1918* (Cambridge: Cambridge University Press, 1990), p. 366.

unions to secure their approval, but it also contained the Clause 4 commitment to socialism. It gave the party a vision for the future which made sense of 'war socialism' as a stage in the evolution of society from pre-war progressivism to a fully socialist society. In 1918 it increased the apparent dangers to be expected of a Labour government amongst those who feared its professed radicalism.

The unpredictability of the outcome of the election was amplified by the extension of the franchise from the pre-war 8.5 million to 21 million and the redrawing of constituency boundaries by the Representation of the People Act of 1918. Both changes could only exacerbate Liberal problems in view of the party's disorganisation in the constituencies. The number of ex-Liberals now running Labour campaigns was noted by both parties.[22] By creating more exclusively working-class constituencies, boundary revision was, nominally at least, an added advantage to Labour. In the event, politicians found mostly apathy, with enthusiasm only for revenge on Germany to which most pandered in the course of the campaign. The result was no watershed. The coalition swept the board with 526 of the 707 seats; Sinn Fein with 73 was its nearest challenger in numbers, but those not in prison refused to attend at Westminster. Labour won only 22.7 per cent of the vote and fifty-seven seats (sixty-one if four Independent Labour MPs are included). The Liberals taken together did better than this because 133 Coalitionists were returned from the 159 seats allocated; of the 258 Asquithian candidates, only 28 were returned.[23] The 1918 election was a 'khaki' election taking place a month after war ended and resulted in an overwhelming victory for the coalition that won the war. Those associated with failure, like Asquith, were censured, whilst 'uncouponed' Conservatives benefited from their association with successful patriotism. The result carried few implications for a future in which the political system remained molten.

Inertia: the Independent Liberals

The election of 1918 marked another stage in the disintegration of the Liberal party in that the Coalitionists clearly supported Conservatives against supposedly fellow-Liberals, and in places Asquithian Liberals supported Labour against the coalition.[24] The edges of the

22. Pugh, *Making of Modern British Politics*, p. 199.   23. Ibid. p. 194.
24. Wilson, *Downfall*, pp. 164–74.

conflict were nevertheless still blurred by the uncombative stance of Asquith, the central organisation, the NLF and the constituency associations which had remained largely under Asquithian control in the split of 1916. In 1918, party officials were content to provide central support for any Liberal candidate, Coalitionist or Asquithian, duly adopted by the local association. Their attitude was generally reciprocated by the Coalitionists who continued to proclaim their essential Liberalism, just as many uncouponed Liberals proclaimed their support of the government, or avoided the issue and spoke only of policy. The Liberals fought the election nominally as a single party. Such goodwill could hardly survive the result. After the election, one wing had enjoyed considerable success, the other had been devastated. Defeated Asquithians blamed the 'coupon' for their defeat, and were understandably resentful.

Such resentment found expression when parliament reassembled. On 3 February, at a meeting attended by only twenty-three MPs, the Asquithians formed themselves into a separate group of Independent Liberals, soon nicknamed the 'wee frees', in opposition to the coalition and its Liberal members. Overtures from Coalitionists, many of whom still considered themselves Liberals and the coalition as a temporary, if indefinite, expedient, were rebuffed. The Liberal split was thus institutionalised although the opposition did not initially extend into the constituencies. The 'liberalism' of Coalition Liberals was still strong, especially on fiscal issues. In June 1919, seventeen Coalitionists voted against the extension of the protective McKenna duties into peacetime, and the proposed anti-dumping bill brought further protests in November.[25] Nevertheless, for the moment at least, it was the Coalitionist Liberals who were in political limbo.

At the beginning of 1919 the Independent Liberals enjoyed a brief revival, winning three by-elections against the Conservatives: Leyton West, Central Hull and Central Aberdeenshire (where the prospective candidate who wanted to run as a Coalitionist was forced to withdraw by his local association which insisted on independence, and his replacement won as an Independent Liberal).[26] At the end of the year, the convention that the Liberal candidate chosen by the local association would be accepted by both sides, which had hitherto avoided open conflict, finally collapsed. In Spen Valley, a former Coalition Liberal seat, the local association not only chose an Independent but, in what amounted to a rejection of

25. Ibid. pp. 191–2.   26. Douglas, *Liberal Party*, p. 141.

Lloyd George and all his works, chose the anti-conscriptionist, Sir John Simon. A Coalitionist Liberal candidate was run against him, but came third, although his intervention was enough to hand the seat to Labour on a split vote. The episode marked the beginning of a new animosity within the divided Liberal camp. The Independent Liberals adopted a policy of retaliation, promising to challenge Coalition Liberal candidates even if selected by a local Liberal association, although this was increasingly unlikely as Liberal organisations turned against the coalition.

The Independent Liberals, however, had little to justify their independent stance. They represented no clear region or interest, suffered lethargic leadership and were deeply divided on policy. The Liberal electoral base had been destroyed during the war. In 1918, of 144 three-cornered contests, the Liberals won only 12, but most significantly, they came third in 92.[27] In mid-1919, these conditions reappeared as Labour resumed its attack. The Liberals gained only one more seat before the 1922 general election, and out of twenty-four three-cornered by-elections, came third in fifteen. A considerable number of seats were left uncontested altogether.[28] The lack of dynamic leadership was in part a by-product of the electoral position. Asquith saw no 'logical antithesis between Liberalism and Labour',[29] and Independent Liberals believed, against all the evidence, that Labour would come to an agreement with them, and that the next 'Liberal' government would involve both parties.[30] Liberals supported Henderson in the Widnes by-election to encourage cooperation, but reciprocity was not forthcoming. Shortly afterwards, the Rusholme Liberals found themselves facing a Labour candidate, and the split vote handed the seat to the Conservatives in what was to become a familiar pattern.[31]

The delusion of Labour cooperation reflected a lack of faith in the future. Lloyd George's feeling that the Liberal party was 'dead' was echoed on the Asquithian side.[32] Asquith was the despair of his colleagues, roused to aggression only in defence of the past, but his colleagues themselves were the despair of the younger radicals within the party. Much of the new initiative came from the Manchester Liberal Federation under the inspiration of E.D. Simon and Ramsay Muir, who continued to proclaim the radical interventionist policies of pre-war New Liberalism. Muir's *Liberalism and Industry*, published in 1920, called not only for the nationalisation of the mines and

27. Wilson, *Downfall*, p. 183.   28. Ibid. pp. 206–7.   29. Ibid. p. 197.
30. Ibid. p. 217.   31. Ibid. p. 206.   32. Ibid. pp. 125–6.

railways 'with representative government by all the factors concerned', but 'regulation, taxation and, if necessary national ownership' of trusts and cartels,

> the taxation of land values and increments with large powers of
> public purchase, large public provisions for housing, health and
> education, public guarantees for minimum wages, leisure and un-
> employed pay coupled with a taxation policy in which indirect
> taxation (except of luxuries) disappears, and income taxes and
> death duties form the sources of normal revenue with a capital levy
> as an emergency measure for reducing the war debt to manageable
> dimensions.[33]

Written during the post-war euphoria, when many things seemed
possible, *Liberalism and Industry* was adopted by the Manchester
Liberal Federation, and formed the basis of the NLF's industrial
programme of 1921, where, however, it attracted rather more controversy and seemed to some, not unreasonably, veiled socialism.[34]

The leadership took little notice either way. Asquith's acceptance
of the 'national minimum' in 1918 proved merely nominal, and in
general senior Liberals appeared to have forgotten that there had
even been a 'New Liberalism', reverting to that dry biscuit of orthodox political economy that even Fowler had denounced twenty years
earlier. As boom became depression in the summer of 1920, Sir
John Simon demanded 'a crusade against wasteful expenditure'.
Sir Donald MaClean, chairman of the Independent Liberal party
and its leader in the House of Commons until Asquith's return in
March 1920, similarly had 'nothing heroic to offer', just 'simple
common-sense and homely wisdom' which told him that 'the only
way to get back to national health was by way of economy'.[35] As
early as 1919 E.D. Simon, proposing redistributive taxation, had
warned that it was questionable 'whether the progressive wing of
the Liberal party was to continue to cooperate with the Liberal
party'.[36] Most did, but the drift of left-wing Liberals to Labour that
had begun during the war continued. Retrenchment had at one
time been a Liberal cause, but by 1920 it had been appropriated by
the Conservatives, and as 'anti-waste' by the conservative right. The
Liberal party would not find a political role in the defence of the
ideas of nineteenth-century political economy.

33. Ibid. p. 91.
34. Michael Freeden, *Liberalism Divided* (Oxford: Oxford University Press, 1986),
p. 81; Wilson, *Downfall*, p. 215.
35. Ibid. p. 216.   36. Ibid. p. 216.

Movement: Lloyd George and 'fusion'

For better or worse, the future of progressive Liberalism lay with
Lloyd George. Lloyd George had not, despite the coalition and his
pursuit of political realignment, ceased to be progressive according
to his own lights. These had never been the lights of orthodox
Liberalism, and the war had strengthened his belief in reform from
above. His interpretation of pre-war New Liberalism, wartime administration and post-war reconstruction ran on similar lines, towards
efficiency rather than liberation. Many of the domestic ideas of
New Liberalism could easily be adapted to become the doctrine of
a party of social-imperialism, or, as Lloyd George unfortunately but
revealingly termed it, 'Nationalism-Socialism'.[37] Both the programme
for reconstruction and the creation of a coalition to carry it out
were the products of wartime predictions founded, not unreasonably, on the possibility of military stalemate and a negotiated peace
which would leave Germany still powerful, especially economically.[38]
The objective, expressed in the Paris Resolutions of 1916, was to
establish conditions in which the Allies would maintain economic
superiority over Germany by controlling world trade in essential
commodities.[39] An alternative scenario predicted German economic
weakness, but also a world shortage of food and raw materials that
might lead to chaos.

Either way, the forecasts were of a post-war world in which
British power and social stability were threatened, and where
determined government action, however costly, was required to
meet these dangers. 'You must', Sir Eric Geddes declared, 'be prepared to spend money on after-the-war problems as you did during
the during-the-war problems. . . . It is the period of reconstruction,
and money has to be spent generously.'[40] The coalition programme
offered much to Conservatives, especially those like Bonar Law,
Milner, Lord Birkenhead, and even Austen Chamberlain despite
his later caution, who came from the radical tariff-reforming wing
of the divided pre-war Conservative party. Social-Imperialism, like
the 'national efficiency' of the Liberal Imperialists, was the product

37. Riddell, *War Diary*, p. 324.
38. P. Cline, 'Winding down the war economy: British plans for peacetime recovery, 1916–1919', in K. Burk (ed.), *War and the State* (London: Allen & Unwin, 1982),
pp. 159–61.
39. Ibid. pp. 166–7.
40. P. Cline, 'Reopening the case of the Lloyd George coalition and the post-war
economic transition, 1918–1919', *Journal of British Studies* 10 (1) (1970), 169.

of a siege mentality. The siege reality of 1914–18 enhanced the standing of its ideas and advocates whilst that reality lasted. State intervention to defend Britain's economic position by protecting and promoting trade against rivals abroad, and by improving the health, housing and education of the workforce at home, was not necessarily unprogressive in effect, whatever the motives.

The same concerns removed any dogmatic objections to nationalisation or a minimum wage if the national interest or a fit and disciplined people capable of shouldering the burdens of empire required. Reconstruction was a joint electoral promise, and in 1919 a joint governmental commitment, predicated on wartime cooperation and wartime projections. Even the far-right National party of Lord Croft proposed a 'comfort wage'[41] in what, as Lloyd George promised, was to become a land 'fit for heroes to live in'. The coalition of 1918–22 rested on the same bases as the proposed coalition of 1910, and Lloyd George's aspiration that from the coalition might come a National or Centre party with 'Nationalist-Socialist' policies was not as ridiculous in 1917–18 as it seemed by the autumn of 1920. Lloyd George was not a 'centrist' in the conventional sense that the centre was the location of the moderates of both parties, as the Whigs had believed. His vision of a so-called Centre party involved a fusion of the radical or 'left' wing of the Liberal party with the radical, and arguably 'right', wing of the Conservative party. It was a union of interventionist, authoritarian radicals, not conservative Liberals and liberal Conservatives.[42] Nor did it mean that Lloyd George had become a Conservative, still less a conservative.

Lloyd George's response to the challenge of the Independent Liberals in the spring of 1920 followed the same wartime perceptions not yet modified by post-war disillusion. To Lloyd George, the views of the Independent Liberals and to a lesser degree of the local Liberal associations, were not significant. ' "Wee Freeism" is almost an extinct force; it simply gathers to its flag the mere sectarian.'[43] Facing what he described as 'a serious crisis', he outlined his alternatives as: retirement, offering occasional support to the government; resignation and the reorganisation of the Coalition

---

41. W.D. Rubinstein, 'Henry Page Croft and the National Party 1917–22', *Journal of Contemporary History* 9 (1) (1974), 142.

42. Martin Pugh, 'Left in the centre? Lloyd George and the centrist tradition in British politics', in Judith Loades, *The Life and Times of David Lloyd George* (Bangor: Headstart History, 1991), pp. 21–2, 26.

43. Peter Rowland, *Lloyd George* (London: Barrie & Jenkins, 1975), p. 548.

Liberals into a political party, or the fusion of the two wings of the coalition into a Centre party. He did not mention reconciliation with the Independent Liberals.[44] He still believed that he negotiated from a strong position, and the first two options were undoubtedly a threat to any opposition to his chosen option of fusion in a form which would increase his independence by splitting the Conservative party as the Liberal party had been split, to remove its most conservative elements.

A joint 'Centre party' committee of Coalition Liberals and Conservatives had existed since May 1919, its secretary, significantly, being the future leader of British Fascism, Sir Oswald Mosley. The idea of a Centre party had also been publicly canvassed by Churchill, Birkenhead and Guest.[45] Their findings were not encouraging. Guest reported that the Coalition Liberals were not keen, and personally doubted if the Unionists would cooperate.[46] Lloyd George himself discussed the idea with Fisher and Addison in September,[47] and on 6 December at Manchester opened his own public campaign for 'fusion', elaborating on the theme of the dangers to be expected from Labour and socialism. There, he stressed his Liberalism and his willingness to accept the resolutions of the National Liberal Federation that had met at Birmingham the previous month, despite its strongly anti-Coalitionist tone. Privately he was more explicit, rejecting being tied

> to the Tory party pure and simple: I want a National Party; but I want Liberals in it. I should be quite content if I got such a party by dropping some of the people at both ends who would not agree. . . . I want strong government. I want private enterprise. But private enterprise must give the workers a chance and *certainty*.

But in arguing that 'a Labour government would land the country in revolution' he revealed how far Liberals had gone in accepting that Labour was now the main opposition party.

In February, he pursued the subject further with a conclave of Coalitionist Liberal ministers, and Fisher, who remained committed to social reform, was allotted the task of drawing up the programme of the new party that Lloyd George would announce. Lloyd George presumed too much. His reference to the NLF resolutions forced Bonar Law, who assented to fusion without enthusiasm, to soothe irate Conservatives demanding a full repudiation.[48] Balfour took

44. Ibid. p. 519.   45. Douglas, *Liberal Party*, p. 146.
46. Rowland, *Lloyd George*, p. 514.   47. Ibid. p. 518.
48. Ibid. p. 518; Wilson, *Downfall*, pp. 193–4; Douglas, *Liberal Party*, pp. 142–3.

exception to Fisher's draft programme and characteristically objected to any 'concrete list of changes. . . . In substance what the Coalition stands for is Reform versus Revolution', with the nature of reform left vague in the extreme. Lloyd George accepted the criticism that Fisher's programme was potentially divisive and distanced himself from its 'challenging details'. He now stressed only that

> unity on fundamental issues is essential. The general line of demarcation between the contending forces is clear, and becoming clearer every day. It is embodied in your formula of reform as against revolution. . . . The gravity of the labour onset will force us to an early decision. The Socialist movement has behind it most of the organised labour of the country. A more serious development, however, is the extent to which it is attracting the lower middle classes.

Lloyd George further distinguished his position from socialism by denouncing the nationalisation of the mines that he had supported earlier in the year.[49] More significantly, he also told Fisher in January 1920 that reform must be replaced by 'a period of administration'; this was the real meaning of the Balfour 'formula'.[50]

Lloyd George's belief that his position was 'Liberal in the real, and not the party sense'[51] depended upon a distinction that others did not recognise. He had agreed with Bonar Law and Balfour that he would secure Coalition Liberal support before the launch of the new party. Surprisingly, in view of their dependence upon the Conservatives, and the belief of some, like Hilton Young, that the Liberals were a 'party of the Right',[52] the Coalition Liberals in the government whom Lloyd George met on 16 March totally rejected the idea, proclaimed their Liberalism, and refused to abandon those 'Liberal labels' that Lloyd George thought 'we must be prepared to burn'.[53] This meeting ended the possibility, although not Lloyd George's hopes, of fusion. At the full meeting of Coalition Liberals two days later, he spoke only of the need for closer cooperation in the constituencies. Protestations of steadfast Liberalism, however, could not save Lloyd George's followers from the wrath of their Independent compatriots, and the party took another step towards dissolution in May, when several senior Coalitionists rashly attended the NLF meeting in Leamington. Their claim to be the true inheritors of the Liberal tradition so offended the predominantly Independent meeting that they were

49. Rowland, *Lloyd George*, pp. 519–29.   50. Wilson, *Downfall*, p. 204.
51. Rowland, *Lloyd George*, p. 569.   52. Morgan, *Age*, p. 200.
53. Wilson, *Downfall*, p. 197.

shouted down, and obliged to stage a walk-out that could not disguise their rejection.

The failure of fusion demonstrated the isolation of the Coalition Liberals, and left Lloyd George more dependent upon the Conservatives than ever, and thus upon their continued willingness to support social reform. For the moment, he was thrown back upon his second alternative, the formation of a distinct Coalition Liberal organisation. The Coalition Liberal councils that resulted were regional bodies not constituency associations, and even the establishment of these was not accomplished without some difficulty. The ready availability of funds, accumulated in part from the sale of honours, made creating a *Lloyd George Liberal Magazine* as a counterpart to the official *Liberal Magazine* considerably easier, but did not guarantee readers. The National Liberal party that was officially launched in January 1922 proved no lifeline to an increasingly stranded prime minister.

The failure of Coalitionism

The expectations of social reform from the coalition were not initially disappointed. During 1919 and much of 1920, despite mounting criticism of the cost, the government had proceeded with reconstruction. The extension of unemployment insurance, the increase in old-age pensions, a new Education Act, accelerated school building and a revised scale of pay for teachers, the extension of assistance to agriculture, and the creation of a new ministry of health, headed by Addison, with the prospect of poor-law reform, were all evidence of the government's sense of purpose. Housing, which addressed a pre-war shortage and had been a central element in the land campaign before the war was, however, the 'ultimate test' of 'the worth of the Coalition's social intentions'.[54]

Addison's Housing Act passed in July 1919 obliged local authorities to provide houses assisted by state subsidies. Addison aimed to build 500,000 houses under the scheme, but confronted by the reluctance of already indebted local authorities, the rising cost of materials, the shortage of skilled labour in the building industry and the resistance of the building unions to government intervention, the scheme rapidly ran into difficulties. The collapse of the postwar boom and the imposition of high interest rates by a treasury

54. Morgan, *Consensus*, p. 88.

bent on fiscal orthodoxy sealed its fate. The target was progressively reduced to 300,000 in February 1921, then 250,000 and finally to 176,000 in July. Addison himself was removed from the ministry in March 1921, and resigned from the government in July.

The commitment to minimum wages followed the same course. In 1919 both sides of industry on the short-lived National Industrial Council recommended legislation to establish universally applicable minimum wages and maximum hours, which the cabinet approved in April. Between 1918 and 1921, the number of trade boards increased from eleven to sixty-three, and the number of workers in minimum wage schemes from half to 3 million. In 1921 the process stopped; only six more boards were set up in the inter-war period. Treasury control and the internal weakness of the ministry of labour were significant factors, but the key was again the failure of political will. Ministers did not support reforming civil servants against the treasury, and lacked the conviction to pursue a consistent interventionist policy.[55]

For much of the war, business interests appeared to share the government belief in an insecure economic future. Nevertheless, the siege mentality on which intervention and reconstruction was posited did not long outlast the war, if it lasted that long. The ministry of labour remarked on the 'revulsion of feeling' against the extension of state control during the war, and reported early in 1918 that 'Everybody – employers and workers alike – are saying they don't want the State to act, they want the State to keep out and let them handle their own problems.' In true bureaucratic fashion it complained that 'they are *not* handling their own problems. They are doing nothing – except abuse the State', but the fact remained that the state was unwanted.[56] Minimum-wage legislation was all but unenforceable in the face of potential public non-compliance. A Portsmouth court refused to convict drapers accused of paying illegally low wages, and the government backed away from its own legal obligation to enforce the wages imposed by the Grocery Trade Board.[57]

Recession from the middle of 1920 provoked a cry from the political right for retrenchment, although such was the confusion of political alignments that their views were shared by the Asquithian leadership; and within Labour, despite its left-wing pose, Snowden proved the epitome of fiscal rectitude. Reconstruction failed because

55. Rodney Lowe, 'The erosion of state intervention in Britain 1917–24', *Economic History Review* 31 (1978), 270–86.

56. Ibid. p. 286.　　57. Ibid. pp. 285, 276.

such demands caught the public mood. Politically stifled by the coalition, retrenchment found expression in the anti-waste campaign, a grass roots movement favoured by sections of the Conservative press and right-wing independents which threatened the Conservative members of the coalition as much as Lloyd George. An Anti-Waste candidate won the Dover by-election in January 1921, and the Abbey division of Westminster in June. In August, Lloyd George appointed a committee under the chairmanship of the former spendthrift, Sir Eric Geddes, to investigate ways of reducing government expenditure, despite the opposition not only of Fisher but of Churchill and even Baldwin. As a 'sop to anti-waste' it backfired. A businessman's committee, consisting largely of men from the transport sector, in February 1922 recommended cuts of £75 million, including £18 million from the education budget.[58] The high hopes born of wartime reconstruction lay in ruins, amidst the debris of 'a land fit for heroes'.

The fall of the coalition

The failure of reconstruction entailed the failure of the coalition as a political experiment. For the Conservatives, especially the backbenchers whose commitment to both the coalition and reconstruction was markedly less strong than that of the leadership, this was an increasingly desirable outcome. For the Coalition Liberals it was a disaster. Pulled between their allies and their Liberalism and devoid of their *raison d'être*, they began, like the Independent Liberals, to fall apart into Conservative- and Labour-inclined sections. Lloyd George vainly sought to hold the coalition together. In the absence of fusion by consent, the only alternative was an election fought as a coalition since this would almost certainly result in institutional realignment.[59] His success in negotiating an Irish agreement during 1921 appeared to offer the opportunity just as it increased the necessity. The treatment of Ireland since 1918 demonstrated at its bleakest the difference between executive and libertarian Liberalism. Government determination to restore order in Ireland led to the proscription of Sinn Fein in August 1919 and of the Dail in September, and the use of the 'Black and Tan' irregulars to counter Sinn Fein attacks. The reprisals and counter-reprisals of 1920 and 1921 outraged Liberal opinion, and added one more item to

58. Morgan, *Age*, p. 202.   59. Wilson, *Downfall*, p. 220.

the growing catalogue of Lloyd George's betrayals of Liberalism, which did not concern Lloyd George since he was not, at this point, seeking Liberal reunion.

Lloyd George's opening of discussions in December 1921 for an early election to achieve fusion by subterfuge was enough to frighten away his prospective Conservative victims. Unionists up and down the country responded to the inquiries of the new party leader, Austen Chamberlain, by denouncing not only plans for an early election, but the coalition itself. Chamberlain himself feared the emergence of many 'independent Conservatives, unpledged to the support of the Coalition', and the party's chief agent, Malcolm Fraser, feared that 'it would split the Unionist party from top to toe'. Lloyd George's designs for fusion, in effect a new 'Centre party', were founded on just this prospect: the division of the Conservative party into a majority tied to his coalition and a diehard anti-coalitionist rump. He had, in fact, been rumbled. In the face of these protests, astutely leaked to the press, and the outspoken opposition of the party chairman, Sir George Younger, who reinforced them, Lloyd George was forced to abandon his plans in mid-January.[60]

The Conservative party was rapidly moving beyond the control of its leaders. Lloyd George was forced to threaten resignation to evoke pledges of loyalty from leading Coalition Conservatives, but the pledges meant little. Confident of backbench support, Younger ignored efforts to discipline him. A deputation of backbenchers to Chamberlain on 13 February protesting against the continuation of the coalition reinforced the point.[61] The crisis marked, as another alienated Conservative backbencher, W.A.S. Hewins, noted,

> the disintegration of the Coalition. The idea of a general election at once was not welcome to any section of Conservatives ... but the prevailing feeling amongst Conservative M.P.s, and still more in the constituencies is that they will not have another coalition election. Opinion, however, is not sufficiently formed to prevent some split in the Conservative ranks if LL.G. forced an election now. Fusion is out of the question. ... So these people want to wait until Conservatives can go to the country as a party[62]

Until then, the Coalitionist Liberals continued to suffer humiliation from a Conservative party unleashed as a result of its chairman's

---

60. Morgan, *Consensus*, pp. 271–9.   61. Rowland, *Lloyd George*, pp. 561–2.
62. Ibid. p. 550.

defiance. In March, to their unabashed delight, Montagu was forced to resign after a disagreement with Curzon, the foreign secretary, over the propriety of publishing a dispatch from the Indian viceroy, the Marquess of Reading, criticising the government's anti-Turkish policy in the Middle East. *The Times* echoed Hewins in seeing the coalition 'dying before our eyes'.[63]

Lloyd George looked abroad, to the coming conference at Genoa in April 1922 to achieve 'European pacification' and 'restore his star to the zenith'.[64] Undermined by French intransigence and the prior Russo-German agreement at Rapallo, the conference was a failure like its numerous predecessors. Lloyd George's plan 'to fight on Genoa' as 'the real test of whether the Coalition is to be progressive or reactionary'[65] never got off the drawing board. Instead, his purpose in attending the conference, to gain conditional recognition for communist Russia, provided another reason for the Conservatives to reject the coalition, if another reason was needed. Lloyd George was further discredited by the 'sale of honours scandal' in June. The award of honours for political services or contributions was a long-established practice, but the Coalition Liberals, in need of funds of their own after the split with the Asquithians, were too blatant in their approaches and sometimes insufficiently scrupulous in their choice of recipients. Conservative reaction was conditioned by the fear that Lloyd George was stealing their own hopefuls and diverting money from Conservative-party coffers to his own, but the affair provided another stick with which to beat Lloyd George, who was driven to refer the question to a royal commission. The dubious origins of his political fund haunted Lloyd George throughout the remainder of his political career.

By the summer of 1922, Conservative backbenchers needed only an occasion and a lead to overthrow the government and destroy the coalition. The occasion developed out of the crisis in the Middle East where, at the end of August, the resurgent Turks threatened the small British garrison at Chanak as they proceeded to tear up the post-war settlement of the region which had greatly favoured the Greeks at their expense. Lloyd George's aggressively pro-Greek and anti-Turkish stance produced a rift in the government and another outcry from outraged Conservatives for whom support for Turkey had been traditional party policy since the time of Disraeli. Disillusionment with the coalition was now so great that in September the Conservative chief whip predicted that over 180 independent

63. Ibid. p. 569.   64. Ibid. p. 570.   65. Ibid. p. 569.

Conservative candidates would be run against the coalition at the next election.[66]

Despite the manifold indications of discontent, and the now familiar opposition from Younger and Conservative-party officials, still fearing a party split,[67] Lloyd George and his closest cabinet colleagues, which included Austen Chamberlain, decided on 17 September in favour of an early election. Insofar as this was designed to exploit popular patriotism aroused by the international crisis, Lloyd George had misread the national mood. The Chanak crisis did not offer the opportunity for a desperate prime minister to restore his reputation and secure his government, but confronted an exhausted nation with an unwanted war. Popular feeling was more accurately reflected by Bonar Law, briefly restored to health by his rest, who noted in a letter to *The Times* that Britain could no longer act as the policeman of the world. The re-emergence of Law was crucial in the events that followed, providing the lead that the disaffected Conservatives required.

The Chanak crisis was resolved by negotiation just before final collapse of the coalition, for which it was only indirectly responsible. Already in its death-throes, the end of the coalition was brought about by the determination to prove that it was still alive. The decision in mid-September to hold an early election showed senior members of the government to be out of touch with their largely Conservative supporters both in parliament and the country, but convinced that they could impose their will and eager to force the issue before disaffection grew even stronger. After Chanak, however, the revolt had spread too far, and embraced not only backbenchers and junior ministers, but members of the cabinet itself, including both Curzon and Baldwin. In summoning a party meeting at the Carlton Club on 19 October to assert his authority and secure assent to an early election as a coalition, Chamberlain over-reached himself. Nevertheless, it was Bonar Law's intervention in favour of independent action rather than Baldwin's perceptive criticism of Lloyd George as a 'dynamic force' who had already split the Liberal party and was bent on splitting the Conservatives, that ensured Chamberlain's failure. The meeting voted to withdraw from the coalition and rallied to Bonar Law. Technically the Conservatives did split, in that Chamberlain, Birkenhead and Balfour remained loyal to Lloyd George, but it was not the deep vertical split that Lloyd George sought and Younger feared. The backbench rebellion proved decisive. The resignations of Chamberlain as party leader and Lloyd George as prime minister followed as a matter of course.

The end of the coalition left the Liberal Coalitionists without a political home or a political purpose. Fusion was part of Lloyd George's vision for post-war reconstruction in which all parties would split, leaving impotent rumps of diehard Conservatives, anachronistic Liberals and fanatical socialists outside the new national party. Its aim was to transform society, but if society showed no wish to be transformed, then there was no place for the party that was to carry out the transformation. The general election of 1922 confirmed this verdict. In places, Coalition Liberals fought with Asquithian support, elsewhere they relied on the Conservatives as in 1918; in some twenty-four constituencies Independent Liberals attacked Coalitionists, in five constituencies Coalitionists attacked Independents; in Berwick and East Ham, there were three Liberal candidates. The Conservatives, even though they left 174 seats uncontested and suffered a net loss of 15 seats, gained a clear overall majority. The Liberals won 117 in total, but were outnumbered in the new House of Commons by Labour which now included 11 former left-wing Liberal MPs, the 'brains' that Henderson considered the great lack of the Labour party.

The great losers were the Coalition Liberals, who recorded only three gains against eighty-one losses, demonstrating yet again the dependence of the former coalition on Conservative support in the constituencies as well as in parliament.[68] The Independent Liberals won fifty-six seats, primarily from Conservatives and ten from the Coalitionists, but only one from Labour. For Liberals generally the emerging pattern was disturbing. Labour had run over 400 candidates and won 142 seats, but above all it was establishing a socio-regional basis of support in the industrial constituencies; Conservatism predominated in its old heartland of southern England and in middle-class suburban constituencies. The pre-war polarisation was re-emerging, albeit with Conservatism much stronger, and with Labour increasingly occupying the old Liberal bases.[69]

Coalition Liberalism: the wrong turning

By 1922 it was clear that the war had not revolutionised either society or politics. The coalition experiment was an attempt to realise

68. Wilson, *Downfall*, pp. 285–7.   69. Ibid. pp. 235–40.

the potential that appeared to exist in pre-war politics for a realignment of parties into collectivist and anti-collectivist groups by harnessing the energies released by the war. The experience revealed that a coalition of social-imperialist and New Liberal collectivists was no more viable in 1918 than it had been in 1910. Whatever radicals of the right and of the left may have had in common, their radicalism remained unwanted by the country which had demonstrated a widespread rejection of wartime priorities and the siege mentality. In their place, there had been a considerable reassertion of Liberal values that censured the penal peace treaties of 1919 and entrusted the future to the League of Nations. Even decontrol and the demand for retrenchment were expressions of an individualism and economic orthodoxy that was at root Liberal, even if the Liberalism was of a rather old-fashioned kind. Not only had there been no 'strange death of Liberal England' before the war, but 'Liberal England' had survived the war itself. Yet the Liberal party failed to benefit from this revival of Liberal values.

The perpetuation of the division of 1916 beyond the war by continuing the wartime coalition into the coupon election of 1918 was obviously partly responsible for this. The split of 1916 concerned the conduct of the war, and resulted from political pressures that required the shunting or sacrifice of Asquith to preserve a government of national unity in a wartime emergency. There was no clear line dividing the bulk of Liberals into two separate camps to prevent reunion once the war ended, however uncomfortable the initial moments. The bitterness and the institutionalisation of the division followed from the coupon election. This does not make Lloyd George solely responsible for the split, still less for the collapse of the Liberal party. Bitterness was the prerogative of the Asquithians; they first institutionalised the split and rejected the Coalitionists at Leamington. Nor was Lloyd George responsible for the lacklustre leadership provided by Asquith and his senior colleagues, or their failure to tap the dynamic radicalism of the constituency activists.

Nevertheless, in taking a section of the Liberal party into coalition, Lloyd George fatally misjudged the attitude of the electorate. Labour unrest during the war confirmed Lloyd George's views about the inability of the working classes not only to govern the country, but to govern themselves.[70] It was a conclusion he was predisposed to reach but it confirmed the direction in which he wished to take

70. Rowland, *Lloyd George*, p. 452.

Liberalism. 'He wants to improve the world and the condition of the people,' Riddell observed, 'but wants to do it in his own way.'[71] This entailed not the empowerment of labour, politically or industrially, but labour docility, cooperating with their employers. Riddell was extremely sceptical of Lloyd George's plans for national unity under a National Party, but captured the tone. 'The rich must give to the poor, but the poor must not ask too much. They must be good children. I wonder.'[72]

Lloyd George welcomed confrontation with the miners in 1920 as an opportunity to enforce government authority. 'Now is the acceptable moment for putting everything to the test. We must show Labour that the Government mean to be masters.'[73] The same outlook produced the insistence on the restoration of order in Ireland that led to the introduction of the 'Black and Tans', and his remark that if the Greeks misbehaved, Athens could be levelled by the British fleet.[74] The benefits of his 'Nationalist-Socialist' reforms were only available to those who behaved 'properly'.[75] There was, as Smuts observed, 'a curious element of brutality in George . . . George believes far too much in force'.[76] Lloyd George was, like Joseph Chamberlain, a 'radical authoritaire'.[77] Both sought radical change using the power of the state, disrupting political parties in pursuit of the political leverage to do so. Baldwin's description of Lloyd George as 'a dynamic force' was, from Baldwin's point of view as a conventional party politician, correct.

In pursuit of dynamic leadership, Coalition Liberalism turned its back upon the working classes, which had become crucial to Liberal party success by the end of the nineteenth century. After the 'great cleavage' Lloyd George envisaged relying 'on the business classes to a great extent', and his concerns were adjusted accordingly.[78] The abandonment of the excess profits duty was justified by the need to conciliate the government's 'principal supporters and those on whom the permanent commercial prosperity of the country largely depended'.[79] Far from leading the middle classes into a brave new world, however, Lloyd George, and thus Liberalism, became their prisoner. In 1921, when 'the middle classes mean to insist upon a drastic cut down [of government expenditure]; nothing will satisfy

71. Lord Riddell, *Lord Riddell's Intimate Diary of the Peace Conference and After 1918–1923* (London: Gollancz, 1933), p. 179.
72. Riddell, *War Diary*, p. 334.   73. Rowland, *Lloyd George*, p. 528.
74. Wilson, *Scott*, p. 395.   75. Rowland, *Lloyd George*, p. 418.
76. Wilson, *Scott*, p. 398.
77. Austen Chamberlain, *Politics from Inside* (London: Cassell, 1936), p. 81.
78. Rowland, *Lloyd George*, p. 447.   79. Ibid. p. 522.

them next year except an actual reduction in taxes', they had to be satisfied: 'ruthless reductions . . . are inevitable'.[80] This put an end to any hope that Coalition Liberalism resting on the business classes, especially when envisaged as an administrative elite, would bring about a radical politically led reconstruction of the country.

The electoral consequences, veiled in 1918 by nationalist revanchism and coalition unity soon became apparent. Convinced that 'as far as the industrial north is concerned, our real peril is Labour', Lloyd George was rightly concerned 'lest we find ourselves caught between Labour in the north and "Anti-Waste" in the south'.[81] Lloyd George sought to occupy a middle ground that did not exist. Since it did not, he competed with Conservatism for the middle classes, and abandoned the Liberal heartland to Labour. So, however, did the Independent Liberals. Asquith's refusal to fight the 1918 election in determined opposition to the coalition virtually invited any Liberal who wished to oppose the Conservative party to vote Labour. The calls for retrenchment were but a pale reflection of the anti-waste campaign; where Lloyd George praised the 'captains of industry', Asquith defended the coal-owners, and radical policies such as the redistribution of wealth or a capital levy were simply ignored.

Lloyd George identified, but apparently failed to comprehend, the fateful choice made by the Liberal leadership during and after the war. 'If the working classes are united against us, the outlook is grave and the gravity would be intensified if what I call intellectual liberalism unites with Labour against us.'[82] It was this continuation of what had been the Edwardian progressive alliance, in which the working classes and intellectual Liberalism were united with the Liberal party, that he and Asquith shunned in 1918. To survive, as the Edwardian experience had shown, the Liberal party had to continue to evolve, but as Liberalism, not as 'Nationalism-Socialism'. Lloyd George's attempt to provide organisation and leadership for radical Liberalism after 1924 came too late to revive the Liberal party. Moreover, it remained radicalism from above offered to a society which had shown itself highly conservative in a liberal sense.

80. Ibid. p. 538.   81. Ibid.   82. Ibid. p. 528.

CHAPTER NINE

The End of Liberal Politics

Despite the recriminations of the previous six years, reunion rapidly reappeared on the agenda of the Liberals returned to parliament in 1922, but the various calls for reunion were marked by distrust, insincerity and confrontation. Leading Coalitionists like Guest still preferred the idea of cooperation with the Conservatives as anti-socialists as if the Centre party scheme was still alive[1]; leading Asquithians inclined, or thought they inclined, towards cooperation with Labour, although their position on this remained rather nebulous. Asquith reiterated in March that the Liberals had no fundamental dispute with Labour,[2] and his appointment of Vivian Phillips, MP for West Edinburgh and a pronounced anti-Coalitionist, as chief whip was a direct affront to Lloyd George. Statements by both Asquith and Lloyd George and a memorandum signed by seventy-three MPs in favour of reunion meant little; in practice the old animosities remained.

Liberals reunited

It was typical both of the condition of the Liberal party and of the electorate's outlook that Liberal reunion and Liberal revival were ultimately the result of external pressure to defend the ancient Liberal cause of free trade. In November 1923 Baldwin, who had succeeded the ailing Bonar Law as leader of the Conservative party in May, suddenly cast himself in the unlikely role of dynamic force

1. Roy Douglas, *The History of the Liberal Party 1895–1970* (London: Sidgwick & Jackson, 1971), pp. 166–7.
2. Trevor Wilson, *The Downfall of the Liberal Party* (London: Collins, 1966), p. 247.

and announced the need for protective tariffs and imperial preference to cure unemployment. Whether an aberration, the sincere
belief of a tariff reformer, which Baldwin was, or a political manoeuvre to pre-empt Lloyd George and reunite leading Conservative
dissidents with the party, Baldwin's announcement stirred the Liberals into action. Asquith and Lloyd George succeeded in agreeing
a single Liberal manifesto, Lloyd George contributed £160,000 to
the campaign from the Lloyd George Fund, and Liberals in the
constituencies were urged to unite behind a single candidate. The
weakness of the Lloyd George Liberal organisation in the constituencies facilitated this, although there were still occasional places
with rival Liberal candidates.[3]

The return of 158 Liberals in the general election of 1923
appeared superficially as a success for the reunited party, which
presented itself as the alternative to both protection and socialism.
The victory, however, was won on the negative defence of free
trade rather than the manifesto's references to public works to ease
unemployment. The party reaped the benefits of a conservative
stance against more radical proposals from both Conservatism and
Labour. Sixty-nine of the eighty-three Liberal gains were from the
Conservatives reflecting a protest vote by free-trade Conservatives,
not a conversion to Liberalism. Liberals did well in old Liberal
areas of Nonconformity like the west country, in the cotton regions
of the north-west and in retirement and spa towns where 'old Tory
tabbies' disliked innovation of any kind and feared the impact of
protection on their fixed incomes.[4] The party made little impression on Labour, gaining only thirteen seats. Above all, it failed to
reassert its supremacy in the Celtic and northern-England heartland of Victorian and Edwardian Liberalism.

Many of the Liberal victories were insecure, reliant on the high
number of seats uncontested by the Conservatives, and were won
with narrow majorities or in straight fights.[5] As the 1924 election
was to show, these gains were untenable once the Conservative
party resumed the path of negation upon which Salisbury had
founded its late-Victorian recovery. Even in 1923 they remained the
largest party with 258 seats, and in an election fought on the Liberal issue of free trade, Labour came second with 191. When Baldwin
resigned after his defeat by Labour and Liberal votes in a vote of

---

3. Ibid. p. 251.   4. Ibid. p. 259.
5. Ibid. p. 263. The Conservatives left twenty-three seats uncontested, Labour
sixty-eight. More than a quarter of Liberal victories were with majorities of under
1000 votes, and over half were won in straight fights.

confidence, Labour formed a minority government. The alternative of a caretaker Liberal government with general Conservative and Labour support has received more support from Liberal historians than it did from Liberals at the time.[6]

Although Ramsay MacDonald had shown no inclination to negotiate, the Liberals expected some degree of cooperation from a Labour government which included several ex-Liberal figures and depended upon Liberal votes to keep it in office. There appeared to be sufficient common ground on both domestic and foreign policy to recreate a form of the Edwardian progressive alliance, albeit with the party roles reversed. Such expectations, heavily conditioned by patronising disdain for Labour's ability to govern and a continued assumption of Liberal indispensability, were rapidly removed. In the constituencies, even when the Liberals showed restraint, Labour consistently attacked Liberal candidates – even at the cost of a Conservative victory.

Apart from Snowden's completely orthodox free-trade budget, it also soon became clear that there were basic disagreements between Liberal and Labour policies, but the Liberals backed away from confrontation, fearing that the defeat of the government would precipitate a general election. As early as February 1924, Lloyd George's former private secretary, Edward Grigg, thought that MacDonald 'is definitely established as the national leader of the Left [and] will take with him a very large section of the Liberal Party when next he goes to the country'.[7] Liberal anger at Labour's uncompromising attitude increased with the realisation of their powerlessness to control a government which was dragging them to certain doom. In August, the government's proposed trade treaty with Russia, which included loan guarantees, finally found the limits of Liberal tolerance. Faced with certain defeat, the government chose to go out on the 'Campbell' case, a similarly 'Bolshevik' issue in which the Liberals demanded a select committee to consider the dropping of charges of incitement to mutiny against the editor of the *Workers' Weekly*. The Liberals were left to explain why, in the light of their criticisms, they had maintained such an irresponsible government in office for so long.

6. Douglas, *Liberal Party*, p. 175: 'Asquith rejected the idea of playing for a Liberal administration . . . it is arguable that this decision was the most disastrous single action ever performed by a Liberal towards his party.' See also Chris Cook, 'A stranger death of Liberal England', in A.J.P. Taylor (ed.), *Lloyd George: Twelve Essays* (London: Hamish Hamilton, 1971), pp. 287–313.

7. Wilson, *Downfall*, p. 270.

Elections since 1918, even when the issue favoured Liberalism as in 1923, showed that the Liberals fared badly in three-cornered contests. The effect of the Labour government of 1924 was to focus attention on the three-party nature of the system, and the virtual irrelevance of the Liberal party in that situation. Moreover, within the Liberal party the suppression of factionalism to defend free trade was only temporary. The legacy of the past continued to provoke acrimonious disputes over control of the organisation, which in turn inhibited recovery. The official party machine, still controlled by Asquithians, was crippled by lack of money. The threat to free trade had brought donations in 1923, but by 1924 such sources of income had all but dried up. Support for the Labour government frightened away several wealthy supporters; awareness of the Lloyd George Fund discouraged more. Because of its poverty the party was, as Herbert Gladstone, now director of the Liberal party's head-quarters, frankly admitted to Asquith, 'at L.G.'s feet'.[8]

In 1923, the *Lloyd George Liberal Magazine* had ceased publica-tion, and National Liberal organisations wound down as part of 'reunion', but Lloyd George rejected Gladstone's proposed pool-ing of funds and retained his separate headquarters. The Fund was Lloyd George's trump card, and his only defence against the hos-tility of the leading Asquithians. Grigg, who supported Lloyd George's retention of his funds, believed that 'they have no desire except to strangle him at the earliest possible opportunity'.[9] Lloyd George knew this, just as the Asquithians knew that Lloyd George sought to wrest control of the Liberal party from them by exploit-ing their poverty. The result was paralysis. Throughout 1924, until the very eve of the election when he grudgingly made £50,000 available (Gladstone thought £130,000 the minimum required), Lloyd George resisted both pressure and concessions and refused any commitments. In 1924 the party was able to put forward only 346 candidates, thus making apparent to all that it was a third party with no pretensions to office.

Such bickering was suicidal for both factions. By 1924 the Lib-eral party, however moribund, was the only institutional base left to Lloyd George. The official party possessed the framework of a national constituency organisation which he lacked, together with the Liberal-party tradition; but without the money which only Lloyd George could provide, that organisation was steadily decaying. Moreover, without some new policies which could give meaning to

8. Ibid. p. 293.   9. Ibid. p. 280.

the assertion that the Liberal party offered a real alternative to both socialism and Conservatism, there was little reason for its continued existence. After the experience of the previous six years of Asquithian leadership, it was clear that these too could only come from Lloyd George. The 1924 election drove this lesson home. With Conservatism now re-established as the party of resistance, and Labour nominally as the party of change, the Liberals for the first time felt the force of the squeeze that the British electoral system applies to third parties. The Conservatives won an overwhelming victory with 415 seats, Labour fell to 152, but the Liberals were all but obliterated, with only 43 MPs.

The Liberal party had in practice behaved as a third party since 1918. Devoid of an independent identity as Liberals proclaiming a specifically Liberal policy, and equally devoid of electoral strength, sections of the party defined themselves relatively, and inclined towards either Conservatism or Labour. In the post-war context, the majority of the Lloyd George Liberals saw Liberalism as a movement of the right, a tendency encouraged by the need for Conservative support, or at least acquiescence, for the safety of their seats. Whilst the bulk of the Liberal party favoured the attempt to cooperate with Labour in 1924, a group of some twenty Liberals, mostly ex-Coalitionists, voted regularly with the Conservatives against the Labour government.

Their outlook at least had the virtue of consistency. The experience of a Labour government in 1924 also exposed the vapid assertions and patrician arrogance of the Asquithian leadership. With far less awareness of what they were doing, they too drifted towards the Conservative party. At the end of 1923 the *Liberal Magazine* had maintained that Liberals and Conservatives 'are separated in their fundamental aims, in thought, in idea, in principle: and there is neither any event nor any formula that can ever bridge this gulf'.[10] By 1924, however, the gulf had been bridged. The party campaigned against Labour, frequently in cooperation, and sometimes in alliance, with Conservatism. 'Both the old political parties in this election,' Asquith argued, 'have found themselves, as they believe, confronted with a common danger, which, without any loss of identity or compromise of principle on one side or upon the other, they are making reciprocal sacrifices to avert.' Asquith welcomed Conservative supporters on to his platform, and like Lloyd George, was spared a Conservative opponent, although he still lost to Labour,

10. Ibid. p. 265.

whose candidate, Rosslyn Mitchell, was another former Liberal. The promise of reunion, and above all the promise that Liberalism represented an alternative to both Conservatism and Labour, remained unfulfilled.[11]

Summer-school radicalism

Insofar as being reduced to a leading member of an insignificant rump can be said to benefit any politician, the election of 1924 benefited Lloyd George at the expense of the Asquithians. The great majority of Liberals returned were his supporters, and he quickly realised his ambition to be elected chairman of the party. It was symptomatic of continuing division that the Asquithian dissidents responded by forming a 'radical group' under Runciman. Runciman's statement that the group 'would take a pronouncedly Radical line, regarding Tories equally with Socialists as their political foes',[12] reiterated a familiar third-party theme, but was, in this case, directed less against the Conservatives than the former Liberal Coalitionists. Runciman was no radical by post-1906 standards, and the group's choice of title revealed yet again that the bulk of the Liberal party, and especially the Asquithian element, had reverted to a mid-Victorian mentality. Although they were slow to realise it, and still thought of themselves as 'radicals', in the post-1918 world they had become 'conservative' in a way that was undynamic even by the standards of the Conservative party.

Herein lay the importance of the return of Lloyd George in 1923, and of the struggle for control of the party machinery. Masterman's view, that 'when Lloyd George came back to the party, ideas came back to the party'[13] was not entirely accurate. Ideas had been bubbling in the Liberal summer school that E.D. Simon had founded in 1921. The summer school, however, was not only unofficial, but had been deliberately set up as a forum for Liberal ideas independent of the party, although its success rapidly drew in party involvement.[14] By 1927 the *Manchester Guardian* saw 'the primary object with which these Liberal summer schools are held' as 'the definition of . . . Liberal policy'.[15] The summer schools were 'the success story of the liberalism of the 1920s',[16] a conclusion that

11. Ibid. pp. 302–3.   12. Ibid. p. 321.   13. Ibid. p. 287.
14. Michael Freeden, *Liberalism Divided* (Oxford: Oxford University Press, 1986), p. 82.
15. Ibid. p. 104.   16. Ibid. p. 15.

itself signifies the bankrupt state of the Liberal party as a political force. Their success was none the less flawed.

The problem lay in the nature of the ideas themselves. The war and its aftermath had dealt a severe blow to Liberal confidence in Liberalism as an ideology, even when wartime compulsion was justified on the grounds of temporary emergency and regarded as not 'necessarily anti-Liberal or anti-democratic'.[17] The extent and nature of wartime intervention revealed to Liberal theorists the coercive character of the state that had previously been apparent only to its selected targets. Hobhouse now discovered that compulsion destroyed 'the moral autonomy of the individual' that was 'the kernel of the *modern* principle of liberty'.[18] The reaction was not, and could not be, complete. Hobhouse retained his allegiance to the principle of the 'common good' and to 'the rights of the community as a whole' implicitly over-riding the rights of the individual. A letter to the *Nation* in 1925 still argued that man derived all his liberty and all his rights from his relation to society, and 'fulfils himself and gains true significance through his association with the community and through nothing else'.[19] The state had nevertheless lost some of its aura as the embodiment of the common good, and thus as an ethical absolute, that it had enjoyed in the most extreme expressions of pre-war New Liberalism and, to a lesser degree, in the Whig view of legislation.

The war also revealed another problem that pre-war Liberals had attempted to ignore: the existence of competing groups within society, rather than, as they supposed and hoped, competing individuals. Typically, but one-sidedly, they saw this most clearly in the growth of trade-union power and the rise of its political wing, the Labour party. Masterman, despite his pre-war reforming radicalism, saw unions as 'a repetition of the tyranny of the old feudal and landlord system'. By 1925, Hobhouse had reversed his previous supportive position just because trade unions, once essential for the emancipation of the working classes, had become not only 'powerful but dominating'.[20] The enhanced awareness of competing interest groups within society challenged the very foundation of Liberalism, the belief that rational behaviour, good legislation and the right institutions could, as an evolutionary process, bring harmony out of conflict. Liberalism was no longer a doctrine that transcended conflict, nor could the Liberal party rely on that doctrine in its claim

17. Ibid. p. 21.   18. Ibid. pp. 23, 270.   19. Ibid. pp. 277–9.
20. Ibid. pp. 200–1.

to be a national party. In accepting the emergence of conflicting sections, Liberalism was forced to consider mediation between sectional interests, in political terms to find a middle way, to become a party for which compromise was a policy in itself. This in turn exacerbated the problem of an ideological and political identity.

Rather belatedly, the Liberals gained some insight into what the worker wanted. 'It used to be thought that the working man wanted two things – good wages and security. It is now evident that he wants something more – a sense of freedom and responsibility in his work . . . the working classes are, in fact, trying to demand the introduction of the atmosphere of democracy into their working lives.' As always, Liberals overlooked material factors and over-intellectualised, yet seemed incapable of grasping that whilst 'the old labour questions were bread and butter questions [and] the new ones are rather those of responsibility, independence, and . . . industrial self-government', these issues were not mutually exclusive. Insofar as workers did want control it was to safeguard their bread and butter. The *Nation* was more perceptive in deducing that for the workman 'the State, its institutions, its industries, these are not to be active forces pressing on his life, ruling his habits; they are to be a world that feels and reflects his power'.[21] The working classes were looking, as usual, to an industrial world of free collective bargaining. The state remained more a potential instrument of oppression than of liberation. Liberals still failed utterly to understand the defensive mentality of the working classes and the defensive purpose of working-class institutions. Control of the state secured the position of trade unions, determined the incidence of taxation, and regulated the operations of the bureaucracy, police and army. They could not be de-politicised.

Liberal theories in pursuit of a middle way thus started on false assumptions about the nature of industrial confrontation. Their ideal solution still lay with incorporation. The Whitley report of June 1917 attempted this through the establishment of joint industrial councils with equal representatives of employers' associations and unions to discuss not only wages, conditions and security of employment, but industrial research and legislation. Samuel, as a moderate, thought that in this way 'the workman would become a citizen of the workshop as well as of the state'. The New Liberal *Nation* saw in the councils the principle that 'an industry is not the property of an employer, but a form of national service undertaken

21. Ibid. pp. 50–1.

by a body of persons, all of whom have a recognised share in its control'. In another way, however, the Whitley councils could be interpreted as an attempt to reconstitute mid-Victorian factory paternalism enabling 'philanthropic employers to break up the solidarity of the union and to create a special community of interest between themselves and the workers in their factories, as opposed to the solidarity that united, or could unite, their workers to unionised workers in other firms'.[22] Such a community of interest was precisely what Liberals sought, but the belief that it could be engendered simply by creating the institutions within which it might operate reduced Liberalism to a pious aspiration.

The difficulty emerged when the NLF considered its industrial report in 1921. The *Manchester Guardian* inadvertently assumed that the recommended national industrial council and its subordinate committees would have compulsory powers to fix wages and hours, only to be rebuked by Ramsay Muir, who pointed out that the issue of compulsion was left undetermined. Since the state was at that time finding minimum-wage awards impossible to enforce, the dispute mattered little except to reveal Liberal uncertainty. A far more significant manifestation of ambivalence towards the state was the desire to use industrial councils to take industrial relations outside the sphere of politics. Councils were, for Muir, the basis of 'a real and powerful system of industrial self-government, subject always to the control of the State, but not to the incessant intervention of its agents'.[23] For Hobhouse, the Whitley councils might become the basis for a structure of government parallel to the state, 'such that the definition of their relations with the State . . . may become the central question of politics',[24] rather than industrial regulation itself.

Suspicion of the state that led post-war Liberalism to devolve complex issues to essentially voluntarist bodies like the Whitley councils, and to propose that the regulation of trusts could be left to public opinion, transformed the relationship of Liberalism and social reform that had been the core of the pre-war creed. In the post-war context of great hopes and shattered economies, direct state intervention, as briefly proposed by the Lloyd George coalition, was both too little and too much: too little because it offered only material improvements, not social and human regeneration; too much because it was essentially redistributive and in the post-war depression there was not enough to redistribute. In consequence,

22. Ibid. pp. 56–9.   23. Ibid. p. 63.   24. Ibid. p. 56.

'further large measures of social reform (of the public expenditure type) must be ruled out for the time being'.[25] Behind the failure of the coalition in the wake of 'anti-waste' and the Geddes report, and the failure of the Asquithian leadership to raise the issue, lay a belief that the country could no longer afford redistributive social reform. As the *Nation* wrote in 1929, 'the a priori justice or injustice of redistributing wealth by taxing the rich for the benefit of the poor is beside the point . . . we should eschew for the time being measures which are primarily redistributive in character and concentrate our energies for the next few years on the attempt to restore and improve our national productivity'.[26]

The NLF had said as much in 1921. The primary role of its national industrial council was 'to promote increased production'. Once 'the returns to capital are on the increase', it might also turn its hand to 'the full and proportionate reward of labour'.[27] Liberals were still convinced that capital, not labour, was the essential element in industry, or perhaps, as Muir argued, 'it is not capital which controls industry, it is expert direction – acting . . . in the interests of capital'.[28] They were equally convinced that capitalism only functioned with the profit incentive. Throughout the 1920s, Liberalism spoke with many voices. Nineteenth-century individualism and retrenchment still bumped against the New Liberal 'common good' and individual potentiality as expressions of the Liberal 'spirit', but in turn both ran into the more cautious Liberalism, if it was that, of the 1920s. The coup that secured the *Nation* for the organisers of the Liberal summer school in 1923 was symbolic of the new, less expansive, mood. The *Nation* passed from the ethically inspired optimism of Massingham and New Liberalism to what C.P. Scott rightly called 'the arid intellectualism of Keynes'. So did Liberalism. In policy terms, as the first edition of the revised *Nation* warned, 'the development of social services involving public expenditure, and the raising of money by stiffer taxes upon wealth' was no longer possible.[29] The new focus of attention was to be the management of the economy, with particular emphasis on monetary policy.[30]

In making the transition, Liberalism became even more elitist. Monetary policy was, as the new *Nation* also noted, a 'technical'

25. Ibid. p. 143.   26. Ibid. p. 165.   27. Ibid. p. 61.   28. Ibid. p. 147.
29. Ibid. p. 94.
30. John Campbell, 'The renewal of Liberalism: Liberalism without Liberals', in Gillian Peele and Chris Cook (eds), *The Politics of Reappraisal 1918–1939* (London: Macmillan, 1975), p. 95; Freeden, *Liberalism Divided*, pp. 90–4.

question.[31] Liberalism in this form became increasingly a technical creed by and for technicians. The technicians were more or less well-intentioned, and in focusing on unemployment they attacked the main social evil of the inter-war years. But managed capitalism with the emphasis on productivity was not pursued primarily for the sake of social justice, and the rights and rewards of industrial workers were hardly even a secondary consideration. Nor was it either easily comprehensible or easily presented in a comprehensible fashion. In 1925 E.D. Simon wondered privately 'whether a somber [*sic*] constructive Summer School policy can ever be made to appeal to more – or even be understood by – the mass of voters. I don't think any democracy has ever been interested in such a policy of reason and hard thinking.'[32] Unable to understand, the masses were to depend on 'a kind of trust on the part of politicians and the feeling of responsibility on the part of the more or less independent experts'.[33]

The resurrection of Lloyd George

The ideas developed by the Liberal summer-school movement, if not his own relegation to the role of observer, were grist to Lloyd George's mill. Riddell noted his awe of businessmen: 'he constantly refers to the great services rendered by captains of industry and defends the propriety of the large share of profits they take. He says one Leverhulme or Ellerman is worth more to the world than 10 000 sea captains or 20 000 engine drivers and should be remunerated accordingly.'[34] After the failure of the coalition, Lloyd George's ideas moved in the same direction as those of the Liberal intellectuals, towards improved productivity through managed capitalism, with the state exercising residual control rather than direct intervention. In the *Nation* in April 1924 he signalled his change of emphasis: 'It is of no avail to spend time on distribution if production lags behind the common need. The best means of achieving production seems to be the most urgent task of our industrial and political leaders at this hour.'[35] His speech to the London Liberal Federation in May 1924 identified Labour as well as Conservatism

31. Ibid. p. 95.   32. Ibid. p. 101.   33. Ibid. pp. 273–4.
34. Lord Riddell, *Lord Riddell's Intimate Diary of the Peace Conference and After* (London: Gollanz, 1933), p. 179.
35. Campbell, 'Renewal', p. 98.

as the enemies of Liberalism, and called for a new Liberal crusade for the creation of greater wealth and against vested interests that impeded national development. Amongst these he included the trade unions, as well as the familiar Liberal evils: the land and drink monopolies. Nevertheless, the 'great Liberal campaign' which followed, while drawing large audiences, was largely ineffective, as the 1924 general election result showed. In this it was a harbinger of 1929.

Unable to work within the framework of the official Liberal organisation, in 1924 Lloyd George reverted to his pre-war practice of developing and advocating novel policies through semi-private 'expert committees' and *ad hoc* leagues. From this developed his cooperation with the summer-school group of intellectuals. The first report, *Coal and Power*, was issued in 1924 over Lloyd George's name, but with clear input from the summer-school discussions, especially McNair's proposal for the nationalisation of coal and mineral royalties which could then be leased to private mining companies. The mines themselves were to remain in private hands, as was their management. *Coal and Power* was endorsed by Asquith, although neither he nor the party leadership had been consulted about its production or contents, and it figured in the party's election programme of 1924, which was fought under the slogan 'Peace, Social Reform and National Development'.

The second of Lloyd George's policy reports, *The Land and the Nation* (1925), the so-called 'Green Book', was similarly orientated towards increased productivity, but aroused a controversy that threatened to split the party. The evolution of a new policy and a new identity could not be disentangled from the struggle for control that had festered since the so-called 'reunion' of 1923. Throughout 1924, Lloyd George had justified his refusal to make his Fund available to the party on the grounds of the inefficiency of the party organisation. Electoral annihilation in the general election resulted in the appointment of a committee of enquiry which made party organisation more democratic by placing it under a representative administrative committee largely drawn from the NLF. In the long run, the change gave Lloyd George greater control, but at the time it represented no more than a recognition that in the absence of funding from headquarters, the constituencies would have to assume greater responsibilities. It went hand in hand with the 'million fund' appeal directed by Vivian Phillips to raise money from constituency supporters which was clearly intended to gain independence from Lloyd George. Its failure, and Lloyd George's continued refusal to contribute, left the party desperately poor, and its provincial organisation deteriorated further. Agents went unpaid,[36] and at one point Phillips feared that the party headquarters might have to close altogether.[37]

Under these circumstances, Lloyd George's use of his Fund to finance his committees, and in October 1925 to form the Land and Nation League to agitate the 'Green Book' policy, was provocative. Protests by Phillips at the use of the money induced Lloyd George to offer the party £20,000 a year for three years, but only if the party adopted his land policy. The principal proposal, 'cultivating tenure', in which the state would take over land but let it out on permanent lease subject to good cultivation, while similar in principle to the proposals of *Coal and Power*, smacked too much of land nationalisation for the conservative wing of the party, and led to the defection of Sir Alfred Mond, the former Coalitionist minister of health. Protests against both the policy and Lloyd George's usurpation of the party name resulted in open conflict between the party and Lloyd George's league by the end of 1925.

By the time of the Land Convention in February 1926, Lloyd George had moderated his policy by conceding that land would only be acquired by the state when it came on to the market. On this basis, the party accepted Lloyd George's new policy and cooperated with the Land and Nation League in publicising it, but both the party and the policy suffered from the repetition of the tawdry disputes over finance with which they became embroiled, and the visible persistence of the old feuds amongst the leadership. It was another round of self-destructive Liberal blood-letting. The general strike, some six months later, brought matters to a head. Lloyd George openly defied the Asquithian leadership, which was vocal in its denunciation of the unions, by endorsing negotiation. Asquith, with the full support of his colleagues, seized upon Lloyd George's refusal to attend a shadow cabinet meeting as an opportunity to humiliate him, and perhaps drive him from the party.

The attempt backfired when it became clear that the party, although it had forced Lloyd George to retreat on land policy, would not support his proscription. The issue, moreover, was ill-chosen. The shadow cabinet's policy was typical of the political drift of the Asquithian leadership, but it placed the party in outright opposition to organised labour. The NLF's expression of confidence in Asquith was rendered meaningless by the reiteration of its desire 'to retain

36. Wilson, *Downfall*, pp. 314–18.   37. Ibid. p. 339.

the cooperation of all Liberals in pressing forward a vigorous and constructive policy of social and industrial reform'.[38] Asquith, ill during the summer, recognised the rebuff to his authority, and resigned the leadership in October.

Asquith's resignation was ten years too late. He was as responsible as Lloyd George for the split of 1916 and the subsequent factionalism. In 1916, Asquith was forced from power not from office, and might have remained a figurehead prime minister for the duration of the war for the sake of party unity. The Asquithians had a genuine grievance against Lloyd George. His continuation of the coalition into peacetime deprived the party of the opportunity to treat the war and its political repercussions as aberrations, and draw a veil over the disagreements the war had provoked. But Asquith contributed. He was offered, and refused, office in the post-war coalition. His failure to develop the positive alternatives offered by the radicals in the NLF left the party in no man's land, separated but not divorced. Domestic disputes, conducted largely in public, continued to poison reunion after 1923, further delaying reorganisation and removing any chance of recovery. Whatever their complaints against Lloyd George as a result of the coup of December 1916 or the continuation of the coalition in 1918, Asquith and the senior members of the Asquithian faction had shown themselves not only unable, but unwilling, to formulate a distinctive Liberal programme that would mark post-war Liberalism out as something more than an 'attitude of mind'. By 1924 they had made Liberalism only Conservatism without conviction.

Even so, the Asquithians did not accept defeat. As chairman of the party's organisation committee, Phillips still controlled party finances, including the 'million fund' for what it was worth. To gain control Lloyd George again used his financial power, offering to assist party headquarters and to finance 500 candidates at the next election. The acceptance of the offer and the complete renewal of the organisation committee was a victory for Lloyd George which gave him effective control of the party. In reaction, the Asquithians created the Liberal Council under Grey which included most of the Asquithian old guard – Phillips, Runciman, Maclean, Pringle and the last remnants of individualist radicalism, Holt and Leif Jones. Not only did they look to the Liberal past, they vaulted beyond the New Liberalism of 1908–14 to rest on the mid-Victorian principles of free trade and retrenchment with all the rigidity of

---

38. Ibid. p. 332.

men who understood neither the world they had lost nor the world in which they lived. In this they were truly representative of the Asquithian outlook after 1918.

Disagreement was nevertheless half-submerged until the general election of 1929. With the appointment of Herbert Samuel as chairman of the organisation committee in February 1927, the party gained an able administrator who was both neutral and respected. Samuel had been a cabinet minister before the war, and played an active role in ending the general strike in 1926, but as high commissioner for Palestine until 1925 he had remained outside the factional disputes which rent the post-war party. The years 1927–9 saw the last flourishing of progressive Liberalism in association with the Liberal party before its ideas were annexed by Labour as the basis of its reforms after 1945. An injection of financial support to the district federations revitalised provincial organisation in most areas, and with this came candidates, by-election successes and renewed optimism.[39]

Britain's industrial future

As a result of the cooperation of Lloyd George and the summer-school group, the Liberal party also gained a more distinctive policy. In 1926 Lloyd George had given the summer school £10,000 to finance an industrial inquiry. Its secretary noted, 'The spelling of Enquiry was amended to Inquiry when it was pointed out that the abbreviation to LIE would provoke rude scoffing.'[40] Some hostages were not given to political fortune. Early in 1928, the committee on industry, which included the economists Keynes, Layton and Henderson, Lloyd George's former backroom advisors, Rowntree, Kerr and Masterman, and the Manchester radicals, Muir and E.D. Simon, published the 'Yellow Book', *Britain's Industrial Future*. The 'Yellow Book' expressed the post-war Liberal concern with efficiency and productivity. It expressed also the underlying belief that efficiency was best achieved by private enterprise, under state supervision but freed, as far as possible, from direct intervention.

Managed capitalism still left a considerable role for the state, and there were traces of New Liberal organicism in the function ascribed to it of 'harmonising individual liberty with the general good, and personal initiative with a common plan'.[41] To this end,

39. Ibid. pp. 342–3, 346.   40. Campbell, 'Renewal', p. 101.
41. Freeden, *Liberalism Divided*, p. 107.

the report proposed a board of national investment to channel
national savings into the development of national resources, and
an economic general staff to provide expert advice to government
on economic problems. Further expertise on industrial affairs was
to come from a representative council of industry advising a newly
created ministry of industry. In general, however, the state was
ascribed a residual rather than an initiating role, plugging gaps left
by private enterprise, and adjusting relations between the two sides
of industry, rather than acting as an instrument of social justice.

There were still some shades of the old moral foundations of
Liberalism. High wages were

> a primary interest of the whole community, and not merely of the
> wage-earners themselves . . . and the chief reason for desiring indus-
> trial progress is that higher wages should be made possible in order
> that the general standard of life may be raised. Industry is not an
> end in itself: it exists in order to provide livelihood for the whole
> community. . . . The social justification for paying high wages is not
> merely that this will lead to better production, though it often does
> so; high real wages are an end in themselves, because high wages
> mean general well-being.[42]

In a similar vein, the report also recommended that every industry
had 'a duty to fix minimum wage-rates . . . and these minimum rates
should be made legally enforceable in the same way as Trade Board
rates'.[43] More usually, however, workers' remuneration, whether by
wages alone or supplemented by profit-sharing and share ownership schemes, was considered in terms of the gains in efficiency
and industrial cooperation that resulted from giving the worker a
feeling of participation. For the same reason, the report strongly
recommended consultation of the workforce through the creation
of works councils at the factory level. Like the Whitley councils, this
had the potential to break union solidarity by creating a revived
form of factory paternalism and factory loyalty. That, if not the
weakening of the unions, was its explicit objective.

Published two years after the general strike, there was an air of
unreality in many of the report's recommendations for industrial
peace and economic well-being. Its tone was all sweet reasonableness, far removed from the passion of industrial confrontation and
the sense of betrayal that pervaded many areas of post-war Britain.
Wary of state intervention, the report fumbled when it considered

---

42. *Britain's Industrial Future* (London: Earnest Benn Limited, 1928), pp. 181–2.
43. Ibid. pp. 212–13.

the means to realise its objectives. It recommended the extension of the system of trade boards, with their powers to enforce minimum wages, but vaguely, 'to every industry in which [they] can be shown to be needed', a principle that, in theory, had existed since 1909. It proposed that joint industrial councils, on the Whitley model, should also receive limited compulsory powers, but only to bring a recalcitrant minority into line when the majority of both employers' and workers' representatives agreed. It was unclear whether these councils were also to enforce minimum wages and, subject to the approval of the Council of Industry, profit-sharing schemes.[44] When it came to the question of enforcement, the report was generally unclear.

In this it again reflected the position of Liberalism throughout the 1920s. Running through the 'Yellow Book' ran the desire to remove the contentious world of industrial relations from the political arena. The industrial inquiry noted with approval, and relief, the 'steady movement of opinion towards the view that the voluntary organisation of industries for self-regulation offered the true line of advance'.[45] Its proposals were designed to encourage such voluntary regulation by suggesting appropriate machinery that might be created. This, too, was the philosophy of the Whitley councils, and the industrial report ran into the same problem, what action to take if the warring sections of industry failed to use that machinery. There were hints of coercion. 'The State', the report argued, 'cannot look on indifferently while civil war rages between organised bodies of its citizens, for its primary function is to substitute the rule of reason and law for that of force.'[46] But there was no policy.

Even so, the hints of coercion could not avoid an anti-union bias. The report attempted to overcome this by including in its rather legalistic definition of trade unions, combinations of employers as well as of workers. In both forms 'these powerful organisations . . . have become essential organs for the common regulation of industry and trade . . . it would seem to be high time that they were in some way worked into the recognised framework of our social system, and given responsibilities corresponding with their power'.[47] Optimistically, trade unions might become rational, realise 'that efficiency in production is of the first importance to them',[48] and work cooperatively within a self-regulating industrial system. If not, then coercive intervention would be required. But whatever that

44. Ibid. pp. 198–204, pp. 222–3.   45. Freeden, *Liberalism Divided*, p. 113.
46. *Britain's Industrial Future*, p. 166.   47. Ibid. p. 159.
48. Freeden, *Liberalism Divided*, p. 112.

intervention was to be, it could not overcome the inequality of power between workers and employers as individuals, and thus the unequal impact that any restriction on collective action would have on industrial relations. Ultimately, the report accepted the supremacy of management and the subordination of the worker as 'inherent in the necessities of industrial organisation'. Any form of workers' control was explicitly ruled out as incompatible with efficiency. The assertion that its proposals meant 'a real advance towards that goal of Liberalism in which everybody will be a capitalist, everybody a worker, as everybody is a citizen',[49] involved a peculiar understanding of the traditional Liberal idea of citizenship.

In one specific respect, however, the residual role allocated to the state produced proposals for active intervention. Mass unemployment was symptomatic 'of fundamental defects in our economic organisation' which were apparently beyond the capacity of private enterprise to rectify. As Keynes observed, it was 'not a question of choosing between private and public enterprise . . . it is a question of the State putting its hand to the job or of its not being done at all'.[50] Part 4 of the report thus proposed using the board of national investment to direct savings into a 'vigorous policy of national reconstruction', road and house building, agricultural improvement, afforestation and land reclamation among other things, to deal with what the inquiry considered to be the serious, but short-term, problem of 'abnormal unemployment'.

Politically, it was this positive action to be taken on unemployment that was emphasised, and it was part 4 of the industrial report that formed the basis of the Liberal party's election manifesto for 1929. In the 'Orange Book', *We Can Conquer Unemployment*, the party claimed that it could, within a year, reduce unemployment to 'normal proportions' by a programme of public works that would, moreover, be virtually self-financing and non-inflationary. *We Can Conquer Unemployment* provided the party with a policy that nominally restored it to its position of a reforming party. This position was, nevertheless, confusing. Criticism of the 'Yellow Book' ranged from the communism uncovered in it by the *Daily Dispatch* to the Conservatism exposed by the *Glasgow Herald*.[51] Both were right. The 'Yellow Book' consisted of a series of familiar pious aspirations which all could applaud. At the same time, both it and its derivative 'Orange Book' contained, by slightly more than implication, a plan for the extensive coercion of all sides of industry into a system of

49. Ibid. p. 114.   50. Ibid. p. 120.   51. Campbell, *'Renewal'*, p. 106.

state-regulated corporatism. Confusion was the price paid for the ambiguity inherent in the approach of both the 'Yellow Book' and the Liberal party to industrial politics. The secretary of the industrial inquiry committee, W. McK. Eagar, hit upon the real problem that a non-ideological policy devised by experts would cause for a party that was already centrist. It would

> (a) . . . convince Labour men generally that Liberalism is Conservatism without the courage of its convictions. (b) . . . prove to Conservatives that Liberalism is Socialism without the moral appeal of Socialism or its intellectual tidyness. (c) . . . settle for a considerable number of Liberals that their philosophy is mainly of antiquarian interest and that they must make up their minds finally whether their intellectual home is in Conservative [sic] or the Socialist Parties.[52]

The 'Yellow Book' was adopted by the NLF in 1928 and the party programme was launched in March 1929, followed by an extensive campaign through to the general election in May. It enjoyed general support, even from Asquithians, as, in some cases grudgingly, did Lloyd George himself. Expectations were high. As early as 1927, the *Manchester Guardian* believed that 'a Liberal majority is not impossible; and a formidable Liberal party in Parliament is almost assured'.[53] In the election, with 500 candidates, the party won 59 seats. The anti-Conservative vote which Lloyd George's new radical programme was designed to win, went to Labour. The 1929 election confirmed that the poor result of 1924 was more than the temporary consequence of Liberal disunity. The party had run far more candidates and a vigorous well-funded campaign in support of an innovative programme for economic recovery, with hardly any improvement in its parliamentary position.

The general election of 1929 was a political judgement on the party and Lloyd George, rather than on Liberalism as an ideology, but it entailed a judgement on Liberalism as it had evolved during the 1920s. Liberalism appealed for working-class votes while offering the working man nothing more than the role of cog in a more efficiently run capitalist machine. Not only did it say nothing about the sectional interests of the working classes and their defensive concerns, which would have been anathema to Liberalism, but it had little to say about the dignity of man that had been central to it. It inclined more in the opposite direction of deriding working-class aspirations. The independence that mattered so much had

52. Ibid. p. 116.   53. Wilson, *Downfall*, p. 337.

become an object of scorn, 'a tell-tale word', an 'absurdity'.[54] The strength of nineteenth- and early-twentieth-century Liberalism, 'old' or 'new', had rested on a belief in human potential which included all men, not just an intellectual or managerial elite. This had vanished. As Michael Freeden has observed, 'the price of Keynsianism was that economics had been, if not depoliticised, de-democratised. *General* control of economics via politics was brought to an end; a new elitism was born, remote in spirit from the inclusivist ethics that had animated the new liberalism.'[55] It was the Liberals' well-deserved misfortune in 1929 that the electorate expected its politicians to have more principles than those that could be reduced to mathematical equations.

Descent into insignificance

With the loss of the election and the withdrawal of Lloyd George's funding, which stopped completely by June 1930, familiar problems resurfaced within the political party. Without money, the party in the country collapsed again. Attempts to find alternative sources of funds failed as the 'million fund' appeal had failed. By 1930, Ramsay Muir, who had succeeded Samuel as chairman in January, saw, much as Phillips had done in 1926, 'a real danger that we may be wiped out'. The peeling facade of unity that had been maintained in a vain attempt to deceive the electorate that all was well cracked completely. Asquithian hostility, embodied in the Liberal Council, once more became vocal, and now found support amidst the rank and file which felt justifiably exploited and betrayed by Lloyd George's withdrawal of support. The inadequacy of the summer-school policies as a Liberal philosophy which could bind the party together in a common system of beliefs stood revealed.

The pressure of a Labour government completed the process of decomposition. The party decided to oppose the Labour government's coal bill in accordance with the industrial policy hammered out in the late 1920s. For both Lloyd George and Samuel, the coal bill was inadequate just because it failed to provide for the rationalisation of the coal industry. In December 1929 the bill survived because two Liberals voted for it and six abstained in defiance of official party policy; it survived again in February 1930 for the same reason.[56] By March, abstention had become party policy to avoid

54. Freeden, *Liberalism Divided*, pp. 276, 282.   55. Ibid. p. 172.
56. Wilson, *Downfall*, pp. 356–7.

the repetition of visible disunity, again demonstrating the super-fluity of the Liberal party.

Apart from radicals like E.D. Simon who wished to work with Labour because it was the nominal party of the left, the coal bill, and indeed the economic policy of the second Labour government as a whole, found its most reliable Liberal support from the right of the party, Runciman, Leif Jones and Maclean of the Liberal Council, because its policies coincided with their own faith in free trade and retrenchment. Whenever Lloyd George tried to cooper-ate with the government by urging it towards bolder policies, he found, as Mosley from within the Labour party found, that Snowden was immovable on any deviation from fiscal orthodoxy. Despite this, attempted cooperation merely alienated another Liberal group, this time led by Sir John Simon who affected to see the Labour party as a left-wing threat. Confronted by another Labour government, Simon followed the well-worn path towards Conservatism, and in June 1931 rejected the Liberal whip altogether.

Simon was nevertheless recognising reality in both electoral and policy terms. He, and some of his sympathisers, had been elected in 1929 through Conservative abstention. By their opposition to Labour they were laying the basis for the continuation of such electoral cooperation in the future. The rise of protectionism within the Conservative party was no impediment to this in the eyes of the so-called 'Simonites'. Tariffs were at last becoming respectable across a broad spectrum. Not only had Churchill finally abandoned the free-trade dogmatism that had led him to join the Liberal party in 1904, but amongst Liberal intellectuals, Keynes and Henderson now proposed revenue tariffs, and even E.D. Simon was prepared to treat tariffs on their merits. When the Labour government finally fell in August 1931, not only was the Liberal party in complete disarray, Liberalism hardly existed as a distinct political position. Most senior Liberals, except Lloyd George who was ill and was not invited, joined the National Government as if there were no major differences between them and the policies of either the dominant Conservatives or the National Labour rump.

The election of 1931 placed the Liberal party in an impossible position. As anti-Labour free traders, most chose to support Con-servative National Government candidates and turned a blind eye to Conservative protectionism. The exception was Lloyd George, who severed his connection with the official party when it refused to leave the National Government, and backed Labour as the free-trade party. Not that it mattered. The Liberals fielded only 160 candidates plus Lloyd George's family group. They did win seventy-two seats, but of these sixty-two were won in the absence of Conservative opposition; thirty-seven were held by Simonite Liberals who were Conservatives in all but name; thirty-one seats were held by free-trade supporters of the National Government, or 'Samuelite' Liberals, and four by Lloyd George's pro-Labour 'family group', secure in their North Wales bastion. There was hardly a Liberal party worthy of the name. 'The poor abject mob', as Lloyd George called them, 'have entirely ceased to count. No one now talks of the extermination of the Liberal Party; for all practical purposes it is annihilated.'[57]

In September 1932, the remaining 'Samuelite' ministers resigned from the National Government against the reintroduction of imperial preference following the Imperial Economic Conference at Ottawa, which marked the triumph of Conservative fiscal ideas over the hallowed Liberal doctrine of free trade. In November 1933, under increasing pressure from the rank and file, the group reluctantly moved into opposition. A rump of some thirty MPs still proclaiming that they aimed to 'give the electorate an opportunity of returning a Liberal Government to power' was little less than absurd, as was the justification for it, that the country needed an alternative to 'a complacent and idle Toryism' and 'a reckless and subversive Socialism'. The Labour party under Arthur Henderson was far from subversive, and the Tories under Baldwin no more complacent than official Liberalism. 'From a party point of view', Lothian (formerly Philip Kerr) observed in 1933, 'Liberalism is in an almost hopeless position.' Both Baldwin and Henderson were

> democrats, liberally minded, supporters of disarmament and the League of Nations, and constitutionalists. Both, too, are moderate tariffists, even friendly, in theory, to free trade. It is obviously . . . impossible for the Liberal party to advocate an immediate and unilateral return to free trade [or] a policy of immediate and unilateral disarmament. We have, therefore, no future by just talking what may be called the general principles of Liberalism. Apart from the stalwart remnant of the old guard the mass of voters will tend to vote for one or other of the two major parties, which at any rate have some hope of coming to power and are both, to-day, liberally minded.[58]

57. Chris Wrigley, 'Lloyd George and the Labour movement after 1922', in Judith Loades (ed.), *The Life and Times of David Lloyd George* (Bangor: Headstart History, 1991), p. 68.
58. Wilson, *Downfall*, pp. 377–8.

What was missing in this assessment was any reference to *Britain's Industrial Future* or the unique policies of the Liberal party for economic recovery. Dingle Foot had shown a similar disregard as early as 1930 when he criticised E.D. Simon's 'indiscretion' on tariffs because to accept tariffs would remove the distinction between Liberalism and Conservatism, as if free trade alone separated them. 'To old-fashioned and plain people,' wrote the veteran, Sir Albert Pease, of the reshuffling of parties in 1931, 'all this is very bewildering, and the old party lines having been obliterated, the very names of Liberal, Labour, Tory, Conservative and Unionist now appear to be meaningless.'[59] For the Liberals at least this was true. Liberalism was either so broad a stream that it failed to distinguish one party from another, or it was so narrow, deep and dark that no one could tell what it was, and everyone just ignored it.

As far as the Liberal party was concerned, this was certainly what the electorate did for the next half century. At the general election of 1935, the Liberals fielded only 161 candidates,[60] and won only 17 seats. Lloyd George's family group of four returned to the party after the election, and made a total of twenty-one. Sir Archibald Sinclair, MP for Caithness and Sutherland, replaced Samuel as leader because of the latter's defeat at Darwen, but in reality he had little to lead, and nowhere to lead it to. Ultimately he led it into the Churchill coalition in 1940, becoming in the process minister for air, and the last Liberal to hold cabinet office. After 1935 the party entered into a pattern of behaviour not unlike that of a mouse in a maze, sometimes excited by the prospect of success, more often depressed by failure, pausing for thought in periodic reorganisation committees (1936, 1946, 1969), floating the idea of 'United Front' (1937) or a 'Government of National Unity' (1974), but confronted at every turn by a dead end.

The return to party politics in 1945 revealed that in seeking to occupy the mythical centre, the Liberals occupied only the killing ground of modern politics, caught in the crossfire between the two major parties. They were accordingly mown down. In 1945, despite participation in the victorious wartime coalition, providing, through Keynes and Beveridge, the basic framework for post-war reconstruction, and running 307 candidates, the party secured only 9 per cent of the vote and 12 seats in the new House of Commons. Sinclair

---

59. Michael Bentley, *The Liberal Mind 1914–1929* (Cambridge: Cambridge University Press, 1977), p. 121.
60. Wilson, *Downfall*, p. 377.

himself, the chief whip, Sir Percy Harris, and even Beveridge were all defeated. Yet there was worse to come. In the general election of 1950, 319 of the 475 Liberal candidates lost their deposits and parliamentary representation fell to 9. In 1951, the party all but collapsed. It fielded only 109 candidates, over half of whom again lost their deposits, secured only 2.6 per cent of the vote and won only 6 seats, which it at least succeeded in retaining in 1955. In 1957, however, with the by-election loss of Carmarthen to Labour despite the absence of Conservative opposition, its parliamentary representation fell to five, an all-time low.

In 1951, with a parliamentary majority of fifteen, safe but not altogether comfortable, Churchill as the incoming Conservative prime minister offered the Liberals a coalition. The proposal occasioned earnest discussion, but was refused without great heart-searching. Herein lay the crux of the Liberal problem. Access to power realistically meant cooperation with one or the other of the major parties. Yet combination involved the risk of being absorbed, as the Simonite Liberals had been. The Conservatives trod gently on Liberal toes, leaving five of its six MPs without Conservative opposition in 1955, but failed to grasp the mentality of residual Liberalism. The Liberals had still not come to terms with the emergence of the Labour party, and still thought of themselves as the natural opposition to Conservatism.

In part the product of their long, successful history, this also reflected a particular approach to politics. Whereas the major parties and their respective electorates focused upon the material problems arising from Britain's economic and imperial decline after the Second World War, committed Liberal voters, perhaps some 7 per cent of the electorate, were more concerned with the issues of traditional Victorian Radicalism, liberty, internationalism and the constitution. Similarly, whilst Conservative and Labour voters reflected the class divide around which politics had rapidly repolarised after 1945, the Liberal vote came from all classes and reflected an indifference to, or rejection of, categorisation by class. The Victorian legacy of Nonconformity and rationalism remained a strong influence. Conviction Liberals had a different set of political values to those of the committed supporters of Conservatism and Labour, and were not, in that respect, simply centrist in a common spectrum.[61]

61. Michael Steed, 'The Liberal party' in H.M. Drucker (ed.), *Multi-Party Britain* (London: Macmillan, 1979), pp. 83–7.

But the Liberals were also perceived as centrist, a rather vague, unthreatening party whose very title embodied the generalised liberalism that all shared, but few could, or needed to, define. Voting Liberal was the shortest step that disaffected Conservative and Labour voters could take to express their dissatisfaction with their party. As a result, the Liberals enjoyed, in addition to their small and eccentric core vote, the sympathy of a substantial section of the electorate and from time to time sizeable but extremely volatile support. In the two general elections of 1974, nearly half of those who voted Liberal in February did not do so in October.[62] Mistaken though it was, the Liberals were thus encouraged in their belief that there existed a latent moderate majority that could be persuaded to return to its former Liberal allegiance, and the Liberal party to its natural position as the leading progressive party.

They were encouraged, too, by the manifest failure of the Labour party in the 1950s to loosen the Conservative grip on office. Conservative majorities increased steadily from 15 in 1951 to 70 in 1955 and 100 in 1959. Under the more radical leadership of Jo Grimond, who replaced Clement Davies as Liberal leader in 1956, the Liberals became more actively radical, and looked to a realignment of the left to restore both their own position and an alternative to Conservatism. It was, nevertheless, still a confused and potentially divided party. At the 1955 general election, the Liberal peer, Lord Moynihan, advised Liberal voters to vote Conservative in the absence of a Liberal candidate, which was the usual situation throughout the decade. He subsequently defected to the Conservatives. At the same election, Lady Megan Lloyd George advised Liberals to vote Labour, and became, in 1957, the successful Labour candidate at that Carmarthen by-election which reduced to the Liberals to only five MPs. This was not quite what the Liberals had in mind by realignment.

The 1950s were the nadir of post-war Liberalism. In 1958, a good showing in the Rochdale by-election with 35.5 per cent of the vote, followed a fortnight later by Mark Bonham-Carter's victory in the Torrington by-election, began a sort of recovery. In the 1959 general election, the party was able to run 216 candidates, and although it again won just 6 seats, at least only 56 candidates lost their deposits. In the next two years, a succession of good by-election performances seemed to indicate that the recovery might be sustained. Eric Lubbock's victory in March 1962 in the apparently

62. Ibid. p. 84.

safe Conservative seat of Orpington suggested more, a real break-through that would allow the Liberals to expand from the remote areas of Britain, the Scottish Highlands, Wales, Devon and Cornwall into which they had been driven, and to eat into the Conservative suburban heartland.

It was an illusion. Orpington was the crest of a slight Liberal resurgence, not a new beginning, another indication of the volatile vote which the Liberals could attract at times and in places but not hold or extend. With 365 candidates in 1964, the party polled 11.2 per cent of the vote, but won only nine seats. The gains, Bodmin (Cornwall) and three Highland constituencies, were all on the periphery. So, too, despite an advance to twelve MPs in 1966, was the Liberal party. Far from realignment, the real recovery on the left was that of the Labour party, which won a bare majority in 1964 but ensured its continuation in government with a majority of ninety-eight in 1966. By 1970, the Liberal party was back where it had started, with over half of its 332 candidates losing their deposits, 7.5 per cent of the vote and only 6 MPs. Some slight adjustment was clearly required.

What emerged was a rift between the radicalism of the Young Liberals, whose militant direct action against the South African rugby tour had done some damage to the party in 1970, and the more conservative party leadership. Radical 'community politics', working at local level and involving the local community in local issues, developed in the late 1960s and led not only to municipal success in the larger English cities, especially Liverpool and Birmingham, but a surprising by-election victory in 1969 in the formerly safe Labour seat of Ladywood (Birmingham). In 1970, with few alternatives on offer and the election a disaster, the party conference accepted the Young Liberal resolution that the party should begin again at the community level. But as the former Young Liberal chairman, Peter Hain, observed, 'the party leadership does not understand what community politics is all about, and if they did, they wouldn't like it'.[63]

Success, nevertheless, followed almost immediately, with a succession of by-election victories in 1972–3 in Rochdale, Sutton and Cheam, Lincoln, Ripon, the Isle of Ely and Berwick-upon-Tweed. With success came renewed hope. In an optimistic mood and with a radical programme including minimum wages, profit sharing and

63. Chris Cook, *A Short History of the Liberal Party 1900–1976* (London: Macmillan, 1976), p. 151.

improved pensions, the party put forward 517 candidates drawn strongly from young middle-class professionals at the general election of February 1974. But although it improved its share of the vote to 19.3 per cent, it still won only fourteen seats. However, in the close parliamentary situation that resulted from the election, with Labour having only a five-seat advantage over the Conservatives, this was enough to give the Liberal party a significance that it had not enjoyed since 1931, and to open up new prospects, even if they ultimately turned out to be no more than mirages.

The rise of the Liberal party in the early 1970s offered the potential of coalition, but also the vision of the long-awaited decline of one of its rivals or the disintegration of the two-party system itself. Dick Taverne's disagreement with the Labour party, and his successful defence of his Lincoln seat for 'Democratic Labour' against an official Labour candidate in a by-election in March 1973 and again in the general election of February 1974, nourished such hopes. Taverne lost his seat in October, but post-war Liberals were adept at living off illusions. They were less able to make difficult choices. Irrelevance allowed the party to maintain its purity and dream of a return to a Liberal government. The prospect of merely sharing power, both in the 1970s and the 1980s constantly threatened a split between purists and collaborators.

This was one consequence of the difference between the core Liberal vote and the volatile Liberal vote, between eccentric and centrist perceptions of Liberalism. The former dictated purity, the latter compromise, if the Liberal party was ever to convert that vote, on which its periodic electoral revivals depended, into a stable electoral base. In 1974, the knowledge that the Liberal leadership was even considering an approach from the defeated Conservative prime minister, Edward Heath, about the possibilities of a coalition, was enough to arouse alarm and protest within the party. The unity re-established on the basis that this was not the right opportunity did not disguise the difference between those, like the then chief whip, David Steel, who thought the circumstances wrong, and those who disliked coalition under any circumstances. Steel, indeed, contacted his future Social Democrat ally, Roy Jenkins, on the possibility of a deal with Labour.[64]

Coalitionism was thus firmly on the agenda of the Liberal leadership, if not of the Liberal party as a whole. In June, the Liberal

64. David Steel *Against Goliath: David Steel's Story* (London: Weidenfeld & Nicolson, 1989), pp. 78–81.

leadership proposed a 'Government of National Unity', promptly rejected by Labour, but taken up with some interest by Heath, in preparation for the general election of October 1974. Both this and the prospect of Labour disintegration were encouraged by the defection of Christopher Mayhew, Labour MP for Woolwich East. Mayhew was, however, like Dick Taverne a lone figure. The polarisation of post-war politics which the Liberals sought to end rested upon the class polarisation of the electorate and its industrial expression, the conflict between management and labour. However much Liberal critics might point to the waste and inefficiency of repeated industrial clashes and their contribution to Britain's apparently inexorable economic decline, breaking the two-party system involved, as the Liberals were to discover, more than occasional political defections.

The massive onslaught that the Liberals prepared for the general election of October 1974 with 619 candidates and a manifesto – 'Why Britain Needs Liberal Government' – which seemed to consider this a possibility, reflected Liberal illusions rather than political realities. The party won only thirteen seats, and notwithstanding the greater number of candidates, only 18.3 per cent of the vote. Once again, however, the political situation was such that the Liberals could not be completely ignored, which in turn fed delusions of grandeur. In 1977 the party acquired an indirect role in government as the ailing Labour administration was obliged to find outside support to maintain itself in power. In return for Liberal support in parliament, the Lib-Lab 'pact' agreed between the Labour prime minister, James Callaghan, and David Steel, now the Liberal leader, set up a joint consultative committee on government policy and regular meetings between the chancellor of the exchequer and his Liberal opposite number. Those meetings between Denis Healey and John Pardoe were explosive, and the 'pact' once again created severe tensions within the Liberal party even though it fell well short of a coalition. Most significantly, it carried no electoral implications. This became fully evident at the general election of 1979, when the Liberals again won only 14.1 per cent of the vote and eleven seats. The Conservatives had a secure majority of forty-four and the prospect of the Liberals acquiring power through a coalition with one of the major parties disappeared.

The prospect, or mirage, of the disintegration of the system, or at least of significant secessions from the major parties, did not disappear. In the early 1980s, both Conservatism and Labour vacated the centre and abandoned consensus in favour of confrontation.

Under the leadership of Mrs Thatcher, Conservatism became abrasive both in outlook and in its 'new right' policies of monetarism, privatisation and 'union-bashing', especially after the cabinet purge of September 1981. In turn, the Labour party moved to the left under pressure from its constituency activists who met little resistance from the new leader, Michael Foot, himself from the left wing of the party. Centrists of both parties, which included the disaffected Conservative ministers purged in 1981, were restive. By 1981, Mrs Thatcher was not only deeply unpopular in the country, but according to political gossip in danger of a revolt in her own party.

It was, however, the Labour party that provided the apparent opportunity for Liberalism to realise its long-frustrated ambitions. In 1981 Labour moderates revolted against the left-wing trend, when the 'gang of four' – David Owen, Shirley Williams, William Rodgers and Roy Jenkins, all former Labour cabinet ministers – left to form the Social Democratic Party. Twenty-nine Labour MPs eventually joined the SDP, but despite discussions between David Steel and some Conservative dissidents,[65] only one Conservative, Christopher Brocklebank-Fowler, MP for North West Norfolk, followed suit. The new party won immediate success, gaining Crosby (Liverpool) and Croydon from the Conservatives, and in March 1982, Glasgow Hillhead from Labour. In the previous month the Liberals themselves gained Bermondsey, a safe Labour seat since 1918. An alliance was forged between the two parties in the autumn of 1981, and the opportunity to 'break the mould' of political and industrial confrontation seemed to have arrived at last. The euphoria of the early 1980s was captured by David Steel's exhortation to delegates at the Liberal party conference in 1981 to 'go back to your constituencies and prepare for government'. As late as June 1983, Tony Benn from the Labour left thought that 'the Alliance is beginning to grow at the expense of the Tories and it is possible that enough Tories will vote for the Alliance to allow Labour to slip in'.[66]

Yet the apparent opportunity provided by Conservative unpopularity, Labour disarray and the formation of the SDP proved to be no opportunity at all. Mrs Thatcher's reputation was revived by the wave of jingoism which greeted the Falklands war in the spring of 1982. Coming in the wake of the war and the defeat of Argentina, which endorsed the hardline politics of Thatcherism with success, however irrelevant to Britain's domestic troubles, the 1983 general

65. Ibid. p. 226.
66. Tony Benn, *The End of an Era: Diaries 1980–1990* (London: Hutchinson, 1992), pp. 289–90.

election gave little latitude to soft centrists. The Alliance between the Liberal and Social Democratic parties was very much an alliance of electoral convenience, contrived to avoid splitting the vote between the two minor centrist parties, and offered no clear image to the electorate. It polled well by the recent standards of the Liberal party, gaining 26 per cent of the vote and almost closing the gap on a demoralised Labour party which gained only 27.6 per cent. But the electoral system, which had penalised the Liberal party in the past, continued to penalise the Alliance. Its reward was a mere 23 seats, 17 Liberals and 6 Social Democrats, against the 209 won by Labour and the 397 won by the Conservatives, on only 42.9 per cent of the vote.

The lack of realism nevertheless persisted. In 1985, Alliance morale was boosted by widespread success in the local-government elections, victory in the Brecon and Radnor by-election and a Gallup poll in which it was significantly more popular than either the Conservatives or Labour. At the party conference in Dundee, Steel again advised Liberals that 'we must seriously prepare ourselves for government', and expressed the belief that the next government would be formed by the Alliance.[67] The Alliance did, indeed, continue to make gradual progress in this mid-term of a parliament, as the Liberals had done on earlier occasions. In 1986, it made further considerable gains in the local elections, and won the Ryedale by-election in what had been a safe Conservative seat. In 1987, it secured two further by-election successes, gaining Greenwich from Labour and retaining Truro.

Nevertheless, the Alliance was more likely to fall apart at the top than to form the next government. Under the mercilessly satirised dual leadership of the two Davids, Owen and Steel, it never fully escaped from its improvised origins. Whilst Steel sought greater unity leading to merger, Owen cautiously regarded the Alliance as the cooperation of two separate and distinct groups. Policy differences, especially over nuclear defence where the Liberal party's hostility to nuclear weapons constantly clashed with Owen's belief in their necessity, increased the tensions. The differences that emerged between 1984 and 1986 were smoothed over, but contributed to the image of the Alliance as an indefinite, confused and even divided grouping of barely compatible political opportunists. They re-emerged again in the election campaign itself, when Owen ruled out cooperation with Labour in the event of a hung parliament

67. Steel, *Liberal Party*, p. 261.

because of its defence policy, whilst Steel described cooperation with Mrs Thatcher as 'unimaginable'. The Alliance had become 'scarcely more than a rabble'.[68] It still took 22.6 per cent of the vote, but won only twenty-two seats. Those discontented with Thatcherite Conservatism, as in 1983 the majority of the electorate, turned towards Labour which crept back to 30.8 per cent of the vote and 229 seats.

In the aftermath of the 1987 election débâcle, merger between the two wings of the Alliance acquired a new importance and urgency. Even so, it was achieved only by splitting the SDP and to a lesser extent the Liberal party itself in what David Steel later described as a 'summer bloodbath'.[69] Only two of the five SDP MPs, both Scots, ultimately joined the Liberals in the still somewhat improvised 'Social and Liberal Democrats'. The Liberals were markedly more enthusiastic. But in supporting union in February 1988, the special assembly of the Liberal party at Blackpool voted the historic Liberal party of Gladstone, Asquith and Lloyd George out of existence. They did so with regret, in the hope of an unknown future. Thus far, the story of the Liberal Democrats (the new party's final title) has been depressingly familiar, at least to post-war Liberals.

1988 marked the formal end of a party that had been intellectually vibrant but political moribund since the 1920s. By the second half of the twentieth century, the Liberal party had become clearly identified as a party for the protest vote. It was able to achieve victories in mid-term by-elections, and to poll well in safe Conservative, and to a much smaller extent safe Labour, seats, but was squeezed by the major parties whenever the government of the country was at stake. After 1929, the Liberal party also behaved as a third party, whatever its aspirations to office or its inconsistent belief in single-party government. The most telling indication was the sudden discovery of the importance of proportional representation or the alternative vote by a party which in 1912 was confident enough, or complacent enough, to drop the proposal with hardly a second thought, and still confident enough to reject it in 1918.

In 1924, in an acknowledgement of their third-party status and lack of a future, the Liberals sought proportional representation, but did not make it a condition for continued support of the government; in 1931 the condition was imposed, and so, with the exception of 1977, it remained until the end. In it the Liberals saw

68. Kenneth O. Morgan, *The People's Peace* (Oxford: Oxford University Press, 1992), p. 490.
69. Steel, *Liberal Party*, p. 286.

their only hope of political salvation, even though the most likely outcome would be perpetual coalition, and the loss of that purity they struggled so long to maintain. 'It is hard', wrote a Liberal commentator on the tenth Liberal summer school in 1930, 'to think that all this bubbling energy, this zeal for social betterment and reform, this real knowledge and sparkling wit is nothing but a Midsummer Night's interlude in the rather frowsy drama of modern politics.'[70] But all fairy tales must come to an end.

70. Freeden, *Liberalism Divided*, p. 125.

CHAPTER TEN

Reflections

In retrospect, it is clear that the Liberal party was finished by 1924, by which time the Liberals were no longer regarded by the electorate as a possible government, whatever their policies. Between 1922 and 1924 the realignment of British politics, anticipated by prophets of doom since the first emergence of Labour, was finally realised. As early as 1895, Rosebery mused on the possibility 'that that may happen which has happened in Belgium – the elimination of Liberalism, leaving the two forces of Socialism and Reaction face to face'.[1] Rosebery was acutely aware of the potential danger to Liberalism in the politics of class, but he did not see this development as inevitable.

Nor was it. The argument that the downfall of the Liberal party and its replacement by its Labour rival was the inevitable outcome of class politics assumes, to a greater or lesser extent, that the working classes were, or became by the 1920s, a relatively undifferentiated working class with similarly undifferentiated political objectives; that politics was seen as the proper arena for the realisation of those objectives, and that the Labour party was the best vehicle to that end. None of these is necessarily true. Since the working classes enjoyed a majority in the electorate after 1884, the central question is why, after the dramatic arrival of Labour in 1906, the replacement of Liberalism by Labour was delayed until the 1920s.

One factor was the constraints placed on the growth of Labour by the restricted franchise still in place in 1914, which disfranchised many potential Labour voters. The extension of the franchise in 1918 trebled the electorate and, it is argued, enfranchised the

1. Robert Rhodes James, *Rosebery* (London: Weidenfeld & Nicholson, 1963), p. 386.

lower strata of the working classes, enabling Labour for the first time to realise the full voting strength of its natural constituency. Liberal difficulties with class politics in a new mass electorate were compounded by the absence of a permanent party organisation of the kind enjoyed by the Conservative and Labour parties, a situation made worse still by the decay of such Liberal organisation as there was during the war. Furthermore, the Liberal style of appealing to the voter's reason was singularly ineffective in 'a new electorate . . . less likely to respond to policies that demanded a comparatively high level of political intelligence' in contrast to the restricted Edwardian electorate which was 'so defined that a fair part of it would respond to appeals of this sort'.[2]

Some of this is pure supposition, especially the relative effectiveness of politicians' arguments on the attitude of the electorate. But the basic premise has also been called into question. Recent work on the Edwardian electorate suggests that, whilst there was a slight bias against the working classes, it was far less than previously believed. Rather, the pre-war bias built into household suffrage was against the young and unmarried of all social classes. The 1918 reforms did not enfranchise a new, lower class of voters, but extended the franchise to the disfranchised within social groups that already had the vote. They had only a limited impact on the class composition of the electorate.[3] Taking this into account, the inevitability hypothesis has gone on to incorporate generational and political culture arguments in favour of the emergence of a 'labour generation'[4] in the 1920s. Thus, in the last two or three decades of the nineteenth century, 'similar educational experiences [through the introduction of elementary education], increasingly similar leisure pursuits and increasingly similar working conditions moved these youths towards a more inclusive and less hierarchical identification of their class and its particular needs'.[5] In sum, in

---

2. H.C.G. Matthew, R.I. McKibbin and J.A. Jay, 'The franchise factor in the rise of the Labour party', *English Historical Review* 91 (361) (1976), 723–52; P.F. Clarke, 'Liberals, Labour and the franchise', *English Historical Review* 92 (364) (1976), 582–90.

3. Duncan Tanner, 'The Parliamentary Election System, the "Fourth" Reform Act and the Rise of Labour in England and Wales', *Bulletin of the Institute of Historical research* 56 (134) (1983), 205–19; Duncan Tanner, *Political Change and the Labour Party 1900–1918* (Cambridge: Cambridge University Press, 1990), pp. 99–129; Neal Blewett, 'The franchise in the United Kingdom 1885–1918', *Past and Present* (32) (1990), 27–56.

4. Michael Childs, 'Labour grows up: the electoral system, political generations, and British politics 1890–1929', *Twentieth Century British History* 6 (2) (1995), 144.

5. Ibid. p. 142.

the younger generations, the working classes were becoming a working class, even without the accentuation of class consciousness by the war.

The argument concedes that 'Labour was unlikely to have made much headway under the existing franchise in any hypothetical 1914 election . . . it is not even likely that it would have captured a majority of working class votes with universal suffrage', because the emerging Labour generation would not have fully matured. But 'conversely, it is hard to see how the Liberal Party could have avoided demise in the long run as its working class supporters died and were not replenished in like proportion'.[6] Even before the war, sections of the Liberal party were wary of the effect of enfranchising young workers against whom the pre-war franchise was particularly biased. Several Liberal federations in northern England and Scotland believed that if given the vote they would support Labour, not Liberalism.[7]

Even so, there are problems unresolved. The expansion of the electorate cannot be entirely discounted, particularly in the light of the organisational deficiencies of the Liberal party by 1918, but it may have been at best only a slight advantage to Labour. Indeed, in 1918, it appears that Labour success was in inverse proportion to the number of new electors.[8] The 1918 general election was fought in peculiar circumstances, but the post-war municipal elections, held under a franchise which excluded 75 per cent of the new parliamentary electors, tell a similar story. Labour's municipal success, especially in 1919, suggests that the party was converting older, established voters from both of its political rivals.[9] The move to Labour may have been that of a household, rather than a generation. The factors creating the putative 'Labour generation' would seem to apply to all young workers. But a substantial proportion of the working classes voted, or continued to vote, Conservative during the inter-war years. The 'Labour generation' appears to have materialised only amongst that section of the working classes who would, in other circumstances, have inclined towards Liberalism.

Moreover, working-class consciousness, both before and during the war, developed in an industrial form that did not translate easily or automatically into political behaviour, as the Labour party was to find to its cost. During the inter-war period Labour failed to

6. Ibid. p. 143. 7. Ibid. pp. 132–3.

8. Martin Pugh, *The Making of Modern British Politics 1869–1939* 2nd edn (Oxford: Blackwell, 1993), pp. 198–9.

9. Duncan Tanner, *Political Change* pp. 410–12.

gain even 50 per cent of the working-class vote, and peaked at 38 per cent of the total vote.[10] In a predominantly working-class electorate, a substantial proportion of the working classes still refused, as they had before the war, either to regard themselves as a working class or to recognise Labour as their political vehicle. In consequence, throughout the twentieth century Labour has been notoriously less successful as a political force than Liberalism in the nineteenth century. To that extent, the inevitability argument provides a complicated explanation for an event that did not happen.

The British political system is severe on third parties, but the electorate is merciless to divided parties that present contradictory messages and a confused image. Between 1880 and 1886 the Liberals disintegrated and subsequently spent twenty years in the political wilderness; between 1900 and 1906, the divided Conservatives crashed from a secure majority to a landslide defeat. Six years is a long time in politics, ample to change the public image of a political party and effect that small transfer of votes required to produce a marked shift in the balance of the parties in parliament. The activities of the political elite are significant just because they determine the image of the party presented to the electorate. As Rosebery also remarked in 1895, whether Liberalism was eliminated or not 'depends on the Liberal party'.[11]

After 1918 neither of the quarrelling Liberal factions, one entangled with Conservatism in an anti-socialist crusade, the other aloof and invertebrate, did much to endear themselves to the working classes, especially organised labour. Working-class politics was about improved working and living conditions, but it was also about recognition and status. Lloyd George promised the former, was dismissive of the latter, and delivered on neither. The succession of broken promises, the aura of corruption, and the cooperation with Conservatism destroyed Lloyd George's credibility as a reformer. Asquith offered only platitudes, and in 1924 defaulted even on those. Lloyd George was right to regard the party split that developed after 1916 as one of ideology as much as of personality[12]; at root the dispute turned on the proper role of the liberal state. Because they could not agree on this, the Liberals continued to present the image of a divided party, even whilst Lloyd George was attempting to construct a new programme.

10. Pugh, *Making of Modern British Politics*, pp. 252–3.
11. James, *Rosebery*, p. 386.
12. Trevor Wilson, *The Downfall of the Liberal Party 1914–1935* (London: Collins, 1966), p. 340.

The danger of division was always inherent in Liberal politics by the very nature of the party. The party achieved mid-Victorian dominance primarily as a result of the Conservative split of 1846, which for almost two decades reduced that party to the position of an impossibilist right. Under Palmerston, the Liberal party secured the political centre by occupying it, marginalising both Conservatives and Radicals. The price of inclusiveness was the breadth of opinion contained within the Liberal party itself, and the potential for fragmentation both of the party and the party system. As a party of 'action' united around major issues by Gladstone, the party moved left, leaving the centre as a contested area. Confronted with Radical pressure and Gladstone's 'unreliability', the Whigs wavered between the containment of Radicalism from within and resistance from without by offering independent support to a Conservative government. Their attitude was that of a centrist third party without the power to rule independently, seeking to moderate both extremes under pressure from the Radicals within their own party.

The last quarter of the nineteenth century exposed the coalition nature of the party that had dominated mid-Victorian politics. The formation of the Irish Home Rule party brought about the virtual extinction of Irish Liberalism in less than a decade; the defection of the Whigs to the Conservatives was accompanied by that of a substantial section of the middle classes; Labour was sufficiently independent by 1903 to require negotiation to secure its support, even if the desertion of the working classes took longer. Having lost the Whigs by moving to the left, the Liberals were unwilling to accept the consequences of the decision. Gladstone was too restricted by his concern for the rights of property and freedom of contract to reform Irish land tenure decisively and prevent the junction of agrarian discontent and nationalism. Nor were any efforts made to integrate the newly enfranchised working classes into the party structure. In different ways, Ireland and Labour raised the same issue of the empowerment of the dispossessed. Neither mounted a serious threat to property, despite their respective radical fringes, but the Liberals were too conservative for too long, trapped in the general view that neither the Irish nor the working classes were capable of government, and that the consequences would be anarchy and despoliation.

Support from the working classes compensated the Liberal party for its middle-class losses. Until the First World War, labour remained largely loyal to the Liberal party. The reverse was much less true, with local Liberal associations refusing to select working-class candidates, and being inclined to make common cause with local Conservatives when threatened by independent working-class candidatures in municipal elections. Fifty years further on, the most noticeable feature of Liberal candidates was still the virtual absence of manual workers. The evolution of the party required a recognition of social mobility to include the MacDonalds, Snowdens and Hendersons, along with the Runcimans, Simons and McKennas, just as the Whigs recruited Bright, Forster and Chamberlain. The Liberal party as a whole was never prepared to accept this whilst it was still possible. What was lacking was conviction, both social and intellectual.

The late-Victorian strength of the Liberal party can easily be overstated, particularly by regarding the 'Conservative hegemony' of 1886–1906 as an aberration caused by Liberal abstentions, and the election of 1906 as restoring the normal pattern of Liberal power. The Liberals won an absolute majority only twice after 1868. For the rest they were dependent on the outside support of groups that had formerly been either virtually or actually within the mid-Victorian Liberal party/coalition. This was the significance of its disintegration. The 1906 success was not the continuation of Victorian supremacy, but the aberration from the emerging pattern of Liberal weakness, caused primarily by the renewal of Conservative divisions and their adoption of deeply unpopular policies which reignited old Liberal passions for one last time. The vast majority of 1906 had vanished by January 1910.

By that time, the consequences of the socially exclusive attitude of the party were beginning to be felt. The inclusion of Ramsay MacDonald in the cabinet, which Lloyd George wanted, would not have revitalised the Liberal party. Rather, it would have recreated in more visible form a coalition which in itself was an indication that the Liberal party was becoming too weak to stand alone. The Liberals made little effort to overcome this weakness. Labour support for national insurance had to be bought by the passage, at long last, of the one measure crucial to its involvement in national politics, the payment of MPs. National insurance revealed the new, coercive direction of Liberalism. This coercive quality might have been mitigated, either by the minimum wage, or by bringing the interventionist state more under working-class control by the recruitment of working-class MPs. But as the instrument of a coercive alien culture, the state remained unloved.

The difficulties of the social transition required of late-nineteenth-century Liberalism were thus compounded by an ideological confusion of a kind not met by the mid-Victorian party. In moving to the Conservatives, the Whigs also appropriated to Conservative use key elements of Liberal ideology, in particular the connection between property, freedom of contract and individual liberty. Without a new programme, the Liberal party was left advocating only a moderate version of what was fast becoming the Conservative position in politics within shared liberal values. New Liberalism filled the ideological gap and provided a new ideology for the reformist left. Indeed, it filled the gap so well that it provided the inspiration for post-war reconstruction by a reformist Labour party between 1945 and 1950.

Nominally, New Liberalism built upon the Liberal tradition of liberation, but it ran too easily to expert committees that bore more relation to the ideas of Milner than those of Gladstone. It compounded social with intellectual condescension. The working classes were to be administered, inspected, policed and reformed, their incomes were to be compulsorily reduced for their own good, their choices restricted, but they were not to share power. The elevation of the state, as a positive force, the embodiment of the 'common good' through which the individual achieved his own liberty, provided a rationale for top-down government by bureaucracy. New Liberal ideology did not just build upon traditional Liberalism; it turned it inside out, providing the ideological basis that few understood for reforms that few wanted. Moreover, it was, like the economic policies that succeeded it in the 1920s, not only unintelligible in terms of traditional Liberalism, but often just unintelligble. Nothing had changed by 1929.

New Liberalism appealed most to those maverick Liberals like Churchill and Lloyd George, coalitionists who saw nothing amiss in cooperation with at least a section of the Conservatives, even if cooperation in practice proved more difficult. The majority of the Liberal leadership had ridden the New Liberal tiger with varying degrees of discomfort before the war; only Lloyd George appeared to feel that it could be domesticated. For Lloyd George, the tutelary state not only presented no intellectual difficulty, but was in itself a positive good. Coalitions which eliminated parliamentary criticism and electoral choice, ministries driven by unelected businessmen, small cabinets which reduced the area of debate, and extensive state regulation, represented his idea of good government. It was this, and the patriotic attitudes that only fully emerged during the war, that finally clarified his affinities with social imperialists like Milner, half-concealed before the war by his partisan attacks on the landed interest. 'Milner and I', he remarked in 1917, 'stand for very much the same things. He is a poor man, and so am I. He does not represent the landed or capitalist classes any more than I do. He is keen on social reform and so am I.'[13] Such an outlook made it possible to imagine a chimaera like the Centre party for as long as politics remained influenced by the war. The proposed 'Centre party', however, belonged to the margins of British politics, as did the views of Milner and Lloyd George.

The evolution of electoral politics from sectarianism to a loose form of class redefined liberty to mean the self-determination of the working classes rather than that of Nonconformists, but it did not alter the basic equation of liberty with the enfranchisement of the individual against the state rather than through the state. Lloyd George's policies contradicted the libertarian view of liberty central to the popular perception of Liberalism. Popular perception was not simply the product of over a century of Liberal theorists, politicians and publicists from Adam Smith to Gladstone hammering home the merits of the minimal state. Nineteenth-century Liberals, Radicals and Nonconformists in their various ways drew strength from, and at the same time reinforced, a historical tradition that stretched back through the revolution of 1688, the Puritan revolution and Magna Carta to the Saxon mists before the coming of 'the Norman Yoke'. The tutelary state ran straight into the popular belief in the 'freeborn Englishman'.

The war affected the political parties more than it changed fundamental popular attitudes. It gave the Labour movement a new self-confidence, and provided, as a result of working-class patriotism, a moral justification for what had hitherto often appeared mere sectionalism. But above all, war rescued the Conservative party from its pre-war disarray. As the party of patriotism and strong defence, after the formation of the 1916 coalition it became the party that won the war. It profited accordingly in 1918, and profited thereafter from the divisions of the left, both within the Liberal and Labour parties, and between them. Labour replaced the Liberal party as the principal party of the left, but it never achieved the Liberals' nineteenth-century status as the normal party of government. Despite the attention focused on the rise of Labour in the twentieth century, the rise of the Conservative party was far more significant as the principal beneficiary of Liberal collapse.

13. Lord Riddell, *Lord Riddell's War Diaries* (London: Ivor Nicholson & Watson, 1933), p. 243.

The Liberals were the losers. The war both corroded traditional Liberal values and aggravated the ideological confusion and the tensions evident before 1914. In 1918 the Liberal party faced again those questions of social reform and its relationship to labour, both industrial and political, that it had faced before the war, but in circumstances of greater urgency. In confronting them, its intellectual wing developed a doctrine of the managed economy that was both elitist and materialist, and Liberalism lost contact with its central ideals. As the *Nation*, then still in the hands of Massingham, pointed out, 'with any . . . dissociation from the principle of life and growth in the modern state, the function of Liberalism, as its masters conceived it, comes to an end'.[14] Ironically, the lack of 'heart' in the Liberal success story of the 1920s, the summer schools, killed Liberalism as a creed.

By then, however, the Liberal party was so divided, confused and lacking in confidence that its leaders misjudged the post-war political situation. The choices made, whilst confirming tendencies visible before the war, were coloured by the experience of the war. The Asquithian leadership lapsed more completely into that smug conservatism towards which it was already inclined; Lloyd George moved more strongly towards executive radicalism which he mistakenly believed could be carried through by a Conservative alliance. The result if other decisions had been taken is incalculable; those actually taken, dictated by Lloyd George's assumption that Liberalism was already dead, merely ensured that the Liberal party died.

The irony lay in the survival of traditional liberalism. Whilst the Liberal party became separated from Liberalism as a reforming but libertarian creed, the electorate remained liberal. The Liberal party was not, to re-work a familiar metaphor, run down by a 'rampant omnibus (the First World War)' whilst loitering without intent. None of the parties was that passive. The Conservatives recognised the bus and jumped on board; the Liberals mistook the direction it was travelling and threw themselves in front of it; the Labour party stepped aside, and stripped the Liberal corpse of its valuables when the bus was safely gone. The robbers were led by men who had been driven from Liberalism, including several who had attempted to become Liberal candidates. The final verdict on the party is not inevitable decline through old age, nor accidental death, but suicide while the balance of politics was disturbed.

14. Michael Freeden, *Liberalism Divided* (Oxford: Oxford University Press, 1986), p. 142.

A Guide to Further Reading

It is a fair commentary on the history of Liberal politics that general texts covering the nineteenth century cannot avoid the Liberal party, while those on the period after 1931 can hardly find a reason to mention it. For the context, try N. Gash, *Aristocracy and People: Britain 1815–1865* (London: Arnold, 1979), M. Bentley, *Politics without Democracy 1815–1914* (London: Fontana, 1984), R. Shannon, *The Crisis of Imperialism 1865–1915* (London: Granada, 1976), M. Pugh, *The Making of Modern British Politics 1867–1939* (2nd end, Oxford: Blackwell, 1993), and K.O. Morgan, *The People's Peace: British History 1945–1990* (Oxford: Oxford University Press, 1992). Histories of the Liberal party usually cover a limited time-span. M. Bentley, *The Climax of Liberal Politics: British Liberalism in Theory and Practice 1868–1918* (London: Arnold, 1987) is complex; G.R. Searle, *The Liberal Party: Triumph and Disintegration 1886–1929* (London: Macmillan, 1992) is a stimulating survey with an excellent bibliography. Chris Cook, *A Short History of the Liberal Party 1900–1976* (London: Macmillan, 1976) is certainly short, but useful for raw information. In general, a more detailed history of the Liberal party is better built up from that layer of books between surveys and specialised monographs.

For the Whigs, the basic work is now J.P. Parry, *The Rise and Fall of Liberal Governments in Victorian Britain* (New Haven: Yale University Press, 1993), although T.A. Jenkins, *The Liberal Ascendancy 1830–1886* (London: Macmillan, 1994) is more accessible. Both are usefully supplemented by E.D. Steele, *Palmerston and Liberalism 1855–1865* (Cambridge: Cambridge University Press, 1991). John Vincent, *The Formation of the Liberal Party* (London: Constable, 1966) remains a classic. Gladstone towers over mid-Victorian politics and the subsequent history of the Liberal party. H.C.G. Matthew, *Gladstone*, 2 vols. (Oxford: Oxford University Press, 1986 and 1995) discusses both the 'grand old man' and his setting. D.A. Hamer, *Liberal Politics in the Age of Gladstone and Rosebery* (Oxford: Oxford University Press, 1972) links Gladstone with his successors. Peter Stansky,

Ambitions and Strategies (Oxford: Oxford University Press, 1964), and H.C.G. Matthew, *The Liberal Imperialists* (Oxford: Oxford University Press, 1973) discuss the feuding between them.

Paul Adelman, *Victorian Radicalism: The Middle Class Experience* (London: Longman, 1984) provides an introduction to the mid-Victorian Radicals. Miles Taylor *The Decline of British Radicalism 1847–1860* (Oxford: Oxford University Press, 1995) is detailed, as is D.A. Hamer, *The Politics of Electoral Pressure* (Brighton: Harvester, 1977) on the largely Nonconformist pressure groups. G.I.T. Machin, *Politics and the Churches in Great Britain 1832–1868* (Oxford: Oxford University Press, 1977) is wide-ranging because of the centrality of sectarian rivalry to politics. A second volume with the same title covers 1869 to 1921 (Oxford: Oxford University Press, 1987), but for this period see also S. Koss *Nonconformity in Modern British Politics* (London: Batsford, 1975) and D.W. Bebbington, *The Nonconformist Conscience: Chapel and Politics 1870–1914* (London: Allen & Unwin, 1982). On popular politics in the later nineteenth century, both Eugenio F. Biagini, *Liberty, Retrenchment and Reform* (Cambridge: Cambridge University Press, 1992) and Patrick Joyce, *Work, Society and Politics* (London: Methuen, 1982) are outstanding.

On 'New Liberalism', Peter Clarke, *Liberals and Social Democrats* (Cambridge: Cambridge University Press, 1978) is entertaining as well as informative, M. Freeden, *The New Liberalism* (Oxford: Oxford University Press, 1978) difficult but essential. J.R. Hay, *The Origins of the Liberal Welfare Reforms 1906–14* (London: Macmillan, 1975) provides a brief, clear introduction to the major legislation. The crucial budget of 1909 is explained in Bruce Murray, *The People's Budget* (Oxford: Oxford University Press, 1980). P. Rowland, *The Last Liberal Governments*, 2 vols (London: Barrie & Rockcliff, 1968 and 1971) is a strictly chronological account, requiring much use of the index to pursue particular issues, but very useful for information, as is his *Lloyd George* (London: Barrie & Jenkins, 1975). John Grigg, *Lloyd George*, vol. 2 *The People's Champion* and vol. 3 *From Peace to War* (London: Methuen, 1978 and 1985), and B.B Gilbert, *David Lloyd George*, vol. 1. *The Architect of Change* and vol. 2 *The Organiser of Victory* (London: Batsford, 1987 and 1992) are better biographies, but less easy for simple reference. Neither has yet got beyond 1916. Asquith is still impenetrable. Roy Jenkins, *Asquith* (London: Collins, 1964) probably gets closest to the man, S. Koss, *Asquith* (London: Allen Lane, 1976) closest to his politics.

Two of the party's pre-war problems are clarified in D. Morgan, *Suffragists and Liberals* (Oxford: Blackwell, 1975), and P. Jalland, *The*

Liberals and Ireland (Brighton: Harvester, 1980). For the emergence of the Labour party, D. Tanner, *Political Change and the Labour party* (Cambridge: Cambridge University Press, 1990) is dense but unavoidable. R. McKibbin, *The Evolution of the Labour Party 1910–1924* (Oxford: Oxford University Press, 1974), includes the Labour party's internal development. Trevor Wilson, *The Myriad Faces of War* (Oxford: Polity Press, 1986), can be used selectively for the political ramifications of war. John Turner, *British Politics and the Great War* (New Haven: Yale University Press, 1992) is a standard work, as is K.O. Morgan, *Consensus and Disunity* (Oxford: Oxford University Press, 1979) for the post-war coalition. Trevor Wilson, *The Downfall of the Liberal Party* (London: Collins, 1966) is thin on detail by modern standards, but remains the basic political history. M. Freeden, *Liberalism Divided* (Oxford: Oxford University Press, 1986) is essential for the intellectual developments, although M. Bentley, *The Liberal Mind* (Cambridge: Cambridge University Press, 1977) still has much to say.

Further reading can be found in the footnotes, and in the bibliographies of the books mentioned above. Most leading politicians have had biographies written about them. The great Victorian and Edwardian 'tomb' biographies should not be dismissed simply because their authors often shared the outlook of their subjects. In recent years, few senior politicians, and some less senior, have neglected to publish their autobiographies or diaries.

Glossary

This glossary is aimed primarily at non-specialist and overseas readers who may not be entirely familiar with the British political and legal systems. In addition, it provides brief explanatory summaries of some subjects which appear in the text as important issues in the history of British liberalism, but which go beyond the scope of the book itself.

alternative vote: a system of voting designed to eliminate the situation in which, when there are three or more candidates, a candidate can be elected on less than 50 per cent of the vote. Voters are asked on the ballot form to rank candidates in order of preference. If, when first preferences are counted, no candidate has secured 50 per cent, the candidate with the lowest number of first preferences is eliminated, and his second preferences allocated to the remaining candidates. If there is still no candidate with 50 per cent of the vote, the process is repeated until one candidate does secure 50 per cent. This system is used in Australia.

annual parliament: a parliament dissolved each year, resulting in annual elections. Extreme Radicals (e.g. Chartists) demanded this to secure greater control by the electorate over its representatives. *See also* triennial parliament.

army estimates: the money that the government estimates will be required for the upkeep of the army for the current year. Such estimates must be submitted to parliament for approval, producing a debate, and ultimately a vote, on the government's policy towards the army, and more generally on national defence. *See also* navy estimates.

blackleg: a worker who continues to work during a strike, or takes the job of a striking worker.

borough franchise: the qualification determined by act of parliament to vote in a parliamentary election in an urban constituency (borough). The 1832 Reform Act fixed the level as occupancy of a house of £10 annual value (the £10 householder). The Reform Act of 1867 extended the vote to almost all householders (householder franchise) by reducing the £10 requirement to that of simple payment of rates (local taxes).

bowdlerise: strictly, the removal of supposedly indecent passages from a text, after Thomas Bowdler (1754–1825) who published an emasculated edition of Shakespeare. More generally, oversimplification.

Chartists: the 'People's Charter' was drawn up by the radical London Working Man's Association in 1838. It demanded six major reforms: manhood suffrage, the payment of MPs, equal electoral districts, annual parliaments, the secret ballot, and the abolition of the property qualification for MPs. During the economic distress of the late 1830s and 1840s, it acquired mass support among the unemployed and impoverished. In so doing it developed a violent 'physical force' wing alongside the advocates of 'moral force', who worked within the law and attempted to persuade parliament to introduce its reforms by mass petitions. Despite the threat of disorder, the occasional violent outbreak and the submission of three petitions to parliament, the last in 1848, the movement achieved none of its objectives in the short term, although all except annual parliaments are now part of the British political system. The movement petered out with the return to prosperity in the 1850s, leaving a tradition and a mythology to both the trade-union movement and the later Labour party.

chief whip: the officer of a political party responsible for the organisation and discipline of the party in parliament. The term is derived from hunting, where the 'whippers-in' assisted the huntsman to control the hounds. In the mid-nineteenth century, the chief whip also had the responsibility of maintaining links with party agents and members in the constituencies and for election campaigns. Subsequently, this extra-parliamentary role was met by the appointment of a chief agent and a party chairman, leaving the chief whip and his subordinate whips to concentrate on parliamentary matters. *See* whips.

church rates: rates for the upkeep of the church and churchyard, the ordinary expenses of church services and the payment of the clerk's salary were levied on all occupiers of property except the occupiers of Crown property and proven destitutes since at least the reign of Edward I. Dissenters (q.v.) objected on both conscientious and financial grounds to paying for the upkeep of a church to which they did not belong and whose spiritual truth they denied. With the growth of militant Dissent (Nonconformity), church rates became a symbol of the tyranny of an established church. Opposition was closely related to the parallel growth of voluntaryism (see voluntaryist) in the late 1830s and 1840s. The Church Rate Abolition Society was formed in 1836 after the Whig government had failed to abolish the rate, but the failure of another abolition bill in 1837 marked the last attempt by a government to settle the issue until 1866. In parliament, it was taken up in private members' bills (there were thirty-six attempts to abolish church rates between 1834 and 1860) and in the country Nonconformist resistance and agitation continued. There were numerous cases of imprisonment for non-payment, whilst agitation was led by Edward Miall, whose property was seized for non-payment in 1836, in the *Nonconformist* newspaper he launched in 1841, and by the Anti-State Church Association formed in 1844 and renamed the Liberation Society in 1853. The attack on church rates became increasingly associated with the campaign for the complete disestablishment of the church, an association which in turn stimulated the resistance of the church's supporters who formed a Committee of Laymen of the Church of England in 1856. Nevertheless, the abolitionists gained ground. In 1858 a church rates abolition bill was passed in the House of Commons for the first time, although it was soundly defeated in the Lords, and liberal churchmen of both major parties were seeking compromise in the belief that the continued dispute was doing harm to the church itself. Abolition of compulsory church rates was finally achieved in 1868 by a compromise, necessary to secure the agreement of the House of Lords, negotiated by Gladstone with the minority Conservative government, which left voluntary payment untouched. The Irish equivalent of the church rate, the church cess, was abolished in 1831.

church tithes: the payment of one tenth (nominally) of produce by parishioners for the maintenance of the parish church and its priest. Voluntary in origin, tithes were enforced in the tenth century, but the payment was widely resented by Dissenters in England and

The Rise and Fall of British Liberalism

Scotland, and especially by Catholics in Ireland, whose resistance was often violent. *See* tithe war.

coal and mineral royalties: payments, usually on a percentage basis, made to a landowner for the exploitation of coal and mineral resources beneath the land.

Commons: shorthand for the House of Commons, the lower, but most important, house in the British parliament.

consensus politics: the situation when both major parties are broadly agreed on a range of fundamentals, and policy differences become matters of detail and administration. The opposite of adversarial or confrontational politics.

constituency association: the local organisation of a political party in each electoral division, or constituency. Constituency associations emerged gradually during the nineteenth century as part of the development of political parties. It was not until the 1870s that attempts were made to integrate them into national bodies, the National Union of Conservative and Constitutional Associations and the National Liberal Federation, to achieve greater coherence. Even then, constituency associations retained considerable local autonomy, and resented interference from such national organisations or the chief whip and the party central office.

cooperative movement: a movement designed to prevent the exploitation of consumers by middlemen by integrating production, distribution and sale within a single organisation, or cooperative society, with profits being redistributed to members. The Rochdale Pioneers are credited with the first cooperative store in 1844. Cooperatives secured legal recognition in 1852, and the Cooperative Wholesale Society was formed in 1863. The Cooperative party was formed in 1917 in the peculiar circumstances of the Lloyd George coalition. Subsequently it has been closely associated with the Labour party.

Corn Laws: legislation intended to prolong into peacetime the protection that British farmers had enjoyed through the interruption of trade during the French Revolutionary and Napoleonic Wars (1793–1815). The Corn Law of 1815 prevented the import of foreign grain until the price had reached 80 shillings per quarter. Despite amendment to a nominally less restrictive sliding scale in 1828, the Corn Laws were attacked as class legislation by manufacturers who blamed them for raising costs, thereby reducing trade, profits and employment; by workers for increasing the price of food, still further reducing their standard of living; and by Nonconformists because the established church (the Church of England) had a vested interest in high grain prices in its capacity as a landowner. Increasingly undermined by such opposition and the prevalence of liberal economic ideas commending free trade, the Corn Laws were repealed in 1846.

Country faction: a faction composed mainly of country gentlemen, with articulate leaders and pamphleteers, that emerged after the revolution settlement of 1688–9 and lasted virtually until the end of the eighteenth century. Nominally it might have included almost half of the House of Commons, but country gentlemen were not assiduous in attendance. It included both radical Whigs (the 'Commonwealthmen') who were not unfavourable to a more equitable distribution of property since aristocratic wealth encouraged dependence and corruption, were sympathetic to Dissenters and sought an extension of civil and religious liberty, and strongly conservative Tories who defended the social hierarchy and the established church. Divided on general politics, the Country faction was united in its distrust of the Court, ministers, Crown patronage and the placemen it created. This corruption of the political system, and its destruction of civic virtue would, the Country faction argued, destroy the balanced constitution of king, Lords and Commons, give all power to the Court and ministry, and subvert the liberties of Englishmen. *See* Crown patronage.

county franchise: the qualification determined by act of parliament to vote in rural (county) constituencies. The Reform Act of 1832 retained the franchise in existence since 1430 of residents with a freehold worth 40 shillings (the '40 shilling freeholder'), who still made up the bulk of the county electorate. It added £10 leaseholders, with some security of tenure and independence and, on a Conservative amendment, £50 tenants-at-will, with little or none. The Reform Act of 1867 reduced the qualification requirements to £5 leaseholders and £12 occupiers. The Reform Act of 1884 went further still, and introduced for the counties the householder qualification set for the borough electorate by the Act of 1867.

Crown patronage: political patronage was an essential feature of the eighteenth-century political system, whether exercised by wealthy landowners through their control of parliamentary seats (*see* pocket borough, rotten borough), and ecclesiastical livings (*see* lay patronage) or by the Crown through the distribution of offices and favours. The scope for the exercise of Crown patronage increased with the expansion of the treasury, the customs and excise and the armed forces. MPs who held their seats as the result of Crown patronage were called 'placemen' and were expected to support the party favoured by the Crown, usually the government of the day, which was appointed by the Crown and in turn advised the Crown on the exercise of its patronage. In 1701 there were 113 such 'placemen' out of a total of 513 MPs. In the absence of organised political parties offering steady support, the system relied upon such management for much of its stability. In the 1780s, the movement for 'Economical Reform', an expression of the concern for parliamentary reform, progressively reduced the numbers of placemen and the effectiveness of Crown patronage by such measures as the disfranchisement of Crown revenue officers and the exclusion of the holders of government contracts from the House of Commons. *See* Country faction.

death duties: introduced by Sir William Harcourt in his budget of 1894 to replace the estate duty of 1859, death duties were a tax on capital levied at the death of the owner. The duties were graduated, rising in incidence according to the capital sum taxed. They were replaced by Capital Transfer Tax in 1975.

decontrol: after the First World War the removal of government controls and restraints imposed by the government during the wartime emergency. Refers particularly to the removal of economic controls and the return to a free market (q.v.) and free competition.

derating: complete removal from the liability to pay rates (local taxes) on certain types of land or improvements (usually buildings) thereon, or alternatively assessing certain types of land or improvements at a lower level. Thus, to relieve the burdens on farming land during a period of depression, agricultural land was rated at half its assessed value by the Agricultural Rates Act of 1896. Thus also, assuming a valuation which distinguished the two, provision for which was made in the budget of 1909, rates could be removed from buildings (improvements) and levied solely upon the assessed value of the site on which they stood. Hence 'site value rating'. *See* land values taxation, rating relief.

direct tax: a tax levied on individuals directly. The most obvious and widespread is income tax.

disposable income: the income left for individual use after compulsory deductions, usually by the state in the form of direct taxation and, after the 1911 National Insurance Act, insurance contributions. Depending on legislation, such deductions might also include pension payments and even trade-union contributions.

Dissenters: Protestants who did not conform to (i.e. 'dissented' from) the established Church of England. Persecuted since the reign of Elizabeth I, Dissenters became strong supporters of civil and religious liberties during the late seventeenth and eighteenth centuries. They were associated in this cause with the Whigs, and subsequently during the nineteenth century with the Liberal party. The term is virtually synonymous with 'Nonconformists', although the latter, the familiar nineteenth-century description, expresses a more self-confident, even aggressive, outlook. *See* church rates, voluntaryist.

double-member constituency: a constituency which returned two members to the House of Commons. Traditionally a feature of the British political system, and vigorously defended in 1832 as tending towards compromise and facilitating minority representation, the double-member constituency was eroded during the course of the nineteenth century. The Reform Act of 1885 established the single-member constituency (q.v.) as the norm, although even then fifty-two double-member constituencies survived. *See* proportional representation.

dumping: the marketing of goods overseas at prices below the home market price, or even below the cost of production. An extreme version of what Protectionists (q.v.) considered 'unfair competition' made possible by government subsidies or high tariff barriers which allowed losses abroad to be covered by high profits from artificially high prices at home. The object of dumping is to capture the foreign market by destroying local competitors, a short-term operation after which prices can be raised to even higher levels.

electorate: the whole body of those qualified to vote. After the 1832 Reform Act, approximately 20 per cent of the adult male population had the vote, rising to some 35 per cent after the Reform Act of 1867 and to 66 per cent after the Act of 1884. The Representation of the People Act of 1918 introduced manhood suffrage and gave the vote to women over thirty, enfranchising some 74 per cent of the population. Women over twenty-one were given the vote in 1928, theoretically enfranchising the whole adult population. In practice the figure is reduced to approximately 97 per cent because of the six months residence qualification before voters were placed on the electoral register. *See* registration campaign.

Enlightenment: an intellectual movement in the eighteenth century that was sceptical of traditional authority, especially ecclesiastical authority, to which it opposed human reason. It accordingly emphasised the right of the individual to liberty, particularly of free thought and expression, and from the arbitrary rule of existing political and religious authorities. These authorities should be tested for their utility in maintaining the rights of the individual, and reformed or abolished if found wanting.

entail: in English property law, the restriction of inheritance to designated heirs and their successors. Until 1925 limited to landed estates, thereafter applicable to all property by the creation of trusts. Used by landowners to prevent the break-up of estates by creating a life-interest in the estate which permitted use of the income, but prevented disposal of the capital (the estate) which had to be handed on intact to successive heirs designated in the entail. An impediment to the free sale of land which nineteenth-century radicals regarded as essential if more land was to be brought into productive use, and what they termed 'the land monopoly' was to be broken. More generally the word is used to mean a necessary consequence that follows from an action.

Erastian: from Thomas Erastus (1524–1583), a Swiss theologian who asserted the supremacy of the state over the church. In England state supremacy was instituted during the reign of Henry VIII with the monarch as head of a church by law established, i.e. the Church of England. The doctrine was much favoured by the Whigs, who saw in an established church under state control a means to reduce doctrinal disputes and sectarian rivalry. By adopting a broad-church policy, especially in church appointments, the Whigs sought to make the established church as inclusive as possible.

fair rent: in Ireland, the second of the 'Three Fs' (*see also* fixity of tenure, free sale) that were the basis of Irish demands for land tenure reform from the middle years of the nineteenth century until they were conceded by the Irish Land Act of 1881. The establishment of a rent the tenant could pay was essential to the working of the first demand of the 'Three Fs', fixity of tenure (q.v.), since without it the landlord could engineer the removal of a tenant by increasing his rent beyond the tenant's capacity to pay. Such a rent, however, might not be 'fair'. 'Fairness' might be derived either from the profit the tenant could extract from the land, or from supply and demand in the market for tenancies. Under the Land Act of 1881 tenants could apply to have their rents fixed by a rent court, and applications flooded in – on one occasion, 12,000 in a single day (12 November 1881). The Act, however, gave no guidance to the rent tribunals on the principles they should adopt in fixing rents. Ability to pay appears to have been the main criterion, and the Irish Land Act of 1881, despite its length and complexity, has been denounced as no more than 'simply a rent control act', for the political purpose of reducing Irish agitation. *See* tenant right.

Fenian: member of an Irish revolutionary society committed to Irish independence formed in the United States in 1858 which spread to Ireland by the mid-1860s. Fenian bombing of Clerkenwell prison and the murder of a policeman in Manchester in 1867 aroused Gladstone's interest in the Irish question. Subsequently known as the Irish Republican Brotherhood (IRB), but superseded after 1916 by the Irish Republican Army (IRA).

fiscal reform: a term used, both by contemporaries and historians, as a synonym for 'tariff reform', the programme of import duties (2 shillings per quarter on imported wheat, a corresponding duty on imported flour, a 5 per cent duty on dairy produce and a duty of up to 10 per cent on imported manufactured goods) outlined by Joseph Chamberlain at Glasgow in 1903. The duties were to be remitted in whole or in part on colonial products, creating a structure of imperial preference (q.v.) intended to bind the empire together. The term can also be used to distinguish the more explicitly fiscal proposals made by Balfour in 1907 from Chamberlain's tariff reform. Balfour proposed revenue duties which might be remitted to provide imperial preference, but which were primarily aimed at 'broadening the basis of taxation' to provide revenue for Conservative policies of national defence and social reform without recourse to higher direct taxes on the rich, of the kind that Lloyd George introduced in his 'People's Budget' of 1909.

fixity of tenure: one of the 'Three Fs' (*see also* fair rent, free sale) that were the programme of the Irish Tenant Right League formed in 1850. Subsequently the 'Three Fs' became the basis of Irish demands for land tenure reform until they were conceded by the Irish Land Act of 1881. Most Irish tenancies were yearly, but fixity of tenure, derived from Ulster customary tenure, meant security of tenure, that the landlords would not evict a tenant as long as the tenant continued to pay his rent. Although a principal demand, fixity of tenure was not the real issue, which was rent (*see* fair rent). On the other hand, with fixity of tenure, secured by fair rent, the tenant acquired an interest in his holding which he could sell on removal. The 'Three Fs' therefore stood together. *See also* tenant right.

franchise: the right to vote in elections to the House of Commons, or other representative bodies, such as county councils. *See* borough franchise, county franchise.

freedom of contract: contracts are, in theory, legally binding agreements between free and equal individuals. Freedom of contract expressed the individualism at the heart of nineteenth-century liberalism, based on the view that rational individuals (adult males, not women or children) were the best judges of their own interests. Accordingly, neither the state, nor organisations, of which trade unions were the most relevant, should interfere with the exercise of that judgement. Increasing appreciation of the manifest inequality between contracting parties led to legislation, for example the legal recognition given to trade unions and the protection to Irish tenants. *See* minimal state.

free market: a commercial system that allows the laws of supply and demand to regulate the economy, including the market for labour, without government interference. It does, however, require government interference to maintain its preconditions, property and legally enforceable contracts.

free sale: in Ireland, under Ulster custom (extended to the rest of Ireland by the Irish Land Act of 1870) and the Irish Land Act of 1881, the right of a tenant to sell his right, or interest in his holding, to an incoming tenant. One of the 'Three Fs' (*see also* fair rent, fixity of tenure) that formed the basis of Irish demands for land tenure reform from the middle years of the nineteenth century until they were conceded by the Act of 1881. *See also* tenant right.

friendly society: a benefit society in which individuals combine to pay regular dues into a common fund in return for payments at time of need, usually sickness and burial benefits. In the nineteenth century they were, with building societies and trade unions, one of the classic self-help institutions of the skilled working class. Successive legislation protected the societies and their funds since 1792, and a national register of friendly societies was set up in 1846.

general warrant: warrants are given under the authority of the Crown by magistrates and similar judicial or executive officials usually to authorise an arrest or the search of premises (as in 'search warrant'). Customarily the individual or premises are named in the warrant, but in a general warrant the individual or premises are not specified, allowing them to be used at discretion. The Wilkes affair established that general warrants were unlawful.

government patronage: *see* Crown patronage.

habeas corpus: a writ issued by the courts requiring prison keepers to bring a detainee to court to determine whether there were sufficient grounds for continued imprisonment. As such, an effective means of guarding against arbitrary arrest and detention, and of protecting individual liberty.

Home Rule: a movement to repeal the Act of Union (1801) between Britain and Ireland. Home Rule was a demand for self-government rather than for complete independence, for a separate Irish parliament for Irish domestic affairs but one which was subordinate to the British (usually called the 'Imperial') parliament at Westminster. Home Rule bills thus reserved to the imperial parliament such matters as control of foreign policy, defence, and customs. The movement first achieved prominence under the leadership of Daniel O'Connell in the 1830s and 1840s. It was revived by the activities of the Fenian Society (*see* Fenian) in the late 1860s, and by the formation by Isaac Butt in 1870 of the Home Government Association. Some fifty-nine Irish MPs were committed to Home Rule after the general election of 1874. Under the more resolute leadership of Parnell the Irish Parliamentary Party became a formidable force in the 1880s, reinforced by the agrarian distress and violence in Ireland that erupted after 1879. The 1885 general election left the Irish party holding the balance in a hung parliament (q.v.). Gladstone secured Irish support by adopting Home Rule as Liberal party policy, but the first Home Rule bill (1886) split the party and was defeated by the votes of secessionist Liberal Unionists, predominantly Whigs but including Joseph Chamberlain and a small group of Radicals. Dependent again upon Irish support in 1892, Gladstone's second Home Rule bill passed the House of Commons but was overwhelmingly defeated in the House of Lords. Dependent again on Irish support after the general election of January 1910, Asquith's Liberal government introduced a third Home Rule bill in 1912, which passed under the provisions of the Parliament Act in 1914, but was suspended owing to the outbreak of the First World War. The major political difficulty facing Home Rule, especially after 1912, was the resistance of Ulster, whose fervently Protestant population objected to incorporation into Catholic Ireland. By 1914 the country was on the brink of civil war and the government was obliged to consider schemes for the exclusion of Ulster. Irish Home Rule was finally achieved by the Anglo-Irish Treaty of 1921, but Ulster remained part of the United Kingdom.

householder franchise: the right to vote by virtue of occupying a house, and the payment of rates thereon, subject to a certain period of residence. The Reform Act of 1867 introduced the household qualification in urban constituencies (boroughs). The Reform Act of 1884 extended this qualification to the county constituencies.

household suffrage: *see* householder franchise.

hung parliament: when neither major party in the House of Commons has an absolute majority, and is unable to form a stable government without the support of minor parties whose influence is accordingly increased.

imperial preference: an arrangement by which duties on imports are so structured that goods from the countries of the empire are taxed at a lower (i.e. preferential) rate than goods of foreign origin, thus, assuming similar costs of production and transport, allowing them to sell at a lower price in the home market, to the benefit of the imperial producers. Primarily associated with Joseph Chamberlain, the tariff reform campaign that he launched in 1903 saw preference as a means to achieve imperial federation rather than as simply an economic policy. Imperial preference finally became British policy as a result of the Imperial Economic Conference at Ottawa in 1932, but as a response to economic depression rather than an expression of the imperial idealism that had characterised the pre-war campaign.

indirect tax: a tax imposed on goods or services, usually collected either when goods move from one region to another (customs duties), or at the point of sale (sales tax, value added tax).

jingo: adopted from a music-hall song backing Disraeli's anti-Russian policy during the eastern crisis of 1877–8, the term subsequently denoted anyone with an ultra-patriotic and aggressive attitude on foreign and imperial affairs. The most notable outbreak of jingoism occurred in 1900 during the riotous celebrations that followed news of the relief of Mafeking, and coined another term for jingoist behaviour, 'to maffick' or 'mafficking'.

labour exchange: labour exchanges were established in 1909 as places where unemployed workers could register in pursuit of work, and employers could announce vacancies. By bringing the unemployed and job vacancies together, the government hoped not only to reduce unemployment, a primary cause of poverty, but also to increase national efficiency and reduce welfare costs. In modern terminology, 'job centre'.

land values taxation: in simple terms, the imposition of a tax on the capital value of land, preceded, of course, by land valuation. The simplicity was deceptive. Land values taxation came to incorporate under a single vague head, a variety of objects and schemes. The incidence of the tax, as of all taxes, could vary from a low level for revenue purposes to a tax equal to the total value of the land as proposed by the English and Scottish Land Restoration Leagues, in effect land nationalisation through taxation. The tax might be applied to all land, or to particular categories of land, for example building sites, whether built upon or merely potential, as 'site value taxation'. Under the general heading came proposals to tax the unearned increment (q.v.) which was at least a mild form of land values taxation, and proposals to tax ground rents, which had little connection with it. Much of the considerable agitation for the taxation of land values came from local authorities, who wanted to impose local taxes on land values and thus really meant land values rating. By 1906, 518 local authorities supported the taxation (i.e. rating) of land values. The 'land taxes' in Lloyd George's budget of 1909, despite their notoriety, were comparatively mild, a 20 per cent tax on unearned increment (q.v.) and a half penny in the pound on undeveloped land and minerals. Their real value lay in requiring a land valuation, after which land values taxation, or rating, in any of its forms on any category of land, became a possibility. Without such a valuation, it was an impossibility, as Lloyd George discovered with his proposals for site value rating in his 1914 budget. Despite its complexity and variety, land values taxation appealed strongly to Radicals (including Labour) and Liberals. It drew upon a long radical tradition of the expropriation of the people by an alien aristocracy, on resistance to feudal oppression, and on the idea that ownership of the land, as a limited resource, constituted a monopoly. As such it focused on the Liberal party's traditional enemies, the landowners. Moreover, for a party in danger of division on class lines, and of losing its middle-class elite, land values taxation had the advantage of distinguishing between wealth created by individual enterprise through labour, manufacturing and trade, and wealth that was, so land values taxers argued, created by society and to which, accordingly, its owners had no right. *See* unearned increment.

lay appropriation: taking possession of church property or revenues by a member of the laity (i.e. one who is not a clergyman). This might be an individual, usually a landowner, or a government, a lay institution. For example, the attempts by Whig (q.v.) governments during the 1830s to appropriate (seize) the surplus revenues of the Anglican Church in Ireland, in order to finance measures to assist the wider Irish population, most notably its education proposals.

lay patronage: the right of a member of the laity (i.e. one who is not a clergyman), usually a landowner, to present to a living, that is to choose the clergyman (parson, vicar, priest, minister) for a parish of which he was the patron. The living was exactly that, the house (parsonage, vicarage, manse), the land attached and the parish revenues, most notably the church tithe (q.v.). Literary examples abound, but, for example, in Jane Austen's *Pride and Prejudice*, Mr Collins was given his living by Lady Catherine de Bourgh and in *Sense and Sensibility* Edward Ferrars was given the living of Delaford by Colonel Brandon.

libertarian: a believer in the greatest possible freedom of thought and action for the individual, and his right, either natural, historic or constitutional, to exercise that freedom. Government interference should be minimal. *See* minimal state, voluntaryist.

lockout: used by employers to discipline workers, or counter a strike, by excluding workers from their place of work, literally by locking the gates. Successfully used, for example, by engineering employers against the once powerful Amalgamated Society of Engineers in the strike and lockout of 1897–8.

Lords: shorthand for the House of Lords, the upper house in the British parliament.

Magna Carta: the Great Charter granted by King John to his rebellious barons in June 1215. Amongst many clauses relating to feudal obligations, the charter promised to summon a 'common counsel' before assessing aids (taxes) and trial by peers according to the law. From the charter, despite its feudal nature, subsequent generations, especially during the disputes between parliament and the Crown in the seventeenth century, derived the right to consent to taxation, trial by jury and the rule of law. Moreover, although the charter explicitly 'granted' the liberties it listed, it was later regarded as simply declaratory of those historic rights of freeborn Englishmen which thus did not depend on the grace or grant of a monarch. Less often noted, clause 61 contained what amounted to an affirmation of the right of resistance to oppression.

malt tax: a tax bitterly resented by farmers, particularly during periods of agricultural depression, as between 1829 and 1833, when they had difficulty paying rents. It was alleged that the tax not only reduced the consumption of barley, but also increased the price of beer. Despite rural agitation, pressure from country MPs and a wish by both Whig and Conservative governments to repeal the tax, the revenue it brought in was too valuable to give up. The tax survived until 1880, when, at the onset of another period of agricultural depression and amidst mounting unrest from farmers, Gladstone finally converted it into a beer duty.

manhood suffrage: the right of all adult males to vote. Manhood suffrage (except for peers and lunatics) was introduced by the Representation of the People Act (the fourth reform act), in 1918.

minimal state: the ideal of classical liberalism in the nineteenth century, in which the three principal sources of British liberalism – the myth of historic liberties, eighteenth-century rationalism, and religious dissent – converged. With the individual constrained by economic laws to pursue the advantage of society despite his selfish motivation, progressively educated by good laws to obey the rule of law, and made moral by the teachings of Christianity, the individual should be freed to enjoy the liberty that was his historic right under a free constitution. The role of the state could, and should, be reduced to the minimum consistent with the enforcement of free contracts between free individuals, the preservation of order and the protection of property through the operation of the law, and the defence of the realm. For some, e.g. Cobden and Gladstone, the role of the state even in matters of national security should diminish as the combined pressure of free trade (as a law of nature governing economic relations) led to increasing economic inter-dependence, and the moral injunctions of international law drove nations, as individuals writ large, towards peaceful cooperation in their own self-interest. The corollary of the minimal state was low taxation, further freeing the individual by allowing him control of more of his own income and, in theory, maximum economic growth since state expenditure, unlike individual investment, was regarded as unproductive. Conversely, since the state should not intervene to provide education or any form of welfare support, the individual was thrown back on his own resources or on charity. The ideal was never realised as the state intervened in the interests of public health, to protect the weak (women, children, Irish tenants, etc.), and to provide education, but nineteenth-century liberals never developed a coherent justification for such intervention. *See* freedom of contract, voluntaryist.

ministerial responsibility: ministers are responsible to parliament for their actions and those of their subordinates, and have to resign if unable to secure parliamentary support for them. However, those subordinates also remain personally liable for their actions if they break the law, and cannot plead obedience to orders from their superiors in extenuation.

minority government: a government lacking a majority in the House of Commons. Since governments are usually formed from a single party, the Liberal governments of 1892–5 and 1910–15 were technically minority governments, dependent upon the outside support of the Irish Parliamentary Party and, after 1910, of the Labour party. In practice, deals with those parties on Home Rule and the payment of MPs gave them a comfortable majority, at the price of policy concessions.

natural rights: rights which are alleged to belong to all humans, based on the assumption that in a state of nature, logically or chronologically prior to society, individuals neither were, nor could be, subject to any legitimate authority. For the preservation of their most important rights, individuals agreed to form societies, each giving up some of his rights on the basis that others did the same (the social contract), and instituted governments to ensure that this agreement was adhered to. The purpose of society and government was thus to maintain the rights of the individual which the individual retained, and which some theorists (e.g. Locke) argued, could not be given up. Such rights included life, liberty, security, property and 'the pursuit of happiness'. If the government proved oppressive, the individual retained the right, in defence of his natural rights, either to migrate or to overthrow the government. Natural rights, now known as human rights, were embodied in various constitutions in the late eighteenth and nineteenth centuries (e.g. USA, France), and in the United Nations Declaration of Human Rights.

navy estimates: the sum estimated by the government as necessary for the maintenance, and, more usually in the later nineteenth and early twentieth centuries, the expansion of the navy. Like the army estimates, the navy estimates required parliamentary approval, initiating a debate and ultimately a vote on government naval policy. For a Liberal party committed to reduced expenditure on defence, the naval estimates were usually difficult, and often critical. Gladstone resigned on the navy estimates proposed by his cabinet in 1894, and the estimates of 1908–9 and 1913–14 almost broke up the government.

open question: in parliamentary terms, a debate and vote in which party discipline is not exercised, and members are permitted to vote according to conscience.

paper duties: excise duties on the manufacture of paper. The repeal of the paper duties, proposed by Gladstone in 1860, provoked a political crisis when the Lords rejected the bill, partly at least because of Palmerston's well-known opposition. Palmerston, however, objected to the timing, because repeal sacrificed revenue needed for national defence, not to the principle. In 1861 Gladstone increased income tax by 1d. to cover the lost revenue, and incorporated repeal of the paper duties into his budget, taking advantage of the constitutional convention that the Lords should not interfere with a money bill, to ensure that repeal would pass. Together with the repeal of the stamp duty in 1855, the repeal of the paper duties facilitated the emergence of a new cheap democratic press, especially in the provinces and greatly to the advantage of the Liberal party.

parish relief: each comprising a district in the care of a priest, parishes became the basic unit of local government in the sixteenth century when they were given responsibility for the administration of the Poor Law (q.v.), providing relief for those unable to work, but also disciplining the simply idle. Contributions to relief were initially voluntary, but following precedents of 1563 and 1597 when justices of the peace were empowered to raise funds compulsorily, the Poor Law Act of 1601 introduced a poor rate levied on property. The Workhouse Test Act of 1723 forced the poor to enter workhouses for relief, but Gilbert's Act of 1782 excluded the able-bodied poor from the workhouse and obliged parishes to provide work or what was called 'outdoor relief', known as the 'Speenhamland system'. The expense of this system, which became virtually a subsidy for low wages during the difficult years of the early industrial revolution, led to pressures for reform, resulting in the 'New Poor Law' created by the Poor Law Amendment Act of 1834. The Act grouped parishes together in Poor Law unions managed by boards of guardians elected by ratepayers, and restored the workhouse as the only place of relief. *See* Poor Law.

parliamentary party: here used to distinguish the party in parliament, i.e. the MPs belonging to the party, from the members of the party in the country.

parliamentary privilege: the right of each house of parliament to control its own affairs and maintain internal discipline without outside interference. Members of the House of Commons enjoy the privilege of free speech, which exempts them from legal proceedings for statements made within parliament, freedom from arrest, except that arising from criminal charges, preventive detention, bankruptcy or contempt of court. Civil suits are unaffected. The House may take action against violations of its privileges but where this involves the rights of individuals outside the House, the limits of privilege are determined by the courts.

parliamentary sovereignty: the theory that parliament is the supreme authority in Britain, and that there can be no appeal against its decisions, whether to natural rights, the will of the people, or even God. Parliament can thus make laws on any subjects it chooses in any form it chooses. It can pass retrospective laws, and does so in the form of indemnity acts safeguarding officials against possible criminal proceedings for actions taken in time of emergency, such as the suspension of habeas corpus (q.v.). However, since each parliament is sovereign, no parliament can bind its successors. It is sometimes argued that in Britain legislative sovereignty resides in parliament, but political sovereignty with the electorate, because the latter can change the composition of the predominant house of parliament, the House of Commons. *See* popular sovereignty.

picketing: pickets were strikers who stood outside a works or factory to prevent other workers from going to work. Legally pickets could only attempt to dissuade by 'peaceful picketing', which was made lawful by the Conspiracy and Protection of Property Act of 1875, and reaffirmed by the Trade Disputes Act of 1906. This not only gave trade unions but also their officials immunity from prosecution for acts in furtherance of a trade dispute, including picketing. The development of mass picketing, 'flying pickets' who rushed from one site to another, and secondary picketing by unions not involved in the original dispute led to closer definitions, particularly after the coal strike of 1972 and the mass picketing of the Grunwick photo-processing plant in 1977 when on one day (11 July 1977) there were 18,000 pickets. The Employment Act of 1980 outlawed secondary picketing, and the Code of Practice on Picketing (1980) recommended that there should not be more than six pickets at any entrance. The Employment Act of 1982 removed the immunity from prosecution of trade-union officials engaged in unlawful picketing, and unlawful secondary action. *See* sympathy strike.

plebiscite: a direct vote by the electorate. Usually reserved for questions of special significance, particularly affecting national integrity or sovereignty, such as self-government for Scotland, or British membership of the EEC. The same as a referendum.

plural voting: a system that entitles a voter to vote more than once in a general election. In nineteenth- and early-twentieth-century Britain, voters who owned property in several constituencies were entitled to vote in all of them. Twenty-three appears to be the verifiable maximum number of votes held by any single individual, although the Radical MP, Sir Charles Dilke, claimed to know an individual with thirty-seven. In 1911, there were some 500,000 to 600,000 plural voters, some 7 per cent of the electorate. The plural vote existed until 1948, when university seats were finally abolished.

pocket borough: similar to rotten borough, a borough constituency with few electors controlled by a landowner or one or two land-owning families who thus had the borough 'in their pocket' and were able to nominate the MP. Many were abolished by the Reform Act of 1832, but many also survived, perhaps as many as fifty-two.

political levy: the levy imposed by trade unions on their members for political purposes, in practice to support the Labour party. It was imposed compulsorily by some unions until successfully challenged by W.V. Osborne, secretary of the Walthamstow branch of the Amalgamated Society of Railway Servants, in the courts. The Osborne judgement by the House of Lords, as the final court of appeal, in 1909 left the Labour party short of funds, and sixteen Labour MPs without even a salary. This was rectified by the introduction of the payment of MPs in 1911, and the political levy was restored by the Trade Union Act of 1913, but subject to a ballot of members before it could be introduced, and with the right of individual members to opt out. Following the general strike of 1926, the Conservative government's Trade Disputes and Trade Union Act of 1927 placed the initiative for payment of the political levy on the individual trade-union member by substituting 'opting in' for 'opting out'. The result was to reduce the Labour party's income from the trade unions by a third. In 1946 the Labour government repealed the 1927 Act, restoring the 'opting out' position of the 1913 Act. Further Conservative legislation in the 1980s altered the position slightly by insisting on periodic ballots to decide whether the political levy should be continued, but a careful campaign by the trade-union leadership ensured that the ballots resulted in continuation.

Poor Law: here used to refer to the 'New Poor Law' set up by the Poor Law Amendment Act of 1834. The New Poor Law abolished the outdoor relief provided by parishes under Gilbert's Act (1782) which in the difficult years of the early nineteenth century proved both expensive and inefficient. It also abolished the parish as the unit of poor law administration that it had been since the sixteenth century, grouping parishes together in 600 new Poor Law unions managed by boards of guardians elected by ratepayers. The thinking behind the larger units was to build larger workhouses in which different categories of the poor could be handled separately, with relief for the old and infirm, treatment for the sick, training for the young and discipline for the idle. The practice did not live up to the ideal. Relief was available only in the workhouse, where conditions were kept deliberately harsh to provide an incentive for the poor to seek work rather than relief. Application for admission to the workhouse thus became, as intended, a test of genuine destitution, and the workhouse one of the most hated institutions of the nineteenth century and beyond. Although different attitudes to unemployment and poverty by the early nineteenth century led to a new approach, for example old-age pensions and national insurance, aspects of the Poor Law remained until the establishment of the National Health Service in 1948.

popular sovereignty: the theory that sovereignty resides in the people, or, realistically, the electorate. Frequently embodied in written constitutions, such as the French constitution of 1791. Nominally, it requires all legislation to be ratified by plebiscite or referendum, and makes all representatives subject to recall, i.e. direct democracy. In practice, it is assumed that the legislature represents the will of the people, i.e. representative democracy, with occasional reference to the sovereign people on matters of supreme importance, such as amendments to the constitution. *See* plebiscite.

populist: in specific use the term applies either to Russian history (the narodniks) or more usefully to members of the US People's Party formed by agricultural producers to contest the 1892 presidential election. In general use, one who appeals directly to the 'ordinary' or 'little' man in opposition to 'big' organisations, whether large business or large landowning interests. There are overtones of class in this, but the appeal to the 'ordinary' man is directed not only to workers as a class, but to small producers, farmers and shopkeepers who feel threatened by, and powerless against, large corporations, unless they secure government support. There are also hints of demagoguery.

preferential tariff: a duty on overseas imports which is lower for one country or group of countries than for others. The former thus receive preferential treatment. In Britain preferential tariffs were usually associated with the empire. *See* fiscal reform, imperial preference.

primogeniture: a method of ensuring that the whole inheritance descends to the eldest son to the exclusion of younger sons. Together with entail (q.v.) a means of keeping estates intact. It did not apply to female inheritance, where the estate was equally divided, nor to personal or moveable property.

proportional representation: a system in which the number of seats held by any party in the legislature reflects the proportion of votes gained in a general election. The two best-known systems of proportional representation are that used in Germany, and the Single Transferable Vote (STV) as used in local elections in Northern Ireland and for both local and parliamentary elections in the Republic of Ireland. Under the German system, voters have two votes and cast one for a constituency candidate and one for a party, each making up half of the legislature. Constituency representatives are elected on a simple majority; the party representation is proportional. The number of seats due to a party is calculated by determining how many seats the party should have gained on a strictly proportional representation, deducting from that the number of seats it has already gained in the constituency elections, and making up the difference by additional seats. Any party which does not gain 5 per cent of the national vote, or three constituency seats, is excluded from the allocation of proportional votes and seats. STV was invented in the mid-nineteenth century, and endorsed by John Stuart Mill in *Considerations on Representative Government* (1861). It might be considered a sophisticated extension of the double-member constituency (q.v.) then prevailing in England. Under it, voters rank candidates in order of preference, as in the alternative vote (q.v.), but in multi-member constituencies. They can thus choose not only between parties, but between members of the same party. The number of votes required for a candidate to be elected, the 'electoral quota', is calculated by dividing the total votes cast in a constituency by the number of candidates. The candidate with the lowest number of votes is eliminated, and his votes transferred to the second-choice (and progressively third-choice, fourth-choice etc.) candidates. However, since a candidate will, at some point in the allocation of preferences, secure not only the votes required for election, the 'electoral quota', but a surplus beyond that level, those surplus votes are also reallocated according to the voters' preferences. This complex process then continues until the required number of candidates has been elected. Proportional representation was proposed in Britain during the debates on the representation of the people bill (1918), but was defeated. It became the policy of the Liberal party, using the STV system, in 1922, and remained party policy until the merger of the party into the Liberal Democrats. It is still Liberal Democrat policy.

Protectionist: one who supports the imposition of tariffs on overseas imports to limit, or prohibit, the entry of such imports into the home market, thus 'protecting' home producers from competition, as in a 'tariff wall'. The antithesis of free trade. Frequently associated with preferential systems. *See* fiscal reform, imperial preference, preferential tariff.

rating relief: partial or complete exemption from the requirement to pay rates (local taxes), as for example in the Agricultural Rates Act of 1896 which levied rates on agricultural land at half its assessed value. *See* derating, land values taxation.

registration campaign: voters, even if they met the qualifications of age, property ownership, etc. laid down by act of parliament, still required (and still require) to be entered on the electoral register. After the Reform Act of 1832, when qualification remained complex, entry in the electoral register a matter of personal initiative, and constituency associations (q.v.) sufficiently large to be beyond the control of local magnates, yet small enough for a few votes to tip the scale, political parties campaigned to place their supporters on the register, and to object to the registration of their opponents.

rental qualification: a qualification to vote based on the amount of rent paid by the householder.

reproductive capital: capital used productively, primarily in the sense of providing employment, wages and profits, but also through the re-investment of profits to reproduce and augment itself.

revanchism: a foreign policy directed at revenge against another state. Most frequently associated with the French attitude towards Germany after the Franco-Prussian War of 1870–1 and the loss of Alsace-Lorraine.

rotten borough: a borough constituency with few or no inhabitants, for example Gatton, Old Sarum, and the most glaring case, Dunwich, which had fallen into the North Sea. An extreme version of pocket boroughs, or nomination boroughs, where the landowner, or sea-bed owner in the case of Dunwich, simply nominated the MP. They were largely abolished by the Reform Act of 1832. *See* pocket borough.

royal prerogative: the residual powers of the monarchy to act without consultation of ministers or parliament. Royal prerogative was once far-reaching, almost absolute, but has been steadily eroded by the growth of parliamentary power, especially since the seventeenth century. Among its nominal powers, the Crown can still create peers, summon and dissolve parliament, appoint and dismiss ministers, pardon or reprieve criminals, declare war and make peace, but in practice these are only done on the advice of ministers, and ministers themselves are appointed from the party with a majority in the House of Commons. Political independence exists in practice only when there are two rival leaders in a majority party between whom the monarch can choose, as when Queen Victoria asked the Earl of Rosebery rather than Sir William Harcourt to form a government when Gladstone resigned in 1894, or, to a limited degree, in the event of a hung parliament (q.v.).

royal warrant: authorisation by virtue of royal prerogative (q.v.). The use of a royal warrant to abolish the purchase of army commissions in 1871 was possible because purchase had been made illegal by an Act of 1809, and the system had been continued after that by royal warrant which created exceptions (almost all commissions) from the operation of the Act.

sectional (Labour party): critics of the Labour party argued that it was sectional in that it represented, and sought to represent, only a section of the nation, the working class, rather than the interests of the nation as a whole, in contrast to the attitude of the Liberal and Conservative parties, which sought to be national parties. It can be answered either with Marxist theory, which holds that as a result of the inexorable historical process the proletariat will become the nation, with the exception of a small minority of exploiting capitalists, or, as British gradualists like Ramsay MacDonald argued, that socialism represented the ethical growth of the nation, not the dominance of a class.

sectionalism: largely used critically by political opponents to allege that organisations, especially pressure groups, were pursuing the interests of a section of the nation, rather than the interests of the nation as a whole. Thus pressure groups such as the United Kingdom Alliance in its pursuit of temperance, or the Welsh Liberals in pursuit of the disestablishment of the Anglican Church in Wales, were accused of being sectionalist. The same criticism was applied to trade unions as protagonists of the interests of a class, and to the Labour party.

seditious libel: a crime committed by publishing libels which bring into hatred or contempt the Crown, the government, parliament or the judiciary, thereby inciting disturbance and disaffection and jeopardising the stability and security of the state. Sedition is a similar, but less serious crime than treason, being more a question of intent than action.

single-member constituency: a constituency which returns only one MP. Single-member constituencies became the norm in British politics following the 1884 Reform Act. *See* double-member constituency.

standing army: an army in permanent existence. Cromwell's New Model Army (1645) was perhaps the first example in England. The experience of the Cromwellian protectorate, and the fear of the absolutist tendencies of the Stuart monarchs, led standing armies to be regarded as threats to English liberties. James II was condemned for maintaining a standing army in the Bill of Rights (1689). The Mutiny Act of 1689 gave control of the army to parliament by providing only temporary authorisation for army discipline. The Act, and in effect the army, lasted initially for six months, later extended to a year, after which a new act was required if the army was to remain in being. The Mutiny Act was superseded in 1879 by the Army Discipline and Regulation Act ('the Army Annual Act') which, like its successors, the Army and Air Force (Annual) Acts, maintained parliamentary control over the armed forces in the same way.

'sweating': the employment of labour in poor conditions for long hours at low rates of pay. Usually found in the domestic trades, tailoring, furniture, hat- or flower-making, etc., where workers, often immigrants, were too desperate and too dispersed to form trade unions in their own defence. Sweated conditions became a political issue, along with other aspects of poverty and ill-health, in the late nineteenth and early twentieth centuries leading to government intervention. The Trade Boards Act of 1909 thus established boards empowered to set minimum wages in trades designated as 'sweated trades'.

sympathy strike: a strike by workers not immediately involved in the original dispute who sympathise with, and strike in support of, their fellow workers. Hence also secondary strikes. Sympathy strikes were widespread during the labour unrest of 1911–14, particularly by workers in trades related to those on strike, or living and working in the same area as the strikers. After the general strike of 1926, the Trade Union and Trade Disputes Act of 1927 made sympathy strikes illegal, but this act was repealed by the Labour government in 1946. Sympathy, or secondary, strikes became widespread again during the labour unrest of the 1970s. They were again made effectively unlawful by the removal of immunity from prosecution of trade-union officials who organised them by the Conservative government's Employment Acts of 1980 and 1982. *See* picketing.

syndicalism: a militant trade-union movement, begun in France, which advocated violence in industrial disputes and the seizure by workers of their places of employment (mines, docks, railways, factories, etc.) which they should then own and manage free of capitalist exploitation and state interference. British syndicalists usually thought in terms of about twenty syndicates (a single trade union for each industry) whose representatives would meet in a 'parliament of industry' to determine economic and industrial policy, prices, wage rates and conditions of work. Syndicalism rejected political participation in favour of direct industrial action, regarding the state itself as an instrument of exploitation. It was thus a direct challenge to parliamentary sovereignty (q.v.).

tellers: those, usually whips except on private members' bills, appointed to count and report the votes given for each side on a division in either house of parliament.

temperance: usually applied to the consumption of alcohol where temperance, whilst it might mean moderation, more commonly means total abstinence, as in 'tee-total'. The temperance movement sought to restrict or totally prohibit the consumption or sale of alcohol. The movement drew strong support from the frequently puritanical Nonconformist churches, and was consequently most closely associated with the Liberal party, although its most formidable pressure group, the United Kingdom Alliance formed in 1853, tried, unsuccessfully, to act independently of political parties, and severely criticised the Liberal government's Licensing Act of 1872.

tenant right: in Ulster custom and subsequently Irish land legislation, the right of a tenant to an interest in his holding, and to sell the same on removal to an incoming tenant. Tenant right could be regarded as compensation for unexhausted improvements made by the outgoing tenant during his tenure, but in Ireland, the belief among tenants that they had rights in their holdings derived from the continuation of tenancies in a single family for generations amounted to a claim to co-ownership with the landlord. In the face of agrarian violence, the English government felt obliged to give legal recognition to this tradition in the Irish Land Acts of 1870 and 1881. *See* fair rent, fixity of tenure, free sale.

'Three Fs': *see* fair rent, fixity of tenure, free sale.

tithe war: term used to describe the violent resistance to the payment of tithes (*see* church tithes) in Ireland, particularly during the early 1830s. The largely Catholic Irish population resented paying for the upkeep of a small and alien church, but religious motives were reinforced, even outweighed, by economic pressures. From the late eighteenth century Irish agriculture increasingly converted from pasture to arable and became commercialised, growing corn for the market generated by the expanding population of both Ireland and mainland Britain. Falls in grain prices in 1813–16, 1819–22 and the early 1830s each provoked renewed revolts against the payment of tithes. The grievance was removed, or evaded, by the commutation of tithes into a rent charge, set at 75 per cent of the income from the tithe, in 1838.

triennial parliament: a parliament dissolved every three years, thus resulting in elections every three years to renew the House of Commons. Like annual parliaments, but less drastically, a means to ensure that the electorate retained some control over its representatives in parliament.

unbalanced budget: a budget in which receipts from taxation do not cover the expenditure of the year, leaving a deficit and forcing the government to borrow.

unearned increment: the increase in capital value of assets without effort on the part of the owner. The concept is nominally applicable to all forms of capital, as in Hobson's theory of socially created wealth, but usually applied to land. Land reformers argued that the value of land, and particularly the increase in its value, was created by society through urban expansion, which turned agricultural or waste land into valuable building sites, and the provision of transport facilities. The classic case in Edwardian England was the opening of Golders Green underground station, which gave the district access to central London, and raised the value of surrounding property overnight. Land reformers argued that the increment should be taxed to recover for society the increased wealth it had created. *See* land values taxation.

unproductive wealth: wealth not used to produce employment, wages and profits. The concept was particularly applied to land left lying as waste, parkland or moorland for shooting. Hence Lloyd George's criticism of 'idle land in the hands of idle men', but it could also apply to 'idle' capital.

voluntaryist: generally a Nonconformist who supported the principle (voluntaryism) that churches, and by extension education, which was inseparable from religion in the nineteenth century, should be maintained by voluntary payments from individuals and not by the state. Voluntaryism became politically significant in the 1840s, and voluntaryists were prominent in the campaign against church rates (q.v.) and against the education provisions of the Conservative factory bill of 1843, the Maynooth Grant of 1845 and the Whig Education Act of 1847. None of the early voluntaryist organisations – for example, the Religious Freedom Society or the Evangelical Voluntary Church Association – flourished, but the success of Miall's newspaper, the *Nonconformist,* and of the Anti-State Church

Association, formed in 1844, which became the powerful Liberation Society in 1853, indicated the growing strength of voluntaryism. The disestablishment of the Anglican Church was the ultimate goal of voluntaryism, and most clearly expressed its attitudes. Those attitudes were rooted in individualism and the freedom of the individual conscience, and had close affinities with other aspects of individualism which sustained the liberal creed, especially free trade. Voluntaryists often described their objective as 'free trade in religion'. Not only were many manufacturers Nonconformists, but Nonconformist ministers were notable supporters of the Anti-Corn Law League, and the Anti-State Church Association modelled its organisation on that of the League. Driven by religious fervour, voluntaryists were often obsessive, and from the point of view of the Liberal party, disruptive, as in Edward Baines's activities in West Yorkshire in late 1840s. *See* church rates, minimal state.

welfare state: a system in which the state is mainly responsible for ensuring the social and economic security of its citizens 'from cradle to grave' by providing hospital care, education, unemployment and sickness benefits, old-age pensions and similar social services. The foundations of a welfare system in Britain that contrasted fundamentally with the Victorian approach were laid by the Liberal governments of 1906–14. The first major innovation was the establishment of old-age pensions in 1908. Old-age pensions were paid from general taxation, but following the National Insurance Act of 1911, which provided sickness and unemployment benefits, the system has been based on the principle of compulsory insurance contributions to the state. Old-age pensions were brought into the contributory structure in 1925. The provision of welfare services was greatly expanded during the 1940s under the impact of war, culminating in the National Health Service in 1948.

Whig: the Whig party emerged in 1679 as the opposition to the succession of James, Duke of York (James II) because he was a Catholic. It subsequently dominated the politics of the early and mid-eighteenth century. After an extended period of opposition between 1784 and 1830, the party returned as the advocates of moderate reform to pass the 1832 Reform Act. More a group of wealthy landed families reliant on patronage (*see* Crown patronage) than a political party, the Whigs needed allies to survive in the post-reform political system and their party evolved into the more broadly based Liberal party for which they provided the ministerial elite until at least the party split over Irish Home Rule in 1886. At that point the great majority, as opponents of Home Rule, left to work with, and ultimately to join, the Conservatives.

whips: the officers of a political party who, under the chief whip, are responsible for the organisation and discipline of the party in parliament. The term is derived from hunting, where the 'whippers-in' assist the huntsman to control the hounds.

Index

Note: Page numbers in *italic* refer to glossary entries.